WTO Law and Trade Policy Reform for Low-Carbon Technology Diffusion

World Trade Institute Advanced Studies

Series Editor

Thomas Cottier

VOLUME 5

The titles published in this series are listed at *brill.com/wtia*

WTO Law and Trade Policy Reform for Low-Carbon Technology Diffusion

Common Concern of Humankind, Carbon Pricing, and Export Credit Support

By

Zaker Ahmad

BRILL

LEIDEN | BOSTON

Open access publication of this book has been made possible by the Swiss National Science Foundation grant 10BP12_20057.

Library of Congress Cataloging-in-Publication Data

Names: Ahmad, Zaker, author.
Title: WTO law and trade policy reform for low-carbon technology diffusion: common concern of humankind, carbon pricing, and export credit support / by Zaker Ahmad.
Description: Leiden ; Boston : BRILL, 2021. | Series: World trade institute advanced studies, 2405-9331 ; 5 | Includes bibliographical references and index.
Identifiers: LCCN 2020048848 (print) | LCCN 2020048849 (ebook) | ISBN 9789004446083 (hardback) | ISBN 9789004446090 (ebook)
Subjects: LCSH: Carbon offsetting–Law and legislation. | Emissions trading–Law and legislation. | World Trade Organization. | Carbon taxes–Law and legislation. | Climatic changes–Law and legislation. | Technology transfer–Law and legislation. | Green technology. Classification: LCC K3593.5.C37 A36 2021 (print) | LCC K3593.5.C37 (ebook) | DDC 343.08/7–dc23
LC record available at https://lccn.loc.gov/2020048848
LC ebook record available at https://lccn.loc.gov/2020048849

Typeface for the Latin, Greek, and Cyrillic scripts: “Brill”. See and download: brill.com/brill-typeface.

ISSN 2405-9331
ISBN 978-90-04-44608-3 (hardback)
ISBN 978-90-04-44609-0 (e-book)

This book is printed on acid-free paper and produced in a sustainable manner.

For Shammo

Contents

Acknowledgements

This book is the culmination of my doctoral journey at the World Trade Institute. I must admit that as journeys go, the sum total of its rewards spans far beyond this volume. I remain grateful to all who have empowered me, helped me cope, and successfully conclude what has not only been a great learning experience, but also a process of self-discovery over the past few years.

In particular, my thanks to the Swiss National Science Foundation (SNF) for the grant extended to the research project 'Towards a Principle of Common Concern in Global Law'. The PhD research, done as a part of that project, would not have been possible otherwise. Also, open access publication of this volume would not have been possible in absence of the additional SNF grant. Thanks for that too! I am also very grateful to my research supervisors Professor Thomas Cottier and Professor Michael Hahn. The trust, mentorship, and guidance provided by Professor Cottier, both as the project leader and the primary supervisor, have been a key driving force. Professor Hahn's careful comments from time to time also played an important part in tempering the runaway ideas chasing the horizon.

Thanks also to my project teammates – Lucia Satragno, Alexander Beyleveld, Iryna Bogdanova, as well as fellow PhD colleagues working on the same theme – Judith Schaeli, Rosa Maria Losada, for their kind cooperation. This research stands atop that foundation of teamwork. The colleagues at the Institute for European and International Economic Law (IEW) – Rachel Liechti, Andrea Schlaepfer, and Brigitta Imeli have always been the greatest listeners. They provided help when needed, and healthy critique too. Thanks to my colleague Anqi Wang for her support in making my remote access to the WTI library possible. I also gratefully acknowledge the support of the experts in the field, especially Gabrielle Marceau, Cedric Ryngaert, Peter Tobias Stoll, Krista Nadakavukaren Schefer, Duncan French, Klaus Zimmermann, and Oisin Suttle, for kindly accepting our invitation to come to Berne and hear our ideas.

I thank the WTI doctoral school, under the guidance of Ilaria Espa, and later Doris Oberdabernig for the institutional support. The routine academic events were useful to get feedback from in-house experts, including Professors Peter Van den Bossche, Manfred Elsig, and Joseph Francois. Thanks to Christian Haeberli, and Octavio Fernandez for maintaining a keen interest in my research over the years. Those conversations over coffee brought out helpful insights. Thanks to Rodrigo Polanco for setting the standard on the timely finishing of work for us PhDs. The WTI librarians, Wulfhard Stahl and Yvonne Motzer have been of the greatest assistance. Making books hot off the press appear on my desk was their magic, for which I remain grateful! Thanks to the staff at Brill, especially Kelley Baylis and Marie Sheldon, for coordinating the publication process. Thanks to the designers, typesetters and the production staff for their patience and efforts. Thanks also to Monica Matthews for agreeing to look at my manuscript on very short notice. Her close scrutiny has helped to get rid of many errors in the volume. Needless to say that the remaining errors in the volume are to attributed to me only. Many thanks to Sandra Joseph for all the administrative and logistical support. Thanks to all the MILE students from the four corners of the world whom I have met over the years, for sharing your positive spirits.

To Monica, Jin, Sascha, Clarence, Alex, Andrea, Brigitta, Anqi, Rachel, Iryna, and Sophie – your gifts of friendship and support have helped me through some of the toughest times. I wish life returns you generously of what you gave me. To my old pals, Chaity and Tasrin – thanks for your help. Lastly, a great big special thanks to Margrit Vetter, for always looking out. I miss you all!

Zaker Ahmad
Chittagong, November 2020

Boxes and Figures

Boxes

Figures

Abbreviations and Acronyms

AB	Appellate Body
ARSIWA	Articles on the Responsibility of States for Internationally Wrongful Acts
BTA	Border Tax Adjustment
CDM	Clean Development Mechanism
COP	Conference of Parties
CBDR	Common but Differentiated Responsibility
CIRR	Commercial Interest Reference Rates
CTCN	Climate Technology Centre and Network
CTE	Committee on Trade and Environment
DSB	Dispute Settlement Body
DSU	Understanding on Rules and Procedures Governing the Settlement of Disputes
ECA	Export Credit Agency
EGS	Environmental Goods and Services
EUR	Euro
GATS	General Agreement on Trade in Services
GATT	General Agreement on Tariffs and Trade
GCF	Green Climate Fund
GEF	Global Environment Facility
GHG	Greenhouse Gas
GPG	Global Public Good
GSP	Generalized System of Preferences
HS	Harmonized System
ILA	International Law Association
ILC	International Law Commission
IMF	International Monetary Fund
IPCC	Intergovernmental Panel on Climate Change
IPR	Intellectual Property Rights
LCT	Low-Carbon Technology
LDC	Least-Developed Country
MEA	Multilateral Environmental Agreement
MFN	Most-Favoured-Nation
MPR	Minimum Premium Rate
NAMA	Nationally Appropriate Mitigation Action
NDC	Nationally Determined Commitment
NIEO	New International Economic Order
NT	National Treatment

OECD	Organization for Economic Cooperation and Development
PPM	Process and Production Measures
PTA	Preferential Trade Agreement
PV	Photovoltaics
SATAP	so as to afford protection
SBSTA	Subsidiary Body for Scientific and Technological Advice
SCM	Subsidies and Countervailing Measures
SDG	Sustainable Development Goal
TEC	Technology Executive Committee
TF	Technology Framework
TM	Technology Mechanism
TNA	Technology Needs Assessment
TRIPS	Trade-Related Aspects of Intellectual Property Rights
UNCTAD	United Nations Conference on Trade and Development
UNEP	United Nations Environment Programme
UNFCCC	United Nations Framework Convention on Climate Change
UNGA	United Nations General Assembly
UNSC	United Nations Security Council
USD	United States Dollar
VCLT	Vienna Convention on the Law of Treaties
WIPO	World Intellectual Property Organization
WGTTT	Working Group on Trade and Technology Transfer
WTO	World Trade Organization

Introduction

> Institutions – the rules and norms that guide human interactions – enable or impede the structures, mechanisms and measures that guide mitigation and adaptation. Institutions, understood as the 'rules of the game', exert direct and indirect influence over the viability of 1.5°C-consistent pathways.
>
> IPCC Special Report 2018[1]

The current relationship between trade and climate change can be aptly described as a clash of objective truths with narrow politico-economic interests. While the science calls for rapid improvements in transfers of mitigation technologies among others, existing legal infrastructure prioritising commercial and political interests retard that process. It is not altogether novel to hold that transboundary economic transactions like trade and investment greatly enhance the level and scale of the dissemination of technologies necessary to combat climate change. Researches to this effect have been in existence since the early 2000s.[2] Unfortunately however, this insight has not permeated into the institutions regulating such economic transactions. Institutions, being the 'rules of the game' as quoted above, are creations of public international law at their very core. Despite this shared root, linkages between different rule-frameworks regulating international trade on the one hand and climate change on the other still remain only in the realm of possibility. One key drawback that prevents strong interlinked institutions from developing is that global rules can only go so far as the least willing participant is ready to venture. On one end, the talk of trade measures for climate technology diffusion is unpalatable in the climate domain. James Bacchus recently noted how conflicts of sentiments have relegated trade issues to the position of being 'taboo' in climate

1 Heleen de Coninck and others, 'Strengthening and Implementing the Global Response' in Valerie Masson-Delmotte and others (eds), *Special Report: Global Warming of 1.5°C* (World Meteorological Organization (WMO) 2018) 352 <http://www.ipcc.ch/report/sr15/> accessed 15 October 2020.

2 IPCC, *Methodological and Technological Issues in Technology Transfer* (Bert Metz and others eds, Intergovernmental Panel on Climate Change 2000).

discussions.[3] On the other end, a growing number of trade disputes challenge measures touching upon climate change one way or the other.[4]

Against this backdrop, the present volume offers an alternative narrative, putting the need for clean technology diffusion at the forefront, at the same time making suggestions to tune the trade law regime to play a complementary part therein. This is done upon the foundation of a proposed doctrine and framework of 'Common Concern of Humankind' (hereafter referred to also as 'Common Concern', for short). The notion is itself well-established, especially in the field of climate change. While its lingering presence has been interpreted as a clarion call for concerted efforts to be made by all involved parties, specifics of the required actions have never been detailed. The proposed doctrine facilitates that step. It calls for assuming – (i) responsibilities of good faith cooperation by the stakeholders, (ii) diligent measures to tackle a concern domestically, and as a last resort, (iii) recourse to unilateral countermeasures against negligent non-compliance.[5] In brief, the doctrine of Common Concern of Humankind is a propositional framework of norms to conceptualise, also respond to the collective action problems regarding global public goods (GPG s) of critical importance. To distinguish the proposed normative framework from the traditional understanding of 'common concern of humankind', a terminological distinction is maintained throughout the work.[6]

The chief attraction of having a normative structure and specific legal consequences, possibly as a principle of public international law, lies in the possibility of resolving the conflicts briefly outlined above. It cannot be denied that having in place an international law principle that can objectively guide suitable responses as new global hazards emerge, is indeed lucrative. Unlike the current practice of understanding common concern of humankind by

3 James Bacchus, 'What Is a Climate Response Measure? Breaking the Trade Taboo in Confronting Climate Change' (Centre for International Governance Innovation (CIGI) 2019) 220.

4 For example, *Canada – Certain Measures Affecting the Renewable Energy Generation Sector / Canada – Measures Relating to the Feed-in Tariff Program* [2013] Panel Report WT/DS412/R and Add.1; WT/DS426/R and Add.1, DSR 2013: I 237; *India – Certain Measures Relating to Solar Cells and Solar Modules* [2016] Appellate Body Report WT/DS456/AB/R; 'China – Certain Measures on the Transfer of Technology: Request for Consulatation by the European Union (Revision)' (2019) WT/DS549/1/Rev.1; G/L/1244/Rev.1; IP/D/39/Rev.1.

5 For a detailed introduction to the doctrine, see, Thomas Cottier (ed), *The Prospects of Common Concern of Humankind in International Law* (Cambridge University Press 2021). The first chapter of this book also elaborates the doctrine in the particular context of low-carbon technology diffusion.

6 When referring to the traditional usage of the term, small letters are used, e.g. 'common concern' or 'common concern of humankind'. The proposed enhanced attributes of the concept are referred to as a doctrine, using capital letters, e.g. 'Common Concern'.

assigning it a reluctant meaning, one that reflects the lack of bold steps in climate affairs, the doctrine takes a more forward-looking approach. The avenues of normative consequences proposed by the doctrine as emerging from the expression of Common Concern, are geared towards effective solution of that 'concern'. It is pragmatic at its very core, making the case for a new realism, as Thomas Cottier suggested.[7] While the doctrine in some aspects just states the obvious regarding the climate change discipline (e.g. the duty to cooperate, or to take adequate response actions domestically), others offer substantial provocation (e.g. unilateral trade countermeasures) to begin dialogues.

Research in this book will examine the intersections of and linkages between low-carbon technology diffusion and trade using the doctrine of Common Concern as the principal theoretical framework. This attempts to serve two purposes. One is, as already mentioned, to supply a blueprint of an alternative approach to trade and technology diffusion in the climate context. The second purpose is to make specific observations on the practical utility of the doctrine itself. Therefore, with respect to the problem of trade and low-carbon technology (LCT) diffusion, the research touches upon, step by step, all the normative facets of the doctrine, i.e. (i) cooperation, (ii) homework, and (iii) unilateral compliance enforcement through countermeasures.

The first chapter acquaints readers to the factual, conceptual and regulatory specifics of the research. It begins with a portrayal of the need for low-carbon technology diffusion and the potential role of trade regulation. Upon that foundation, the doctrine of Common Concern of Humankind is introduced and its potential utility in meeting the technology needs using trade law and policy measures is elaborated. The second chapter takes a deep dive into the institutional expressions of technology development and transfer in the climate and the trade regimes. The findings therefrom are then assessed against the current empirical understandings of the barriers to low-carbon technology diffusion. This leads to a clear understanding of the nature of cooperation required to tackle the absence of effective regulation. The conclusions feed into the third chapter, which outlines the new narrative of trade cooperation and policy measures to facilitate LCT diffusion. The principal argument in that chapter is that it is possible to fashion factually informed, and mutually beneficial trade measures that would enable the LCTs to spread further. Cooperation among the WTO members, within the organization and also beyond, should be geared to bring such measures into effect.

7 See, Conclusion, Thomas Cottier, 'The Principle of Common Concern of Humankind' in Thomas Cottier (ed), *The Prospects of Common Concern of Humankind in International Law* (n 5).

Corresponding to the homework aspect of the Common Concern doctrine, chapters 4 and 5 each present a case study of a specific trade measure that can facilitate the diffusion of low-carbon technologies in a given context. While constraints of space and scope prevent extensive analyses of all possible trade-related actions, these two studies provide a glimpse of issues that may arise in practice. Chapter 4 examines the implications of an emission pricing measure coupled with utilisation of the generated revenue for technological improvements in the developing countries. This leads to the long-standing and unresolved issue of discrimination claims regarding the non-product related process and production measures (PPMs). In a similar-structured analysis, chapter 5 looks at the ramifications of easier terms of credits offered by the governments for exports involving LCTs. This leads to yet another lingering issue of amending the WTO agreement on subsidies and countervailing measures. Both chapters look at the proposed measures' compliance with the existing WTO rules and highlight the possible benefits of a recourse to the proposed Common Concern doctrine. Necessary suggestions are made in both cases.

Chapter 6, the final chapter of the volume, delves into a study of the utility and the practical applicability of unilateral trade countermeasures deployed as part of the Common Concern framework. While it is true that unilateral self-help measures for perceived breaches of trade commitments are explicitly prohibited under the WTO rules, it is also true that in some limited areas (e.g. the security exceptions), members enjoy greater freedom to impose restrictive measures on others. The chapter also explores the possibility of using the Common Concern doctrine to retain the benefits of unilateralism while taming the opportunistic use of such a power.

In the end, a conclusion summarises the overall findings of the research, including the lessons learnt on the utility of the proposed normative framework of Common Concern of Humankind. A brief outlook, as part of the conclusion, forecasts potential areas where this field of research can further expand into.

CHAPTER 1

Climate Technology, Trade, and the Doctrine of Common Concern

The urgency attached to the need for diffusion of LCTs[8] is a consequence of its indispensable role in the mitigation of climate change. A habitable climate is a global public good.[9] Maintaining safe climatic conditions is arguably the toughest cooperation challenge ever faced by the international community since the World Wars.[10] A number of factors contribute to the complexity of the climate change problem; for example, its all-encompassing nature, the difficulty of pinpointing a critical threshold of catastrophic emission, a commonly perceived negative effect on the interests of domestic economic growth, and the difficulty to represent, also quantify the interests of the future generations.[11] The challenge of finding a package of workable solutions to all these issues goes to the root of the current inability of the international legal system to provide an adequate framework of response to contain adverse climate change impacts. While there is an international treaty-based body of climate rules, not only does it lack sufficient normative strength, but also the level of influence it exerts upon other relatively stricter regimes (e.g. international trade regulation) is ambiguous.[12] Therefore, the sense of urgency to spread LCTs is not translated into actual law.

The role of this opening chapter is to lay out a broad factual and theoretical background to assess the above. It has two general segments. The first segment (sections I & II) supplies a factual context, in particular, the needed levels of

8 For details on the meaning and scope of low-carbon technologies, See section IIB at p. 14 below.
9 Scott Barrett, 'Aggregate Efforts: Global Public Goods That Depend on the Combined Efforts of All States', *Why cooperate? : the incentive to supply global public goods* (paperback ed, Oxford University Press 2010).
10 Daniel Cole, 'Climate Change and Collective Action' (2008) 61 Current Legal Problems.
11 Harro van Asselt, *The Fragmentation of Global Climate Governance: Consequences and Management of Regime Interactions* (Edward Elgar 2014) 3–4; Scott Barrett, 'Climate Treaties and Approaching Catastrophes' (2013) 66 Journal of Environmental Economics and Management 235; Scott Barrett, 'Rethinking Global Climate Change Governance'; Simon Caney, 'Cosmopolitan Justice, Responsibility, and Global Climate Change' in Stephen Mark Gardiner and others (eds), *Climate ethics: essential readings* (Oxford University Press 2010).
12 For more see p. 22 below.

emission mitigation for a safe climate, also the hazards otherwise. The importance of low-carbon technology diffusion and the facilitative role of international trade in that regard is outlined as well. The second segment (sections III &VI) outlines the legal and theoretical framework, eventually presenting the hypothesis that the goal of building a positive coherence between the trade and the climate rule system will benefit from the integration of the doctrine of Common Concern of Humankind in those systems. Such coherence would further enable the deployment of trade policy measures for the diffusion of low-carbon technologies.

I Mitigation of Climate Change: Fact vs. Law

As human-induced changes to the earth's climate were agreed to be a common concern of humankind,[13] the international community responded by making a binding commitment in 1992 to "[a]chieve, [...] stabilization of greenhouse gas concentrations in the atmosphere at a level that would prevent dangerous anthropogenic interference with the climate system".[14] Great may it have sounded back then, but the hindsight of almost three decades of failed attempts at making a rule system capable to do just that now brings to mind brave Achilles' fabled struggle to catch up with the Tortoise.[15] As the scientific forecasts of our long-term future keep getting bleaker, the success to build an effective framework of rules continue to slip away repeatedly. The initial 1992 agreement where the commitment was made was a framework arrangement, waiting to be fleshed out over time. The first attempt to that end was the Kyoto Protocol. Despite its strong obligatory language, the Protocol has been largely unsuccessful in bringing forth necessary emission reduction as the large developed country emitters left the process over time. Coming pages will show that the recent Paris Agreement has not yet been of much effect either.

In stark contrast to the rulemaking challenges, climate scholarship is a thriving field. Scientists report that the risks posed by anthropogenic climate change are dynamic and they affect in many different levels. Not only does unabated emission of greenhouse gases worsen the natural environment, but it also has a further knock-on effect on social and economic ecosystems that depend on

13 For an account of the inception of the expression, see p. 29 onwards.

14 United Nations Framework Convention on Climate Change 1992 (1771 UNTS 107).

15 Nick Huggett, 'Zeno's Paradoxes' in Edward N Zalta (ed), *The Stanford Encyclopedia of Philosophy* (Spring 2019, Metaphysics Research Lab, Stanford University 2019) <https://plato.stanford.edu/archives/spr2019/entries/paradox-zeno/> accessed 25 October 2020.

those environments. The Intergovernmental Panel on Climate Change (IPCC) periodically collects and communicates information on the 'key risks'[16] arising out of human-induced climate change.[17] These risks are combined together in groups to form five broad types of threats, each communicated by the IPCC as a 'reason for concern'.[18] These five reasons for concern are – (i) danger to the unique and threatened systems, (ii) extreme weather events, (iii) uneven distribution of impacts, (iv) global aggregate impacts, and (v) large-scale singular events. As a depiction of the risk levels, the figure in the next page (Figure 1) usefully portrays the immediate necessity of additional mitigation efforts. The top panel of the figure shows six different ranges of temperature rise compared to pre-industrial levels due to different levels of greenhouse gas (GHG) concentrations (in CO_2-equivalent terms) by the end of this century. The bottom panel shows the way each of the reasons for concern worsens with the increase of average global temperature. Together it is possible to read the figure as a carbon concentration goal for any temperature limitation target (top) and the consequences thereof in terms of global risks (bottom).

The figure above shows that in the case of the global average temperature rising more than 2°C above the pre-industrial levels by 2100, 'high' to 'very high'

16 The key risks are those that are widely agreed upon by the experts as having the most severe adverse consequence for the human and socio-ecological systems. A risk becomes 'key' due to its hazardous consequence or the vulnerability of the systems exposed to it. Other factors of consideration to determine 'key risks' are: (i) magnitude of the consequence, (ii) probability of the risk to materialise, (iii) irreversibility of impact and (iv) limited ability of the impacted.

17 These risks are- (i) Risk of death, injury, ill-health, or disrupted livelihoods in low-lying coastal zones and small islands due to storm surges, coastal flooding, and sea-level rise; (ii) Risk of severe ill-health and disrupted livelihoods for large urban populations due to inland flooding in some regions; (iii) Systemic risks due to extreme weather events leading to breakdown of infrastructure networks and critical services; (iv) Risk of mortality and morbidity during periods of extreme heat, particularly for vulnerable urban populations and those working outdoors; (v) Risk of food insecurity and the breakdown of food systems linked to warming, drought, flooding, and precipitation variability and extremes; (vi) Risk of loss of rural livelihoods and income due to insufficient access to drinking and irrigation water and reduced agricultural productivity; (vii) Risk of loss of marine and coastal ecosystems, biodiversity, and the ecosystem goods, functions, and services they provide for coastal livelihoods; (viii) Risk of loss of terrestrial and inland water ecosystems, biodiversity, and the ecosystem goods, functions, and services they provide for livelihoods. Michael Oppenheimer and others, 'Emergent Risks and Key Vulnerabilities' in Christopher B Field and others (eds), *Climate Change 2014: Impacts, Adaptation, and Vulnerability – Part A: Global and Sectoral Aspects. Contribution of Working Group II to the Fifth Assessment Report of the Intergovernmental Panel on Climate Change* (Cambridge University Press 2014) 1069–1071.

18 ibid 1043, 1051–1052, 1074.

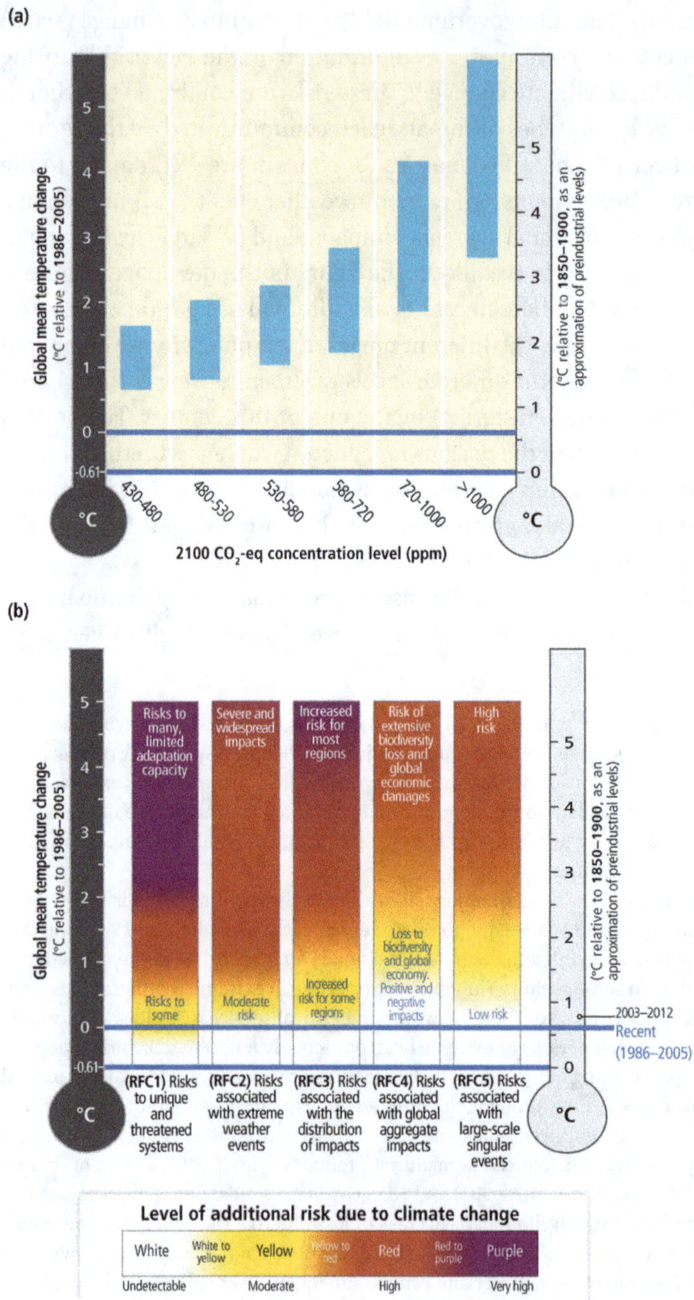

FIGURE 1 Reason for concern. Figure 19–7, (n 17) ibid 1082

risks start setting in. The level of ecosystem damage through the extinction of large fractions of freshwater, marine and terrestrial species will rise with the increasing rate and magnitude of climate change.[19] Rising marine temperature will also result in the redistribution of global marine resources and loss of marine biodiversity. Increased acidification of oceans will cause loss of the coral reefs and will damage polar ecosystems.[20] Frequency of submergence, flooding and erosion will continue to increase in the coastal areas as the sea levels will continue to rise well beyond the 21st century.[21] The ecosystem impact then affects human livelihood, increasing the existing vulnerabilities of the communities.[22] As global warming is projected to reduce the surface and ground freshwater resources in the subtropical regions, it will make existing water crises in those regions more acute. An increase of the global average temperature will reduce the yield of staples; for example, wheat, maize and rice in the tropical and temperate regions, worsening the food security conditions.[23] Human health will also be adversely impacted as climate change would intensify existing health risks from natural hazards and nutrition loss. All these impacts would affect poor and vulnerable locations many times more than other areas. Besides, climate change will make poverty reduction slow, and sustainable development difficult to achieve for many parts of the globe.[24]

Limiting the adverse impact of climate change is only possible through mitigation up to a scale wherein the cumulative anthropogenic emission of greenhouse gases does not exceed a certain threshold, known as the carbon budget. According to a special report released by the IPCC after the signing of the Paris Agreement, for a 50% chance of staying within the 1.5 degrees temperature limit, the remaining carbon budget must be about 580 $GtCO_2$.[25] For a 66% probability, the same must be only around 420 $GtCO_2$.[26] A portion of this budget (about 100 $GtCO_2$) would be automatically exhausted by the natural events already triggered, e.g.

19 IPCC, *Climate Change 2014: Synthesis Report. Contribution of Working Groups I, II and III to the Fifth Assessment Report of the Intergovernmental Panel on Climate Change* (RK Pachauri, Leo Mayer and Core Writing Team eds, IPCC 2015) 67.

20 ibid.

21 Peter U Clark and others, 'Consequences of Twenty-First-Century Policy for Multi-Millennial Climate and Sea-Level Change' (2016) 6 Nature Climate Change 360.

22 IPCC, *Climate Change 2014* (n 19) 69.

23 ibid.

24 ibid 73.

25 IPCC, 'Summary for Policymakers' in Valerie Masson-Delmotte and others (eds), *Special Report: Global Warming of 1.5°C* (World Meteorological Organization (WMO) 2018) 33 <http://www.ipcc.ch/report/sr15/> accessed 25 October 2020.

26 ibid.

thawing of the permafrost and methane emissions from the wetlands.[27] Almost all climate scientists agree that the current annual rate of consumption of the carbon budget is around 42(±3) $GtCO_2$, which means that unless it slows down significantly, the budget would be fully depleted around the 2050s.

Against the backdrop of such bleak forecasts and after much struggle, the international community delivered the Paris Agreement in 2015 – a beacon of hope.[28] The Agreement is nothing short of a miracle given the level of consensus and ambition it stands for. Just like the 1992 Framework Convention, the Paris Agreement showcases a near universal commitment to climate action. Taking into account the forebodings from the scientific community, the Agreement updated the global emission mitigation target in the following terms:

> This Agreement, in enhancing the implementation of the Convention, including its objective, aims to strengthen the global response to the threat of climate change, [...] including by:
>
> a. Holding the increase in the global average temperature to well below 2°c above pre-industrial levels and to pursue efforts to limit the temperature to 1.5°c above pre-industrial levels, recognizing this would significantly reduce the risks and impacts of climate change; [...][29]

Nevertheless, the price for a global agreement on an overall mitigation target was paid in the form of legal ambiguities built into the system – so much so that it remains possible to fail to attain the abovementioned target and not break any strict rules of the agreement at the same time.[30] The mitigation commitment of each participant country is nationally and thus unilaterally determined, albeit subject to an obligation of being progressive over a five years cycle.[31] Although the parties are encouraged to submit clear, transparent and methodologically consistent commitments,[32] those submitted in the first round vary widely and hence remain beyond any meaningful comparison.[33]

---

27 ibid.

28 Paris Agreement 2015 (Report of the Conference of the Parties in its twenty-first session, Decision 1/CP 21, Annex, FCCC/CP/2015/10/Add1).

29 Article 2, ibid.

30 Richard N Cooper and others, 'Why Paris Did Not Solve the Climate Dilemma' in Peter C Cramton, David JC MacKay and Axel Ockenfels (eds), *Global carbon pricing: the path to climate cooperation* (MIT Press 2017).

31 Article 4, Paris Agreement (n 28).

32 Article 4.8, ibid.

33 This makes tracing of the 'ambitious' elements in the NDCs with respect to a common baseline difficult. United Nations Environment Programme, *Emissions Gap Report 2018* (UNEP 2018) 7–15.

Moreover, detailed guidelines on market-based approaches[34] to emission mitigation remain up in the air. Further guidance has been detailed in the evolving Paris rulebook,[35] impact of which will not be witnessed until the second round of commitments come in by 2020.[36] Given the onset of the global economic downturn in the wake of the COVID 19 pandemic, mitigation is not a priority policy agenda for governments. Moreover, the United States, one of the biggest polluters, has already formally communicated its withdrawal from the Paris Agreement.[37]

The latest IPCC special report is a reminder that even if all the nationally-determined contributions (NDCs) pledged under the Paris Agreement were duly realised, the global mean temperature would rise about 3°C higher than the pre-industrial period by 2100 and would keep rising.[38] This is again confirmed by the latest UNEP Emissions Gap Report. It shows that meeting all the conditional and unconditional NDC commitments would still see global mitigation fall short by 26–31 $GtCO_2$ in 2030, compared to the level required to reach the 1.5°C target.[39] For all except one of the predicted 1.5°C pathways, annual average global emission must remain below 35 $GtCO_2eq$ per year, whereas the same average emission according to the current global mitigation commitment is between 52 and 58 $GtCO_2eq$.[40]

Clearly, effective response to the global concern of climate change by reaching the adequate levels of mitigation in time will require efforts going beyond the polite suasion of the core climate law system (i.e. the UNFCCC and the

34 Article 6, Paris Agreement (n 28).

35 Information to facilitate clarity, transparency and understanding of nationally determined contributions, referred to in decision 1/CP.21, paragraph 28 2019 (Meeting of the Parties to the Paris Agreement on the third part of its first session, Decision 4/CMA1, Annex, FCCC/PA/CMA/2018/3/Add1).

36 For more see p. 64 below.

37 Michael R Pompeo, 'On the U.S. Withdrawal from the Paris Agreement' (*U.S. Department of State*) <https://www.state.gov/on-the-u-s-withdrawal-from-the-paris-agreement/> accessed 25 October 2020.

38 IPCC, 'Summary for Policymakers' (n 25) 24; Jaime Nieto, Óscar Carpintero and Luis J Miguel, 'Less than 2°C? An Economic-Environmental Evaluation of the Paris Agreement' (2018) 146 Ecological Economics 69; UNFCCC, 'Synthesis Report on the Aggregate Effect of the Intended Nationally Determined Contributions' (UNFCCC 2015) Synthesis report FCCC/CP/2015/7 <http://unfccc.int/resource/docs/2015/cop21/eng/07.pdf> accessed 25 October 2020; UNFCCC, 'Aggregate Effect of the Intended Nationally Determined Contributions: An Update' (UNFCCC 2016) Synthesis report FCCC/CP/2016/2 <http://unfccc.int/resource/docs/2016/cop22/eng/02.pdf> accessed 25 October 2020.

39 United Nations Environment Programme, *Emissions Gap Report 2018* (UNEP 2019) 23–25.

40 IPCC, 'Summary for Policymakers' (n 25) 24.

Paris Agreement). It is highly unlikely that over the next decade, rules of the existing climate regime would succeed in exponentially increasing the parties' level of commitment and ambition. This rising probability of failure triggers the need to look past the traditional limits of the regulatory domain for effective solutions. Like the saying that one must not put all the eggs in the same basket, instead of putting all our hopes on the success of the Paris platform, it would only be prudent to explore for additional and complementary avenues of effective mitigation options, especially in the regulatory realm governing global economic activities.

The domain of the international economic law (IEL) is the most fitting area to search for effective accompaniments to climate rules. IEL is a branch of public international law that covers an ever expanding sphere of transboundary public and private economic activities,[41] as well as related social issues. This field of law is comprised of areas such as trade, investment, monetary regulations, taxation, related concerns regarding competition, labour welfare, development, and also cross-cutting issues such as multi-level governance and global value chains.[42] On one hand, some of these activities (e.g. transport emissions) are direct contributors to climate change and therefore must be controlled. On the other hand, IEL offers powerful tools to discipline the behaviour of the different types of actors in the market to curb emissions. Regulatory reforms and policy measures falling within the scope of the IEL can complement climate action by creating new opportunities for climate-friendly production, consumption, and investment choices. So far the disciplines of IEL have remained on the sidelines of international climate action, but this must change. With this motivation, the current research trains its focus on one particular part of the IEL, i.e. international trade regulation under the umbrella of the WTO.

To reflect the need for spreading LCTs for climate mitigation, the rest of the chapter would outline the preliminaries of a coherent trade and climate change rule system to that effect.

---

41 John Jackson, 'International Economic Law: Reflections on the "Boilerroom" of International Relations' (1995) 10 American University International Law Review 596–599.

42 Jeffrey L Dunoff, 'Subject-matter of International Economic Law' in Thomas Cottier and others (eds), *Elgar encyclopedia of international economic law* (Edward Elgar Publishing 2017).

II The LCTs as an Important Puzzle Piece

A *Technology in Mitigation Pathways*

Although a variety of predicted emission reduction pathways can successfully limit global emission within 1.5°C, all of those require quick adoption of new technologies at an unprecedented scale, enabling deep decarbonisation of the global economy across all sectors.[43] Emission pathways that successfully model achievement of the target with limited or no overshoot, are built upon assumptions that include rapid and immediate system changes all across the board, including changes in production and consumption patterns, as well as international cooperation to enhance sustainability and reduce energy demand.

To illustrate, successful emission pathways predict a necessary increase in the share of renewables in electricity generation to be around 70–85% by 2050.[44] Within the same time period, the share of coal is expected to go down to virtually zero. The emission from the industry sector is projected to be 75–90% lower in 2050 compared to the 2010 levels.[45] According to the IPCC, sector-specific transitions can be attained through combinations of existing technologies and practices like electrification, product substitution, and techniques of carbon capture and storage. However, deployment of the new technologies at an unprecedented scale is challenging due to economic, financial, and institutional constraints.[46] In other GHG emitting sectors like transport, buildings, and infrastructure, deep emission cuts require adoption of energy efficiency practices, as well as changes in urban and land planning. For example, the share of low-emission fuel in the transport sector should rise from the current less than 5% to about 35–65% by 2050.[47] Again, such transitions are challenged by economic, institutional, and socio-cultural barriers.[48]

Pathways that attain the 1.5°C target while accounting for an initial phase of emission overshoot, are even more dependent on expensive and uncertain carbon dioxide removal (CDR) technologies in the later phases. Instead of immediate decarbonisation, such models predict an emission intensive lifestyle

---

43 The sectors are: energy, industry, buildings and infrastructure, transport, land usage, and waste.

44 IPCC, 'Summary for Policymakers' (n 25) 17.

45 ibid.

46 ibid 21.

47 ibid 18.

48 An extensive discussion focusing on the market-related barriers preventing low-carbon technology diffusion can be found in Chapter 2, Section III. at p. 76 below.

leading up to 2050. Only by an extensive deployment of CDR technologies from that point, negative emission is planned to be reached before other models, thereby resulting in the attainment of the target. The problem is that delayed mitigation allows some of the climate hazards to set in early on–often in regions that were not responsible for those emissions, increasing the burden of climate adaptation. Also, dependence on non-existing CDR technologies assumes technological breakthroughs, which do not happen regularly.[49]

Keeping aside the long-term temperature limitation goals, technologies play a crucial role even to attain the existing insufficient levels of emission reduction commitments registered under the Paris Agreement. According to Brandi, 63% of all mitigation contributions pledged by the parties under the Paris framework is conditional upon technology transfer.[50] UNFCCC Secretariat reports that almost all the developing countries mention technology in one form or other in their intended nationally determined contribution (INDCs) documents.[51] More than 100 developing countries mention the need for technology-related support to be able to pursue their planned commitment.[52]

In sum, appropriate technologies and their global dissemination are an indispensable component for stepping up current and future climate mitigation efforts. In the absence of access to necessary mitigation technologies, not only is it impossible to reach the global mean temperature target set in the Paris Agreement, but also the sustainability of the Agreement itself will be threatened.

B *The Concept and Scope of LCTs*

The term 'low-carbon technologies' (LCTs), or alternative formulations[53] are used in this volume to mean "technologies that aim to minimise greenhouse gas (GHG) emissions, especially carbon dioxide emissions, relative to those

---

49 Leon E Clarke and others, 'Assessing Transformation Pathways' in Ottmar Edenhofer and others (eds), *Climate Change 2014: Mitigation of Climate Change. Working Group III Contribution to the Fifth Assessment Report of the Intergovernmental Panel on Climate Change* (Cambridge University Press 2014) 433.

50 Clara Brandi, *Trade Elements in Countries' Climate Contributions under the Paris Agreement* (International Centre for Trade and Sustainable Development (ICTSD) 2017) < https://ictsd.iisd.org/sites/default/files/research/trade_elements_in_countries_climate_contributions.pdf > accessed 25 October 2020.

51 UNFCCC, 'Technology and NDCs' <http://unfccc.int/ttclear/tna/ndcs.html> accessed 25 October 2020.

52 ibid.

53 Alternatively, the expressions 'mitigation techology', 'climate technology', and 'clean technology' has been used throughout the volume to refer to the same notion.

technologies currently in use in a particular context".[54] The notion is somewhat flexible in scope, as it seeks to cover all forms of emission mitigation options. The LCTs can be final products destined for end consumers, capital equipments used for production and processing, and also practical knowledge or skills.[55] The scope of the notion would therefore comprise of, e.g. tangible products, intangible know-hows, and institutional settings.[56] Although not a treaty term, low-carbon technology is a notion that is frequently employed by the researchers. Compared to the term 'environmentally sound technology' (EST) used in the treaty language,[57] low-carbon technology is narrower and focuses exclusively on climate mitigation. It ought to be noted at this stage that this narrow specification is only to maintain analytical rigour. It does not convey any explicit or implicit order of importance or prioritisation of climate mitigation over adaptation.

To a degree, what falls within the domain of appropriate 'low-carbon technology' for any country depends upon respective overall environmental context (e.g. economic situation, income levels, and position relative to the technology frontier).[58] The annex at the end of this volume provides a detailed overview of the scope of such technologies as individually identified by many developing countries. Although the list is fairly expansive, there is a degree of convergence in what countries take to be preferred mitigation technology.

The IPCC special report on limiting global warming to 1.5°C sheds useful light on the scope of LCTs. For example, power generation from solar, and

---

54 David Ockwell and Alexandra Mallett (eds), *Low-Carbon Technology Transfer: From Rhetoric to Reality* (Routledge 2012) 3.

55 Jørgen Boldt and others, *Overcoming Barriers to the Transfer and Diffusion of Climate Technologies* (Second Edition, UNEP Risø Centre 2012) 7; Ivan Nygaard and Ulrich Elmer Hansen, 'The Conceptual and Practical Challenges to Technology Categorisation in the Preparation of Technology Needs Assessments' (2015) 131 Climatic Change 371.

56 Nygaard and Hansen ibid 374.

57 Used formally in the UNFCCC Article 4.5, ESTs has come to mean "technologies which protect the environment, are less polluting, use all resources in a more sustainable manner, recycle more of their wastes and products, handle residual wastes in a more acceptable manner than the technologies for which they were substitutes, and are compatible with nationally determined socio economic, cultural and environmental priorities". IPCC Working Group III, *Methodological and Technological Issues in Technology Transfer: Summary for Policymakers: A Special Report of IPCC Working Group III* (Intergovernmental Panel on Climate Change 2000) 52.

58 To give an example, for a less-developed country, end of pipe carbon capture method for a coal-fired power plant may be considered as low-carbon technology. However, this would not be so for a rich economy having access to better ways to mitigate. See Annex for details.

wind energy has grown dramatically in recent time. To cope with that, the grid systems and storage capacities need to be adapted to the intermittency of renewable energy.[59] Carbon capture and storage technologies (CCS) are important for fossil-fuel dependent power sectors. In the land usage sector, soil management through conservation agriculture, livestock management, efficient irrigation, and agroforestry reduces emissions overall. The reduction in demand for emission-intensive food items (e.g. meat products) is also useful. Better consumption management to reduce food waste and food loss can further relieve the pressure on food production.[60] To reduce the amount of energy consumed by urban buildings, the focus remains upon better designs for building heating and cooling, and also on the use of efficient appliances.[61] Management of urban transport needs using efficient mass transit systems, lowering dependencies on private cars and modal shifts resulting in a lesser need for travel will reduce emissions in that sector, as well as improve urban air quality.[62] Some domestic aviation can be cut down by high-speed rail connectivity. Also, energy efficiency improvement measures and operational modifications in the industries can contribute to emission reduction.[63] Lowering emissions in the industrial sector would be feasible when the required capital costs do not raise competitiveness concerns. Energy efficiency improvements can result from general purpose technologies (e.g. information technology), and also from cross-sector technologies (e.g. motor systems, steam systems, recovery of waste heat). Increase in the rate of recycling can also push us towards a more circular economy.[64]

III International Trade for Low-Carbon Technology Diffusion

A *Aspects of the Relationship between Trade and Technology*

Technology transfer is often understood only as a legacy claim made by the developing WTO members to their developed counterparts.[65] While this is an

59 de Coninck and others (n 1) 324–5; Thomas Cottier and Ilaria Espa (eds), 'Introduction and Overview', *International Trade in Sustainable Electricity: Regulatory Challenges in International Economic Law* (Cambridge University Press 2017).

60 de Coninck and others (n 1) 327–9.

61 ibid 331.

62 ibid 332.

63 ibid 333.

64 ibid 335–6.

65 For more see pp. 81 & 85 below.

important aspect, it is not the whole picture.[66] The often overlooked fact is that the act of trading between partners across different markets and related cooperation across borders is the biggest conduit for spreading new technologies. Trade triggers cross-border transmission of knowledge in both 'hard' and 'soft' forms, the outcome of which is new products or processes finding markets in the partner economies.[67] Therefore, transfer of technology also includes situations where multiple stakeholders, both public and private, interact with each other creating flows of knowledge, commodities, and services embodying new technologies.[68] The IPCC lists a number of pathways through which the stakeholder interactions lead to technology transfer. The list includes, *inter alia,* direct purchase, licensing, franchising, foreign direct investment, joint ventures, subcontracting, research cooperation, export of products and capital goods, education and training, exchange of scientific and technical personnel, and government assistance programs.[69] Each of these pathways are categorised by the IPCC as public, private, or community-driven ones, also holding that the private-sector driven pathways are the dominant mode of technology transfer.

In this spontaneous process of technology diffusion, the role of international trade policy, and regulation is facilitative. Domestic tariff and non-tariff measures, as well as global trade rules set the terms of interaction for firms engaged in LCT transactions across borders. By doing so, trade regulation provides the overall framework within which transactions–both voluntary and compulsory–will take place. Therefore, trade rules are important determiners of how a novel technology is taken up by the market actors.

In more theoretic terms, diffusion is a key stage (Figure 2) in a new technology's journey from the drawing board to the market. At that sage, a new technology spreads along different trade-related pathways (e.g. imports, license

66 We discuss the existence and evolution of such legal commitments in the trade and the climate regimes extensively in the Chapter 2, Sections II and IV, below.

67 Boldt and others (n 55) 12.

68 IPCC Working Group III (n 57) 51, 55, 60.

69 ibid 57; Cristina Tébar Less and Steven McMillan, 'Achieving the Successful Transfer of Environmentally Sound Technologies: Trade-Related Aspects' (2005) Working Paper 2005–2 <https://www.oecd.org/environment/envtrade/35837552.pdf> accessed 25 October 2020; Przemyslaw Kowalski, Daniel Rabaioli and Sebastian Vallejo, 'International Technology Transfer Measures in an Interconnected World' <https://www.oecd-ilibrary.org/trade/international-technology-transfer-measures-in-an-interconnected-world_ada51ec0-en> accessed 25 October 2020; UNCTAD categorises four avenues of technology and knowledge transfer, namely – trade, licensing, FDI, and movement of people. See, Chapter 2, UNCTAD, 'Transfer of Technology and Knowledge Sharing for Development – Science, Technology and Innovation Issues for Developing Countries' (United Nations 2014) UNCTAD/DTL/STICT/2013/8.

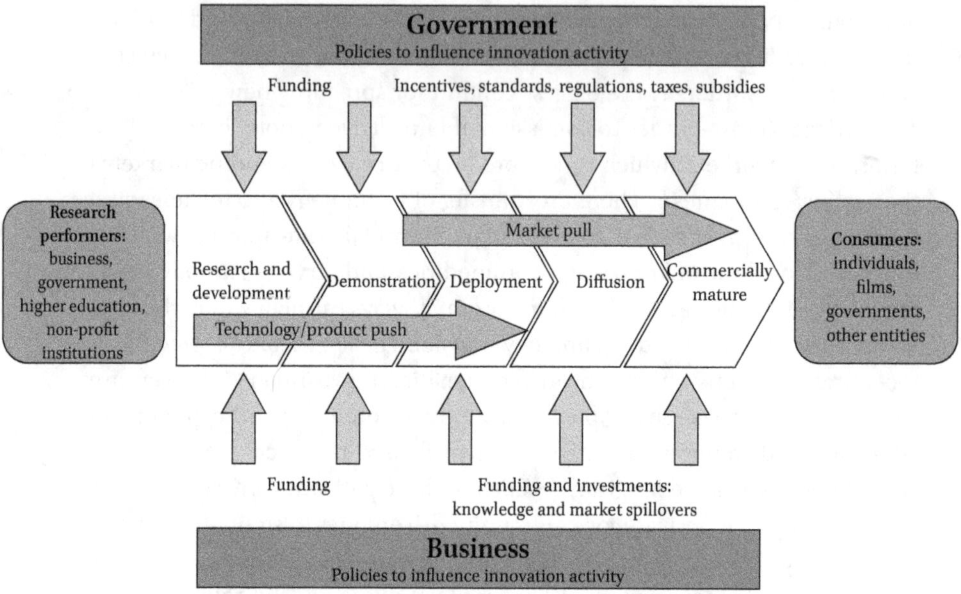

FIGURE 2 The innovation cycle. EGTT, 'Recommendations on Future Financing Options for Enhancing the Development, Deployment, Diffusion and Transfer of Technologies under the Convention' (2009) FCCC/SB/2009/2 8

agreements etc.), given that adequate enabling conditions exist. The following figure shows that while the 'technology push policies' (e.g. R&D funding, incentives) ensure that a new technology reaches the deployment stage, whether it would progress further or not depends on the existence of appropriate 'market pull' measures.[70] This is what Gallagher proposes as market formation policies for LCTs.[71] Therefore, to the extent trade rules are concerned, their role can hypothetically be to allow, also promote such a push and pull dynamic to take place.

Furthermore, economic theory often talks of a 'technique effect'[72] arising from increased cross-border trade between partners, which may also

70 de Coninck and others (n 1) 370; Jeffery Atik, 'Technology Transfer' in Thomas Cottier and others (eds), *Elgar encyclopedia of international economic law* (Edward Elgar Publishing 2017) 606.

71 Kelly Sims Gallagher, *The Globalization of Clean Energy Technology: Lessons From China* (MIT Press 2014) 16–19. More on this can be found in Chapter 2, pp. 83-84 below.

72 'Trade and Environment – The Impact of Trade Opening on Climate Change' (*World Trade Organization* (WTO)) <https://www.wto.org/english/tratop_e/envir_e/climate_impact_e.htm#:~:text=Finally%2C%20trade%20opening%20can%20lead,generates%20less%20greenhouse%20gas%20emissions.&text=First%2C%20freer%20trade%20will%20increase,friendly%20goods%2C%20services%20and%20technologies.>

potentially influence LCT diffusion. It is predicted that the technique effect may take place in two ways–one is that increase of income would make consumers want products with a lower carbon footprint; the other is that the producers would have access to and adopt better production technologies.[73] Overall the technique effect may eventually counteract and nullify the growth of the scale of emission due to increased trade. This is the essence of an Environmental Kuznets Curve (EKC). Though theoretically sound, different factors make an actual finding of technique effect difficult. Torras and Boyce argue that technique effect is further dependent on how the income benefit due to trade is distributed throughout the economy.[74] Fernandez-Amador and others also do not find the technique effect in the economy.[75] It may, therefore, suffice to submit that proactive domestic trade policies can help induce low-carbon technology diffusion through triggering the technique effect.

Domestic trade policies are also a relevant issue to reap the technology benefits from the global value chains (GVCs). Cross-border trade in intermediates also involves low-carbon technologies, especially in areas such as the manufacturing of solar photovoltaic (PV) products. While it is true that developing country firms' participation in such supply chains open up possibilities to obtain efficiency improving technologies from the lead firms in developed countries, this does not automatically happen.[76] The GVCs tend to be semi-independent relationship among businesses where climbing up the

accessed 25 October 2020. Open trade can impact aggregate GHG emissions of an economy through 'scale', 'composition', and 'technique' effects. Scale effect indicates the increase in emission with the economic growth in terms of scale. The composition effect indicates that with increasing sectoral efficiency, overall emission level would be influenced by the compositio of the economy. Lastly the technique effect indicates that energy efficiency improvement due to trade would lower the level of aggregate emissisons. Technique effect is always positive, while the scale effect is otherwise.

73 Ludivine Tamiotti, World Trade Organization and United Nations Environment Programme (eds), *Trade and Climate Change: A Report by the United Nations Environment Programme and the World Trade Organization* (World Trade Organization; United Nations Environment Programme 2009) 51–53; Octavio Fernández-Amador and others, 'Carbon Dioxide Emissions and Economic Growth: An Assessment Based on Production and Consumption Emission Inventories' (2017) 135 Ecological Economics 269, 270–271; van Asselt (n 11) 159; David I Stern, 'The Rise and Fall of the Environmental Kuznets Curve' (2004) 32 World Development 1419.

74 Mariano Torras and James K Boyce, 'Income, Inequality, and Pollution: A Reassessment of the Environmental Kuznets Curve' (1998) 25 Ecological Economics 147.

75 Fernández-Amador and others (n 73) 274.

76 UNESCAP, 'Global Value Chains, Technology Transfers and Innovation', *Asia-Pacific Trade and Investment Report 2015: Supporting Participation in Value Chains* (United Nations 2015) 148, 149.

chain involves enduring competitive pressures.[77] Studies show that developing countries falling back in terms of capability improvement remain stuck on low to medium skill-intensive supply chains.[78] While factors such as obtaining foreign investment, domestic trade openness, and better human capital improve chances of direct technology transfer within the GVC, those factors are themselves dependent on governance reforms, improvement of business environments, and efforts to develop the domestic skill base.[79] A study exploring vertical integration of Chinese firms in solar PV supply chains was possible due to advantageous market policies abroad, mobilization of global talents, flexible manufacturing possibilities at home, and availability of domestic industrial policies.[80]

Two additional arguments can be put forward to further highlight the importance of trade rules in relation to LCTs. One is that supporting the technological upgradation of exporting countries is important particularly for the developed nations to assume full responsibility for their total consumption emissions. Fernandez-Amador and others show that a key reason behind the developed countries' successful reversal of the emission trend is the outsourcing of emissions.[81] Once the emission inventories of the OECD countries are made to account for the full spectrum of consumption emission, the reversing trend vanishes. The authors recommend adoption of consumption-based trade regulation by the importing countries to account for the emission leakage. Such regulations would also have a technology diffusion benefit as the exporting countries would be further compelled to adopt greater efficiency and mitigation technologies.

Another argument is that trade measures are the best option to tackle price and incentive distortions in the market operating as barriers to the diffusion

77 ibid 149.

78 Padmashree Gehl Sampath and Bertha Vallejo, 'Trade, Global Value Chains and Upgrading: What, When and How?' (2018) 30 The European Journal of Development Research 481, 498.

79 UNESCAP (n 76) 150–158; Satoshi Inomata and Daria Taglioni, 'Technological Progress, Diffusion, and Opportunities for Developing Countries: Lessons from China' in World Trade Organization and others (eds), *Technological innovation, supply chain trade, and workers in a globalized world: global value chains development report 2019* (World Trade Organization 2019) 94–96.

80 Fang Zhang and Kelly Sims Gallagher, 'Innovation and Technology Transfer through Global Value Chains: Evidence from China's PV Industry' (2016) 94 Energy Policy 191, 199–200.

81 Fernández-Amador and others (n 73); Octavio Fernández-Amador, Joseph F Francois and Patrick Tomberger, 'Carbon Dioxide Emissions and International Trade at the Turn of the Millennium' (2016) 125 Ecological Economics 14.

of LCT. These barriers, commonly grouped as market failures, pose great challenges to these technologies' penetration of the market and becoming commercially viable. A known economic phenomenon surrounding a public good,[82] theoretically market failures affect the diffusion of clean technologies, because – (i) potential users of the technology do not bear the full social cost of non-adoption, or (ii) appropriate information to make the right choice is not present, or (iii) innovators are unwilling to produce ideas that would benefit others.[83] Trade measures such as pricing of carbon emission or removal of fossil fuel subsidies can correct existing distortions and thereby cure market failures. On a level playing field, actors are then easily attracted towards LCTs. These issues will be further expanded upon in the next chapters.

Before venturing further, one pertinent point ought to be reiterated regarding the scope of this research. This volume focuses on the role of the public international law on trade (i.e. WTO law) and domestic trade policy measures for greater LCT diffusion. It is not meant to prejudice the significance of other important avenues of technology transfer, e.g. cross-border investments, different forms of partnerships, research and development collaborations, and most importantly licensing agreements.[84] While each of these avenues plays an influential role in clean technology diffusion, current research does not engage with all of those.

In addition, certain caveats should also be kept in notice. When it comes to LCT diffusion, the efficacy of domestic policies to trigger transfers would require complementary actions in non-trade sectors (e.g. education and training), as well as steps from actors beyond the domestic jurisdictions. Moreover, the impact of a trade measure is naturally limited to only trading nations. Countries that are not open to trade, especially poor ones, would need support and assistance to be integrated into any trade related scheme of technology diffusion. Lastly, trade is a transaction where market size matters. Therefore, it is unavoidable that some countries will be better endowed to deploy specific

---

82 Kenneth Gillingham and James Sweeney, 'Barriers to Implementing Low-Carbon Technologies' (2012) 03 Climate Change Economics 1250019, 1250019–2. The authors note that 'consumer and producer decision-making in unfettered markets face barriers that lead to less market penetration of low-carbon technologies than would be most economically efficient. We refer to such situations as "market failures." '

83 Adam B Jaffe, Richard G Newell and Robert N Stavins, 'A Tale of Two Market Failures: Technology and Environmental Policy' (2005) 54 Ecological Economics 164; Adam B Jaffe, RG Newell and Robert N Stavins, 'Technological Change and the Environment' in KG Mäler and JR Vincent (eds), *Handbook of Environmental Economics*, vol 1 (Elsevier Science 2003).

84 See UNCTAD (n 69) above.

trade tools (e.g. process and production measures) than others. Nevertheless, given the fact that the top GHG emitters are large, well-integrated trading nations, the principal argument of the importance of trade in relation to the diffusion of LCTs remains valid. These issues are again taken up in the third chapter.

B *The Disconnect between Trade and Climate Legal Regimes*

There are some basic differences between the treaty regimes of international trade and climate change. The climate change regime tackles the challenge of allocating burdens upon individual state actors to produce shared global benefits, whereas, the trade regime is more transactional, offering exclusive benefits in return for the costs incurred.[85] This difference between the regimes is also manifested in their orientation towards domestic law. While the WTO rules seek to ensure that domestically adopted measures do not veer off the internationally agreed standards, the domestic commitments are the standard setters for the global climate regime. Finally, the core principles underlying the regimes prioritise different sets of interests. Similar difference is also observable in the motivation of states animating these legal institutions. To illustrate, while non-discrimination is the guiding rule in the trade regime, in climate law it is the principle of common, as well as differentiated responsibilities that carry the day.

As a result, despite the influential role of international trade transactions to facilitate LCT diffusion, the distinct rule systems that govern international trade on one hand and climate change on the other, are disconnected.[86] The trade rules do not proactively respond to the urgency of combatting climate change. Also, there is no formal appreciation of the role of the regime in spreading low-carbon technologies.[87] In climate law, trade-related aspects of technology development and transfer never saw clear enunciation,[88] mainly because of the difficulty in agreeing to a market based approach. De Coninck and Sagar observed recently that "[m]ost developed countries favour an approach that exclusively promotes markets through enabling environments, while most developing countries are of the view

85 Pauwelyn viewed the multilateral trade regime as an amalgamation of bilateral relationships between states. J Pauwelyn, 'A Typology of Multilateral Treaty Obligations: Are WTO Obligations Bilateral or Collective in Nature?' (2003) 14 European Journal of International Law 907.

86 The next chapter addresses this issue in even greater detail.

87 See Chapter 2 II D at p. 76 below.

88 See Chapter 2 II A at p. 61 onwards.

that support for developing capabilities, regardless of market-conformity, is also needed."[89] Institutional idiosyncrasies driven by distinct sets of interests pursued by parties through them contribute to this disconnect. The result, as Humphreys surmises, is 'structural ambiguity'- a situation where the understanding of a term of art (i.e. technology transfer) takes an ambiguous, or irreconcilably different meaning in different regimes.[90] Over time, this entrenches the divergent approaches of the actors and the regimes towards a common problem.

But the lack of connection between the trade and the climate regimes does not mean that there are necessarily conflicts. The fear of the WTO's anti-environment bias is a thing from the past. The underlying principles in both regimes have lead to repeated attempts in bringing forth a harmonised and complementary coexistence. In the case of the WTO, it is manifest from repeated allusions to the mutual supportiveness of trade openness and environmental protection, giving meaning to sustainable development.[91] However, the legislative part of the institution did not succeed either in making new rules reflecting trade and environment coherence,[92] or in initiatives to liberalise trade in environmental goods and services. In contrast, progressive interpretation from the WTO Appellate Body (AB) has developed a predictable jurisprudence to the effect that trade measures can be maintained to promote environmental concerns, given that the opportunity exists in law. In the very second dispute heard by the AB, it was held that WTO laws are not "to be read in clinical isolation

89 Heleen de Coninck and Ambuj Sagar, 'Technology Development and Transfer (Article 10)' in Daniel Klein and others (eds), *The Paris Agreement on Climate Change: Analysis and Commentary* (Oxford University Press 2017) 261–262.

90 Stephen Humphreys, 'Structural Ambiguity: Technology Transfer in Three Regimes' in Margaret A Young (ed), *Regime Interaction in International Law* (Cambridge University Press 2012).

91 The parties to the WTO maintained that, '[…] the aims of upholding and safeguarding an open and non-discriminatory multilateral trading system, and acting for the protection of the environment and the promotion of sustainable development can and must be mutually supportive'. 'Doha Ministerial Declaration' (WTO 2001) WT/MIN(01)/DEC/1 para 6.

92 For details regarding progress on trade and environment cooperation agenda, See, Mereille Cossy and Gabrielle Marceau, 'Institutional Challenges to Enhance Policy Co-Ordination – How WTO Rules Could Be Utilised to Meet Climate Objective?' in Thomas Cottier, Olga Nartova and Sadeq Z Bigdeli (eds), *International trade regulation and the mitigation of climate change: World Trade Forum* (Cambridge University Press 2009); Also, Henrik Horn and Petros C Mavroidis, 'Multilateral Environmental Agreements in the WTO: Silence Speaks Volumes: MEAs in the WTO' (2014) 10 International Journal of Economic Theory 147.

from public international law."[93] Since then, many environmental instruments have found a way into the factual considerations serving as the background to a better understanding of WTO rules,[94] in particular, the exception clauses therein.

In the climate regime, a desire to avoid conflict with the trade rules appeared in the language of the 1992 Framework Convention, holding that "[m]easures taken to combat climate change, including unilateral ones, should not constitute a means of arbitrary or unjustifiable discrimination or a disguised restriction on international trade".[95] While obliging the developed countries to mitigate emission, the Kyoto Protocol also urged those countries to do so in a manner that minimises the adverse effect on international trade. Taking a different path in the next decade, the issue of reconciliation with the trade rules was buried in the latest Paris Agreement.[96]

Putting all together, a reasonable conclusion to be drawn is that a coherent, constructive relation between trade and LCT diffusion rules remain an incomplete agenda. Despite fundamental differences, the two regimes exist in the shared plane of public international law without significant conflict–not because the overlap between the two systems are well managed, but because their interactions remain at a bare minimum. The task of coherence building between these two regimes should therefore entail predicting the potential areas of overlap and charting of a path for their integration and co-evolution. We take up these tasks in subsequent chapters. The remainder of the current

93 *United States – Standards for Reformulated and Conventional Gasoline* [1996] Appellate Body Report WT/DS2/AB/R, DSR 1996:I 317.

94 For example, the AB took note of the Law of the Sea Convention, Biodiversity Convention and the Agenda 21, *United States – Import Prohibition of Certain Shrimp and Shrimp Products* [1998] Appellate Body Report WT/DS58/AB/R, DSR 1998:VII 2755 48–49; A Panel took note of the WHO classification of asbestos as carcinogenic, *European Communities – Measures Affecting Asbestos and Asbestos Containing Products* [2001] Panel Report WT/DS135/R, DSR 2001:VII 3305 [8.247]; Another Panel took note of the WHO Framework Convention on Tobacco Control, *United States – Measures Affecting the Production and Sale of Clove Cigarettes* [2012] Panel Report WT/DS406/R, DSR 2012:XI 5865 [2.29–2.32, 7.229–7.232]; Panel took note of the Agreement on the International Dolphin Conservation Program *United States – Measures Concerning the Importation, Marketing and Sale of Tuna and Tuna Products* [2012] Panel Report WT/DS381/R, DSR 2012:IV 2013 686; Panel examined whether the UNFCCC has direct effect in India, *India – Certain Measures Relating to Solar Cells and Solar Modules* [2016] Panel Report WT/DS456/R [7.285–7.301].

95 Article 3.5, United Nations Framework Convention on Climate Change 1992 (n 14).

96 To be noted in this regard that the Paris Agreement does not have any direct reference to trade issues at all.

chapter will focus on the theoretical aspects of the coherence building and the impact of the doctrine of Common Concern thereupon.

C *Fragmentation, or Regime Interactions*

The phenomenon of 'disconnect' as outlined above is a result of the fragmentation of the international legal order. Fragmentation is the natural consequence of having multiple specialised rulemaking bodies in a globalising world order, with the corresponding absence of a common coordination mechanism.[97] In international relations literature, it is termed as a 'regime complex', referring to the fact of increasing density of international institutions that are not in a hierarchical relationship in a given area–as a result, creating overlaps and potentially giving rise to conflicting rules reflecting different sets of interests.[98] Both disciplines attribute this phenomenon to the path-dependent rulemaking by institutions in a way that ideas, expectations, and interests animated in different fora are not aligned to generate a set of core applicable norms.[99] As van Asselt identifies, fragmentation can manifest itself in various ways–as that of rules, or institutions.[100] With respect to the fragmentation of rules, one can further distinguish between that of primary, and secondary norms.[101] Fragmentation can also be at the point of governance when one takes into account the increasing role of non-state actors in making rules.[102] The downsides of having a fragmented legal order, or a regime complex is that it creates opportunities for forum shopping, leads to loss of legal coherence across rule systems,

97 Study Group of the International Law Commission, 'Fragmentation of International Law: Difficulties Arising from the Diversification and Expansion of International Law – Finalized by Martti Koskenniemi' (UNGA 2006) A/CN.4/L.682; A/CN.4/L.702 10–17; Thomas Cottier and others, 'Introduction: Fragmentation and Coherence in International Trade Regulation: Analysis and Conceptual Foundations' in Thomas Cottier and Panagiotis Delimatsis (eds), *The prospects of international trade regulation: from fragmentation to coherence* (Cambridge University Press 2011) 9–12; Joost Pauwelyn, 'Fragmentation of International Law', *Max Planck Encyclopedia of Public International Law* (Online, Oxford University Press) <http://opil.ouplaw.com/view/10.1093/law:epil/9780199231690/law-9780199231690-e1406> accessed 25 October 2020.

98 Kal Raustiala and David G Victor, 'The Regime Complex for Plant Genetic Resources' 58 International Organization 277, 295–6.

99 Andreas Fischer-Lescano and Gunther Teubner, 'Regime-Collisions: The Vain Search for Legal Unity in the Fragmentation of Global Law Diversity or Cacophony: New Sources of Norms in International Law Symposium' (2003) 25 Michigan Journal of International Law 999.

100 van Asselt (n 11) 35–36.

101 ibid 37.

102 ibid 38–39.

makes consistent rule implementation difficult, and racks up costs of compliance for poor countries.[103]

As argued by Biermann and others, fragmentation cannot be avoided in current world affairs and it need not necessarily be resented. The authors classify forms of fragmentation into synergistic, cooperative, or conflictive depending on the convergence or divergence regarding the number of participating parties, issues covered, and the decision making procedures.[104] On one hand, there are synergistic fragmentations where the same parties tackle similar issues in institutionally different, but well-integrated regimes – for example, treaty and protocol relationship.[105] On the other hand are conflictive fragmentations where regimes' memberships, underlying principles, and operating procedures hardly overlap (e.g. Convention on biological diversity and the TRIPS Agreement of the WTO).[106]

Keohane and Victor have also reached similar conclusions while examining the climate change regime complex. Despite the risk of forum shopping, the authors hold that a regime complex is not necessarily undesirable, as different regimes provide a variety of options to build cooperation among smaller groups of actors (i.e. the club approach) in a way that willing participants can make desirable rules. Regime complexes also have higher adaptability over time.[107] The authors hold that for the climate regime complex to be of a beneficial nature, it needs to be coherent, have clearly discernible normative content based on scientific information, and be accountable, fair, and sustainable.[108]

D *Paths that Lead to Coherence Building*

Given that fragmentation of international legal regimes is an indispensable reality, it is worthwhile to pursue an agenda of coherence building. It need not be for the appeasement of a postmodern angst,[109] or with a view to preserve a perceived unified essence of international law.[110] Coherence is necessary for

103 Raustiala and Victor (n 98) 299–303; van Asselt (n 11) 40–42.

104 Frank Biermann and others, 'The Fragmentation of Global Governance Architectures: A Framework for Analysis' (2009) 9 Global Environmental Politics 14, 19–21.

105 ibid 20.

106 ibid 21.

107 Robert O Keohane and David G Victor, 'The Regime Complex for Climate Change' (2011) 9 Perspectives on Politics 7, 14–16.

108 ibid 16–17.

109 Martti Koskenniemi and Päivi Leino, 'Fragmentation of International Law? Postmodern Anxieties' (2002) 15 Leiden Journal of International Law 553.

110 Martti Koskenniemi, 'Hegemonic Regimes' in Margaret A Young (ed), *Regime Interaction in International Law* (Cambridge University Press 2012).

international law to be 'responsive'–i.e. able to perform the task the law is set out for. Here we assume that international law must not be construed as incapable to secure the goals states commit to (e.g. containing global temperature rise) through its apparatus (e.g. treaties). The assumption is important to avoid situations of institutionalised paradoxes–outcomes when a regime is ill-equipped to deliver upon its key mandates. Coherence across regimes, based on shared legal principles, would allow complementarity as one regime can gain access to the specialised tools in other regimes to effectively deliver upon the aspirations of the international community.

Therefore, with respect to LCT diffusion, a coherence building agenda is needed to develop a framework that facilitates low-carbon technology flow and thereby better mitigation performance all over. To the extent such coherence among different regimes does not exist, it needs to be built up. Keohane and Victor suggest that a climate regime complex would be successful if it can allow different regime-specific tools to implement the climate goals in a coherent fashion.[111] This task of coherence building is of legal nature at its core. It further depends on the nature of the foundational norms and their conflicting or synergistic interactions. In cases where there are explicit legal norms pertaining to the same issue, conflict can arise if action prohibited or regulated under one regime is permitted, even obliged in another.[112] On the opposite, synergies can exist when regimes are based on shared principles and working towards a common goal. Under both of these circumstances, the fragmentation is manifest. There can also be a potential fragmentation when a principled divergence or convergence among regimes does not actually manifest in conflicts or synergies due to the absence of detailed regulation.[113] With respect to trade and climate regime fragmentation on the issue of LCT diffusion, it is of a potential nature.

Dispute settlement and techniques of treaty interpretation are of great assistance to resolve explicit, conflicting fragmentations *ex post*. A tribunal called upon to find and apply the law will take recourse to the tools of treaty interpretation and find a resolution of the conflict. Available conflict clauses in the treaties or the rules of priority will help to this end. The last resort is the technique of 'systemic integration'. Made famous by the International Law Commission (ILC) report on the fragmentation of international law, this approach calls for use of Article 31(3)(c) of the Vienna Convention on the Law of Treaties (VCLT) as a tool to integrate systemic objective, by interpreting a norm by

111 Keohane and Victor (n 107) 16–18.

112 van Asselt (n 11) 52–54.

113 ibid 54.

reference to its 'normative environment', i.e. general international law.[114] The technique put forward in the ILC report is that any rule of international law exists in a systemic relationship with other laws, and therefore, when facing a manifest conflict there is "[...] a need to carry out interpretation so as to see the rules in view of some comprehensible and coherent objective, to prioritise concerns that are more important at the cost of less important objectives."[115]

However, in cases where there are no rules that manifestly conflict, the above *ex post* techniques cannot be put into use, necessitating a search for alternatives. As mentioned earlier, the fragmentation between the trade and climate regimes is such a situation. As the climate regime is built on soft law foundations, formal disputes do not arise there. Under such circumstances, preventing fragmentation between regimes becomes a progressive task of filling the potential gaps and constructive ambiguities by creating rules and approaches based on common and shared values. In contrast with the former, this approach is of an *ex ante* nature. It will involve synergistic rule generation based on constitutionalism and multi-level governance.

The term 'constitution' implies 'a sum of basic legal norms which comprehensively regulate social and political order of a polity'.[116] A constitutionalist approach will seek to achieve coherence by establishing a clear system of political order, governance, and normative values. Regarding issues that are at the intersection of two distinct legal regimes, such an approach will put an emphasis on identifying the core shared values, which can then be actualised through generating a complementary set of rules. Based on the constitutionalist foundation, the multi-level governance view envisages the global legal order as composed of different interacting governance layers compensating the domestic loss of regulatory freedom by installing the fundamental values in the international system with the overall goal of preserving and promoting those values.[117]

It is through this lens that the doctrine of Common Concern of Humankind is viewed. The conviction presented here is that the proposed formulation of the doctrine and its implementation can further the work of coherence

114 Para 413 Study Group of the International Law Commission (n 97) 208.

115 Paras 417–419 ibid 210–211.

116 Cottier and others, 'Introduction: Fragmentation and Coherence in International Trade Regulation: Analysis and Conceptual Foundations' (n 97) 34; Anne Peters, 'Compensatory Constitutionalism: The Function and Potential of Fundamental International Norms and Structures' (2006) 19 Leiden Journal of International Law 579, 581.

117 Thomas Cottier and Maya Hertig, 'The Prospects of 21st Century Constitutionalism' in Armin von Bogdandy and Rudiger Wolfrum (eds), *Max Planck Yearbook of United Nations Law* (Koninklijke Brill NV 2003) 261.

building between the trade and climate legal regimes; fostering LCT diffusion as a result. In performing this task, the function of the doctrine is much like the norm of sustainable development; building, also strengthening the regime complex of climate change. The following sections elaborate upon the existing and the proposed dimensions of common concern of humankind, and its potential application regarding the diffusion of LCT s.

IV Common Concern of Humankind: History and Meaning

Shared legal concepts are the foundation on which two regimes can develop synergistic interaction.[118] The common concern of humankind is a unique notion that has informed the climate regime over time. As will be elaborated below, the recognition of climate change as a 'common concern' of 'humankind' legally elevates the issue to a higher plane of urgency and also invites all stakeholders to engage in necessary remedial action. This section will provide a brief background of the concept and propose a meaning in which the concept should be shared across regimes. Suggestions will also be made as to the ways in which this notion, when taken as an emerging doctrine, may contribute to a coherent interaction between the trade and the climate regime regarding LCT diffusion.

Further elaboration of the notion of common concern draws upon the theory of global commons and collective action challenge, as well as takes account of related consequences of unregulated negative externalities leading to market failures. It seeks to find a new balance between a strengthened reach of international law responding to crucial common interests and the traditional regulatory independence of the state under the mantle of permanent sovereignty. By so doing, the doctrine of Common Concern may eventually add to the strength of the related norms, such as the *jus cogens* and sustainable development.

A *Inception and Evolution of the Notion*

The very inception of the phrase 'common concern of humankind' is a politically struck settlement in the late 1980s[119] at the United Nations General Assembly (UNGA). While on one hand countries were interested in a norm that

118 van Asselt (n 11) 55–58.

119 UN Doc A/Res/43/53, adopted on 6/12/1988. Paragraph 1 of the resolution "[r]ecognizes that climate change is a common concern of mankind, since climate is an essential condition which sustains life on earth." This was the first ever use of the concept.

can point out the global interest in preserving and promoting transboundary commons anywhere, an expression was required the usage of which did not connote a potential motive of economic benefit.[120] The notion of common concern hence emerged as a duty-focused expression underscoring the need for global action with respect to the issue area, while respecting the sovereign domain of states.[121] Nevertheless, expression of concern does constrain a sovereign entity from acting in a wayward fashion.[122]

Since its inception at the UNGA declaration on climate change, the expression has influenced a number of hard and soft law instruments.[123] Apart from climate change, it has been used to mark the importance of protection and preservation of biodiversity,[124] plant genetic resources for food and agriculture,[125] intangible cultural heritage,[126] also the relation between environment and development.[127] The International Law Commission (ILC) vigorously debated whether or not the common concern of humankind can also be considered as a foundational norm in the area of protection of the atmosphere. Eventually, there was a preambular expression of concern, albeit with different

---

120 This was the reason for not using the expression of Common Heritage of Mankind with respect to climate change, despite the proposition from Malta in the UN General Assembly.

121 Jutta Brunnée, 'Common Areas, Common Heritage, and Common Concern' in Daniel Bodansky, Jutta Brunnée and Ellen Hey (eds), *The Oxford Handbook of International Environmental Law* (First Edition, Oxford University Press 2007). The author's comment is oft-referred that '[t]he concept focuses upon the essence of what renders a given concern "common", and treads gingerly around both common property regimes and the territorial sovereignly of individual states'.

122 ibid 566. The author further conditioned her position by maintaining that '[common concern] signals that states' freedom of action may be subject to limits even where other states' sovereign rights are not affected in the direct transboundary sense envisaged by the no harm principle'.

123 A comprehensive account of the notions evolution can be found here, Shinya Murase, 'Second Report on the Protection of Atmosphere – 67th Session of the International Law Commission' (2015) A/CN.4/681; Also see, Cottier, 'The Principle of Common Concern of Humankind' (n 7); Earlier influential work include, Laura S Horn, 'Common Concern of Humankind and Legal Protection of the Global Environment' (PhD Monograph, The University of Sydney 2000); A A Cançado Trindade and David J Attard, 'I Meeting of the UNEP Group of Legal Experts to Examine the Implications of the "Common Concern of Mankind" Concept on Global Environmental Issues' (1991) 13 Revista IIDH 247.

124 Convention on Biological Diversity (adopted June 5, 1992, entered into force December 29, 1993) UNTS vol. 1760 p. 79.

125 International Treaty on Plant Genetic Resources for Food and Agriculture 2001.

126 Convention for the Safeguarding of the Intangible Cultural Heritage 2003.

127 IUCN, *Draft International Covenant on Environment and Development* (Fourth Edition, 2010).

wording.[128] The reasons behind non-inclusion of the norm in the operative part were, *inter alia,* that there is no state practice to indicate that the term is used with a consistent meaning as was suggested by the special rapporteur.[129]

It is in the growing climate treaty regime that common concern of humankind truly found a home. Not only has the expression played an iconic, and heralding role to the benefit of the budding treaty regime, but it also has activated scholarly contemplation for decades afterwards. In 1992, the preamble to the UN Framework Convention declared that anthropogenic changes to earth's climate are a common concern.[130] The Washington conference of the International Law Association (ILA) produced an agreed list of principles of the climate regime, where the common concern of humankind was provided with a similar contextual role.[131] The draft Article 2, titled 'objectives' reiterates the Framework Convention's position as the earth's climatic change and the adverse effect thereof are a common concern of humankind. Prepared by the most noted environmental law scholars, the ILA document serves to clarify the majority position of the experts in this regard.

The Paris Agreement, as well as the decision of the Conference of Parties (COP) containing the Agreement reaffirmed in 2015 that climate change is a common concern of humankind. This reiteration was unique in ways more than one. It puts to question the wisdom behind the earlier reluctance of the ILC in using the expression in relation to the protection of the commons.[132]

---

128 International Law Commission (ILC), 'Report of the International Law Commission: Sixty-Seventh Session' (2015) A/70/10 22–27. The expression the ILC chose to refer is 'pressing concern of international community as a whole'. It is interesting to note that while the ILC was very explicit about the non-normative nature of the expression used, in the next sentence it admitted that the commision uses it as a guide for its action, i.e. inclusion of new topic in its work program (page 27). For a critical take, see, Cottier, 'The Principle of Common Concern of Humankind' (n 7); Nadia Sanchez Castillo-Winckels, 'Why Common Concern of Humankind Should Return to the Work of the International Law Commission on the Atmosphere' (2016) 29 Geo. Int'l Envtl. L. Rev. 131.

129 International Law Commission (ILC), 'Provisional Summary Record of the 3246th Meeting, Held 6 May 2015' (2016) A/CN.4/SR.3246 See in particular, the intervention by Mr. Murphy; Daniel Bodansky, Jutta Brunnée and Lavanya Rajamani, *International Climate Change Law* (First Edition, Oxford University Press 2017) 51; Georg Nolte, 'The International Law Commission and Community Interests' in Eyal Benvenisti and Georg Nolte (eds), *Community Interests Across International Law* (Oxford University Press 2018); Cottier, 'The Principle of Common Concern of Humankind' (n 7) s 1.2.2.2.

130 Preamble, United Nations Framework Convention on Climate Change (n 14).

131 Shinya Murase and others, 'Washington Conference: Legal Principles Relating to Climate Change' (International Law Association 2014) 3–4.

132 International Law Commission (ILC), 'Provisional Summary Record of the 3246th Meeting, Held 6 May 2015' (n 129) 4. One representative at the ILC pointed out that the common concern has not been used in the negotiation since inception.; Georg Nolte later

Furthermore, the wording of the preambular paragraph in the Paris Agreement also shows a growing normative import. The introductory text of the Agreement mentions:

> *Acknowledging* that climate change is a common concern of humankind, Parties should, when taking action to address climate change, respect, promote and consider their respective obligations on human rights, the right to health, the rights of indigenous peoples, local communities, migrants, children, persons with disabilities and people in vulnerable situations and the right to development, as well as gender equality, empowerment of women and intergenerational equity,[133]

Compared to the previous expressions recognising the common concern of climate change, the above paragraph differs slightly. It is appended with an additional list of issues connected by the obligations of 'respect, promote, and consider'. While on one hand, this could be seen as confusing the scope of the expression and diluting its meaning; on the other hand, it could be seen as an example of its maturity. A plain reading suggests the drafters intend the expression 'common concern of humankind' to trigger climate action, in the course of which the ancillary considerations come to play.[134]

As hinted above, common concern also has a very vibrant life in the scholarly literature. International institutions like the UN Environment (UNEP), also other legal experts have been well invested over time in the growth of this notion. No prominent treatise on environmental law or climate change law is complete without a mention and contemplation on the topic. The existence of the concept has also spread beyond the confines of climate law. This chapter turns next to specify the scope of the concept of common concern.

B *Making of a Common Concern*

Though it is already well-accepted that climate change is a common concern of humankind, it is nevertheless useful to recapitulate the path that has led to

---

admitted that the ILC may have underestimated the utility of the expression, Nolte (n 129) 54–55.

133 Reference to 'common concern of humankind' in the Paris Agreement preamble appeared in connection with a range of other obligations, including human rights, rights of special groups and right to development. Paris Agreement (n 28).

134 Castillo-Winckels (n 128) 142–143; Zaker Ahmad, 'Trade Related Measures to Spread Low-Carbon Technologies: A Common Concern Based Approach' in Thomas Cottier (ed), *The Prospects of Common Concern of Humankind in International Law* (Cambridge University Press 2021).

this outcome; especially because the exercise elucidates the key attributes of a shared problem amounting to a common concern. This then informs the task of taking appropriate responses thereto and translating the same into legal language. Also when the notion of common concern is sought to be employed from one legal regime to another as a shared concept, clarity is necessary not only for application but also to delimit the influence of the concept in the other regime.

Formal designation of an area of shared interest as a common concern of humankind is a function of objective and subjective variables. Objectively, the attributes of a problem should be definable as a 'concern' that is 'common'. Subjectively, the dictates of political expediency would determine whether the governments would agree on such a decision. These are detailed below.

The objective variable is literal at the outset, surrounding the meaning of the phrase 'concern' that is common to 'humankind'. Based on the translation of the notion in several languages, Thomas Cottier concluded that "[c]oncern not merely describes a fact, a problem and adverse effects, but equally entails a normative component that the matter needs to be addressed".[135] Therefore, marking an issue as a common concern does not only underscore an agreement that the issue is worrisome, but also attaches great importance to it, and urges the stakeholders to address the matter.[136] Through a comparative reading of the relevant preambular recitals of the biodiversity and climate change conventions, Duncan French concludes that a subject-matter earns the significance of common concern of humankind when there is a large consensus that the level and scale of the problem impacts humanity at large, including future generations.[137] Also, French notes that assigning of concern is important to take the issue out of the "conceit of an exclusive domestic domain" and to put it as a matter of global interest.[138]

Another aspect of the objective component is to attempt to glean the essential characteristics of a common concern by finding a common denominator among the range of problems where the notion has been formally invoked. In that regard, the starting point is that common concerns arise when global

135 Cottier, 'The Principle of Common Concern of Humankind' (n 7) s 1.3.3.

136 ibid.

137 Duncan French, 'Common Concern, Common Heritage and Other Global(-ising) Concepts: Rhetorical Devices, Legal Principles or a Fundamental Challenge?' in Michael Bowman, Peter Davies and Edward Goodwin (eds), *Research Handbook on Biodiversity and Law* (Edward Elgar 2016) 345.

138 ibid 343–344.

common is adversely affected.[139] Friedrich Soltau, after consulting a number of resources, supplied three fundamental characteristics of common concerns of humankind. Those are – first, that the interests in question are transboundary and "touch on values or ethics of global significance"; second, that the interests are of concern because of the gravity of the threat, or potential irreversibility of the impact; third, that it is not possible to safeguard the interests of concern without collective action.[140] We will see later that the formulation of Common Concern of Humankind advanced as a doctrine further develops the objective parameters as independently verifiable constructs.[141]

Turning to the subjective variable, all the issue areas that have received a formal designation as a 'common concern of humankind' share the seal of political approval in common. Not only do the subject-matters falling within the current formal scope of the term vary to some extent, but also there are pertinent subject-matters that have, despite being logically worthy, not formally received the designation.[142] There also are areas that have expressions that resemble common concern either in wording or in effect.[143] This suggests that the influence of the notion beyond the recognised treaty regimes like climate change remains in flux and would indeed benefit from a structured plan of growth.

The involvement of the political factor in the establishment of a common concern of humankind can limit its import across other regimes where the notion is not agreed upon. It is without doubt that in the climate regime common concern of humankind is a core notion that influences the development and operation of particular principles and rules. However, there is only very limited possibility that this shared concern and related need for action would

---

139 For example, in the UN Framework Convention on Climate Change, its not the climate, rather the anthropogenic change of it is declared a common concern. Brunnée, 'Common Areas, Common Heritage, and Common Concern' (n 121) 564–565.

140 Friedrich Soltau, 'Common Concern of Humankind' in Cinnamon P Carlarne, Kevin R Gray and Richard G Tarasofsky (eds), *The Oxford handbook of international climate change law* (First edition, Oxford University Press 2016) 207–208.

141 See p. 33-4 below.

142 Cottier, *The Prospects of Common Concern of Humankind in International Law* (n 5). Each of the chapters from 3 to 8 of this volume deals with specific issue areas that can objectively be considered as common concerns. French (n 137). French notes that desertification can be a candidate for being termed as a common concern of humankind.

143 Judith Schaeli, 'Marine Plastic Pollution as a Common Concern of Humankind' in Thomas Cottier (ed), *The Prospects of Common Concern of Humankind in International Law* (n 5). Schaeli traces normative consequences similar to that of the common concern in the UN Law of the Sea (UNCLOS) convention. However, as the author pointed out, the UNCLOS does not refer to marine pollution as common concern of humankind.

spontaneously spill over onto other treaty regimes, like for example, the WTO laws. As will be discussed in subsequent chapters, the ability to take trade policy measures to foster diffusion of LCT s can be impacted by such a limitation of the notion's cross-regime influence. The proposed doctrine of Common Concern admits the importance of the process of 'claims and responses' – taking place among the key stakeholders, eventually garnering political clout.[144]

C *Legal Consequence*

Scholars, especially experts on environmental law have at length pored over the possible implications of common concern of humankind as a legal expression. In contrast to the reluctance of the ILC in admitting any legal implication arising from the designation, most experts writing on the topic agree to its having some normative effect. However, as to the extent of the capacity of common concern to trigger legal consequences, opinions vary. While some note the indeterminacy of the exact content of the expression,[145] as well as doubt its independent existence in the absence of a treaty framework;[146] there are also optimistic perspectives that see the notion gradually developing into a legal doctrine or a principle of customary international law.[147] This section will briefly cover the generally shared view among experts on the legal consequences of common concern. Building upon this, the next section will elaborate upon the proposed doctrine of Common Concern of Humankind–a forward-looking structure advanced by Thomas Cottier and others.[148]

At the very initial stage, a meeting of experts convened by the UNEP in the run-up to the UNFCCC convention saw a wide range of views regarding the meaning and possible implication of common concern of humankind. It was highlighted that the notion could be applied not only to environmental problems but also beyond.[149] The note from the UNEP secretariat envisaged

144 See p. 46 below.

145 Patricia W Birnie, Alan E Boyle and Catherine Redgwell, *International Law and the Environment* (3rd ed, Oxford University Press 2009) 129–130.

146 Brunnée, 'Common Areas, Common Heritage, and Common Concern' (n 121); Daniel Bodansky, Jutta Brunnée and Lavanya Rajamani, 'Climate Change and International Law', *International climate change law* (First Edition, Oxford University Press 2017) 51–52.

147 Thomas Cottier and others, 'The Principle of Common Concern and Climate Change' (2014) 52 Archiv des Völkerrechts 293; Cottier, 'The Principle of Common Concern of Humankind' (n 7); Frank Biermann, '„Common Concern of Humankind ": The Emergence of a New Concept of International Environmental Law' (1996) 34 Archiv des Völkerrechts 426, 446–450.

148 Cottier, *The Prospects of Common Concern of Humankind in International Law* (n 5).

149 Laura Horn, 'Climate Change and the Future Role of the Concept of the Common Concern of Humankind' (2015) 11 Australian Journal of Environmental Law 33, 28.

an obligation to cooperate stemming from the concept and involving all countries.[150] The following expert discussion[151] posited the expression of common concern in the chain of the evolution of common interest in international law, which saw to reduced domestic jurisdiction and also the emergence of *erga omnes* obligation.[152] It was noted that what would be elements of common concern could be detected in different doctrines, e.g. those of *res communis,* international public domain, and public trust.[153] Constitutive elements of common concern were identified to be – (i) involvement of all state, and non-state actors, (ii) long-term temporal dimension with intergenerational issues, and (iii) burden-sharing.[154] The issues of intergenerational equity and equitable burden-sharing in the discharge of a concern was especially highlighted.[155]

The unquestionable core implication of common concern of humankind is introducing a responsibility to act upon the international community in general.[156] This responsibility obligates the international community to cooperate in response to the concern.[157] International cooperation triggered by common concern is geared towards the establishment of appropriate institutional and normative framework, built upon the principle of equitable sharing of benefit and burden.[158] Tracing the growth of the climate legal regime towards a decentralised, bottom-up process guided by domestic preferences of the stakeholders, Jutta Brunée argued that instead of enforcing rules in a strictly top-down

150 Mostafa K Tolba, 'The Implications of the "Common Concern of Mankind" Concept on Global Environmental Issues' (1991) 13 Revista IIDH 237, 243.

151 Participants in the discussion were, *inter alia,* Judge Manfred Lachs, Professor (later Judge) Cançado Trindade, and Professor (later Member of the ITLOS tribunal) David Attard.

152 *Barcelona Traction, Light and Power Company, Limited (Belgium v Spain); Second Phase* [1970] ICJ Rep 1970 3 (International Court of Justice (ICJ)) 32; Trindade and Attard (n 123) 248.

153 Trindade and Attard (n 123) 248.

154 ibid 249.

155 ibid 250.

156 Alexandre Kiss, 'The Common Concern of Mankind' (1997) 27 Environmental Policy and Law 244, 246–247. Kiss maintained that common concern, as a concept supplies the basis for the international community to act. Such right and duty of the international community to be concerned requires to be balanced with national sovereignty. Many years later, Shelton echoed the same position,; Dinah Shelton, 'Common Concern of Humanity' (2009) 5 Iustum Aequum Salutare 33, 38; Michael Bowman, 'Environmental Protection and the Concept of Common Concern of Mankind', *Research Handbook on International Environmental Law* (Edward Elgar Publishing 2010) 503.

157 Brunnée, 'Common Areas, Common Heritage, and Common Concern' (n 121) 566.

158 ibid.

fashion, cooperative facilitation of compliance is the key consequence to be drawn from common concern.[159]

Even though scholars concur that the responsibility arising from a recognised common concern has an *erga omnes* character,[160] its actual operation is difficult in practice. As the responsibility is understood to be commonly held by the international community, transforming it to individualised duties upon states amenable to be invoked by others is met with scepticism. There is an apprehension shared by environmental lawyers, especially those specialising in climate change, regarding strictly defined duties. As experience with the Kyoto Protocol suggests, strict duties can backfire when stakeholders leave the forum in consequence thereof.[161] Brunée identifies 'self-help' measures to be potentially reactive, confrontational, and eroding long-term legitimacy of the climate governance framework.[162] Another problem is that even when there is an *erga omnes* obligation upon individual states, it is difficult to effectively invoke their breach.[163] Also, any potential breach will be difficult to settle through disputes because breach of duty, even of an *erga omnes* nature, does not mean that the injured party has an automatic access to courts.[164]

The compilation by the ILA of climate law principles and the commentaries thereto closely echoes the position outlined above. As mentioned previously, the ILA document notes the common concern of humankind as a goal, thereby giving it an overarching status as a guide. While noting the universal agreement that climate change is a common concern of humankind, the commentary declares that "[…] all states have a common responsibility to take appropriate measures to address the concern".[165] Furthermore, the common responsibility is to be discharged 'through' the principles of sustainable development, common but differentiated responsibility (CBDR), equity, and international cooperation. With respect to sustainable development, the commentaries note the

159 Jutta Brunnée, 'The Global Climate Regime: Whither Common Concern?' [2012] Coexistence, Cooperation and Solidarity (2 vols.) 721, 731. We revisit this issue in Chapters 3 and 6.

160 Shelton (n 156) 39; Horn (n 149) 30.

161 Amanda M Rosen, 'The Wrong Solution at the Right Time: The Failure of the Kyoto Protocol on Climate Change' (2015) 43 Politics & Policy 30; Christopher Napoli, 'Understanding Kyoto's Failure' (2012) 32 SAIS Review of International Affairs 183.

162 Brunnée, 'The Global Climate Regime' (n 159) 725.

163 ibid 724; French (n 137) 352–354; Zaker Ahmad, 'State Responsibility Aspects of a Common Concern Based Approach to Collective Action' in Samantha Besson (ed), *International responsibility : essays in law, history and philosophy* (Schulthess, éditions romandes 2017). Further discussion on this issue can be found in Chapter 6 below.

164 Shelton (n 156) 39; French (n 137) 353.

165 Murase and others (n 131) 4.

importance of concerted action on the basis of common concern but propose the execution of such action in the broader context of sustainable development.[166] Similarly, with respect to CBDR, it is submitted that common concern is the basis of the common responsibility part of it, while the incontrovertible operation of the principle of equitable burden-sharing leads to differentiated responsibility.[167] We recall these terms of interaction between the key foundational principles in the final section of this chapter while suggesting implications for LCT diffusion.

It is submitted that although the above formulation of the legal implications of common concern is neatly squared off with the structure of international law in general and the climate regime in particular, it falls short of resolving the concern. The case on point is the concern of climate change. At the beginning of this chapter, it was outlined that a climate regime built upon voluntary, bottom-up commitments is not strong enough to generate sufficient ambition.[168] There is a potential in the notion of common concern to be read as requiring a specific end goal to be achieved. With respect to climate change that goal must be, among others, keeping within a safe carbon budget by the end of the twenty-first century. If a facilitative compliance-based regime does not lead there, the obligation to resolve the concern should further necessitate and justify complementary actions that contribute to reaching that goal. It is explained below how the proposed doctrine of Common Concern of Humankind may lead us down that path.

V Towards a New Doctrine

Reflecting upon the potential of the common concern norm to evolve further, Thomas Cottier and co-authors promoted a well-calibrated set of propositions to add to the core meaning and consequence of the notion.[169] The term

166 ibid 6–7.

167 ibid 14–20.

168 See section I at p. 6 and onwards.

169 Cottier and others, 'The Principle of Common Concern and Climate Change' (n 147); Thomas Cottier and Krista Nadakavukaren Schefer, 'Responsibility to Protect (R2P) and the Emerging Principle of Common Concern' in Peter Hilpold (ed), *The Responsibility to Protect (R2P): A new Paradigm of International Law?* (Martinus Nijhoff Publishers 2014); Thomas Cottier, 'Improving Compliance: Jus Cogens and International Economic Law' in den Maarten Heijer and Harmen van der Wilt (eds), *Netherlands Yearbook of International Law 2015: Jus Cogens: Quo Vadis?* (TMC Asser Press 2016); Thomas Cottier and Tetyana Payosova, 'Common Concern and the Legitimacy of the WTO in Dealing with Climate

'doctrine of Common Concern' is used throughout the volume to indicate the set of broad procedural and substantive responsibilities to be applicable in a clearly defined factual setting as proposed by the author.[170] Doctrinal scholarship as such, in the tradition of public international law's founding fathers like Vattel or Grotius, plays an important role in the progressive development of international law,[171] even when not serving as the principal source of law in traditional terms.[172]

In addition to supplying specific thresholds for determining the boundary of a Common Concern, the doctrine further argues that when a matter of shared interests finds itself to be of 'Common Concern', it must be resolved through cooperative means. Beyond this already established duty to cooperate, another avenue of action is the homework responsibility to appropriately address concerns within respective jurisdictional boundaries.[173] By doing so, the doctrine adds another layer of action, which is of due diligence nature, making sure that any outcome of cooperation is followed upon by the stakeholders with necessary implementation steps. Furthermore, compliance with a Common Concern is ensured not only in a facilitative process but also with unilateral sanctions and countermeasures as the last resort, when necessary and appropriate.[174]

Before venturing further into detailing the different consequences suggested by the doctrine, some attention is due upon the legal nature of the proposed Common Concern norm. The doctrine holds that Common Concern can eventually emerge as a principle of law. Legal principles are unique in their balance between precision and scope of application. The more widely applicable a principle is, the more general tends the terms of its framing to be.[175] From that perspective, although the doctrine of Common Concern would suggest

Change' in Panagiotis Delimatsis (ed), *Research handbook on climate change and trade law* (Edward Elgar 2016); Cottier, 'The Principle of Common Concern of Humankind' (n 7).

170 Specific reference to the doctrine itself or the framework of action thereof is distinguished by using the term 'Common Concern' in title case.

171 Alain Papaux and Eric Wyler, 'Legal Theory as a Source of International Law: Doctrine as Constitutive of International Law' in Samantha Besson and Jean d'Aspremont (eds), *The Oxford Handbook of the Sources of International Law*, vol 1 (Oxford University Press 2018) 524–525 (in print book) <http://oxfordhandbooks.com/view/10.1093/law/9780198745365.001.0001/law-9780198745365-chapter-25> accessed 25 October 2020.

172 As is well known, Article 38 of the Statute of the International Court of Justice, teachings of the 'most highly qualified' publicists from various nations, may only serve as 'subsidiary means' of determining the rule of law.

173 Cottier, 'The Principle of Common Concern of Humankind' (n 7) s 1.6.

174 ibid s 1.7.

175 Ronald Dworkin, 'The Model of Rules' (1967) 35 University of Chicago Law Review 14.

avenues of action, the actual implementation of these avenues with respect to specific concerns need to be adapted to the exigencies of each regime the doctrine is introduced to. As Cottier mentions:

> Conceptualising Common Concern of Humankind as a principle thus seeks to expound underlying values, broadly defined rights and obligations the application of which depends upon a particular context; accordingly results may vary within the broad framework of the principle. We thus should not expect a detailed set of rules commensurate with the principle. This does not exclude that the principle and its components eventually will produce more detailed and specific rules which may further refine its contents and provide enhanced legal security in different fields of the law.[176]

With that being mentioned, following is a brief account of the scope of the proposed notion and all three avenues of legal consequences suggested to be emanating therefrom.

A *A Dynamic Gateway for 'Common Concerns'*

It has been already mentioned that common concern of humankind is an identifier for threats on a massive scale that challenge human communities and therefore necessitate collective responses. The Common Concern doctrine further supplies a structured framework that links the expression to the theory of collective action failure to produce global public goods (GPG s)[177] for identification purposes. The linkage is useful to distinguish true cooperation problems (e.g. climate change) from issues of mere coordination between parties (e.g. global standard setting), or issues where effort by one is globally optimal (e.g. space research).[178] Conceptualisation of the expression along these lines enjoys the benefit of combining existing legal scholarly work with similar theories in other disciplines, especially economics, resulting in a robust fact-based criterion enabling interpretation of the concept in existing and also in new circumstances.

Given that the doctrine prescribes for enhanced responsibility for all stakeholders to resolve a Concern, only exceptional collective action failures merit

176 Cottier, 'The Principle of Common Concern of Humankind' (n 7) s 1.3.2.

177 Cottier and others, 'The Principle of Common Concern and Climate Change' (n 147) 308–309, 313; Cottier, 'The Principle of Common Concern of Humankind' (n 7) s 1.4.1.

178 Scott Barrett, *Why Cooperate?: The Incentive to Supply Global Public Goods* (paperback ed, Oxford University Press 2010).

falling within the scope of its terms. Cottier further suggests that the boundaries of Common Concern be linked to a high enough threshold that only the extraordinary crises may clear. In this regard, it has been advanced that global peace and stability can serve as the bar.[179] Global peace, stability, and welfare are not understood in the sense of only non-aggression and avoidance of war, but as a fundamental precondition necessary to maintain human society.[180] Only the problems that eventually threaten peaceful coexistence and welfare globally may be considered as a Common Concern of Humankind.[181] This way, the authors turn common concern into a dynamic term, the material scope of which may expand over time,[182] including transboundary resource-related collective action problems, and potentially also economic activities with strong international interdependence.[183]

A well-drawn conceptual boundary of Common Concern helps to liberate the notion from being exclusively subject to a political choice made by parties under the dictates of expediency. Even when operating on a recognised plane of common concern of humankind, i.e. climate change, a designated boundary is helpful especially to limit the influence of the concept upon other regimes. For example, measures taken in the trade regime can be helpful for climate mitigation, adaptation, or necessary transfer of technology. But according to the doctrine, a responsibility to take such measures, or to cooperate to that effect would only exist to the extent such steps do bear a clear and manifest linkage with the defined boundary of the Common Concern.

B *Enhanced Legal Consequences*

The doctrine advances three distinct, yet interrelated channels guiding the stakeholders' responses regarding all Common Concerns of Humankind.[184] The responsibility to cooperate, coupled with the duty to take appropriate domestic measures at home (i.e. homework) arise at the very outset with the emergence of a Common Concern.[185] In situations where effective cooperation

179 Cottier, 'The Principle of Common Concern of Humankind' (n 7) s 1.3.2.4.
180 ibid.
181 ibid.
182 Cottier and Payosova (n 169) 14.
183 Cottier, 'Improving Compliance: Jus Cogens and International Economic Law' (n 169) 350; Cottier, *The Prospects of Common Concern of Humankind in International Law* (n 5). See various case studies in that volume.
184 Cottier and others, 'The Principle of Common Concern and Climate Change' (n 147) 314–320; Cottier, 'The Principle of Common Concern of Humankind' (n 7) ss 1.5-1.7.
185 Cottier, 'The Principle of Common Concern of Humankind' (n 7) ss 1.5-1.6.

is unsuccessful or homework is not forthcoming, the doctrine further advances a duty to undertake unilateral measures to secure compliance.[186]

These normative consequences undoubtedly push beyond the traditional meaning of common concern of humankind elaborated earlier.[187] It happens in at least two specific ways. One is the way the doctrine proposes legal consequences arising exclusively out of the legal expression. In the treaty frameworks already deploying the notion (e.g. climate change or biodiversity), obligations such as cooperation and due diligence co-exist with the expression.[188] The doctrine turns this co-existence into causation, making it possible for the consequences to be invoked also in situations where a 'Common Concern' exists in the absence of a treaty. Another way in which the doctrine goes beyond its traditional understanding is the way the consequences are formulated. Instead of declaring the states' freedom to take action to resolve Common Concerns, the doctrine binds them under a positive duty. This duty to act lies at the heart of the proposed framework, influencing all the three avenues of normative consequences arising therefrom.[189]

Even though the doctrine suggests threefold consequences, some primary conclusions already indicate that all three aspects may not come into play in all the fields of law. The nature of the subject-matter may not always merit for efforts along the three avenues. For example, Lucia Satragno's work on monetary regulation as a Common Concern of Humankind shows that unilateral compliance securing measures currently has very little to do in that area.[190] The following paragraphs elaborate upon the enhanced normative consequences and their relevance in international trade regulation and diffusion of LCTs.

(i) Responsibility to Cooperate

As mentioned before, collective responsibility towards cooperation internationally is the undisputed, as well as an indispensable consequence of common concern of humankind. It is nevertheless important to explicitly mention so because international law is punctuated by respect for sovereign equality.

---

186 ibid s 1.7.

187 See pp 34-36 above.

188 With respect to the international climate change law, scholars see 'no harm' rule as having a customary status. This gives rise to homework obligations like due diligence, and procedural obligations like duty to consult, negotiate and cooperate. For details, see, Bodansky, Brunnée and Rajamani (n 129) 40–43.

189 Cottier, 'The Principle of Common Concern of Humankind' (n 7) s 1.7.3.

190 Lucia Satragno, 'International Monetary Stability as a Common Concern of Humankind' in Thomas Cottier (ed), *The Prospects of Common Concern of Humankind in International Law* (Cambridge University Press 2020) s 1.6.

A duty to cooperate does not ordinarily exist unless provided for in express terms. So far, such duties exist within limited frames, e.g. duty to negotiate in good faith at the WTO, or a duty to settle disputes peacefully. The doctrine of Common Concern indicates that a responsibility to cooperate entails engaging in consultation and negotiation in a transparent manner and with good faith.[191] Such cooperation would eventually result in the building of appropriate institutions to tackle and respond to the concern.[192] With respect to climate change, principles of equity, sustainable development, and differentiated responsibility would inform any cooperation approach. The evolving climate governance framework amply exemplifies this point.

It should be emphasised that the responsibility to cooperate is not solely an obligation of conduct. To be successful, parties to cooperation must do more than merely engage. It must result in specification of the appropriate range of actions to be taken by the stakeholders at different levels of governance. It also means that cooperation itself must not be limited to a specific level or certain type of actors. Again, with respect to climate change, it is important that cooperation spans across institutions, fostering a coherent response to the problem. Cooperation is the basis on which further synergy between the trade and the climate regimes can be built up. Chapter 3 of this volume elaborates upon the dimensions of cooperation in pursuance of the doctrine of Common Concern, focusing on the role of states, and specific to the issue of low-carbon technology diffusion.

(ii) Homework Responsibility

Noting that cooperation alone is insufficient to address any shared concern successfully, the doctrine further calls for necessary actions to be taken within the domestic legal system. Although it is an increment upon current understanding of the legal implication of common concern, it is in no way unreasonable. The common concern of humankind is already understood as limiting the policy autonomy of the sovereign entities with respect to an area of shared concern.[193] This constraint, in itself, is an obligation to make policy choices that cater to addressing a concern and not worsening them. For example, with respect to climate change, the limitation of not worsening the concern would translate into supplying incentives to the renewables industries instead of fossil fuels. The homework obligation as proposed by the doctrine of Common Concern offers to change the current mere encouragement to act (right to act)

191 Cottier, 'The Principle of Common Concern of Humankind' (n 7) s 1.5.2.

192 ibid.

193 See p 36 (nn 156-7) above.

following the expression of concern to a positively worded obligation to act in response to the problem.

The environmental principles of 'no harm' and 'due diligence' informs the homework obligation to a great extent.[194] Harm prevention is akin to the constraining function of common concern mentioned above. The principle of due diligence conditions the application of any further positive obligation envisaged by the doctrine. As a result, appropriate homework measures are required to be taken only after consideration of the reality faced by each country, their capacity, ability to discharge positive obligations, as well as the availability of support.

Within the trade regime, the nature and extent of homework obligations would depend on the legal framework actually in place. Thomas Cottier in his work highlights two ways of implementing homework obligations–through the domestic performance of international obligations, or by adopting autonomous measures. In the former case, Common Concern doctrine should inspire further trade rulemaking relevant to the area of application (e.g. technology diffusion) through a cooperative process. Where there are such rules, homework obligation may only entail carrying them out informed by the tenets of multi-level governance (the principle of subsidiarity, in particular).[195] In the absence of detailed regulation, autonomous trade measures are to be taken to address a Common Concern. This category of actions, when challenged, would possibly fall back on the notion itself for necessary legitimation. In case any such action is challenged in a formal dispute, the question would arise whether the principle of Common Concern of Humankind and the suggested normative implications thereto can be taken to form part of the applicable law. This last answer truly depends upon the development and acceptance of the doctrinal approach through claims and responses, as the next section would elaborate.

It is nevertheless true that matters that touch upon trade, e.g. regulating production and consumption, may also indirectly moderate the behaviour of trading partners. This is highlighted by Cottier as the extraterritorial impact of domestic regulation. Such impacts should be necessary and welcome so long as those are not employed to meet protectionist ends. Subsequent chapters of

194 The International Court of Justice held that the obligation of prevention arises from the due diligence required of a State, *Case concerning Pulp Mills on the River Uruguay* (*Argentiva v Uruguay*) (*Judgment*) [2010] ICJ Rep 14 (International Court of Justice); For a detailed discussion, see, Birnie, Boyle and Redgwell (n 145) 137–150; With particular reference to climate change, see, Bodansky, Brunnée and Rajamani (n 129) 41–42.

195 Chapter 3, sections II, & III provides further details in this regard.

this volume explore the detailed aspects of the homework obligation. A number of useful domestic trade policy measures are identified in Chapter 3. Thereafter, Chapters 4 and 5 look at specific technology diffusion policy measures and their relations with trade regulation and the doctrine of Common Concern.

(iii) Securing Compliance

While the duty to act influences all the normative aspects of the doctrine, it perhaps goes farthest and draws most scepticism in response when applied to the aspect of securing compliance unilaterally. The doctrine of Common Concern dictates that as a last resort, non-compliance with the proposed normative framework must be met with unilateral countermeasures. In practical terms, it therefore implies that the willing and able actors are under a positive obligation to act unilaterally seeking to correct the behaviour of their non-compliant counterparts.[196]

Unilateral countermeasures become obligatory in cases where non-cooperation arises from parochial, self-interested motivation. It is not attracted in situations where the failure of an actor to comply with the dictates of the doctrine stem from lack of capacity or other reasonable shortcomings. We further recall that support and assistance remain essential corollaries to cooperation and homework parts of the framework. It is nevertheless true that the legitimisation of any such countermeasure would require the state responsibility rules regarding the definition of the injured state to change. The benefit of the proposition is that not only does it serve as a final recourse to bring the fractious cohorts back to cooperation, it further offers to discipline unilateral action, which currently takes place in a grey area of public international law.[197]

Chapter 6 of this volume discusses that the aspect of compliance enforcement through unilateral countermeasures, like the homework aspect of Common Concern, would depend on the existing contextual legal framework. It would also depend on the actual nature of the breach itself. In case explicit regulations inspired by the doctrine are put in place within a treaty framework, a breach thereof would first and foremost require taking resort to the mechanism established within such frameworks to address non-compliance. Whether a compliance mechanism would accommodate taking of unilateral countermeasures as proposed here would depend on the specifics of each situation. Also importantly, in an era where multilateralism is threatened to be

196 Cottier, 'The Principle of Common Concern of Humankind' (n 7) s 1.7.3.

197 Ibid s 1.7.1.

abandoned in favour of populist and mercantilist policies, abundant caution is required while advancing a proposition that calls upon the powerful states to act unilaterally.

In situations where the primary obligations of cooperation and homework have not resulted in express substantive commitments from the parties to a treaty framework, the call for compliance using unilateral countermeasure would have a smaller scope of legitimacy. However, unilateral steps as such would nonetheless be required as part of a 'carrot and stick' approach, to induce all the involved parties to come to the negotiations table, also to take diligent homework measures. The legitimacy of this approach would depend on the success of the argument that refusals to cooperate and undertake homework measures breaches obligations of *erga omnes* character arising out of the Common Concern of Humankind doctrine.

C *Forward Evolution*

Although the Common Concern doctrine potentially supplies an integrated framework to deal with critical collective action challenges with global public goods (GPGs) as they arise, it should be noted that it is an evolving process. The gradual fostering of Common Concern of Humankind as a norm entailing stricter legal consequence would take place through 'claims and responses' in the international field.[198] Nolte similarly mentions that community norms do not automatically manifest themselves. Often they are results of claims made by an actor, which then gathers salience due to political or other forms of suasion.[199] Eventually, some or all aspects of the doctrine may obtain a status of a customary or a general principle of international law, of an *erga omnes* nature.

Principles are flexible instruments that suggest a general standard of conduct.[200] The positive aspect of construing the doctrine of Common Concern as a future principle of international law is that it remains possible to envisage its application in a variety of factual settings.[201] This adaptability, as previously

198 Ibid s 1.3.1.

199 Nolte (n 129) 103; This is similar to what Finnemore and Sikkink identified as norm entrepreneurship, Martha Finnemore and Kathryn Sikkink, 'International Norm Dynamics and Political Change' (1998) 52 International Organization 887, 895.

200 Dworkin (n 175); Jutta Brunnée, 'The Rule of International (Environmental) Law and Complex Problems' in Heike Krieger, Georg Nolte and Andreas Zimmermann (eds), *The International Rule of Law: Rise or Decline?* (Oxford University Press 2019). The author maintains that principles like customary principles like harm prevention are not by themselves sufficient to tackle complex global challenges. The latter requires development of treaty regimes.

201 See pp. 40-1 above.

mentioned, comes at the cost of specificity. Principles colour the application of rules, or inspire the making of new ones that eventually operationalises the expression in the real world. Admittedly, therefore, even when Common Concern of Humankind is considered as a principle of international law, its application in a specific setting would probably require new rules, or understanding the existing ones in its light. It remains possible for a multilateral or a regional treaty regime to adopt the doctrine as a guiding principle in part or full, thereby turning it into an *erga omnes partes*.[202] In so doing, manifestation of the doctrine's proposition in different regimes would vary.

Unlike international lawyers, international relations scholars, especially the social constructivists closely study the evolution of norms. Some insight may be obtained therefrom. Finnemore and Sikkink, in their work, indicate three key stages in the life-cycle of a norm, namely norm creation, norm cascade, and norm internalisation.[203] The authors hold that available literature generally concur on two elements for successfully creating a new norm, i.e. having norm entrepreneurs and the existence of an organisational platform. New norms do not emerge from a vacuum. It is rather the existing ones that evolve and take up new meaning. The norm entrepreneurs serve as 'meaning architects' or suppliers of a new 'frame' of interpretation.[204] The evolution of the doctrine of Common Concern can be contemplated along the same line. At the initial stage the norm entrepreneurs need not necessarily be the states. Different non-state actors can organise and disseminate the utility of a norm at various levels of governance. Eventually, however, state endorsement would be necessary for a norm to eventually gather enough salience to be able to pass a 'tipping point' beyond which it becomes self-reliant.[205] That arguably is the point when the norm formally enters the domain of hard law.

It remains a hypothesis of this research that this doctrinal structure may assist in generating a more coherent trade and climate regime and in the process facilitate diffusion of LCT. The following section ventures to outline that process.

VI Application in the Trade-Climate Interface

So far we have concluded that the trade and the climate regimes have key differences in terms of subject-matters, goals, and core principles. While the

202 Brunnée, 'The Global Climate Regime' (n 159) 724.
203 Finnemore and Sikkink (n 199) 895.
204 ibid 897.
205 ibid 900–901.

differences lead to a potential of fragmentation between these two regimes, both have the seeds of mutual cooperation planted in them in the form of a common subscription to sustainable development.[206] Here we initiate application of the proposed doctrine of Common Concern of Humankind upon the incomplete trade-climate coherence building agenda, on which the subsequent chapters will build upon.

We recall that one of the key goals of this research is to introduce the doctrine of Common Concern to the multilateral trade regime with respect to the latter's dealings with climate change.[207] Trade itself is not a Common Concern of Humankind. It forms part of a shared dialogue under the rubric of the Common Concern doctrine only to the extent the WTO law and domestic trade policy measures have an exclusive role to take the climate agenda forward. The doctrine would facilitate better framing of trade-related response measures to climate change. The framing would prioritise coherence by balancing the competing values, as well as preserving the alignment of the guiding norms that define the relationship between the climate and the trade regimes. As we would see later with respect to the diffusion of clean technologies, a coherent trade and climate change agenda has much more to do with harmonised and complementary actions than merely using trade as a means of threat.[208] The act of trade is in itself a facilitative and mutually beneficial endeavour. Questions of unilateral intervention, if ever arising, would only be to tackle instances of egregious non-cooperation.

Also, this research does not deal with the entirety of the space of Common Concern of climate change in the trade field. As already detailed, it addresses the issue of LCT diffusion. Technology development and transfer is not an entirely new issue in the trade regime, especially when the issue touches upon intellectual property protection. As already mentioned, technology transfer can take place spontaneously, as well as through implementation of specific North to South support obligations. Transfer of technology in general is not seen as a Common Concern here. What is a Common Concern of Humankind is the inhibition of wide diffusion of low-carbon technologies, particularly to the developing and the least-developed countries, as it hinders effective, adequate, and timely climate mitigation from taking place globally.

Until a principle of Common Concern of Humankind attains a customary status under public international law, it can influence rulemaking in other

206 See p. 23-4 above.

207 There can be other Common Concerns that may have a bearing upon trade rules. See, Schaeli (n 143).

208 See Chapter 3, section II A below.

treaty regimes like the WTO through express incorporation into the body of treaty rules. The doctrine can also be utilised to interpret existing trade regulation applied with respect to climate change. However, despite originating from a recognised principle of climate law, Common Concern is yet to garner evidence of use and practice by the states in international relations like the principle of sustainable development.

A *Terms of Relationship with Key Notions*

The doctrine of Common Concern needs to be squared off with the current normative basis of synergistic understanding between the two regimes, namely the principle of sustainable development. It is well understood that the principle of sustainable development "add[s] colour and texture" to the commitments of the covered agreements of the WTO.[209] It also sits at the heart of the global sustainable development goals (SDG s) endorsed by the United Nations, including *inter alia,* the goal of ensuring sustainable production and consumption patterns (Goal 12),[210] and the goal of climate action (Goal 13).[211] The question is whether the introduction of Common Concern is in any way subversive to the state parties' commitment to the principle of sustainable development. Similar attention is also required with respect to reconciling Common Concern with the principle of differentiated responsibility.

The doctrine of Common Concern will only supplement the integrative and conciliatory role of sustainable development.[212] The role of Common Concern is to introduce a special emphasis on certain issues from the bulk that are within the panoply of sustainable development. It is submitted that due to the factual circumstances mentioned at the beginning of the chapter, climate change indeed deserves a more than equal share of attention compared to the

---

209 *United States – Import Prohibition of Certain Shrimp and Shrimp Products* (n 94) para 153; See, for more, Christina Voigt, 'Delineating the Common Interest in International Law' in Wolfgang Benedek and others (eds), *The common interest in international law* (Intersentia 2014); Elisabeth Bürgi Bonanomi, *Sustainable Development in International Law Making and Trade : International Food Governance and Trade in Agriculture* (Edward Elgar 2015).

210 United Nations General Assembly, 'Transforming Our World: The 2030 Agenda for Sustainable Development' (United Nations 2015) A/RES/70/1. Goal 12C specifically asks to '[r]ationalize inefficient fossil-fuel subsidies that encourage wasteful consumption by removing market distortions, in accordance with national circumstances, including by restructuring taxation and phasing out those harmful subsidies, where they exist, to reflect their environmental impacts, taking fully into account the specific needs and conditions of developing countries and minimizing the possible adverse impacts on their development in a manner that protects the poor and the affected communities'.

211 ibid.

212 See p. 37 above.

other environmental issues, as well as a quicker and stronger response from all stakeholders. The Common Concern doctrine carries that sense of urgency from the climate change regime and brings it to the trade world. While all the environmental issues coming to the trade regime also come under the fold of sustainable development, not all of them will be considered as Common Concerns. Therefore the doctrine can be used to create an exclusive narrative commanding immediate action to be taken regarding climate change in the trade regime. This can be of use to all the sticking climate-related issues, including that of LCT diffusion.

Respect for differentiated responsibility should also be a part and parcel of implementing the doctrine of Common Concern in trade law. The nature of differentiated responsibility under climate law is slightly different from the special and differential treatment commitments that exist in the WTO covered agreements. The principle of common but differentiated responsibility (CBDR) is a mainstay of the climate regime. While earlier the CBDR entailed a strict bifurcation of responsibility among the Annex-I countries and others as identified in the UNFCCC, over time it has become more dynamic in nature. The doctrine of Common Concern, as well as the WTO law and trade policy attracted under its fold, must be attendant to the demands of this principle. As explained in relation to the homework obligation under the Common Concern doctrine, domestic trade policy measures to facilitate climate action must take place with appropriate considerations for their impact on developing countries. It is all the more important when such measures would entail costs upon the latter. Appropriate settlements of such concerns are only possible through cooperation, which is why equitable consideration plays a core role in the new cooperation agenda outlined later.[213] However, differentiated responsibility should not be taken as an excuse for any actor to shirk off climate responsibility. It would rather be important that the specific needs of the countries are communicated and appropriate assistance provided to ramp up global action.

B *Implications for Low-Carbon Technology Diffusion*

To the extent diffusion of low-carbon technology is a part of the Common Concern, not only would the doctrine suggest for adequate steps to be taken to deal with any existing barriers preventing such diffusion, but it would also call for actions to positively incentivise technology related transactions. This research is devoted to that effect. At this moment, it can only be hypothesised that obligations arising out of the doctrine, i.e. international cooperation and

---

213 See p. 125-7 below.

domestic steps to tackle market barriers, as well as to promote the growth of related industries will have a positive impact upon the diffusion of low-carbon technologies worldwide. To test it out, awareness of the details of current legal and institutional settings, as well as an empirically sound knowhow of the nature of the technology diffusion challenge, is paramount. The next chapter will turn to those issues.

VII Conclusion

This inaugural chapter has supplied a succinct account of the research problem and the theoretical framework, specified the scope of research, and provided a brief glimpse into the coming analysis. It has been shown that climate change is a complex problem, which the current body of rules, including the recently concluded Paris Agreement, remain incapable of addressing. Part of that inability affects the diffusion of LCTs, which is the particular topic of research here. The chapter has also highlighted that various sub-disciplines of IEL, international trade law for example, provide for avenues through which clean technologies are spread across borders. Focusing on international trade, it was argued that trade policy interventions are necessary to enhance the technique effect of trade opening to lower aggregate GHG emissions, to help countries assume responsibility for consumption emissions, and also importantly, to tackle price and incentive related market imperfections that hinder diffusion of clean technologies. However, the reality is that appropriate coherence between trade and climate regimes remain incomplete.

Against this backdrop, the chapter has characterised low-carbon technology diffusion in the light of the legal doctrine of Common Concern of Humankind, proposing tripartite obligations as emanating from it – (i) duty to cooperate, (ii) homework obligations, and (iii) unilateral enforcement through trade countermeasures. It is maintained that subject to the fulfilment of the requirements of state practice, the doctrine can become a future customary principle, or be incorporated into a treaty regime. It is also found that the Common Concern doctrine can make progress upon the incomplete agenda of coherence between the trade and climate regime by supplementing the already applicable principle of sustainable development, and side by side maintaining respect for differentiated responsibility. To the extent that the diffusion of LCTs suffer from trade-related obstacles, it comes under the umbrella of Common Concern and obtains benefit from the novel framing introduced by the doctrine.

CHAPTER 2

Rules and Facts on Low-Carbon Technology Diffusion

This chapter supplies an in-depth factual understanding of the market-related determinants of low-carbon technology (LCT) diffusion, as well as the relevant developments in the climate and the trade legal regimes to date. In doing so, it facilitates a better understanding of the possible linkages between international trade and LCT diffusion, also the implications of using the Common Concern doctrine in that regard. It begins with a brief, yet illuminating account (Section I) of the origins of technology transfer as a political agenda in the form of early attempts to negotiate a technology transfer code. Following the failure of the code negotiations, the unique expression of technology development and transfer is traced through the evolving, predominantly soft law framework of the climate regime (Section II). It is then joined by a sweeping survey of empirical studies from various sources – to clearly understand and establish the role of markets, and economic instruments in facilitating LCT diffusion (Section III). Against the backdrop of this legal and empirical surveys, the chapter finally indulges into an assessment of the trade rules and practices pertaining to technology development and transfer (Section IV), helpful to later highlight the possible areas of action in the next chapter. Summary analyses appear at the end of each section, which then feed into the conclusion at the end of the chapter. The main contribution of this chapter is in supplying an up-to-date and comprehensive regulatory and factual account – useful not only to substantiate later arguments, but also to update the reader on the current developments.

I The Origin of the Polemics on Technology Transfer

Technology transfer originally emerged as a claim made by the developing to the developed countries in the backdrop of the global South's attempts to create a New International Economic Order (NIEO) in the post-world war II era. Although unsuccessful to generate a binding international agreement, it had a lingering impact on the subsequent developments in different legal regimes, where technology transfer retained a contentious character. The origin story of technology transfer as a negotiation agenda is educative of the points where states' views mingle and stray.

A *Unsuccessful Code Negotiations*

The fundamental basis of the demands for technology transfer made by the newly decolonised and other developing countries emerging from the second world war was based on the premise of economic development being a right, coupled with the understanding that access to modern scientific and technological knowledge is an indispensable component to attain the desired quality of growth.[214] Therefore, the claim was essentially of fairness, i.e. the developing country firms should be able to access necessary technologies from their developed counterparts on fair terms. The wording of the UN General Assembly Resolution[215] regarding the NIEO in 1974 followed by a Charter[216] of Economic Rights and Duties of States reflected this sentiment. For example, Article 13 of the Charter mentioned that "[e]very State has the right to benefit from the advances and development in science and technology for the acceleration of its economic and social development".[217] The same provision also called upon the developed countries to "[...] co-operate with the developing countries in the establishment, strengthening and development of their scientific and technological infrastructures and their scientific research and technological activities so as to help to expand and transform the economies of developing countries".[218]

What made the approach contentious was the perceived difficulty in gaining access to modern technologies. The prevalent business practices were considered as posing obstacles to that end. Under the spotlight were practices like the charging of very high fees for transfers, terms in licensing agreements preventing competition, the practice of packaged transfers, etc.[219] Moreover, the

214 The reformist agenda, as Roffe and Tesfachew term the period during 1960s and 1970s. See, Pedro Roffe and Taffere Tesfachew, 'The Unfinished Agenda' in Surendra J Patel, Pedro Roffe and Abdulqawi Yusuf (eds), *International Technology Transfer: The Origins and Aftermath of the United Nations Negotiations on a Draft Code of Conduct* (Kluwer Law International 2001).

215 United Nations General Assembly, 'Declaration on the Establishment of a New International Economic Order' (United Nations 1974) Resolution A/RES/3201 (S-VI).

216 United Nations General Assembly, 'Charter of Economic Rights and Duties of States' (United Nations 1974) Resolution A/RES/3281 (XXIX).

217 ibid 13.

218 ibid.

219 Countess P. Jeffries, 'A Preliminary Evaluation of the Proposed Text' in Surendra J Patel, Pedro Roffe and Abdulqawi Yusuf (eds), *International Technology Transfer: The Origins and Aftermath of the United Nations Negotiations on a Draft Code of Conduct* (Kluwer Law International 2001) 21–24; Dennis Thompson, 'An Overview of the Draft Code' in Surendra

use of intellectual property rights protections (e.g. patents) by the technology supplier firms to prevent working, wider diffusion, and use of the technology to export products was also perceived as a problem. This fuelled demands for a comprehensive multilateral review of the terms of technology transfer agreements and to develop a set of mutually agreed terms in the form of a code on one hand, and also a revision of the standards of intellectual property protection, especially the Paris Convention on Industrial Property on the other.[220]

With the gift of hindsight, scholars see that the absence of a truly shared goal was a key reason for the failure of the NIEO based claims of technology transfer.[221] A number of developing countries were already experimenting with locally suited technology transfer policies domestically, e.g. the parameters for approved license agreements, reducing scope and duration of patents, domestic working requirements, and provision for compulsory licensing. Whereas the developed countries focused on protecting the business interests, calling for adequate protection of intellectual property rights across the borders and also a liberal regulatory environment for businesses and foreign investment. Due primarily to this absence of a shared vision, the Code negotiations that started in 1972 backed by the UNCTAD, failed in 1983 after six conferences.[222]

The failed Code negotiation nevertheless served to clarify the position of the parties. It also portrayed how the issue of technology transfer can spill over from the domain of private contractual transactions to that of inter-state claims. The developing countries sought to use their advantage in numbers to correct a perceived systemic disadvantage to their private firms. Whereas the developed countries refused to influence private sector transactions by regulating the market. All sides nevertheless agreed that transfer of technology comprised mostly of private business transactions, taking place in the

---

J Patel, Pedro Roffe and Abdulqawi Yusuf (eds), *International Technology Transfer: The Origins and Aftermath of the United Nations Negotiations on a Draft Code of Conduct* (Kluwer Law International 2001) 60–64.

220 Wei Zhuang, *Intellectual Property Rights and Climate Change: Interpreting the TRIPS Agreement for Environmentally Sound Technologies* (Cambridge University Press 2017) 47–59.

221 Roffe and Tesfachew (n 214); Padmashree Gehl Sampath and Pedro Roffe, 'Unpacking the International Technology Transfer Debate: Fifty Years and Beyond' (2012) 36 ICTSD, Issue Paper <http://papers.ssrn.com/sol3/papers.cfm?abstract_id=2268529> accessed 25 October 2020.

222 It should be noted that in the same period, the technology transfer based approach towards deep seabed mining also failed, as the United States refused to ratify the UN Law of the Sea Convention and forced a revision of the rules on that issue. For details, see Thomas Cottier, *Equitable Principles of Maritime Boundary Delimitation: The Quest for Distributive Justice in International Law* (Cambridge University Press 2015) 54–57.

backdrop of a domestic and international legal framework. One could see that transfer of technology became a political agenda due to the dissatisfaction over the operation of private commercial transactions. It also failed because of disagreements on that point. The tussle between these two competing views for a dominant narrative position at the international level has coloured the nature and approach of the subsequent legal regimes tackling technology transfer, especially the World Trade Organization (WTO) and the multilateral environmental agreements (MEAs).[223]

B *Regime Specific Trends*

Since the failure of the Code negotiations, the issue of technology transfer, instead of remaining as a self-standing agenda, was subsumed as a component in different issue-specific negotiations (e.g. trade regulation, or protection of the environment). This dispersion of the notion across supra-national forums of varying institutional set-up and strength resulted in a perceptible difference in the way the notion was understood, incorporated, and implemented. The most notable is the divergence in the approach towards operationalisation of technology transfer in the subsequent MEAs *vis a vis* the multilateral trade regime embodied in the WTO.

Provisions for technological and financial assistance are ubiquitous in the soft laws, as well as the treaty instruments regarding environmental issues that came into being in the decades following the United Nations Conference on Human Environment in 1972.[224] A typical example can be Article 10A of the Montreal Protocol on Ozone Depleting Substances. The provision holds that

> Each Party shall take every practicable step, consistent with the programmes supported by the financial mechanism, to ensure:
>
> (a) that the best available, environmentally safe substitutes and related technologies are expeditiously transferred to Parties operating under paragraph 1 of Article 5; and

223 Laurence Boisson de Chazournes, 'Technical and Financial Assistance' in Daniel Bodansky, Jutta Brunnée and Ellen Hey (eds), *The Oxford Handbook of International Environmental Law* (First edition, Oxford University Press 2007).

224 28 multilateral agreements were identified by the UNCTAD in 2001 as containing technology transfer arrangements. All except 9 on that list were multilateral environmental agreements; the rest being intellectual property conventions, WTO covered agreements and the Energy Charter Treaty. See, UNCTAD (ed), *Compendium of International arrangements on Transfer of Technology: Selected Instruments* (United Nations 2001).

(b) That the transfers referred to in subparagraph (a) occur under fair and most favourable conditions.[225]

About the same time, in the then newly established WTO,[226] specific mention of technology transfer as an obligation appeared in the context of intellectual property issues. The WTO Agreement on the Trade-Related Aspects of Intellectual Property Rights (TRIPS)[227] was the outcome of efforts by the developed countries to ensure for their businesses an avenue to secure protection of intellectual property rights (IPR) abroad. The agreement provided for mandatory minimum standards of IPR protection for all the WTO members minus the least-developed countries (LDCs) to establish and maintain. The agreement was founded on the conviction that the protection of intellectual property rights "should contribute to the promotion of technological innovation and to the transfer and dissemination of technology [...]".[228] Moreover, the developed countries were put under a strict obligation to incentivise respective institutions to transfer technologies to the LDC members.[229]

The differences between the trade and the environmental treaty regimes' approach to technology transfer manifest how political interests vary across those regimes, thereby influencing the final bargain struck. In the MEAs, the scope of technology transfer was narrow and specific to the issue at hand. Therefore, the North v South schism over property rights did not dominate the discussions.[230] Moreover, the emergence of integrative notions like sustainable development helped to move the narrative of technology transfer closer towards preservation of commons. The developed countries also found it politically palatable to commit additional financial resources to issues that were of interest to their own citizens.[231] As a result, the practice of finance backed technology transfer provisions became standardised in the MEAs. This

225 Article 10A, Montreal Protocol on Substances that Deplete the Ozone Layer 1987 (1522 UNTS 3; 26 ILM 1550 (1987)).

226 Marrakesh Agreement Establishing the World Trade Organization 1994 (1867 UNTS 154; 33 ILM 1144 (1994)).

227 Agreement on Trade-Related Aspects of Intellectual Property Rights 1994 (Marrakesh Agreement Establishing the World Trade Organization, Annex 1C, 1869 UNTS 299; 33 ILM 1197 (1994)).

228 Article 7, ibid.

229 Article 66.2, ibid. For further details, see section IV B below.

230 Abdulqawi A Yusuf, 'Technology Transfer in the Global Environmental Agreements: A New Twist to the North-South Debate' in Surendra J Patel, Pedro Roffe and Abdulqawi Yusuf (eds), *International Technology Transfer: The Origins and Aftermath of the United Nations Negotiations on a Draft Code of Conduct* (Kluwer Law International 2001) 315.

231 de Chazournes (n 223) 957–958.

approach prioritised making of state-to-state financial and technical assistance to attain the MEAs targets instead of constraining the firms' freedom to contract.[232]

In contrast, the WTO rules were a branch of international economic law that sought to regulate international trade between its members in unprecedented detail and depth. These new set of rules played a significant part in influencing the terms of competition among private firms. In that context, the TRIPS agreement made sure that holders of intellectual property are provided with a minimum level of security in all jurisdictions. This Agreement triggered the code-era conflict of interests in the WTO, in a slightly different formulation. The question became whether rigorous protection of, or flexibilities regarding IPRs would contribute to transfer of technology. While mandatory technology transfer had no place in the WTO agreement, one exception was the strict obligation to transfer technology to the LDCs.

This brief account explains how the absence of a shared understanding of the meaning and determinants of technology transfer resulted in the notion's regime-specific and somewhat kaleidoscopic character. Although the same state-level actors animated the transfer of technology agenda in various regime settings, differences between those regime characteristics and specific political interests of the parties greatly influenced how the key issues were perceived and pursued. To further comprehend the implications of this 'structural ambiguity'[233] that is diffusion of LCT, we explore the evolution of the notion in the relevant treaty regimes, namely those of climate change and international trade.

II Developments in the Climate Regime

The legal regime of climate change shares common traits with other MEAs. Bodansky and others highlight three key characteristics of the climate treaty regime. First and foremost, the regime undergoes a soft law based incremental evolution.[234] This is observable in the framework and Protocol approach to the rulemaking, gradual institutionalisation, and standard setting through diverse bodies managed through the Conferences of Parties (COP).[235] The second trait is that the rules are framed in a fashion that eases participation.[236]

232 Yusuf (n 230) 314, 317.
233 We recall the term coined by Humphreys mentioned earlier. See Humphreys (n 90).
234 Bodansky, Brunnée and Rajamani (n 129) 22–26.
235 ibid 22–26, 56–60.
236 ibid 61–64.

It is evidenced in the practice of shallow initial commitments across a wide range of issues,[237] coupled with a mechanism for progression over time. Participation is further eased by according flexibilities in terms of commitment,[238] also by differentiated standards of treatment.[239] The last feature, another consequence of the soft approach, is that compliance mechanisms related to the regime are mostly non-adversarial and facilitative in nature.[240]

The evolution of the arrangements related to technology development and transfer in the climate regime also manifest the above features. As shown below, the institutional blueprint of technology transfer has emerged through work done at the committee stages, thereupon endorsed by successive COPs. There are also continuous efforts to develop a closely twined relationship between technology transfer and the financial support mechanisms. In addition, parallel areas have also emerged with a potential positive influence on low-carbon technology diffusion. These areas include mitigation mechanisms like the market-based approaches, especially the clean development mechanism (CDM), as well as the non-binding commitment processes like the Nationally-determined commitments (NDCs).

A *Evolution of Institutional Frameworks*

(i) Background: the Framework Convention and the Kyoto Protocol

Provisions relating to technology transfer in the framework convention were, true to the title, of framework nature. To bridge the wide divergence between the developing and developed parties' views,[241] the language of the relevant UNFCCC provisions are vague.[242] The convention lays down a commitment (Article 4.1) upon all members to "promote and cooperate in the development, application, diffusion, including transfer, of technologies."[243]

237 Daniel Bodansky, *The Art and Craft of International Environmental Law* (Harvard University Press 2010) 183–187.

238 Recall Article 4.2 of the Paris Agreement, urging that "[e]ach Party shall prepare, communicate and maintain successive nationally determined contributions that it intends to achieve". Flexibility is also unavoidable as the operational rules are formulated at institutional levels that do not have the mandate to negotiate treaty provisions.

239 Bodansky, Brunnée and Rajamani (n 129) 26–27.

240 ibid 64–68. The Paris Agreement relies upon periodic review in the form of global stocktake (Article 14), and a compliance mechanism (Article 15) that is "expert-based and facilitative in nature and function in a manner that is transparent, non-adversarial and non-punitive".

241 While the developing countries claimed for access to technology on easier terms, possibility of issuing compulsory license and to obtain financial support; the developed nations wanted technology 'cooperation' rather than 'transfer', see, ibid 140–141.

242 ibid 140.

243 Article 4.1(c), United Nations Framework Convention on Climate Change (n 14).

Implementation of that obligation is differentiated, as the developed countries are put under a strict obligation of conduct. Article 4.5 urges the developed parties to "take all practicable steps" to "promote, facilitate and finance" transfer of technologies to other parties, particularly the developing ones. The same essence is also traceable in Article 4.3, which further obliges the developed countries to provide financial support for, *inter alia,* transfer of technology.[244] In contrast, the efforts to be made by developing countries to implement their respective commitments under the convention were made conditional upon reception of financial support and technology transfer.[245] While being unable to indicate practical avenues to implement those commitments, the language of the framework convention already highlighted key issues that would recurrently guide the evolution of the institutional process, namely differentiation, and support. Also, these are the only provisions that are grounded in hard law

Subsequently, the Kyoto Protocol entering into force in 2005, did not contribute much in developing frameworks for technology transfer. As is well known, the language of strict differentiated obligation introduced by the Protocol contributed to its slow demise, as the top emitters gradually abandoned the process.[246] In the same spirit of the Framework Convention, the Kyoto Protocol obliged all parties to cooperate to create effective modalities of technology transfer.[247] It also strengthened the language of urging the developed parties to extend financial support for the transfer of technology to the developing parties.[248] Although unrelated to the formal institutional framework related to technology transfer, the market based mechanisms established under the Protocol, especially the clean development mechanism (CDM), had some technology transfer effect.[249] Nevertheless, for reasons explained later in this chapter, those mechanisms also gave rise to controversies yet to be settled among the participants.[250] Operation of the Kyoto Protocol is extended till 2020 with respect to parties willing to commit thereunder.

244 Article 4.3, ibid.

245 Article 4.7, ibid.

246 Bodansky, Brunnée and Rajamani (n 129) 105–108; Bodansky, *The Art and Craft of International Environmental Law* (n 237) 161–162, 185; Rosen (n 161); Napoli (n 161).

247 Article 10(c), Kyoto Protocol to the United Nations Framework Convention on Climate Change 1998 (UN Doc FCCC/CP/1997/7/Add1; 37 ILM 22 (1998)).

248 Article 11(2)(b), ibid.

249 See pp. 71 & 84 below.

250 See pp. 72-73 below.

(ii) Structural Development at the Conference of Parties (COPs)

The real development of the institutional arrangements for technology transfer took place at the COP level, where efforts have been complex, and multi-pronged. Very early on (COP4), Parties agreed to implement Article 4.5 of the UNFCCC through need-based financing of technology transfer projects[251] with support from the finance arm of the convention. The result was the initiation of the technology needs assessment process (TNA) (Box 1). This process was purposed to provide developing countries with a clear understanding of their technology needs and priorities.[252] Also in COP4, the Subsidiary Body on Scientific and Technological Advice (SBSTA) was mandated to initiate a consultative process for effective implementation of Article 4.5 of the Convention.[253] By 2001, the first regulatory framework was launched with supervision from an expert group, of which the key details are provided in the following sub-section.

Box 1: Technology Needs Assessments (TNAs)[254]

Initiated in 2001, the TNAs have arguably become the most important step that a developing country can undertake to specify its technology needs and obtain necessary support thereupon. Undertaken voluntarily by a developing country member to the UNFCCC, a TNA paves the path to adopt a Technology Action Plan (TAP), which then serves as a basis to develop bankable technology transfer projects.

The TNA process remains loosely linked to the evolving technology-related institutional framework of the climate regime. Currently, the technology executive committee (TEC) discharges guidance and overview functions regarding the TNA, a task previously conducted by the now demised expert group on technology transfer (EGTT). However, the bulk of the activities, i.e. initiation, technical support, advice, and later finance, are carried out by a number of collaborators.

While implementation of the TNA projects have always been in the domain of the Global Environment Facility (GEF), the key finance arm

---

251 Decision 2/CP4, 'Report of the Conference of the Parties on Its Fourth Session' (1998) FCCC/CP/1998/16/Add.1. At that period, the sole financing arm was the Global Environment Facility (GEF). For more on the GEF, see pp 67-69 below.

252 'TNA History' <http://unfccc.int/ttclear/tna/history.html> accessed 25 October 2020.

253 Decision 4/CP4, 'Report of the Conference of the Parties on Its Fourth Session' (n 251); Decision 9/CP5, 'Report of the Conference of the Parties on Its Fifth Session' (1999) FCCC/CP/1999/6/Add.1.

254 'TNA History' (n 252).

of the UNFCCC; the assessment activity was initially assisted by the UN Environment Programme (UNEP) and the UN Development Programme (UNDP). From 2009, TNAs and implementation thereof were carried out as a global project in phases. Finance was still supplied by the GEF under a strategic technology transfer programme, implementation was carried out by the UNEP in partnership with the Danish Technical University (DTU).

So far, there has been three TNA global project phases, which have seen to 85 countries undergoing the assessment. According to the official technology information repository 'tt:clear', while about 260 mitigation project has been floated by developing countries for finance, about 6 so far have been supported. Linked to the TNAs, the GEF also launched 14 pilot projects, which remain at different stages of completion.

a) *Technology Transfer Framework* (TTF)

The technology transfer framework (TTF), adopted in 2001 (COP7), was the result of a consultative process.[255] The TTF envisaged activities around five key themes, namely (i) technology needs assessments (TNAs), (ii) technology information; (iii) enabling environments; (iv) capacity building; and (v) mechanisms for technology transfer. The needs assessment, already an ongoing process, was integrated with the framework with a view to identifying and prioritising the areas of support required by the developing countries. Actual transfers were planned to be attained in two ways- creation of an enabling regulatory environment on one hand, and the developing countries' technological capacity building on the other. This would remain a rare instance when regulatory reform, especially fair-trade policies would find mention in connection with enabling environment in a COP document on technology transfer. Elaborating the tasks under that theme, the developed parties were urged to "[...] promote further and to implement facilitative measures, for example, export credit programmes and tax preferences, and regulations, as appropriate, to promote the transfer of environmentally sound technologies".[256] Equal emphasis, if not more, was put on capacity building efforts for the developing countries, along with an urge to make greater financial resources available for the same.[257] The

255 Decision 4/CP7, 'Report of the Conference of the Parties on Its Seventh Session' (2001) FCCC/CP/2001/13/Add.1.

256 Annex to the Decision 4/CP7, ibid 26–27.

257 Annex to the Decision 4/CP7, ibid 27–29.

dual emphasis on enabling environment and capacity building would become the balancing act for all subsequent technology transfer arrangements.

The institutional mechanism that emerged out of the TTF was in the form of an Expert Group on Technology Transfer (EGTT). The EGTT was mandated to boost stakeholder coordination, cooperation, and to facilitate the development of relevant projects and programs. The goal behind creating an 'expert' group was probably to depoliticise the issues and to work towards objective solutions. Although the group played some facilitative function,[258] it was criticised to be a weak one, having a top-down approach towards technology transfer. It also failed to defuse the tensions between the developed and the developing countries' views.[259] The mandate of the expert group lapsed in 2010.

b) *The Technology Mechanism (TM)*

Work began in 2007 to replace the TTF with a new framework. The Bali Action Plan, which was instrumental in initiating the new process, flagged enhanced action on technology transfer and provision of related finance as two key components of a long-term climate deal.[260] Pursuant to that, the informal Copenhagen Accord decided in 2009 to establish a bottom-up 'technology mechanism' (TM). The decision was formalised in the following year at COP16.[261] Composed of a policy and an implementation arm (technology executive committee (TEC) and climate technology centre and network (CTCN), respectively), the TM was proposed to build upon the previous activities, albeit with redefined priorities and operational structures, as explained below.[262]

The policy arm of the mechanism, i.e. the TEC, is composed of a body of twenty independent technology experts from the developed and the developing countries.[263] The functions assigned to the TEC was mostly deliberative and advisory, including, *inter alia,* making recommendations on technology transfer barriers.[264] Compared to the EGTT, the TEC had a reduced scope, as

258 Efforts included training and capacity building to carry out technology needs assessments. Merylyn Hedger, 'Stagnation or Regeneration: Technology Transfer in the United Nations Framework Convention on Climate Change (UNFCCC)' in David Ockwell and Alexandra Mallett (eds), *Low-carbon technology transfer: from rhetoric to reality* (Routledge 2012) 213.

259 de Coninck and Sagar (n 89) 260.

260 Bali Action Plan, Decision 1/CP13, 'Report of the Conference of the Parties on Its Thirteenth Session' (2007) FCCC/CP/2007/6/Add.1 4–5.

261 Decision 1/CP16, 'Report of the Conference of the Parties on Its Sixteenth Session' (2010) FCCC/CP/2010/7/Add.1 <http://unfccc.int/resource/docs/2010/cop16/eng/07a01.pdf> accessed 25 October 2020.

262 ibid 18–22.

263 ibid 30.

264 ibid 19–20.

some of the issues like capacity building and availability of necessary financial resources were moved to different fora. Based on the assigned mandate, inputs from public, private and institutional stakeholders, and periodic guidance from the COPs, work in the TEC progressed based on a rolling agenda. Such work mostly included different thematic dialogues, workshops, periodic analysis, and guidance support to TNAs.

It is important to note that perception of the kind of steps necessary to be taken for the development of enabling environments for technology transfer changed with the shift from the earlier framework. Between 2012 and 2015, activities undertaken by the TEC touching upon enabling environments and barriers to technology transfers can be summed up to a workshop on national systems of innovation in developing countries,[265] thematic dialogues, and some periodic recommendations made to the COP.[266] It shows that the earlier emphasis on the need for specifically addressing trade-related issues has waned. A plausible reason for this can be the Parties' different positions on market-based approaches to mitigation. In addition, the absence of jurisdiction to discuss trade matters can also be a factor. Among other mandated tasks, the TEC supplied guidance to the TNA process over time.[267] Even in that regard, as we would see later in this chapter, Secretariat reports suggested the significance of barriers that can be tackled by trade policy measures.[268] Despite that, there were no such discussions or recommendations from the TEC. The body, however, made suggestions to develop a permanent linkage with the financial mechanisms

The Climate Technology Centre and Network (CTCN), the other integral part of the TM, is comprised of a central coordinating body connected to a worldwide network of member organisations. Together, the CTCN responds to the needs of technical assistance (TA) submitted by the developing countries. The CTCN is hosted by a UNEP-led consortium and is financed from a variety of sources, ranging from donor countries, the finance mechanism of the convention, as well as contributsions from consortium members. The type of

265 It was held in 2014. 'Joint Annual Report of the Technology Executive Committee and the Climate Technology Centre and Network for 2014' (2014) FCCC/SB/2014/3 8 <http://unfccc.int/resource/docs/2014/sb/eng/03.pdf> accessed 25 October 2020.

266 'Joint Annual Report of the Technology Executive Committee and the Climate Technology Centre and Network for 2015' (2015) FCCC/SB/2015/1 12–13 <http://unfccc.int/resource/docs/2015/sb/eng/01.pdf> accessed 25 October 2020.

267 ibid 10–11; 'Joint Annual Report of the Technology Executive Committee and the Climate Technology Centre and Network for 2016' (2016) FCCC/SB/2016/1 9–10 <http://unfccc.int/resource/docs/2016/sb/eng/01.pdf> accessed 25 October 2020.

268 Synthesis reports on technology needs are discussed in pp. 85-87 below.

technical support provided by the CTCN is request-based, occasionally involving assistance regarding TNAs. The CTCN website reports that so far 180 TA requests have been received, of which 77 have been completed.[269]

The success of the work undertaken by the TEC and CTCN remained closely linked to the availability of adequate financial resources. This is a persistent problem for the network, frequently resulting in its inability to prioritise the support projects.[270] Despite having a finance-backed approach to the transfer of technology, availability of resources to a tune that is adequate to reach the necessary scale of assistance has never become a reality in the context of the TM. This remains a major handicap for the system.

(iii) Technology Framework under the Paris Agreement

Despite being appended as Annex to the COP21 decision, the Paris Agreement can be considered as a treaty from a legal viewpoint.[271] Article 10 of the Paris Agreement, coupled with the relevant parts[272] of the COP21 decision, supply new guidance to the existing technology transfer rules and practices. The new provisions bring adaptation and mitigation activities into equal focus.[273] Apart from that, the Agreement's provisions further underscores the need for linkage between the technology and financial mechanisms. In somewhat ambiguous wording, the Article also supplies one of the rare instances of strict differentiation in the Paris Agreement, holding that additional financial support "shall be provided to the developing country parties".[274] As mentioned, the wording

269 'Request Visualizations' (*Climate Technology Centre & Network*, 20 August 2015) <https://www.ctc-n.org/technical-assistance/request-visualizations> accessed 25 October 2020.

270 'Joint Annual Report of the Technology Executive Committee and the Climate Technology Centre and Network for 2018' (2018) FCCC/SB/2018/2 18–21 <https://unfccc.int/sites/default/files/resource/SB_2018_2.pdf> accessed 25 October 2020. It is mentioned that the CTCN 'continues to experience challenges related to the availability of sufficient and sustained funding as it strives to fund its activities in future years'.

271 Daniel Bodansky, 'The Legal Character of the Paris Agreement' (2016) 25 Review of European, Comparative & International Environmental Law 142, 144–145. Of course it opens the question of priority between the terms of the Paris Agreement and the UNFCCC. Nevertheless, between two sets of relatively flexible commitments, conflict is not immediately apparent. For an alternate view arguing the legal form of the Paris Agreement as a Protocol, see Sandrine Maljean-Dubois, Thomas Spencer and Matthieu Wemaere, 'The Legal Form of the Paris Climate Agreement: A Comprehensive Assessment of Options' (2015) 9 Carbon & Climate Law Review 68.

272 Adoption of the Paris Agreement 2015 (Report of the Conference of the Parties in its twenty-first session, Decision 1/CP 21, FCCC/CP/2015/10/Add1) paras 66–71.

273 Articles 10(1) and 10(2), Paris Agreement (n 28).

274 Article 10(6), ibid.

is ambiguous as it does not clarify who bears that responsibility to extend financial support.

Article 10 also envisioned a new technology framework (TF) that would serve the long-term vision of the Paris Agreement.[275] While the institutional framework of the TM is subsumed into the Paris process, the TF is supposed to provide overarching guidance to the former. The corresponding part of the COP21 decision entrusted the SBSTA with the development of the particulars of technology framework along four themes – (i) undertaking and updating of the TNAs, (ii) provision of enhanced financial support for the TNAs, (iii) assessments of technologies ready to transfer, and (iv) enhancement of enabling environments and removal of barriers.[276] This task was discharged by December 2018, when in COP24 the details of the framework (i.e. the 'Paris Rulebook') were agreed.[277]

The TF envisages five focused areas of action, namely: innovation, implementation, enabling environment and capacity building, collaboration and stakeholder engagement, and support. In many ways, it seems to have successfully picked up the avenues of action, which did not have a strong voice in the technology mechanism and incorporated them to create a long-term, comprehensive work agenda. With respect to trade and diffusion of LCT, the re-introduced theme of enabling environment and also that of collaboration is of special importance.

With respect to creating an enabling environment, the TF holds that it is important to consider the challenges faced by the countries, as well as their different needs. Learning from the decades of insight from conducting TNAs, the activities suggested by the framework to create and enhance enabling environment include, *inter alia,* the following:

> (b) Facilitating countries in enhancing an investment-friendly environment, […] a policy environment, legal and regulatory frameworks and other institutional arrangements; […]

275 Article 10(4) reads as, '[a] technology framework is hereby established to provide overarching guidance to the work of the Technology Mechanism in promoting and facilitating enhanced action on technology development and transfer in order to support the implementation of this Agreement […]'. ibid.

276 Paragraphs 66–71, Adoption of the Paris Agreement (n 272) 9–10; de Coninck and Sagar (n 89).

277 Technology framework under Article 10, paragraph 4, of the Paris Agreement 2019 (Meeting of the Parties to the Paris Agreement on the third part of its first session, Decision 15/CMA1, Annex, FCCC/PA/CMA/2018/3/Add2).

(d) Assisting countries in developing and implementing policies for enabling environments to incentivize the private and public sector to fully realize the development and transfer of climate technologies;

(e) Assisting governments in playing a key role in fostering private sector involvement by designing and implementing policies, regulations and standards that create enabling environments and favourable market conditions for climate technologies;[278]

Yet again, it is submitted that such tasks as mentioned above cannot be executed without the involvement of the trade regulations. However, it is worthwhile to hope that the framework holds collaboration with, and engagement of stakeholders at the local, regional, national, and global levels to be important. It has been mentioned that the necessary action in this regard, *inter alia*, is:

> Enhancing collaboration and synergy with relevant international organizations, institutions and initiatives, [...] to leverage their specific expertise, experience, knowledge and information, particularly on new and innovative technologies;[279]

In sum, it would appear that the TF indicates the existence of a shared will to tackle, among others, economic and market-related barriers to technology development and transfer. To that effect, collaboration with other organisations and institutions are also foreseen. While any effective collaboration is yet to develop, this is a potential opening to establish formal linkages with the trade legal regime to explore policy measures that assist low-carbon technology diffusion. We return to this issue in the following chapter.

At least three compliance enabling mechanisms are linked to the post-Paris arrangement for the transfer of low-carbon technologies. A periodic review will look into the effectiveness of the TM in implementing the agreement, as well as the adequacy of the support provided to the mechanism.[280] The extent to which the mechanism adapts its work to the guidance of the technology framework is a factor in the assessment of effectiveness.[281] Moreover, under a novel transparency framework, the developed country parties are required to

278 ibid 16.

279 ibid 20(d).

280 Adoption of the Paris Agreement (n 272) para 69.

281 Scope of and modalities for the periodic assessment referred to in paragraph 69 of decision 1/CP.21 2019 (Meeting of the Parties to the Paris Agreement on the third part of its first session, Decision 16/CMA1, Annex, FCCC/PA/CMA/2018/3/Add2) para 2(k).

furnish, among others, information on the technology and capacity-building support provided to the developing countries.[282] Information so provided remains subject to a technical expert review. Lastly, the process of 'global stocktake'[283] is also required to take note of the efforts in terms of support provided to the developing country Parties with respect to technology development and transfer.[284] Characteristic to the emphasis upon non-adversariality that epitomizes the Paris Agreement, none of these avenues provides options for strict enforcement when the necessary level of technology transfer is wanting.

B *Evolution of Financial Support Systems*

The account of the institutional evolution of technology transfer arrangements already showcases the importance of adequate finance to bankroll the transfer projects as well as related technical assistance. This entails footing a financial bill of unprecedented scale, actual measurement of which can vary depending on the assumed scope of technologies. For example, the SDG Goal 13 calls for annual contribution of USD 100 billion by 2020 through a fully operationalised Global Climate Fund.[285] One earlier study endorsed by the expert group on technology transfer (EGTT) concluded that development, diffusion, and deployment of mitigation technologies may require annual additional finance of USD 262 to 670 billion.[286] To date, reaching such levels have remained impossible.

The key finance mechanisms of the climate regime, i.e. the Global Environment Facility (GEF), and the new Green Climate Fund (GCF) allocate resources for technology transfer activities at different stages. The aforementioned study finds that out of the overall flow of finance in 2009 for development and diffusion of climate technologies that stood somewhere between 69 to 153 billion US dollars, only 19 million passed through the GEF that was spent in supporting developing countries.[287] Establishment of a permanent linkage with the

282 Article 13, Paris Agreement (n 28); Modalities, procedures and guidelines for the transparency framework for action and support referred to in Article 13 of the Paris Agreement 2019 (Meeting of the Parties to the Paris Agreement on the third part of its first session, Decision 18/CMA1, Annex, FCCC/PA/CMA/2018/3/Add2) para 126.

283 Articles 10(6) and 14, Paris Agreement (n 28).

284 Matters relating to Article 14 of the Paris Agreement and paragraphs 99–101 of decision 1/CP.21 2019 (Meeting of the Parties to the Paris Agreement on the third part of its first session, Decision 19/CMA1, FCCC/PA/CMA/2018/3/Add2) para 36(f).

285 Goal 13, United Nations General Assembly (n 210).

286 EGTT, 'Recommendations on Future Financing Options for Enhancing the Development, Deployment, Diffusion and Transfer of Technologies under the Convention' (2009) FCCC/SB/2009/2 24 <http://unfccc.int/resource/docs/2009/sb/eng/02.pdf> accessed 25 October 2020.

287 ibid 20.

financial mechanism remains an open issue, as described below. Following paragraphs provide a brief overview of the situation of technology finance so far.[288]

(i) The Global Environment Facility (GEF)

The GEF is a consortium of international agencies, countries and civil societies that support and finance implementation activities under several MEAS, including the UNFCCC.[289] It uses periodically replenished contributions made by the participants. With respect to technology development and transfer to tackle climate change, the operational focus of the GEF until 2007 was on removing the market obstacles preventing diffusion of mature technology and supporting development and deployment of promising technologies.[290] In response to the parties' request in 2007,[291] the GEF presented a new strategic program the year after, named Poznan strategy, which still guides the actions of the institution.[292] In light of that strategy, technology finance operation of the GEF takes place under three prongs, namely (i) providing assistance in undertaking of the TNA s, (ii) implementation of pilot projects arising out of those assessments, and (iii) dissemination of the experiences of success.[293] Later, after the launch of the technology mechanism (TM), two additional priorities were added to the previous agenda – (i) support to the CTCN, and (ii) public-private partnerships for technology transfer.[294]

Through the Poznan Strategic Program, the GEF has been continuously supporting the technology activities, though the scale of overall support can be put to question. Regarding the TNAS, a total of eighty-four countries were

288 For additional information on the scale and importance of public financial commitments, see Chapter 5 I at p. 198 onwards.

289 As per decision 12/CP2 at COP2, a memorandum of understanding was struck between the UNFCCC COP and the Council of GEF.

290 GEF, 'Transfer of Environmentally Sound Technologies: Case Studies from GEF Climate Change Portfolio' 3–4 <http://www.thegef.org/sites/default/files/publications/GEF-TechTransfer-lowres_final_2.pdf> accessed 25 October. For a critical take on GEF's market transformation approach, see the studies by Watson & Byrne, and Haum in page 83 and 84 respectively below.

291 Decision 4/CP13, 'Report of the Conference of the Parties on Its Thirteenth Session' (n 260) 26–28.

292 Decision 2/CP14, 'Report of the Conference of the Parties on Its Fourteenth Session' (2009) FCCC/CP/2008/7 3–4 <https://unfccc.int/resource/docs/2008/cop14/eng/07.pdf> accessed 25 October 2020.

293 GEF, *Implementing the Poznan Strategic and Long-Term Programs on Technology Transfer* (2012) 5–6.

294 ibid 6.

provided GEF support in three phases since 2001. Out of those, thirty-six TNAs are completed, twenty-eight underway and twenty about to begin.[295] During this period, only eleven pilot projects arising out of the TNAs have been approved for implementation.[296] Support to the CTCN is provided by the GEF under five ongoing projects. All these add up to nineteen mitigation technology transfer projects (including three cancelled ones) in totoal since 2009, requiring the entity to invest 111.7 million USD of own fund and 709.3 million of co-financing by other institutions.[297] The facility identifies the key perceived obstacles in financing technology projects as – (i) absence of domestic policy frameworks enabling the adoption of EST s, (ii) absence of robust technology options, (iii) information unavailability, (iv) lack of viable business and delivery models to supply the markets, and (v) lack of finance.[298]

(ii) The Green Climate Fund (GCF)

Parallel to the Poznan Strategic Program, the Copenhagen Accord in 2009 floated the idea of a new finance mechanism in the form of the Green Climate Fund (GCF), which was eventually launched in 2010 at the COP 16 in Cancun. The new fund is a response to the voiced demand for new and additional finance to tackle climate change. Like the GEF, the GCF is also an operational entity under the finance mechanism of the Framework Convention, but unlike the former, it deals solely with the climate change issue. Despite having an informal target to mobilise USD100 billion annually and initiate a 'paradigm shift' in low-carbon development, the GCF has been successful in collecting about USD 10.3 in actual pledges so far.[299] As of July 2019, the fund has approved a total of 111 projects in total deploying USD 5.2 billion of its own resources, and triggering another USD 1.5 billion in co-finance.[300] By the same time, the GCF received eleven finance request from the CTCN,

295 UNFCCC, 'Report of the Global Environment Facility to the Conference of the Parties' (2017) FCCC/CP/2017/7 47–49 <http://unfccc.int/resource/docs/2017/cop23/eng/07.pdf> accessed 25 October 2020.

296 ibid 46–47.

297 ibid 44.

298 ibid 103–109; Global Environment Facility, 'Report of the Global Environment Facility on the Progress Made in Carrying out the Poznan Strategic Programme on Technology Transfer' (2018) 122–136.

299 Green Climate Fund, 'Eighth Report of the Green Climate Fund to the Conference of the Parties to the United Nations Framework Convention on Climate Change' (2019) FCCC/CP/2019/3 4–5.

300 ibid 12–13.

of which only six has been approved, amounting to total commitment USD 1.8 million.[301] While there may be some technology transfer benefit arising from the overall GCF engagement, but a system to track such achievement is still in process.[302]

(iii) The Linkage between Technology and Finance

There is no doubt that the level of success of a finance-driven international support mechanism for technology transfer would largely be a function of the amount of resources allocated for the purpose. Current legal arrangements still underperform on this account, as featured by technology transfer being only a partial responsibility in the GEF agenda. While the developing countries demand establishment of a hard linkage between the finance (including the GCF) and the technology mechanism (TM), it was consistently being resisted by the developed countries.[303] In 2015, the COP21 invited the TEC and the operating entities of the finance mechanism (namely the GEF, and the GCF) to sit together and find ways of supporting the TM.[304] In COP22, the parties encouraged the GCF to regularly report the actions being taken to establish the linkage. Later in COP23, an independent review recommended formalisation of the relationships between CTCN, GEF, and GCF through enhanced collaboration of the national focal points of these entities (nationally designated authorities (NDA) for GCF, and nationally designated entities (NDE) for CTCN).[305] The latest reports reveal that the CTCN is partnering with the GCF to access some funds from that latter entity's 'readiness program'.[306] However, partnership with the GEF still remains on an *ad hoc* basis.[307] In the absence of a stronger, and supporting relationship between technology support and finance, the success of the TM would remain a far cry.[308]

301 ibid 18–19.

302 ibid 19.

303 de Coninck and Sagar (n 89) 263.

304 Decision 13/CP.21 'Report of the Conference of the Parties on Its Twenty-First Session' (2015) FCCC /CP/2015/10/Add.2 28–29.

305 'Report of the Independent Review of the Effective Implementation of the Climate Technology Centre and Network' (2017) FCCC/CP/2017/3 para 90.

306 'Joint Annual Report of the Technology Executive Committee and the Climate Technology Centre and Network for 2019' (2019) FCCC/SB/2019/4 para 104; Green Climate Fund (n 299) para 97.

307 ibid para 105.

308 de Coninck and Sagar (n 89) 275.

C *Other Avenues Contributing to Low-Carbon Technology Diffusion*

(i) Market-Based Approaches

a) *The Clean Development Mechanism* (CDM)

While the technology transfer arrangements were too slow to take shape, the market-based mitigation measures agreed under the Kyoto Protocol[309] of the Framework Convention, especially the clean development mechanism (CDM),[310] became an unlikely vehicle for low-carbon technology transfer. It is unlikely because the mandate of the CDM was never related to technology. Opening in 1998, the Kyoto Protocol had the objective of strengthening the mitigation commitments of the UNFCCC parties. To that effect, it provided for strict emission reduction targets, which were possible to be met through domestic, as well as extraterritorial mitigation activities. The latter was known as market-based mitigation measures, comprising of joint implementation, with or without emission trading schemes,[311] and the CDM.

The CDM has a project-centred approach. According to the Kyoto Protocol, entities from the developed countries can invest in mitigation projects in the developing countries and get credit (i.e. certified emission reduction, or CER) for emission reductions that is 'additional' to 'business as usual'. A project developer, with approval from the host country, initially submits the documents for approval. A project is approved when it is registered by the Executive Board (EB) of the CDM. When successfully implemented, the EB issues the CERs, which can then be bought and sold in the market and used by any Annex I party to prove their compliance with the Kyoto limits during the commitment period.[312]

Although studies have shown some limited success and untapped potential of CDM projects to transfer low-carbon technologies,[313] some drawbacks have been pointed out as well. The CDM approach was primarily mandated

309 Kyoto Protocol to the United Nations Framework Convention on Climate Change 1997.

310 Article 12, ibid.

311 Article 4(6), ibid.

312 Joëlle de Sépibus, 'Reforming the Clean Development Mechanism to Accelerate Technology Transfer' (2009) NCCR Trade Working Paper 2009/42 6 <https://www.wti.org/research/publications/7/reforming-the-clean-development-mechanism-to-accelerate-technology-transfer/> accessed 25 October 2020.

313 Eric Haites and others, 'Technology Transfer and the Clean Development Mechanism (CDM)' in David Ockwell and Alexandra Mallett (eds), *Low-carbon technology transfer: from rhetoric to reality* (Routledge 2012); Stephen Seres, Eric Haites and Kevin Murphy, 'Analysis of the Contribution of the Clean Development Mechanism to Technology' (UNFCCC 2010) <https://cdm.unfccc.int/Reference/Reports/TTreport/TTrep10.pdf> accessed 25 October 2020.

to mitigate emissions, not to transfer technology. As a result, the project designs were suited to the needs of the former and not the later. It also became clear that the structure and design of the CDM approval, and issue of CERs were flawed. Moreover, the projects tended to concentrate on only a number of destinations – as private entrepreneurs were reluctant to move elsewhere. De Sepibus identified some of these failures as being: (i) the problem of fixing the emission accounting baseline, (ii) private intervention in auditing, (iii) technology path dependency, (iv) chilling effect on developing country low-carbon policy development, etc.[314]

Along with the rest of the Kyoto Protocol, operation of the CDMs is projected to last till 2020 (i.e. the second commitment period, 2013–20). As it is official that the Protocol would not be extended further, and an alternate plan is underway as the Paris Agreement, the current iteration of CDM would expire after that period. While some were positive about market-based mitigation options like the CDM, the others held deep concerns about its overall impact and reforms.[315] The conflicting views have influenced the negotiation under the Paris Agreement, as shown below.

b) *Difficulty to Renew Market-based Approaches under the Paris Agreement*

In an attempt to address all the divergent views surrounding the market-based approaches to mitigation, Article 6 of the Paris Agreement was drafted in a language that covers and encourages all forms of possible cooperation activities.[316] While creating the opportunity for market-based cooperative mechanisms for emission mitigation, it also underscores the need for ensuring overall emission reduction, stringent accounting, strong oversight, distributional support to adaptation, and contribution to sustainable development. Side by side, it also recognises the need to coordinate and cooperate on mitigation towards the fulfilment of NDCs through non-market approaches. The language of the provision does not, however, indicate any potential technology transfer benefit arising out of such cooperation activities.

The market-based cooperative approaches under the Paris Agreement could further be divided into two types. The internationally transferred mitigation outcomes (ITMOs) possibly envisage transactions like emission trading or other

314 de Sépibus (n 312) 10–13.

315 Andrew Howard, 'Voluntary Cooperation (Article 6)' in Daniel Klein and others (eds), *The Paris Agreement on Climate Change: Analysis and Commentary* (Oxford University Press 2017) 182.

316 Article 6.1, Paris Agreement (n 28).

forms of credit transaction processes[317] subject to the requirement that they promote sustainable development, are transparent, and ensure environmental integrity.[318] Further guidance was sought to be supplied by the SBSTA as part of the Paris rulebook.[319] Article 6.4 to 6.7 lay down further details of a new mechanism, which in broad parts resembles CDM or Joint Implementation (JI) approaches under the Kyoto system. The language of the whole Article avoids using terms like 'credit', 'market' or 'trade' – a result of the strong aversion of certain members.[320] The elaborated mechanism urges ensuring overall mitigation of global emission, support of adaptation activities from the proceeds and avoiding double counting.

Details of the mechanism were left to be developed in the rulebook.[321] By the first session of the conference of parties serving as a meeting of the parties to the Paris Agreement (CMA) in 2018, no consensus on any of these issues has been reached. Key disagreements are regarding methods to avoid double counting of emissions, decision on carrying over Kyoto era CDM credits, means of ensuring overall mitigation reduction, and difficulty to account for trade in mitigation outcomes between parties with varying NDC commitments.[322] Recently concluded COP25 / CMA2 also failed to find an agreement, and the issues have been pushed to the next conference in 2020.

(ii) Technology Aspects of Other Climate Processes

a) *Nationally Determined Contributions (NDCs)*

Nationally determined contributions (NDC), the foremost building blocks of aggregate mitigation under the Paris process, bear a deep connection with the availability and access to low-carbon technologies. According to a UNFCCC secretariat study,[323] almost all of the developing countries (140) refer to

317 Howard (n 315) 185–186; Andrei Marcu, *Carbon Market Provisions in the Paris Agreement (Article 6)* (Centre for European Policy Studies (CEPS) 2016) 5–7.

318 Articles 6.2 and 6.3, Paris Agreement (n 28).

319 'Report of the Conference of the Parties on Its Twenty-First Session' (n 304) para 37.

320 Marcu (n 317) 7; Howard (n 315) 188.

321 'Report of the Conference of the Parties on Its Twenty-First Session' (n 304) 38–39. It should however be noted that while INDC s are an iterative process, TNA s are so far a one-off step leading a technology action plan.

322 See for details, 'In-Depth Q&A: How "Article 6" Carbon Markets Could "Make or Break" the Paris Agreement' (*Carbon Brief*, 29 November 2019) <https://www.carbonbrief.org/in-depth-q-and-a-how-Article-6-carbon-markets-could-make-or-break-the-paris-agreement> accessed 25 October 2020.

323 UNFCCC, 'INDCs and Technology: A Synthesis of Technology Issues Contained in Intended Nationally Determined Contributions' (2016) <https://unfccc.int/ttclear/misc_/StaticFiles/gnwoerk_static/HOME_infobox_2/a61f9f4b94704dd78f06b2bc7cd0b547/f7bbe982812a469db476fd4917714813.pdf> accessed 25 October 2020.

technologies in the NDCs. 70% of all the non-Annex I parties seek international technology development and transfer support to implement their NDC commitments.[324] While the technology mechanism was not frequently referred to, the developing country parties indicated financial as well as non-financial obstacles as barriers to attaining the NDC commitments. In 2018, the technology executive committee (TEC) suggested to use the TNA process to specify, prioritise and update over time the technology aspects of the NDCs.[325]

b) *Nationally Appropriate Mitigation Actions (NAMAs)*[326]

Similarly, nationally appropriate mitigation actions (NAMAs) were an outcome of an earlier process that is still in place. NAMAs share characteristics with NDCs as well as the TNAs. They were made with a view to creating a transparent platform for mitigation projects. While the UNFCCC hosts a registry for the NAMAs prepared and submitted for finance, there is no institutional finance that is allocated for the projects. A donor-supported NAMA facility finances the projects. Many of the NAMAs actually involve introduction of new technologies to a specific domestic emission sector. However, in comparison to the number of NAMAs submitted, very little (about 8.5%) have been financed for implementation.[327]

D *Summary Analysis*

This section summarises the key points emerging from the above discussion.

a) *Balancing and Supporting Function of Technology Transfer*

Effective legal arrangements for technology transfer remains an indispensable part of a long-term global climate deal. Not only does it enable countries to increase the level and scale of emission mitigation, technology transfer, especially providing assistance to the developing countries in that regard, also performs a crucial balancing function. Overall, such arrangement is a key avenue

324 ibid 2.

325 Technology Executive Committee (TEC), 'Updated Paper on Linkages between the TNA and NDC Process' (UNFCCC 2018) TEC/2018/16/7 19–20 <https://unfccc.int/ttclear/misc_/StaticFiles/gnwoerk_static/tn_meetings/40067a60235c4b1c9737e9abf532003a/e8a0bd09bec44237934ee7ed569b2d9d.pdf> accessed 25 October 2020.

326 To be clear, the NAMA here does not have any realation with the non-agricultural market access negotiation at the WTO.

327 Angelica Afanador and others, *Status Report on Nationally Appropriate Mitigation Actions (NAMAs)* (Katja Eisbrenner, Noémie Klein and Xander van Tilburg eds, ECN, ECOFYS 2017).

to implement the ideal of common but differential responsibility in practice. It also enables fostering of inclusivity in the multilateral climate agreement by ensuring the greatest number of participation.

b) *Institutional Evolution is Soft-Law Based, Incremental, and Facilitative*

We find that much of the development of the institutional frameworks regarding technology development and transfer in the climate regime has taken place incrementally, using soft-law based approaches.[328] The upside of such an approach is that the resultant frameworks are inclusive in terms of participants, as well as coverage of interests. However, encompassing different interests and approaches result in systems that are complex and difficult to navigate. This is true for the whole of the Paris Agreement.[329] Also, inclusivity comes at the cost of sacrificing legal stringency of the substantive commitments. As the latest experiences with the Paris Agreement, and the technology framework therein show, aspirational goals and some procedural obligations form the core of the operative rule, emphasising more on a highly participatory and facilitative nature of progress.[330] It is yet to be seen whether such frameworks result in generating effective and adequate levels of technology transfer.

c) *One-Off Projects, the Thrust of Current Actions, Are Inadequately Financed*

In practice, under the current arrangements, the developing countries obtain necessary low-carbon technologies through implementation of standalone projects – e.g. following up a TNA,[331] through CDM s,[332] or by obtaining finance for the submitted NAMA.[333] These processes are only loosely connected to the current legal framework for technology transfer in the sense that the bulk of the work is carried out by autonomous entities (e.g. GEF for project implementation, and the UNEP-DTU consortium for TNA s). These processes are only effective to the extent financial resources are committed to them. Given the slow pace of growth of the scale and volume of institutional finance channelled to

328 Hedger correctly termed the evolution of a working technology transfer process under the UNFCCC as 'slow, laborious and incremental'. Hedger (n 258).

329 Brunnée, 'The Rule of International (Environmental) Law and Complex Problems' (n 200).

330 Jutta Brunnée, 'MEAs and Complex Prevention' (Hague Winter Academy, Hague, January 2019) [on file with the author].

331 See Box 1 at p. 60 above.

332 See p. 71 above.

333 See p. 74 above.

low-carbon technology diffusion, it is only realistic to conclude that exclusive dependence on finance backed technology transfer would be unsuccessful to bring forth the kind of systemic technological change that has been showed to be necessary to avoid climate change.

d) *Systemic Change Would Require Finding New Ways to Enhance Technology Diffusion*

Following the above conclusion, i.e. the inadequacy of financial support, it is important that other complementary avenues of progress are explored. Of key importance are the market-based reform approaches including necessary revision of international trade and investment practices. Experience so far would suggest that although market-based approaches are not alien to the climate regime, they tend to be controversial as their benefits remain limited and execution questionable. The difficulty to deal with it within the climate law framework can arise due to several factors – (i) trade-related issues are subject to the regulatory jurisdiction of the WTO,[334] (ii) this may not be in the interest of all parties, as experience suggests that developed countries prefer market-based approaches, (iii) in terms of impact however, some of these issues may affect developing country process and production, and lastly (iv) there has been some negative experience with such mechanisms under the Kyoto Protocol. Given these factors, it is highly welcome that the enabling environment and capacity building feature prominently in the new technology framework as an integrated agenda.[335]

To throw a clearer light on the contours of the task at hand, the next section undertakes a comprehensive overview of the objective understanding of the barriers to the diffusion of LCT s.

III Growing Empirical Understanding of Technology Diffusion Barriers

This section serves as a synopsis of the current empirical understanding of the barriers to low-carbon technology diffusion that bear a potential linkage with trade rules. It presents the picture that is emerging from the scholarly literature, especially since the late 2000s. This includes – (i) studies that specifically focused on counting and analysing climate technology patents, (ii) those that focus on finding a broader range of barriers in a specific sector, or economy,

334 This is discussed at length from p. 80 onwards. This also forms the crux of Chapter 3.

335 See pp. 65-66 above.

and (iii) the self-assessed barriers to prioritised mitigation technologies, as communicated by the developing countries.

All the studies commonly point out the prevalence of economic and financial challenges to low-carbon technology diffusion. The scope of the available research, however, remain scant both in terms of the sectoral coverage, as well as the number of countries studied. Drawing general conclusions therefrom can be informative, but not highly accurate. However, there is a higher probability for new and more comprehensive empirical analyses to rather corroborate than differ with the insights that are currently available and presented hereunder.

A *Studies on the Relevance of Intellectual Property Rights*

Traditionally, the debate on patent flexibility vs protection grabs the most attention when it comes to the issue of trade and technology transfer barriers. This debate often ends with split discourse of development vs diffusion.[336] The developing countries tend to draw from their experience with IPRs in the field of public health protection, and conclude that easing of IPRs would facilitate access to climate technologies.[337] Whereas, opposite views held by most developed countries indicate the innovation encouraging role of the IPRs through the promise of secured exploitation and the possibility of eventual disclosure.

One of the earliest studies looking at global patenting activities was done by Dechezleprêtre and others.[338] The authors examined thirteen environmental technologies to locate the places of innovation and the role played by the developing countries, also to measure the extent of technology transfer. It was found that between 1978 and 2005, patenting activities in the studied areas were highly concentrated (90%) in twelve mostly OECD member countries.[339] With respect to the number of patents registered, developing countries were

336 David G Ockwell and others, 'Intellectual Property Rights and Low Carbon Technology Transfer: Conflicting Discourses of Diffusion and Development' (2010) 20 Global Environmental Change 729.

337 See for example, Frederick M Abbott, *Innovation and Technology Transfer to Address Climate Change: Lessons from the Global Debate on Intellectual Property and Public Health* (ICTSD International Centre for Trade and Sustainable Development 2009); Ahmed Abdel-Latif, 'Intellectual Property Rights and the Transfer of Climate Change Technologies: Issues, Challenges, and Way Forward' (2015) 15 Climate Policy 103, 106, 112.

338 Antoine Dechezleprêtre and others, 'Invention and Transfer of Climate Change–Mitigation Technologies: A Global Analysis' (2011) 5 Review of Environmental Economics and Policy 109.

339 Namely (in order from top), Japan, US, Germany, China, South Korea, Russia, Australia, France, UK, Canada, Brazil and Netherlands. The ranking changes with Germany on the lead if only high value patents are counted.

found to be lagging far behind.[340] The study concluded, among others, that the domestic policy environment, as well as the price of fossil fuel influence patenting activities. Another key finding, later corroborated by other researchers was a spike in clean technology patenting from the 1990s. This was attributed to the growing number of international environmental regulation. Considering the gathered data on multiple filing of a patent application as a proxy of technology transfer, the study also concluded that such transfers took place largely within OECD countries, followed by 22% of transfers from the OECD to non-OECD countries, mainly China. Transfers between developing countries remained close to none (1%).

In a similar method, Lee et al. examined the patent landscape, concentration of IP, relationships between technology systems and policy implications thereof.[341] Focused on patenting activities in six low-carbon energy technologies[342] spanning from 1976 to 2007, the study confirmed the similar surge in patenting during the 1990s. In addition to the OECD countries, the authors named China as an important innovation hub. It was due to the growing Chinese market since the early 2000s, attracting foreign investments and increased patent filing by their subsidiaries. The authors concluded that patent protection in the studied sector is not a hindrance to technology access as the patent ownerships did not result in the holders' monopolistic dominance in the market. Instead of multiple filing, Lee and others looked at co-assignment of patents as a proxy for the evidence of collaboration and hence technology diffusion. It was found most such activities took place within and between the OECD countries (95%), demonstrating synergistic relationships between firms, universities, and public research bodies.

Clean technology diffusion has been in the focus of the Global Challenges Reports periodically published by the World Intellectual Property Organization (WIPO). As a part of that, Helm and others replicated the abovementioned research by Lee et al. with a longer range of data (till 2011) on four of the six selected technologies.[343] It was found that that over the last five years of the period studied, there has been an immense growth in the number of patent

---

340 Taiwan in 21st, India in 27th and Mexico in 29th position. Dechezleprêtre and others (n 338) 116.

341 Bernice Lee, Ilian Iliev and Felix Preston, *Who Owns Our Low Carbon Future?: Intellectual Property and Energy Technologies* (Chatham House 2009).

342 Wind, solar PV, concentrated solar power, biomass-to-electricity, carbon capture, and cleaner coal.

343 Sarah Helm, Quentin Tannock and Ilian Iliev, 'Renewable Energy Technology: Evolution and Policy Implications – Evidence from Patent Literature' (WIPO 2014) Global Challenges Report. The sectors authors looked at were biofuels, solar thermal, solar PV, and wind.

filings in the selected technologies.[344] Also, in certain cases, specific technologies (e.g. solar PV) outgrew other competitors within the sector. A novel finding was that of the growth of developing country firms. In three of the four selected technologies, the authors noted the position of China as the leading patent family owner, contributed by the public research institutions and universities.[345] Especially in the solar PV sector, the authors found the technological front runners to be based in Asia.[346]

The 2015 WIPO Global Challenges Report, authored by Lybecker and Lohse, focused on the role of intellectual property and other factors enabling the diffusion of green technologies.[347] Based on a survey of secondary literature, the authors concluded that "[w]ell-developed systems to protect and enforce IP rights have been found to stimulate technology diffusion."[348] One work was however mentioned, which finds protection of IPRs resulting in rising costs of green technologies.[349] The authors also highlight a range of market and behavioural failures that slow the rate of diffusion of green technologies.[350] The market failures identified therein are energy market failures,[351] capital market failures,[352] innovation market failures,[353] and information problems[354].

An extensive study of the changing landscape of patents in clean energy technologies (CET)[355] was jointly undertaken by the United Nations Environment Program (UNEP), the European Patent Office (EPO), and the International

344 ibid 4.

345 ibid 34.

346 It is due to the growing dominant presence of South Korean (e.g. LG) and Indian (e.g. Suzlon) firms. ibid 22, 26, 32.

347 Kristina M Lybecker and Sebastian Lohse, 'Innovation and Diffusion of Green Technologies' (WIPO 2015) Global Challenges Report <http://www.wipo.int/edocs/pubdocs/en/wipo_rep_gc_2015_1.pdf> accessed 25 October 2020.

348 ibid 10–12.

349 Global Commission on the economy and climate, *Better Growth, Better Climate: The New Climate Economy Report : The Global Report* (2014) 261–262.

350 Lybecker and Lohse (n 347) 16. The structure was adapted from an earlier work, see Gillingham and Sweeney (n 82).

351 Energy market failure includes causes such as untamed environmental externalities, average-cost electricity pricing, and lack of energy security. ibid.

352 Capital market failure is caused by liquidity constraints. ibid.

353 It arises from the lack of an innovator's ability to prevent R&D spillovers. ibid.

354 This includes information asymmetry, lack of information, principal-agent problem etc. ibid.

355 Fifty technology categories (including renewable technologies like solar PV, wind turbine, geo thermal, and components like rotors and blades) were considered by the EPO within the scope of the term 'clean energy technology'.

Centre for Trade and Sustainable Development (ICTSD).[356] The study again confirmed the fact of patent concentration in the OECD countries, as most of the applications were also found to be coming from a few key jurisdictions.[357] However, when the proportion of CET patents to the overall patenting activity in a location (i.e. relative importance given to CET) is considered, developing countries like Brazil, India, and Mexico come closer to the top in select sectors.

Noting that the data of multiple patent filing is an unsuitable proxy for technology transfer,[358] the abovementioned study undertook a licensing survey to unearth the factors that influence technology owners' tendency towards out-licensing and collaboration. The results indicate that firms that are intensively involved in the CET sectors engage in collaborative IP activities more frequently than other firms.[359] However, very few of such activities involve out-licensing to developing countries.[360] Even where such involvement exists, the partner firm is most often located in China, Brazil, India, or Russia.[361] A survey conducted among the firm managers revealed that key perceived out-licensing obstacles include transaction costs, difficulty in finding partners, and difficulty in finding mutually agreeable terms of license (e.g. pricing, and geographic scope).[362] It was also found that while robust domestic laws on intellectual property protection in the partner country would indeed be a considered factor, it is never the sole determinant of a firm's decision to out-license.[363] Other influencing factors were found to be the presence of scientific capability on the technology receiving side, market conditions, and investment climate.

A study by Copenhagen Economics focused specifically on whether IPRs pose a barrier to climate technology transfer. The answer was negative because it was found that there was no significant price difference between patented and free technologies.[364] The study further tended to argue that IPRs cannot be a significant problem to technology transfer in low-income countries simply

---

356 UNEP, EPO and ICTSD, 'Patents and Clean Energy: Bridging the Gap between Evidence and Policy' (UNEP, EPO, ICTSD 2010).

357 Namely the USA, Japan, Germany, the UK and France, and the Republic of Korea.

358 It is because of the fact that firms apply for patent protection in a specific jurisdiction not only to work it therein, but also for defensive purposes.

359 UNEP, EPO and ICTSD (n 356) 56–57.

360 ibid 58–59.

361 ibid 58.

362 ibid 59.

363 ibid.

364 Copenhagen Economics and The IPR Company, 'Are IPR a Barrier to the Transfer of Climate Change Technology?' (2009) 16–17 <https://www.copenhageneconomics.com/dyn/resources/Publication/publicationPDF/7/27/0/Are_IPR_a_barrier_to_the_transfer_of_climate_change_technology.pdf> accessed 25 October 2020.

because those technologies are hardly ever patented in those regions.[365] In contrast, absence of domestic IPR protection regulation, lack of absorptive capacity, and subsidies counterproductive to the climate protection goal were indicated as areas that may persist to prevent technology transfer.[366]

B *Sector and Country-Focused Studies*

Besides the above, other studies look at low-carbon technology diffusion with respect to specific geographies (mostly China, or India), sectors (e.g. wind, or solar PV based electricity production), or projects (e.g. GEF financed CDM projects). Instead of zeroing in on IPR related concerns, these analyses deal with the opportunities and challenges faced by the private sector operators. They are, as a result, informative of a broader spectrum of hurdles on the path of clean technology adoption.

Barton looked at the relationship between the protection of IPRs and access to clean energy technologies (CETs) in three sectors (solar PV, biomass, and wind).[367] Studying the level of industry concentration[368] in these sectors, he finds that those are mostly clustered in developed countries with the exception of some emerging developing country firms mainly in India (wind), China (solar PV), and Brazil. The conclusion drawn therefrom was that the industries in the studied sectors currently operate in an oligopolistic fashion with very little IPR related barrier to entry.[369] As competition drives the prices of technologies down quickly, entrant firms from the developing countries do not face insurmountable barriers to entry, except for few instances concerning access to state of the art technologies.[370] Barton, however, draws attention to other industry-specific hindrances, e.g. the protected markets of agricultural produce hurting the biofuel industry. Domestic favouritism in allocating public research funds also breeds inefficiency, according to the author. To make the

365 ibid 15–38. Abdel-Latif cautions against drawing such simplistic conclusions.; Abdel-Latif (n 337) 113.

366 Copenhagen Economics and The IPR Company (n 364) 27–33.

367 John H Barton, *Intellectual Property and Access to Clean Energy Technologies in Developing Countries* (ICTSD 2007) <https://seors.unfccc.int/applications/seors/attachments/get_attachment?code=DM9V7CBIEL8AKG3C1YQLDMFTK64UOLUZ> accessed 25 October 2020.

368 Measured by number of shipments made in case of Solar PV, percentage of national production capacity owned in case of Biomass, and percentage of global market share in case of Wind. Data used are collected from secondary sources.

369 Barton (n 367) 4–5. Barton is also one of the first to reject the argument for patent flexibility in clean energy, based upon a drawn parallel with the public health sector.

370 ibid 16.

renewables competitive, Barton advocated for subsidies, designed and implemented in a non-discriminatory fashion.

Lewis made a comparative analysis in the same year between two successful wind energy firms based in developing countries, i.e. Suzlon in India and Goldwind in China. The goal was to look at how the respective national policy contexts have influenced the firms' technology acquisition and assimilation strategies.[371] The study shows that globally successful firms can emerge in developing countries even without needing IPR related flexibilities. Lewis highlights that corporations devise strategies to get the most benefit from the enabling policy frameworks put in place by domestic governments. In the Indian context, key policy enablers for Suzlon consisted of progressive central and regional sourcing commitments, feed-in-tariffs, tax breaks, and certification schemes to ensure the quality of the components. Whereas in China, Goldwind benefitted from a progressive national target for generating renewable energy. The Chinese firms were guaranteed long-term prices if they satisfied the local content requirement.[372] They were also granted research subsidies.[373] Both firms initially depended on licensing with smaller developed country firms to acquire necessary technologies. Subsequently Goldwind capitalised on the growing domestic market, while Suzlon strategically established itself in key supply markets (e.g. USA), and innovation centres (e.g. Germany and the Netherlands), while benefitting from cheaper manufacturing in India at the same time.

Two field studies on clean technology were reported in a volume edited by Ockwell and Mallett on low-carbon technology transfer.[374] One conducted by Pal and Sethi followed the uptake of energy-efficiency technology by Indian SME s in two sectors, i.e. glass foundry, and iron casting.[375] They found that those SME s suffer from high transaction costs, as well as from deficiencies in expertise, knowledge, and information to take up new technologies. The case the authors followed was one where a domestic knowledge institution acted as a conduit between international technology and the SME s. Access to

---

371 Joanna I Lewis, 'Technology Acquisition and Innovation in the Developing World: Wind Turbine Development in China and India' (2007) 42 Studies in Comparative International Development 208.

372 It should be noted that such an approach is in clear violation of current WTO rules regulating subsidies.

373 Lewis (n 371) 217–219.

374 Ockwell and Mallett (n 54).

375 Prosanto Pal and Girish Sethi, 'Case Study: Technology Transfer of Energy-Efficient Technologies among Small and Medium Sized Enterprises in India' in David Ockwell and Alexandra Mallett (eds), *Low-carbon technology transfer: from rhetoric to reality* (Routledge 2012).

long-term and flexible funding was also provided to the businesses. The technologies in question were adapted to the local need and then implemented throughout the industry.

Watson and Byrne reported the other study, dealing with both mature[376] and novel[377] technologies in China. They found a positive effect of government intervention in the market. The researchers concluded that transfer of the mature technologies was made possible due to an incremental policy push by the government over long-term, also at the same time adequate finance options being made available (GEF for boilers, CDM for cement). Acquisition of relevant technologies by the Chinese firms also took place through joint ventures, license agreements with international SMEs, and R&D base acquisitions. Although local firms have acquired significant technological expertise in mature technologies, they still depended on international licenses. Unlike the Indian example above, the Chinese firms often preferred domestic technological solutions over the imported ones due to better access to know-how, and adaptability benefits. Technologies at or closer to the knowledge frontier nevertheless were difficult to gain access to due to non-cooperation by the original owners who are wary of the competition. With respect to the latest generation gas turbine technology for integrated gasification combined cycle (IGCC) power plants, lack of technical skills and access to the technology was found to be key problems. With respect to hybrid electric vehicles (HEVs), lack of government policy backing, and absence of necessary supporting infrastructure were key obstacles.

Gallagher brought her long experience into play when looking at the evolution of four specific technologies[378] in the expanding Chinese clean energy sector.[379] With respect to concerns regarding intellectual property thefts, the author found very little evidence of actual patent infringement on CETs.[380] Based on interviews, patent analysis and examination of domestic dispute settlement practices, Gallagher concluded that the established foreign operators in China take calculated risks and strategically manage their operations for twofold rewards – (i) better access to the Chinese domestic market, and (ii) overall export competitiveness.[381] Protection of intellectual property was found to be concerns for both foreign and domestic firms in China. But none

376 Efficient boilers, and cement production technologies.

377 Offshore wind power generation, hybrid electric vehicles (HEV), integrated gasification and combined cycle (IGCC) technologies.

378 These are gas turbines, solar PV, advanced batteries for vehicles, and coal gasification technologies.

379 Gallagher (n 71). See in particular Chapters 3, 4 and 7 of that volume.

380 ibid 110–114.

381 ibid 130–132.

were so significant as to disrupt the growth of an industry. The most significant issue that calls for intervention is, according to Gallagher, the lack of a 'natural' market with a growing demand for CETs.[382] This led the author to put the principal focus on 'market formation policies' for further improvement.[383] Market formation policies epitomise "stable, predictable, transparent and medium to long-term" policies that help build broad and sustained markets by tackling pervasive externalities and distortions.[384]

Haites and others analysed the CDM projects that referred to technology transfer in the project documents to find out the significant determinants of transfer in their specific context.[385] Apart from finding a declining rate of technology transfer to the recipient countries over time,[386] the authors further discover a positive relationship between the level of technology transfer and project size.[387] Moreover, technology transfer declines if the same country has several projects of the same type.[388] Although the study itself does not report any conclusive findings regarding barriers to transfer, a similar study done by the same authors for the UNFCCC in 2010 presented a counter-intuitive conclusion that countries facing economic or intellectual property rights related barriers experience more technology transfers through the CDM.[389] The authors' conjecture on the possible reason of such finding is that the financial security of the CDM projects may attract to the host country technologies that would otherwise not be introduced by the private entities.[390]

Haum studied an off-grid solar PV project implemented in India, to assess the role of the GEF finance in the development of technological capacity.[391] The study was based on the premise that technology transfer through market transformation should only be considered successful if it resulted in the

382 ibid 74–77.
383 ibid 96–101, 167–173.
384 ibid 96–97, 171–172.
385 Haites and others (n 313).
386 This is due to the fact that once a technology is introduced in the recipient country, it loses novelty for the purpose of analysis. Also given the fact that CDM projects tended to concentrate in a few countries, such decline should be reasonably expected.
387 Haites and others (n 313) 175–179.
388 ibid.
389 Seres, Haites and Murphy (n 313) 18, 22.
390 ibid 22, 50.
391 The Photovoltaic Market Transformation Initiative (PVMTI) is one of the earliest GEF financed market transformation projects. See, Ruediger Haum, 'Project-Based Market Transformation in Developing Countries and International Technology Transfer: The Case of Globel Environment Facility and Solar Photovoltaics' in David Ockwell and Alexandra Mallett (eds), *Low-carbon technology transfer : from rhetoric to reality* (Routledge 2012).

incremental development of the capacity to innovate among recipients.[392] For the new innovative capacity to come out, it was also important that there is steady demand for the technology in the market. Haum found out that the studied project resulted in some new demands for off-grid solar home systems, but the scale or the quality thereof was not adequate for the domestic cell and module manufacturers to further develop their technological capacity. One qualified conclusion drawn by the author is that for market transformation to work as envisaged by the GEF, the size of the market intervention has to be large enough to create incentives at a scale attractive for the domestic manufacturers, which is currently not the case. Haum also indicated a positive influence of the domestic market size, and size of the relevant economic sector on technology transfer, as the suppliers are more interested to cater to bigger markets.

C *Technology Barriers Perceived by Developing Countries*

Technology needs assessments (TNAs)[393] provide an outlook of the barriers faced by the developing countries in adopting, *inter alia,* prioritised mitigation technologies. As of yet, around eighty-five countries have completed the TNA process. Three synthesis reports,[394] published by the UNFCCC secretariat since 2006, allow an aggregate overview of eighty countries.[395] The summary reports describe, among others, the type of mitigation technologies prioritised as necessary by the participating non-Annex I countries, the key barriers in deployment and diffusion of the same, as well as the possible measures necessary to remove such obstacles.

Barrier analysis in the submitted TNAs largely follow the categorisation of barriers in the related guidebooks.[396] The TNA guidebook on barrier analysis indicates that barriers to technology transfer can be classified in ten categories, which are – (i) economic and financial, (ii) market failures, (iii) policy, legal and regulatory, (iv) network failures, (v) institutional and organizational capacity, (vi) human skills, (vii) social, cultural and behavioural, (viii) information and awareness, (ix) technical, and (x) others.[397] The information box (Box

392 ibid 187–190.

393 For a brief description, see Box 1 at p. 60 above.

394 The first published in 2006, the second and the third in 2009 and in 2013 respectively.

395 The second report, which expanded upon the first one focused on all the TNAs until that date, being 70 in total. The third TNA synthesis report was prepared in response to the SBSTA request to provide a summary of the TNAs completed under the Poznan strategic program. Out of the 31 TNAs included there, 10 were from countries which were not available in the second report. All add up to 80.

396 See, for example, Boldt and others (n 55) 15–25.

397 ibid 17–18.

2) below provides an illustrative account of individual non-Annex I members' perception of technology transfer barriers.

A key insight emerging from the synthesis reports is that the need to tackle economic and market-related barriers is perceived as most significant by almost all the parties. The second report showed that this category of barriers was mentioned by most (82%) of the countries with regard to prioritised mitigation technologies.[398] The third report assigned more than 90% of the responses to this category.[399] Economic and market-related barriers include problems such as high cost of the technologies, related affordability problem, and the availability of cheaper but more polluting alternatives, the difficulty of finding finance due to the lack of interest shown by the private sectors (e.g. banks and other financiers), underdeveloped markets, irregularity of supply, etc.[400] Energy technologies, the sector most prioritised by the parties regarding mitigation, also suffered from the same barriers.[401] Apart from economic barriers, the next big obstacles were categorised as policy and regulatory barriers, and technical barriers.[402] The technical barrier category deserves attention, as problems within that category, e.g. the inadequacy of appropriate standards, codes, and certification are particularly related to the WTO rules.[403] Other repeated mentions included lack of human capacity and state resources, shortage of information on appropriate technologies, the complexity of new technologies, institutional capacity shortage, etc.[404] Among the measures highlighted by countries for removal of the barriers included, *inter alia,* state involvement in attracting foreign investment, gaining access to different international and national funding sources, rationalising prices and removal of unreasonable subsidies, introducing energy-efficiency evaluation standards, increasing R&D activities, etc.[405] Most of the parties underscored

398 UNFCCC, 'Second Synthesis Report on Technology Needs Identified by Parties Not Included in Annex I to the Convention' (2009) Note by the secretariat FCCC/SBSTA/2009/INF.1 28–30.

399 UNFCCC, 'Third Synthesis Report on Technology Needs Identified by Parties Not Included in Annex I to the Convention' (2013) Note by the secretariat FCCC/SBSTA/2013/INF.7 25–27.

400 UNFCCC, 'Second Synthesis Report on Technology Needs Identified by Parties Not Included in Annex I to the Convention' (n 398) 28–30.

401 UNFCCC, 'Third Synthesis Report on Technology Needs Identified by Parties Not Included in Annex I to the Convention' (n 399) 25–27.

402 ibid 6, 25–26.

403 ibid 26.

404 UNFCCC, 'Second Synthesis Report on Technology Needs Identified by Parties Not Included in Annex I to the Convention' (n 398) 28–30.

405 ibid 30–31, 39–40.

the need for financial incentives, commonly in the form of tax exemptions on imported technologies. The report further highlighted the need for detailed regulations and standards, technology information availability, also for facilitation of stakeholder networks to overcome policy, technical and network failures.[406] The third report notes that some of the members indicate the need for further clarification of the relationship between intellectual property rights and technology transfer, but it was not registered as a significant barrier.[407]

Recently, Sara Traerup and others prepared a report providing a comprehensive account of barriers and enablers for the technology executive committee (TEC). The report covers the TNAs made by the developing countries so far, their nationally determined contributions (NDCs), also technical assistance requests made by countries to the CTCN.[408] The overall findings echo the conclusions above to a large extent. The authors find economic and financial barriers to be the single most significant hurdle for the least developed countries (LDCs) and the small island developing countries (SIDCs).[409] A new finding was that the examined documents vary on the order of significance of other barriers. While the synthesis of information from the NDCs and the CTCN requests show technical barriers to be the most significant category,[410] the information from the TNA reports appear to put slightly more emphasis on policy and regulatory obstacles, as well as market imperfections.[411] In the technical category, one key problem was poor quality, or performance of clean technologies, which the authors suggested to be tackled through appropriate standardisation initiatives.[412] It was also noted that with respect to none of the desired technologies, economic and financial barriers were the only set of problems. This means that successful technology transfer would require a integrated, system-wide approach to overcome the existing problems.

406 UNFCCC, 'Third Synthesis Report on Technology Needs Identified by Parties Not Included in Annex I to the Convention' (n 399) 28.

407 ibid 41.

408 Sara Traerup, L Greersen and C Kundsen, 'Mapping Barriers and Enabling Environments in Technology Needs Assessments, Nationally Determined Contributions, and Technical Assistance of the Climate Technology Centre and Network' (2018) Background paper TEC/2018/17/4.

409 ibid 7.

410 ibid 6, 9.

411 ibid 6–9.

412 ibid 5, 15.

Box 2: Illustration of Barrier Analysis: TNAs of Moldova and Kenya[413]

The Republic of Moldova completed its TNA in 2012. In respect of the technology prioritised in the energy sector, i.e. combined heat and power generation using internal combustion engines (ICE CHP), the analysis indicated a range of economic, financial, and market-related barriers among others. It was indicated that the implementation of ICE CHP technology has a potential of GHG emission reduction of up to 24,415 tCO_2 by 2020. A key identified problem was high upfront cost of the technology, which meant that the economy of scale was achievable only on high investment levels. This was problematic due to small market size and high cost of finance. Also, there was no incentive (e.g. tax benefit, or pricing of negative externalities) in the markets for shifting to this technology. The barrier was further compounded by an absence of energy efficiency regulation and little experience of the regulating agency in this area. Moreover, some segments of the domestic market, i.e. district heating, were dominated by a few providers under an oligopolistic fashion. Measures planned by Moldova for overcoming the barriers included import duty exemption on the ICE CHP technology, energy efficiency regulation, optimisation of district heating market along with transparent cost allocation on heat and power, informational awareness and strengthening of the regulatory agency.

The barrier analysis done by Kenya in 2013 as a part of the TNA process, solar home systems (SHS) and solar dryers were identified as prioritised mitigation technology in the energy sector. The key problem in mainstreaming SHS technology was found to be prohibitive costs. Requirement of high upfront investment, cost of repair and maintenance, absence of any subsidies on the component prices, and high interest rates (15% to 30%) charged on private loans, cumulatively prevented large scale deployment and diffusion of the technology. Issues that act as barriers to deployment of solar dryers were also found to be similar. Measures planned to remove those barriers in Kenya included steps to strengthen domestic regulatory institutions and standards, and creating linkages with internationally available support funds. Besides, corruption control was also identified as a necessary measure. Kenya planned to overcome supply and cost problems of the required technologies through setting up domestic manufacturing and assembling plants.

413 'TNA Country Reports' (*TT:CLEAR*) <https://unfccc.int/ttclear/tna/reports.html> accessed 25 October 2020.

D *Summary Analysis*

While not exhaustive, the growing body of empirical evidence on the barriers to low-carbon technology diffusion contains important insights that must be reflected in rulemaking and domestic policy formulations. We summarise those as follows -

a) *Low-Carbon Technology Diffusion Is a Developing Country-Specific Problem*

Transfer of technology on commercial terms work well between partners who are equally well-off in terms of technical and financial capability. The large-scale patent and license data surveys revealed that innovation and transfer of clean technologies is not a problem in the OECD member countries. In contrast, developing countries suffer a range of economic, financial, and technical barriers that prevent private commercial transactions from taking place. However, we find that some of the developing countries (especially, China, Korea, India, and Brazil) are increasingly changing this polarisation by catching up and leading the market in specific technologies.

b) *While Patent Protection Is Not an Apparent Major Problem, Further Clarification Is Desirable*

So far, it can be said that a robust domestic system for the protection of intellectual property rights is one of the many factors positively influencing a foreign firm's propensity to transfer technology. Although patenting activity in clean technologies has surged over the recent decades, market competition and availability of alternatives in most sectors have prevented monopolies from arising. This is why the majority of scholarly opinions tend to favour the position that legal protection granted to intellectual property rights is a positive rather than a negative factor for the diffusion of low-carbon technologies. However, given the limited amount of studies, drawing general conclusions is difficult, also premature. To the extent information is available, no such obstacle has been found – especially in sectors where the technology is already commercially available.[414] There is opportunity, and necessity too, to expand the scope of the studies focusing on the relationship between intellectual property rights and clean technologies, especially looking at issues of plant variety protection, or issues other than patents.[415]

---

414 See section III A above.

415 Bradly J Condon, 'Climate Change and Intellectual Property Rights for New Plant Varieties' (2013) 47 Journal of World Trade 897; Abdel-Latif (n 337) 115–116.

c) *Domestic and International Policies Should Target the Actual Obstacles Faced by Private Firms*

While IPRs are not found to pose significant obstacles in the different climate technology areas explored, sector or location-specific studies invariably find a significant positive impact of enabling policy frameworks that ease private firms' access and adoption of the technologies. In varying factual contexts, policy measures such as long-term guaranteed price, access to appropriate finance, local-content requirements, and energy efficiency regulations have been found to be beneficial. In addition, development of understanding and skills to adapt a new technological solution to local needs is important. Considering these aspects, the technology needs assessments (TNAs), and barriers identified in the process are of special relevance.

The available syntheses of the TNA reports overwhelmingly point to the economic and financial problems as the most significant barrier to climate technology diffusion. High prices, difficult financing, and little incentive in the market make technology adoption difficult. These problems are compounded by other issues like skills shortage, and absence of technical standards.

d) *Market Development Is Very Important*

The need for specific and coordinated attention to develop markets for clean technologies is undeniable. The highly shared view of pervasive economic and financial barriers as key obstacles are irrefutable indications of widespread market and system failure affecting climate technology dissemination. Studies therefore correctly highlight the need for medium to long-term policy interventions to tackle different forms of market failures.[416] This is an important insight to carry on to the study of the trade rules, which, if allowed, can positively influence market formation by tackling some of the price barriers, and creating room for enahanced financial supports, as well as other incentives.[417]

The rest of this chapter focuses on tracing the current rules and related developments in the trade regime relevant for low-carbon technology diffusion.

IV Developments in Trade Regulation

References to technology transfer appear in the body of laws of the multilateral trade regime, and also in negotiations and deliberations from time to

416 See p. 79 above. Also in particular, Lybecker and Lohse (n 347).

417 This is discussed further in the next chapter.

time. Concrete provisions regarding technology transfer only exist in the TRIPS agreement. Some provisions regarding technical assistance also appear in other areas of the WTO universe, but those are more tailored towards facilitating a specific objective. That apart, the WTO rules on removal of market access restrictions on trade in goods and services play a direct role in facilitating clean technology diffusion. In addition, one WTO working group is tasked with exploring the linkages between technology transfer and trade – a decades-long endeavour yet to bear fruit.

Beyond the boundaries of multilateralism, references to technological assistance and transfer of technology appears in some preferential trade agreements. Non-reciprocal unilateral preferences like the generalised system of preferences (GSP) and the Enabling Clause can also become of relevance as important routes to support the developing countries. Beyond the domain of the WTO, the UNCTAD is continuously engaged in research and communication in this area.

In the backdrop of the absence of any resounding success along the avenues mentioned above, recently transfer of technology has come up as a contentious point of dispute between key members. All these are discussed hereunder.

A *Existing Multilateral Rules*

(i) The TRIPS Agreement

The WTO Agreement on Trade-Related Aspects of Intellectual Property Rights (TRIPS) is a partial conclusion of the bargain between developed and developing countries that began in the NIEO context and led to the failed code of conduct.[418] It has already been mentioned earlier in this chapter that transfer of technology is one of the objectives of the TRIPS agreement. It is also the subject of a strict obligation imposed on the developed countries for the benefit of the LDCs. Alongside, the TRIPS agreement emphasises the need to maintain effective competition regulations to prevent *de facto* monopolies as a result of the IPR protection.

Articles 7 and 8 elucidate the general approach taken in TRIPS towards technology transfer and its linkage with the protection of the IPRs. Article 7 contains an expectation that technology transfer is achieved through protection and enforcement of the IPRs.[419] Following up, Article 8 recognises that additional measures may be required (e.g. competition regulation) to prevent

418 See the beginning of this chapter.

419 Article 7, Agreement on Trade-Related Aspects of Intellectual Property Rights (n 227). It holds that '[t]he protection and enforcement of intellectual property rights should contribute to […] the transfer and dissemination of technology […]'.

abuse of IPRs in ways that prevent technology transfer.[420] It also mentions that public policy measures need to be consistent with the agreement.[421] The general scheme therefore leads to the conclusion that in the absence of actions in pursuance of the obligation to transfer technology, protection of IPRs is in itself a contribution to the facilitation of technology transfer.

However, the TRIPS agreement provides options, namely, reducing the scope of patent rights, or issuance of a license, which can be of use to further ensure technology diffusion. Articles 27 allows for exclusion of specific areas from the scope of patentability. Such exclusion can be for protection of public order or morality,[422] or can cover therapeutic processes and plant varieties.[423] The latter among those is only allowed subject to the condition that comparable alternate protection is put in place. Article 30 allows limitation of the exclusivity of patent rights subject to the condition that it does not 'unreasonably' interfere with the interests of the holder. Governments can, therefore, issue licenses without the authorisation of the patent holder to, *inter alia,* prevent anti-competitive practices.[424] Under appropriate circumstances, these options can be of use to dismantle patent exclusivity related barriers to the diffusion of any technology.

Article 66.2 of TRIPS imposes a positive obligation upon developed countries to transfer technology in the following terms:

> [...] Developed country Members shall provide incentives to enterprises and institutions in their territories for the purpose of promoting and encouraging technology transfer to least-developed country Members in order to enable them to create a sound and viable technological base.[425]

Although the provision uses strict obligatory language ('shall'), the subject-matter of that obligation is not to transfer technology to the LDCs, but to provide incentives to domestic firms. The goal of such incentives is to 'promote and encourage' those firms to transfer technologies to the LDCs. Therefore, it can be questioned whether successful transfers of technologies from the developed countries to the LDCs are required to effectively discharge this obligation. More on this can be found in the following section.

---

420 Article 8.2, ibid.
421 Article 8.1, ibid.
422 Article 27.2, ibid.
423 Article 27.3, ibid.
424 Sub-paragraph (k) of Article 31, ibid.
425 Article 66.2 ibid.

(ii) Other Relevant Rules under the Covered Agreements

Apart from the TRIPS agreement provisions carrying over some of the earlier political conflicts into the WTO, there are some other relevant commitments with respect to technological assistance, easing of market access and subsidisation. Assistance provisions mentioned here are of soft law nature, and therefore not capable to form the basis of a legal claim. More importantly, as these provisions are not exclusive to the LCT-related goods or services, they can be equally used to facilitate emission intensive trades as well.

a) *Rules for Easing Technology-Related Goods and Services Market Access*

Trade flows of LCT-embedded goods are directly dependent on the market access regulations in the General Agreement on Tariffs and Trade (GATT), especially those on tariffs. While all the WTO members are obliged to submit schedules containing maximum rates of tariffs, the levels mentioned therein are then subjected to multilateral negotiation rounds with a view to their gradual decrease.[426] The negotiations are to be carried out with adequate consideration for the needs and situations of individual members and industries.[427] It is also possible to reduce tariffs unilaterally, as long as the benefit is made equally available to all members.

In a similar fashion, market access regulation in the General Agreement on Trade in Services (GATS) is relevant to ensure that services that are integrated with LCTs are available domestically in competitive terms. For example, construction, engineering and consultancy services play a supportive role in renewable energy projects. Financial services are important to bridge the resource constraints faced by private firms interested in new technologies. Opening of a specific services sector is exclusively a member's prerogative, realised through positive commitments in its Schedule.[428] Similar to the GATT, periodic negotiation rounds should take place to gradually increase effective market access on trade in services for all members, while according flexibility for the developing countries.[429]

The GATS further obliges the developed WTO members, also the developing members to establish contact points to facilitate information availability to the developing country suppliers. Information that is sought to be made easily

426 Article XXVIII bis, General Agreement on Tariffs and Trade 1994 (Marrakesh Agreement Establishing the World Trade Organization, Annex 1A, 1869 UNTS 299; 33 ILM 1197 (1994)).

427 Article XXVIII bis, ibid paragraph 3.

428 Articles XVI, and XX, General Agreement on Trade in Services 1994 (Marrakesh Agreement Establishing the World Trade Organization, Annex 1B, 1869 UNTS 183; 33 ILM 1167 (1994)).

429 Article XX, ibid.

available includes, among others, "the availability of services technology".[430] Special priority is provided to the least-developed countries (LDCs) in such facilitation effort.

b) *Provisions for Assistance Regarding Adoption of Green Standards*

To the extent that adoption of new technologies also involves conforming to technical regulations and standards, the Agreement of Technical Barriers to Trade (TBT) comes in play. Article 11 of the TBT agreement requires WTO members to advise and provide technical assistance to other members upon request, especially when such a request comes from a developing country member. The technical assistance is relating to different regulatory and compliance aspects of conformity assessment procedures between the countries, the establishment of standardising bodies, and participation in international standardising bodies.[431] It is also provided that members shall encourage other bodies within their territories involved in conformity assessments to engage in similar advice and technical assistance.[432] However developing country members are not expected to use international standards as a basis for domestic standard-setting, if such are not commensurate with their financial, developmental, or trade needs.[433] Similar to above, the special needs of the LDCs are to be especially prioritised in this regard.

c) *Easier Subsidy Disciplines for Developing Countries*

The developing countries, especially the least-developed ones, can make use of the relaxed subsidy disciplines to support domestic firms' adoption of clean technology. The WTO agreement on subsidies (ASCM) does not prevent LDCs from export subsidisation.[434] While the developing countries are supposed to phase out prohibited subsidies eventually, some may be maintained on justified grounds subject to review by the subsidies committee.[435] Also, subsidies below a *de minimis* level by the developing countries shall not be countervailed.[436]

---

430 Article IV.2(c), ibid.

431 Articles 11.2 – 11.6, Agreement on Technical Barriers to Trade 1994 (Marrakesh Agreement Establishing the World Trade Organization, Annex 1A, 1868 UNTS 120).

432 Article 11.7, ibid.

433 Article 12.4, ibid.

434 Article 27.2(a) and Annex VII, Agreement on Subsidies and Countervailing Measures 1994 (Marrakesh Agreement Establishing the World Trade Organization, Annex 1A, 1869 UNTS 14).

435 Article 27.4, ibid.

436 Article 27.10, ibid.

Also relevant to note in this regard is the lapse of non-actionable subsidies under the SCM agreement. Article 8 of the ASCM was drafted to keep three broad categories of domestic subsidies beyond scrutiny at the WTO – namely (i) subsidies for research and development,[437] (ii) subsidies for the development of disadvantaged regions,[438] and most importantly (iii) subsidies for compliance with environmental requirements.[439] Each category had to comply with specific threshold limitations to be considered as non-actionable. The disagreements over the continuation of these supports resulted into the dismantling of non-actionable subsidies in 1999.[440]

Similar support measures remain available to members with respect to agricultural products. While Article 6 of the Agreement on Agriculture ensures that a member's aggregate amount of domestic support stay within committed levels,[441] Annex 2 lays out some of the exemptions accorded to public services and programs in this regard, as long as those are not *de facto* price supports. Included in that scheme are government services, including environmental research related to agriculture, training services, extension and advisory services to transfer the knowledge gained from research.[442] These options can be used to domestically explore and promote ways of less emission intensive farming methods. However, like most other provisions discussed, these are also general in nature.

B *Negotiations and Deliberations at the WTO and UNCTAD*

(i) The TRIPS Council

The TRIPS Council is the body responsible for the administration of TRIPS agreement. In 2003, it was decided at the Council that the developed members will be required to report periodically on steps taken to implement Article 66.2 of the agreement.[443] Pursuant to the decision, a number of the developed members have been reporting[444] on the incentives granted by them. Already

437 Article 8.2(a), ibid.

438 Article 8.2(b), ibid.

439 Article 8.2(c), ibid.

440 For details, see, Dominic Coppens, *WTO Disciplines on Subsidies and Countervailing Measures: Balancing Policy Space and Legal Constraints* (Cambridge University Press 2014) 187–189.

441 Article 6.1, Agreement on Agriculture 1994 (Marrakesh Agreement Establishing the World Trade Organization, Annex 1A, 1867 UNTS 410).

442 Annex 2, para 2, ibid.

443 World Trade Organization, 'Implementation of Article 66.2 of the TRIPS Agreement: Decision of the Council for TRIPS of 19 February 2003' (2003) IP/C/28.

444 Every third year, new reports are submitted which are then reviewed and discussed in question and answer sessions.

in 2011, Moon demonstrated the difficulty to measure how much technology transfer actually took place due to the TRIPS provision. The scope of the reports has remained ambiguous due to the absence of a common understanding of what technology transfer actually meant. There was also no specificity as to how a transfer is taking place.[445] Later, while tracing the development up till 2016, Watal and Caminero reemphasised on the absence of a shared understanding, as well as found shortcomings in the conduct of both the developed and the LDC members.[446] On developed countries' front, it was noted that the reports were often compiled from data obtained from different agencies, which appeared to be a recapitulation of the countries' official development assistance (ODA) activities. The authors argued further that a reason behind there not being a meaningful development in reporting is the lack of engagement from the LDC side in the question and response sessions that follow the reports. Authors conclude that "[m]eaningfully improving Article 66.2 implementation and reporting requires continuous and effective engagement of the part of both developed country and LDC member delegations".[447]

The reports submitted since the above assessment[448] show that most members' reports lump a broad range of aid and support activities into technology transfer. To give a sense of how varied the items reported can be, the recent reports included mentions of training events, scholarship programs, specific financed projects, donation to international funds, and etc. One important noticeable issue however is that due to the broad range of activities reported, most are matters that bear no relationship with intellectual property protection at all. This is a consistent subsequent practice, which has given the legal meaning of Article 66.2 a scope that goes beyond the subject-matter limit of the TRIPS. The reports reviewed also show that countries frequently mention climate change related projects, e.g. those for renewable energy generation, as technology transfer incentives.

In a proposal to enable effective implementation of the technology transfer commitment, the LDC group requested the TRIPS council to deliberate and

445 Suerie Moon, *Meaningful Technology Transfer to the LDCs: A Proposal for a Monitoring Mechanism for TRIPS Article 66.2* (International Centre for Trade and Sustainable Development (ICTSD) 2011).

446 Jayashree Watal and Leticia Caminero, 'Least-Developed Countries, Transfer of Technology and the TRIPS Agreement' (World Trade Organization 2018) WTO Staff Working Paper ERSD-2018-01. The paper also contains a succint account of the evolution of Article 66.2 monitoring mechanism.

447 ibid 25.

448 Latest sets of reports, submitted in 2015 (IP/C/W/611/Add.1–6) and 2018 (IP/C/W/646/Add.1–6), were consulted for this purpose.

decide that the developed countries should only report incentives that are extended to the LDCs for technology transfer.[449] Moreover, the LDC group proposal also called for deliberation on the language, "incentives to enterprises and institutions", as found in Article 66.2.

(ii) The Committee on Trade and Environment (CTE and CTESS)

Established in parallel with the WTO itself,[450] the committee on trade and environment has become the hub to share information and deliberate on the trade and environmental issues in general, including issues involving trade and climate change. The regular sessions of the committee serves as a platform to deliberate on a range of matters, in the forefront being the Doha issues – (i) market access impact of environmental measures, including possible economic and environmental benefit of lowering trade restrictions, (ii) relevant provisions of the TRIPS agreement, (iii) labelling requirements for environmental purposes, (iv) issues of technical assistance, and (v) environmental and developmental aspects of the negotiations. The committee is periodically briefed by the WTO members on various environmental issues, as well as international organisations. The UNFCCC has since long been an observer at the committee.

A key contribution of the CTE to attain trade and climate coherence is ensuring transparency through making information available. By the CTE authorisation, the WTO secretariat periodically publishes an updated environmental database, collecting and sorting all the environmental notifications in the WTO. The database is informative regarding the the frequency and nature of climate change related regulations notified to the WTO, although a clear classification is not maintained. Another important contribution is a periodic publication of a matrix of environmental provisions that bear upon trade. The latest version takes account of the Paris Agreement.[451]

Since 2010, the deliberation and briefing activity of the CTE, within the scope of the above-mentioned mandate, has encountered issues that bear upon climate change. Member representatives of the 'friends of the fossil fuel reform' group have kept the committee abreast of the efforts being made in

449 World Trade Organization, 'Proposal on the Implementation of Article 66.2 of the TRIPS Agreement: Communication from Cambodia on Behalf of the LDC Group' (2018) IP/C/W/640.

450 Uruguay Round ministerial decision on trade and environment, 15 April 1994.

451 WTO Secretariat, 'Matrix on Trade-Related Measures Pursuant to Selected Multilateral Environmental Agreements' (World Trade Organization 2017) Note by the Secretariat WT/CTE/W/160/Rev.8; TN/TE/S/5/Rev.6 134–149.

cutting down unreasonable fossil fuel subsidies. There has been a consistent discussion of accounting and implementation methods of carbon footprinting, including a recent briefing on the ISO 14067 standard.[452] Members were also informed on the progress of the plurilateral environmental goods agreement negotiation.[453] Country experiences regarding trade and climate change interrelationships, trade components of respective NDCs were also shared. The UNFCCC also kept the members periodically updated on the progress of the climate negotiations.[454]

The discussion in the regular sessions of the CTE also outlines the hard-lined divergence of views amongst members. For example, with respect to information briefs regarding the removal of fossil fuel subsidies, it was viewed by some as beyond the scope of the committee.[455] A similar view is also shared by some members regarding discussions on climate-related issues, holding that it is of exclusive UNFCCC domain.[456] This position also affected a recent proposal on deepening the understanding of trade and climate relationship.[457] Some others objected to the focus of the platform becoming almost exclusively climate-related.[458] Members' supplied updates on the progress of the plurilateral environmental goods agreement (EGA) was also treated by some as being information only, and criticised by some for breaking out from the multilateral

452 Committee on Trade and Environment, 'Report of the Meeting Held on 20 June 2017: Note by the Secretariat' (World Trade Organization (WTO) 2017) WT/CTE/M/63 16.

453 Committee on Trade and Environment, 'Report (2015) of the Committee on Trade and Environment' (World Trade Organization (WTO) 2015) WT/CTE/22 4–5.

454 ibid 5.

455 It is a consistent position maintained by Saudi Arabia and Venezuela. See, Committee on Trade and Environment, 'Report of the Meeting Held on 28 June 2018: Note by the Secretariat' (World Trade Organization (WTO) 2018) WT/CTE/M/65 5; Committee on Trade and Environment, 'Report of the Meeting Held on 1 November 2017: Note by the Secretariat' (World Trade Organization (WTO) 2018) WT/CTE/M/64 4; Committee on Trade and Environment, 'Report of the Meeting Held on 20 June 2017: Note by the Secretariat' (n 452) 3; Also supported by Qatar, Committee on Trade and Environment, 'Report of the Meeting Held on 14 and 15 November 2016: Note by the Secretariat' (World Trade Organization (WTO) 2017) WT/CTE/M/62.

456 Position held by Saudi Arabia, Russian Federation and Venzuela over recent years, Committee on Trade and Environment, 'Report of the Meeting Held on 28 June 2018: Note by the Secretariat' ibid 14; Committee on Trade and Environment, 'Report of the Meeting Held on 20 June 2017: Note by the Secretariat' (n 452) 26–27.

457 Committee on Trade and Environment, 'Report of the Meeting Held on 14 and 15 November 2016: Note by the Secretariat' (n 455) 19–20.

458 View of Morocco and Bolivia, Committee on Trade and Environment, 'Report of the Meeting Held on 30 June 2016: Note by the Secretariat' (World Trade Organization (WTO) 2016) WT/CTE/M/61 25–26.

platform.[459] The ISO standard on carbon footprint was challenged on grounds of being undemocratic, not differential enough, and a trade barrier for developing country interests.[460]

The negotiation agenda mandated by Article 31 of the Doha declaration was pursued by the WTO members in the special sessions of the CTE. The mandate included negotiation in three areas – (i) relationship between the trade obligations and trade-related commitments in the MEAs, (ii) institutional coordination between the WTO and the MEAs, and (iii) reduction of tariff and non-tariff barriers to trade in environmental goods and services. Over the last two decades, none of the three avenues has resulted in fruition. Developments in policy and jurisprudential approaches in recent times have made the necessity of negotiated rules for trade and environment harmonisation largely redundant.[461] For example, the commendable jurisprudential approach by the Appellate Body has contributed to creating a level of certainty about the expected consequences of environment-conscious trade measures. Also, to the extent trade and climate change institutional coordination is concerned, *ad hoc* approaches have developed, and each institutions is granted observer status in relevant proceedings of the other. However, it is true that neither of the organisation can influence the other's agenda-setting. On the third avenue, the latest available unclassified information (from 2011) suggest deep divides lingering between developed and developing members on the scope of negotiation, and approach to be followed (i.e. list based, project-based, hybrid, or request and offer system).[462] The difficulty of arriving at a multilateral consensus has seen in 2014 the triggering of a plurilateral approach. Though such a breakout signifies stronger ambition on the part of some members, reports and comments thereupon in the regular session suggest that the initiative also resulted in a possible lack of engagement by those members in the multilateral process.[463] The issue remains hamstrung to this day.

459 View shared by Bolivia, Argentina, India and Cuba, ibid 34; Committee on Trade and Environment, 'Report of the Meeting Held on 6 October 2015: Note by the Secretariate' (World Trade Organization (WTO) 2016) WT/CTE/M/60 18.

460 Committee on Trade and Environment, 'Report of the Meeting Held on 20 June 2017: Note by the Secretariat' (n 452) 16–17.

461 Cossy and Marceau (n 92) 391.

462 Committee on Trade and Environment in Special Session (CTESS), 'Report by the Chairman, Ambassador Manuel A. J. Teehankee, to the Trade Negotiations Committee' (World Trade Organization (WTO) 2011) TN/TE/20 2–3, 15–17. According to the Chairman, '[t]he primary area requiring delegations' urgent attention relates to agreeing on an approach to coverage'.

463 Committee on Trade and Environment, 'Report of the Meeting Held on 6 October 2015: Note by the Secretariate' (n 459) 18; Committee on Trade and Environment, 'Report

(iii) The Working Group on Trade and Technology Transfer (WGTTT)

The working group was established in response to the need felt by the developing countries,[464] including the LDCs[465] for a common platform to clarify and implement the special and differential treatment provisions. Unlike the LDCs in the TRIPS council, there was no WTO forum where the developing countries could discuss the need for technology transfer. Nor was there any similar incentive schemes like that of the TRIPS Article 66.2. Prior to the Doha Ministerial Conference in 2001, a large number of developing countries voiced the desire to establish a work program on the issue.[466] In response, the Doha Ministerial Declaration established the WGTTT with a mandate to examine the relationship between trade and technology transfer, also to make possible recommendations to increase technology flow to the developing countries.[467] The Hong Kong Ministerial later provided a rolling mandate to continue work in the group.[468]

The exploratory part of the WGTTT mandate involved hearing from various international organisations engaged in the area and side by side sharing of members' experiences regarding technology transfer. Over the past decade and more, the group heard many presentations and briefings from all the major international organisations.[469] Issues the WGTTT deliberated upon as a result of the briefings included the impact of home country measures, or taxation policies on technology transfer, trends of cross-border technology flow,

---

of the Meeting Held on 30 June 2016: Note by the Secretariat' (n 458) 35. This view is expressed by Venzuela, Argenta, India, Cuba and Bolivia during 2015 and 2016 meetings.

464 The earliest request was made by India, prior to the Seattle Ministerial Conference. 'Preparations for the 1999 Ministerial Conference: Communication from India' (General Council, WTO 1999) WT/GC/W/352.

465 Committee on Trade and Development, 'Proposed Work Programme for the Year 2000: Communication from Zambia' (World Trade Organization (WTO) 2000) WT/COMTD/W/67; Committee on Trade and Development, 'Proposal for Sub-Committee Work Programme: Communication from Zambia' (Committee on Trade and Development, WTO 2001) WT/COMTD/LDC/W/24.

466 'Preparations for the Fourth Session of the Ministerial Conference: Communication from Cuba, Dominican Republic, Honduras, India, Indonesia, Kenya, Malaysia, Pakistan, Sri Lanka, Tanzania, Uganda and Zimbabwe' (General Council, WTO 2001) WT/GC/W/443.

467 Paragraph 37, 'Doha Ministerial Declaration' (n 93). It provided, '[w]e agree to an examination [...] of the relationship between trade and transfer of technology, and of any possible recommendations on steps that might be taken within the mandate of the WTO to increase flows of technology to developing countries'.

468 Paragraph 43, 'Doha Work Programme: Ministerial Declaration' (WTO 2005) WT/MIN(05)/DEC.

469 Institutions that shared research findings with the group included, *inter alia*, UNCTAD, UNIDO, FAO, WIPO, OECD, and the World Bank.

non-equity modes of technology transfer, different sector-specific studies, the role of global value chains, technology diffusion in developing countries, and more. Experiences were also shared by many member countries, including the European Union, Switzerland, the Philippines, and Chinese Taipei. However, the absence of a structure or a progressive work plan kept the discussions very broad, and ultimately no specific insight emerged. Somewhat similar to the earlier mentioned experience in the TRIPS context, there was no agreed understanding of what technology transfer was, or how it would be best assisted within the WTO mandate. Not only was the topic itself complex, but also arguably the inputs received by the working group from different institutional bodies were probably not based on the same understanding of the concept of technology transfer and its many dimensions.

Nonetheless, several common issues could be identified among the whole range of inputs received by the working group. Technological capacity and ability to innovate was universally accepted to be a significant contributor to increased factor productivity and therefore economic growth. Liberal trade regime, especially the import regime facilitating the acquisition of capital goods and intermediates were considered to boost access to technology.[470] Both home and host country incentives to facilitate foreign direct investment (FDI) flows, especially in R&D collaboration is also beneficial.[471] Among others, effective IPR regimes, mobility of scientific and technical professionals, linkage of domestic business and industry associations to international networks and overall integration of innovation to government policy framework was also generally suggested.[472] Not surprisingly, such insights are also in line with the empirical findings of the previous section.

The recommendations part of the working group's mandate fell short, as members' views on the topic did not coalesce enough to generate shared

470 As early as 2008, research findings shared by the World Bank contained these conclusions. WGTTT, 'Report (2008) of the Working Group on Trade and Transfer of Technology to the General Council' (World Trade Organization (WTO) 2008) WT/WGTTT/10; World Bank, *Global Economic Prospects 2008: Technology Diffusion in the Developing World* (The World Bank 2008) <http://elibrary.worldbank.org/doi/book/10.1596/978-0-8213-7365-1> accessed 25 October 2020.

471 WGTTT, 'Report (2004) of the Working Group on Trade and Transfer of Technology to the General Council' (World Trade Organization (WTO) 2004) WT/WGTTT/6.

472 WGTTT, 'Report (2007) of the Working Group on Trade and Transfer of Technology to the General Council' (World Trade Organization (WTO) 2007) WT/WGTTT/9; WGTTT, 'Report (2010) of the Working Group on Trade and Transfer of Technology to the General Council' (World Trade Organization (WTO) 2010) WT/WGTTT/12; WGTTT, 'Report (2014) of the Working Group on Trade and Transfer of Technology to the General Council' (World Trade Organization (WTO) 2014) WT/WGTTT/16.

conclusions. From the very beginning, the developing countries' interests converged around several issues, which include – a substantive review of technical support provisions in different WTO covered agreements, constraints in further implementation of those, and full operationalisation of the Article 66.2 of the TRIPS agreement.[473] Progress in any of those areas was impossible due to several objections.[474] In particular, it was contended that the review activities would result in substantive overlaps with other forum mandates, e.g. that of the TRIPS council.[475] It was also argued that the WGTTT did not have a mandate to negotiate, which was necessary to review existing regulations.[476] Furthermore, some claimed that any recommendation should have an organic linkage with work done under the exploratory part of the mandate.[477] It is assumed that since no headway could be made towards progress, general interest in the group's activity waned over time. Only one recommendation has so far has managed to stay on the agenda, which is about development of a webpage meant to serve as a repository of technologies reasonably available and also to assist business to business matchmaking.

In 2018, the African group proposed a revision of the WGTTT mandate.[478] The proposal sought for concrete tasks to be mentioned, e.g. assessment of developing country needs and constraints, examination of relevant WTO provisions, studying of appropriate incentives in a similar fashion to Article 66.2 of the TRIPS, and more. Although potentially useful for low-carbon technology diffusion, the success of the endeavour is subject to high speculation.

---

473 WGTTT, 'Provisions Relating to Transfer of Technology in WTO Agreements: Communication from Cuba, Egypt, Honduras, India, Indonesia, Jamaica, Kenya, Mauritius, Pakistan and Zimbabwe' (World Trade Organization (WTO) 2002) WT/WGTTT/3/Rev.1; WGTTT, 'Possible Recommendation on Steps That Might Be Taken within the Mandate of the WTO to Increase Flows of Technology to Developing Countries: Communication from Cuba, India, Indonesia, Kenya, Pakistan, Tanzania and Zimbabwe' (World Trade Organization (WTO) 2003) WT/WGTTT/W/6.

474 WGTTT, 'Report (2004) of the Working Group on Trade and Transfer of Technology to the General Council' (n 473) para 8; WGTTT, 'Note on the Meeting of 19 July 2004' (World Trade Organization (WTO) 2004) WT/WGTTT/M/9 para 4; WGTTT, 'Report (2005) of the Working Group on Trade and Transfer of Technology to the General Council' (World Trade Organization (WTO) 2005) WT/WGTTT/7 paras 9, 11; WGTTT, 'Report (2008) of the Working Group on Trade and Transfer of Technology to the General Council' (n 470) paras 22, 24; WGTTT, 'Report (2010) of the Working Group on Trade and Transfer of Technology to the General Council' (n 472) para 33.

475 ibid.

476 ibid.

477 ibid.

478 WGTTT, 'Report (2018) of the Working Group on Trade and Transfer of Technology to the General Council' (World Trade Organization (WTO) 2018) WT/WGTTT/20 para 3.3–3.4.

At the end of the day, the WGTTT remains an ideal platform to initiate the discussion as to which of diverse policy options to trigger low-carbon technology diffusion, would fall squarely in the WTO domain, how to prioritise those, and find the points of convergence among the members' interests to implement them in a positive, and inclusive manner.

(iv) Developments at the UNCTAD

Although the earlier UNCTAD efforts to establish a Code of Conduct on technology transfer practices failed to succeed, the experience gathered therefrom by states was influential to secure the technology transfer obligation enshrined in Article 66.2 of the TRIPS agreement. Since then, work related to transfer of technology at UNCTAD has produced a number of studies and reports, though none exclusively on climate technologies. Issues addressed in this regard include examination of different approaches in investment agreements to ensure transfer of technology,[479] survey of home country measures,[480] and communication of successful country experiences[481]. A range of industry and country-specific case studies was also published.[482] Many of these reports were also presented at the WGTTT. Current mandate of UNCTAD includes, among other areas, continuation of research on the impact of transfer of technology on trade and development.[483]

In 2014, one UNCTAD report made a general survey of issues relating to transfer of technology and development. The report highlighted many existing gaps in knowledge, including the lack of a common definition of 'technology' or 'technology transfer'.[484] The report also mentioned that despite a widening technology gap between the developed countries and the LDC s,[485] a complete understanding of the policies necessary to close the gap remains wanting.[486] The concept of national innovation system, portraying the need for policy

479 UNCTAD, 'Transfer of Technology' (UNCTAD 2001) UNCTAD/ITE/IIT/28.

480 UNCTAD, 'Facilitating Transfer of Technology to Developing Countries: A Survey of Home-Country Measures' (UNCTAD 2004) UNCTAD/ITE/IPC/2004/5.

481 UNCTAD, 'Investment and Technology Policies for Competitiveness: Review of Successful Country Experiences' (UNCTAD 2003) UNCTAD/ITE/IPC/2003/2.

482 UNCTAD, 'Studies in Technology Transfer: Selected Cases from Argentina, China, South Africa and Taiwan Province of China' (UNCTAD 2014) UNCTAD/DTL/STICT/2013/7; UNCTAD, 'A Case Study of the Salmon Industry in Chile' (UNCTAD 2006) UNCTAD/ITE/IIT/2005/12.

483 Paragraph 65(c) 'UNCTAD XIII: Doha Mandate' (UNCTAD 2012) UNCTAD/ISS/2012/1.

484 UNCTAD, 'Transfer of Technology and Knowledge Sharing for Development – Science, Technology and Innovation Issues for Developing Countries' (n 69) 2–3.

485 ibid 13–14.

486 ibid 51.

interventions tackling market and system failures was also comprised in the report.[487] It was further advised that the developing countries should make prudent use of the IPR flexibilities in the TRIPS agreement.[488]

C *Trade Disputes Regarding Technology Transfer and Renewables*

Until recently, technology transfer has not been a contested issue in the vibrant history of WTO dispute settlement. There was one reference to it in the Appellate Body decision in the *US – Shrimp* dispute,[489] where several countries challenged the United States (US) measure of prohibiting the import of shrimp caught in a process that incidentally harms sea turtles. In a landmark judgment, the Appellate Body in that dispute decided that the US measure was provisionally justifiable because endangered sea turtles were exhaustible natural resource and their conservation attempts a valid policy motive to maintain a GATT-inconsistent measure under Article XX(g) of the agreement. However, for any such measure to pass muster, its implementation needed also to be proven as not being arbitrary or unjustifiably discriminatory. The US measure failed that test regarding its varying technology transfer support. The Appellate Body considered that the level of effort made by the US to transfer necessary fishing technology to exclude turtles was connected to the duration of the phase-in period. As those periods were different for the members affected, the AB concluded that the level of effort made for necessary technology transfer was not the same.[490]

It is also relevant to not that trade remedy measures adopted by the developed countries regarding renewable energy production components have become frequent over the past decade.[491] Spearheading these activities are antidumping (AD) and countervailing (CVD) duties imposed by the EU and the US against Chinese solar cells and modules.[492] Massive public funding leading to an exponential rise of the Chinese producers to the forefront of the global

487 ibid 22–23.

488 ibid 28–29.

489 *United States – Import Prohibition of Certain Shrimp and Shrimp Products* (n 94).

490 ibid 157.

491 Johannes Kasteng, 'Trade Remedies on Clean Energy: A New Trend in Need of Multilateral Initiatives' (International Centre for Trade and Sustainable Development (ICTSD), World Economic Forum (WEF) 2013); Kim Kampel, 'Options for Disciplining the Use of Trade Remedies in Clean Energy Technologies' (International Centre for Trade and Sustainable Development (ICTSD), World Economic Forum (WEF) 2017) Issue paper.

492 Kampel, ibid 12–17; Edwin Vermulst and Madison Meng, 'Dumping and Subsidy Issues in the Renewable Energy Sector' in Thomas Cottier and Ilaria Espa (eds), *International Trade in Sustainable Electricity: Regulatory Challenges in International Economic Law* (Cambridge University Press 2017).

solar market[493] has led to other countries scrambling to protect their domestic firms. Treatment of China as a non-market economy (NME) has also contributed to finding higher margins of dumping.[494] While some of the antidumping disputes were settled through price undertaking,[495] one challenge by China to the imposition of CVD by the US has made its way to the multilateral dispute settlement.[496] Recently, the Republic of Korea challenged the imposition of safeguard duties by the United States on its exports of silicon photovoltaic products.[497] China, facing similar US measures, also followed suit.[498] Respective Panels have already been composed to hear the disputes.

It would be useful to note that trade remedy actions usually take place between countries that are competitive with each other in a given sector. Therefore, despite having a negative impact on the volume of trade, these disputes would have little impact on the flow of clean technology to new recipients. For example, during the same period as above, India also undertook an antidumping investigation and found a positive dumping margin regarding Chinese solar components exports, but no duties were imposed due to the domestic dependency on those products.[499]

In addition to above, past years also saw several WTO disputes where domestic subsidies coupled with local content requirements were challenged. Earliest among those was the *Canada – Renewable Energy* dispute, which led to some pathbreaking jurisprudence to be discussed later.[500] Similarly, China

493 Zhang and Gallagher (n 80) 195, 199; Helm, Tannock and Iliev (n 343) 25–30.

494 Vermulst and Meng (n 492) 337–338; Kampel (n 491) 17, 46.

495 Vermulst and Meng (n 492) 345; Christoph Herrmann, Bruno Simma and Rudolf Streinz (eds), *Trade Policy between Law, Diplomacy and Scholarship: Liber Amicorum in Memoriam Horst G. Krenzler* (Springer 2015) 389, European Commission, 'Fact Sheet: The European Union's Measures Against Dumped and Subsidised Imports of Solar Panels from China' <https://trade.ec.europa.eu/doclib/docs/2015/july/tradoc_153587.pdf> accessed 25 October 2020; The minimum price undertaking was withdrawn in September 2018, Becky Beetz, 'EU Officially Ends MIP for Chinese Solar Imports' [2018] *pv magazine International* <https://www.pv-magazine.com/2018/08/31/eu-ends-mip-against-chinese/> accessed 25 October 2020.

496 *United States – Countervailing Duty Measures on Certain Products from China* [2015] Appellate Body Report WT/DS437/AB/R.

497 DS545, United States – Safeguard measures on imports of crystalline photovoltaic products, request for consultations: 14 May 2018.

498 DS562, United States – Safeguard measure on imports of crystalline silicon photovoltaic products, request for consultations: 14 August 2018.

499 Vermulst and Meng (n 492) 346–347.

500 *Canada – Certain Measures Affecting the Renewable Energy Generation Sector / Canada – Measures Relating to the Feed-in Tariff Program* [2013] Appellate Body Report WT/DS412/AB/R; WT/DS426/AB/R, DSR 2013: I 7.

challenged some subsidy programs of EU member countries, which was settled at the consultation stage.[501] In 2016, as a result of US complaint, the Appellate Body confirmed a Panel decision holding that domestic content requirements in an Indian solar energy program as WTO-inconsistent.[502] In response, India also successfully challenged similar requirements prevalent in the incentive schemes of seven states[503] in the US.[504] A similar challenge was also filed by China at the WTO, which has not progressed beyond the consultation phase.[505]

Since early 2018, transfer of technology has become a key sticking point in the relationship of the major trading partners with China. It has manifested in two separate claims eventually resulting in disputes – one complained by the United States, another by the European Union. In both cases, the claims challenge Chinese practice of what complainants term as 'forced technology transfer'. The practice in question involves Chinese requirement to enter into joint ventures, share technology, or perform researches in China in return of investment market access. These are some of the traits that academic literature discussed earlier found at times to be the reasons behind China's ability to swiftly scale up technological competence.[506] In climate change literature, such use of domestic market access as leverage was taken as an example of successful strategy.

The US initiated its dispute (DS542) on 23 March 2018. The request for consultation circulated by the US indicates that the claim involves challenging a range of Chinese domestic regulations regarding import and export of technologies and equity joint ventures with foreign partners.[507] It has been argued by the US that the laws in question limit the scope of a US patent holder's rights as guaranteed by Article 28 of the TRIPS Agreement.[508] On 17 January 2019, a Panel has been composed to settle the dispute.

---

501 DS 452, European Union and certain Member States – Certain Measures Affecting the Renewable Energy Generation Sector, request for consultations 5 November 2012.

502 *India – Certain Measures Relating to Solar Cells and Solar Modules* (n 4).

503 Namely, Washington, California, Montana, Massachusetts, Connecticut, Michigan, Delaware, and Minnesota.

504 *United States – Certain Measures Relating to the Renewable Energy Sector* [2019] Panel Report WT/DS510/R.

505 DS 563, United States – Certain Measures Related to Renewable Energy, request for consultations 14 August 2018.

506 Lewis (n 371); Gallagher (n 71).

507 'China – Certain Measures Concerning the Protection of Intellectual Property Rights: Request for Consulatations by the United States' (2018) WT/DS542/1; IP/D/38.

508 Side by side, the United States has also taken unilateral retaliatory measures. Those are discussed addressed in Chapter 6 below.

The EU launched its own dispute (DS549) against China in June 2018. This dispute challenged thirty-six specific pieces of domestic regulations in China.[509] Among those, one exclusively relates to low-carbon technology, namely China's New Energy Vehicles (NEV) Production Enterprises, and Production Regulation. The European Union contended that the Chinese regulatory requirement upon foreign enterprises seeking to enter new energy vehicles market (including, electric hybrids and fuel cell operated vehicles) to, *inter alia,* master and understand the technology, establish exclusive design and development institution, and establish product information databases, including technical and design specifications is a violation of the commitment made by China in its Protocol of Accession to the WTO.[510] The commitment in question is contained in paragraph 7.3 of Part I of the Chinese Protocol of Accession to the WTO. It precludes the country from imposing performance requirements upon foreign investments, which the EU alleges the Chinese technology transfer practices to violate.

D *Non-Multilateral Approaches*

(i) Plurilateral Initiatives

a) *Environmental Goods Negotiation*

A plurilateral initiative to remove tariff barriers on an agreed list of environmental goods was launched in 2014. Although the initiative was welcomed as taking the process forward, subsequent CTE reports and meeting minutes indicate that some developing countries find such step as stalling the possibility of a multilateral solution.[511] However, the plurilateral initiative itself stalled in 2016. Disagreement among parties on the list of products to be included was considered to be the main reason leading to the deadlock.[512] While on the record, the parties remain committed to finding a solution, ongoing trade war and the US threat to the multilateral trade system have shifted the priorities. It does not seem plausible that the talks would restart any time soon.

Outside the domain of the WTO, however, twenty-one members of the Asia-Pacific Economic Cooperation (APEC) have agreed in 2012 to a fifty-four items

---

509 'China – Certain Measures on the Transfer of Technology: Request for Consulatation by the European Union (Revision)' (n 4).

510 ibid 6.

511 See (n 459) above.

512 ICTSD, 'Ministerial Talks to Clinch Environmental Goods Agreement Hit Stumbling Block' (2016) 20 *BRIDGES* <https://ictsd.iisd.org/bridges-news/bridges/news/ministerial-talks-to-clinch-environmental-goods-agreement-hit-stumbling> accessed 25 October 2020.

list of environmental goods, tariffs upon which are to be gradually lowered to 5 per cent or less.[513] The list covers products relating to renewable energy generation. However, in terms of low-carbon technology, the coverage is not comprehensive.[514] Moreover, as the APEC is a voluntary forum, the commitments do not have a binding effect upon the participants.

b) *Provisions Allowing Green Public Procurement*

The plurilateral governmental procurement agreement (GPA) is in effect since 1994 among 48 WTO members with an aim to open up the government procurement market to the participants. While the GPA requires participants to issue technical specifications and select the most advantageous tender, the revised agreement further mentions that such specifications can be prepared to "promote the conservation of natural resources or protect the environment".[515] This further clarifies the ability of a government participant to the revised GPA to choose low-carbon technologies compared to polluting but cheaper alternatives. Although so far there are only a handful of developing countries participating in the revised GPA, some remain in the process of accession and many others take part as observers.

(ii) Preferential Trade Agreements (PTA s)

According to one report, by 2016 there were thirty-four preferential trade agreements (PTA s) that have specific mention of climate change.[516] To provide context for this number, the same research mentions that general references to the environment are made in 263 PTA s, including the 114 where specific

513 Annex C, '2012 Leaders' Declaration' <https://www.apec.org/Meeting-Papers/Leaders-Declarations/2012/2012_aelm> accessed 25 October.

514 Rene Vossenaar, 'Identifying Products with Climate and Development Benefits for an Environmental Goods Agreement' (ICTSD 2014) <https://seors.unfccc.int/applications/seors/attachments/get_attachment?code=FL5IRCXNKHGQDAD6JQULRT67L7A02OHU> accessed 25 October 2020.

515 Article X(6), Revised Agreement on Government Procurement 2012 (Marrakesh Agreement Establishing the World Trade Organization, Annex 4B, 1915 UNTS 103, (1994)); Marc Steiner, 'The WTO Government Procurement Agreement: Assessing the Scope for Green Procurement' (2015) 9 *BIORES* <https://ictsd.iisd.org/bridges-news/biores/overview?page=6> accessed 25 October 2020; Robert D Anderson and Anna Caroline Muller, 'The Revised WTO Agreement On Government Procurement (GPA): Key Design Features and Significance for Global Trade and Development' 48 60, 960, 970–971.

516 José-Antonio Monteiro, 'Typology of Environment-Related Provisions in Regional Trade Agreements' (World Trade Organization 2016) WTO Staff Working Paper ERSD-2016-13 67. This is the number when explicit reference to climate change is taken into account. When indirect references are included, e.g. provisions on energy efficiency, or renewables, the author notes that the number goes up to 59.

environmental provisions can be found.[517] Climate commitments found in the PTA s so far are of best endeavour nature – mostly involving reciprocal agreements to reduce emission, to cooperate on specific areas like renewable energy, or technological innovations, while allowing for flexibility to accommodate developing country interests.[518] Some specific commitments exist with regard to the promotion of trade in environmental goods, services, and technologies.[519] While the author of the aforementioned report does not specifically highlight it, a quick inspection reveals that most of the PTAs with climate change commitments are those in which the European Union is a party. These include the EU agreements with Colombia and Peru, Georgia, Moldova, Canada, Ukraine, South Korea, Turkey as well as association agreements with Macedonia, and Croatia. This is an example of the positive change a capable and willing country can induce unilaterally. Other significant agreements outside the EU partnership are the PTA s between South Korea and Peru, Japan and Peru, South Korea and New Zealand, as well as South Korea and Turkey.

The PTA between the EU, Peru and Colombia went the farthest in incorporating climate law notions within the agreement. Of special importance is the endorsement of common concern and a related duty to cooperate in the following terms:

> [T]he Parties recognise that climate change is an issue of *common and global concern that calls for the widest possible cooperation* by all countries and their participation in an effective and appropriate international response, for the benefit of present and future generations of mankind.[520]

Against this backdrop, the above legal provision further iterates commitment to differentiated responsibility and equity.[521] The parties articulate the objective

517 ibid 9.

518 ibid 67.

519 ibid 56–57. Based on the author's computation of the data in the WTO RTA database, 17 agreements contain provisions on trade in renewable energy products and services. The same number for energy-efficient goods and services is 13.

520 Article 275.1, 'Trade Agreement between the European Union and Its Member States, of the One Part, and Colombia and Peru, of the Other Part' [emphasis supplied].

521 Article 275.2, ibid. It provides that '[t]he Parties are resolved to enhance their efforts regarding climate change, which are led by developed countries, including through the promotion of domestic policies and suitable international initiatives to mitigate and to adapt to climate change, on the basis of equity and in accordance with their common but differentiated responsibilities and respective capabilities and their social and economic conditions, and taking particularly into account the needs, circumstances, and high vulnerability to the adverse effects of climate change of those Parties which are developing countries'.

as being a rapid transition to low-carbon economies and further agree to promote trade and environment measures that would enhance access, dissemination and use of clean production technologies and the same for mitigation and adaptation. With respect to specific measures, the parties commit to consider steps that would contribute to mitigation and adaptation, including removing barriers to trade in goods and services in mitigation technologies as well as boosting energy efficiency and renewable energy.

In contrast, the United States, as a developed country and still the most powerful player in international trade, casts a strong negative shadow on climate and trade interaction. None of the PTAs to which the US is a party contain specific provisions referring to climate change, although many of them address environmental issues in a highly elaborate fashion. Nowhere is the absence more conspicuous than the recently negotiated USMCA.[522] The environmental chapter of this agreement between the three North American trading partners covers many issues, without mentioning climate change even for once. It cannot but be a deliberate choice. There is also a similar absence of reference to climate change in the CPTPP,[523] which in all probability can be attributed to the initial interest of the United States to get on board. This stance of the United States is a major obstacle in multilateralising any emerging positive PTA language.

It is noteworthy that neither China nor India is a party to any PTAs that is responsive to the need for trade and climate cooperation. This speaks of their conservative attitude when it comes to assuming greater responsibility. While India is less present in the PTA scene in general, its existing PTAs hardly contain any environmental commitment, hard or soft. The Chinese story is similar, although China has a range of preferential trade agreements, especially with the East Asian trading partners. Some of the Chinese PTAs mention environment with respect to the exception provisions. None of the two countries is a party to the mega-regional trade agreements. India, among the two still benefits from a few GSP schemes,[524] preferences wherein are not currently conditional upon any climate-related preconditions.

522 Chapter 24, Agreement between the United States of America, the United Mexican States, and Canada (USMCA), Signed 30 November 2018 https://ustr.gov/trade-agreements/free-trade-agreements/united-states-mexico-canada-agreement/agreement-between, accessed 25 October 2020.

523 Chapter 20, Comprehensive and Progressive Agreement for Trans-Pacific Partnership (CPTPP), entry into force 30 December 2018 https://www.mfat.govt.nz/assets/Trade-agreements/TPP/Text-ENGLISH/20.-Environment-Chapter.pdf, accessed 25 October 2020.

524 The number of GSP donors for India stood at 8 in 2018. UNCTAD, *Generalized System of Preferences: List of Beneficiaries* (UNCTAD 2018). In March 2019 the USA decided to withdraw the GSP beneficiary status of India.

In recent research, Morin and Jinnah have taken the analysis one step forward trying to answer the question as to what extent the merging of climate issues into PTAs accrue beneficial results.[525] Analysing the climate change related provisions in 688 PTAs signed since 1947, the authors come to a sobering conclusion. One key finding is that despite the optimism surrounding preferential agreements serving as building blocks towards multilateral rules, the climate-related commitments, even when concrete, do not really add to the existing mitigation efforts. It is because there is no evidence suggesting that big emitters otherwise not committing to mitigation are doing so in a PTA. The authors guess that it is possibly due to the fact that countries consider long term climate costs are not balanced by the additional economic and political gain of economic integration. Another evidential finding is that climate-related commitments have increasingly become precise over time, especially in the 21st-century PTAs. However, there exists a trade-off between the precision of the commitments and the stringency of the enforcement provisions. The PTAs signed by the EU tend to have relatively detailed and precise commitments, but they are usually backed up with a consultation-based compliance mechanism. Whereas, those signed by the US contain very general climate commitment, but they tend to have stricter dispute settlement provisions often resulting in a binding determination.

(iii) Conditional Unilateral Preferences: GSPs under the Enabling Clause

The generalised system of preferences (GSPs) are unilateral preferential tariff schemes offered by a developed country to developing and least-developed ones. GSP schemes derogate from the standard non-discrimination commitment at the WTO. Such derogations are possible due to a decision by the GATT contracting parties, formalised in 1979.[526] While the GSP can be used to grant special LCT-related tariff benefits to the developing countries, subject to adequate performance prerequisites, no such scheme has yet been put in place. One encouraging example is the EU practice, wherein benefits additional to the regular GSP scheme (named 'GSP plus') are accorded subject to the beneficiaries' participation in a select number of human rights, labour protection and environmental treaties, including the UNFCCC.[527]

---

525 Jean-Frédéric Morin and Sikina Jinnah, 'The Untapped Potential of Preferential Trade Agreements for Climate Governance' (2018) 27 Environmental Politics 541.

526 Differential and More Favourable Treatment: Reciprocity and Fuller Participation of Developing Countries 1979 (L/4903).

527 Annex VIII, Regulation (EU) No 978/2012 of the European Parliament and of the Council of 25 October 2012 applying a scheme of generalised tariff preferences 2012.

E Summary Analysis

a) The Polarised Legacy of Technology Transfer in a Hard Law Framework

Although with respect to technology transfer, the trade and the climate regime started from a common position of the unsuccessful code negotiations, subsequent developments have been markedly different. While a soft-law based approach in the climate regime has led to an incremental formulation of an institutional structure with respect to clean technology development and transfer, no comparable development took place within the trade regime. One reason behind such different outcomes is that unlike the climate rules framework, negotiated rules in the trade regime entail strict legal consequences, resulting in a possible tendency among actors to avoid making of costly new rules. While there are many existing rules that are relevant for low-carbon technology diffusion, most are of general nature.

Yet another reason for the absence of progress in the WTO front is the inheritance of the politically fraught issue of technology transfer and protection of IPRs by the WTO. The TRIPS council is the ideal platform where the developing countries could voice concerns over necessary IPR flexibilities to facilitate technology transfer. This had the effect of drawing all the political capital, leaving little, or none to explore new avenues of technology diffusion.

b) Stalemate as the State of Play at the WTO

Connected to the above, although the existing empirical studies showed that there is a need to influence the markets for greater diffusion of LCTs, any focused and meaningful discussion to that effect is yet to take place in the WTO. The absence of a common understanding of transfer of technology and its determinants have led to a compartmentalisation of discussions in different deliberative fora like the TRIPS council, the trade and environment committee, and the WGTTT, without any meaningful synergies being developed over time. We find some technical assistance and subsidy provision that may be of utility, but those remain of general and best endeavour character.

The deadlock in progress actually serves the members whose interests are vested in keeping the *status quo*. This is conspicuous from the repeated refusals to cooperate by some members at the CTE. To take the agenda of trade and LCT diffusion forward, this stalemate situation must be overcome.

c) Limited Progress Made in Smaller Constellations

Outside the WTO, there have indeed been somewhat successful attempts at liberalising environmental goods – some of which also cover LCTs. While in smaller constellations there are positive alignments of interests, in broader participatory groups, progress is stalled. Evidence of the former is visible in the PTAs where like-minded parties make detailed commitments going beyond the WTO standard. The latter can be noted in the stuck plurilateral negotiation on environmental goods.

d) *Improving Trade Cooperation for Clean Technology Diffusion Is Important*

In the backdrop of emerging disputes involving technology transfer, as well as growing political distrust, it is impossible to overemphasise the urgency of effective cooperation at the WTO in this regard. Cooperation will not only further the cause of LCT diffusion, but will also strengthen the institution's legitimacy.

The doctrine of Common Concern can supply the formal structure and normative content around which an effective convergence of interest of the WTO members is possible. By creating an exclusive dialogue around the need for effective trade-related responses to facilitate climate technology diffusion, the doctrine of Common Concern will attract the parties to engage in meaningful negotiation. This will be elaborated in the following chapter.

V Conclusion

This chapter undertook an important stocktaking exercise. Beginning at the aftermath of the unsuccessful origin of technology transfer as an international agenda, it traced through the regulatory morphosis in the climate and the trade regime. It also presented a comprehensive picture of the existing literature on the determinants of low-carbon technology diffusion.

We found that transfer of technology only becomes a topic in public international law when commercial transactions at private market terms leave some or many actors dissatisfied, almost often involving developing country partners. This leads to general or issue-specific attempts, which at times successfully generate regulatory arrangements for desired levels of clean technology diffusion.

We also found that approaches to technology diffusion arrangements can vary a great deal across legal regimes. The climate regime showcases a multi-pronged approach. Despite an expansive framework based on a deeper understanding of the issue, the approach falls short due to its reliance on financial resources, which is unavailable at the required scales, and also due to its failure to agree on market reform approaches. Avenues in the trade regime remain less successful in striking a common understanding as to the meaning and scope of technology transfer. Efforts made in the trade regime tend to focus on the issue of intellectual property protection, which is of importance in many areas.

Review of the existing empirical studies indicated that legal protection of intellectual property rights is not a significant barrier for the diffusion of climate technologies. The studies rather highlighted a necessity to undertake market development policy measures, i.e. actions that would tackle the existing market failures in the dissemination of LCTs. The part trade rules can play in that regard remains yet to be explored. Moreover, political disagreements and conflicts of views, especially with regard to according a more active role to market reforms in the building up of enabling environments, was found to affect both trade and climate regimes. The outcome of such conflicting positions of countries is not only limited to the absence of adequate progress in rulemaking. It also fuels disputes in the trade regime.

One positive development that is noted, however, is the increasing recognition of the role of the trade policy measures for climate action, including diffusion of technologies in the PTAs. The EU appeared to play the most progressive role in this regard.

CHAPTER 3

Towards a Cooperation Based Trade Action Agenda

After an acquaintance with the market-related determinants of low-carbon technology (LCT) diffusion and highlighting the gaps in the relevant regulatory frameworks in the previous chapter, the question now is that how those gaps may be bridged by creating new opportunities for appropriate responses. Guided by the doctrine of Common Concern of Humankind, this chapter proposes an expansion of the WTO members' responsibility to cooperate to resolve the challenges of LCT diffusion. It begins by pointing out that in purely positivistic terms, the trade rules' falling short of accommodating the interest of LCT diffusion is not illegal *per se.* It is because even if trade-related actions are potentially conducive to an enabling environment for clean technology diffusion, current WTO rules do not compel members to act in the service of the climate protection goal. It is argued that although the independence of a sovereign to make policy choices is the foundation of international law, refusal or avoidance of cooperation with respect to issues that are of Common Concern can raise questions about the legitimacy of its power to act. Moving towards the goal of creating a coherent framework of technology diffusion actions, this chapter lays out a propositional agenda putting the insights from the Common Concern doctrine to use. It is proposed that cooperation within the trade regime should be preceded by formal recognition of the notion, and would thereupon entail the development of coherent rules of action respecting the principles of equity and differentiation. This is moulded into a new proposed narrative to guide trade policy measures for LCT diffusion. Finally, possible ways of implementing the narrative by taking appropriate steps at the multilateral, regional, and domestic levels are explored.

1 'Common Concern' as a Guide to Trade Cooperation

The desirability of trade measures to support climate action is a well-visited topic in scholarly literature. In contributions dealing with the issue, the response is somewhat dichotomous. While many call for the trade regime's involvement,[528] scepticism also exists.[529] Brunnée, for example, highlights that the climate regime has over time evolved into a complex prevention mechanism based on non-adversariality and flexible compliance,[530] making it incompatible with the strict rule-enforcement approach found in the trade regime. Despite the contrasting takes, the search for a path towards stronger trade actions in the service of climate goals is worthwhile for a number of reasons described below.

First of all, the need to facilitate clean technology diffusion is urgent, immediate, and unavoidable, as already articulated.[531] Second, outright refusals to multilaterally address the trade-related issues involved in LCT diffusion at the WTO would not prevent the deployment of climate-motivated unilateral trade measures. In the absence of multilateral efforts, this issue would be relegated entirely to the domestic level, where it would be subjected to varying interests and conflicting approaches in different jurisdictions. The resulting multiplicity would end up being more burdensome for the developing countries on one hand, and threaten the predictability and transparency of the global trade rule system on the other. Third, much of the dichotomous difference between the trade and the climate rules may only be 'imaginary', leading to no big legal conflicts at the operational levels.[532] With the quasi-universal participation of states in both regimes and the common subscription to the goal of sustainable

528 Frédéric Simon, 'Stiglitz Urges Joint EU-China Trade Sanctions against the US on Climate Change' (*euractiv.com*, 28 March 2019) <https://www.euractiv.com/section/climate-environment/news/stiglitz-urges-joint-eu-china-trade-sanctions-against-the-us-on-climate-change/> accessed 25 October 2020; Paul Sammon, 'Could the Threat of Carbon Tariffs Save the Paris Agreement?' (18 September 2018) <https://ictsd.iisd.org/opinion/could-the-threat-of-carbon-tariffs-save-the-paris-agreement> accessed 25 October 2020; Scott Barrett and Robert Stavins, 'Increasing Participation and Compliance in International Climate Change Agreements' (2003) 3 International Environmental Agreements: Politics, Law and Economics 349; S Barrett, 'Climate Treaties and the Imperative of Enforcement' (2008) 24 Oxford Review of Economic Policy 239.

529 See, for example, Alexandra E Cirone and Johannes Urpelainen, 'Trade Sanctions in International Environmental Policy: Deterring or Encouraging Free Riding?' (2013) 30 Conflict Management and Peace Science 309.

530 Brunnée, 'MEAs and Complex Prevention' (n 330); Brunnée, 'The Global Climate Regime' (n 159); Jutta Brunnée, 'Enforcement Mechanisms in International Law and International Environmental Law' in Ulrich Beyerlin, Peter-Tobias Stoll and Rudiger Wolfrum (eds), *Ensuring compliance with multilateral environmental agreements: a dialogue betweeen practitioners and Academia* (Martinus Nijhoff Publishers 2006).

531 See Chapter 1 II A at p. 13 above.

532 Kati Kulovesi, 'Real or Imagined Controversies-a Climate Law Perspective on the Growing Links between the International Trade and Climate Change Regimes' (2014) 6 Trade L. & Dev. 55.

development, it is counterintuitive to assume that commitments made in one regime should conflict with those in others.[533] Fourth, restrictions are not the only tool in the trade regime's repertoire of possible measures supporting climate change. Trade-related measures can be supportive or facilitative in nature as well.[534] In the absence of any overarching regulation, states gravitate towards trade restrictions as a function of the current realpolitik, as those measures entail imposing costs on others while incurring none. Finally, while it may be true that the enforcement of climate commitments through trade sanctions could result in unwanted entanglements of compliance actions between the legal regimes, if negotiated climate-related commitments are part of the multilateral trade rules, there shall be no objection to taking recourse to dispute settlement.

The following paragraphs outline the practical considerations regarding the development of such trade commitments.

A *The Challenge of Cooperation and Common Concern Doctrine*

The actual existence of a state's responsibility to act in pursuance of shared interests in an issue area has a close, often a causal relationship with the prior existence, nature, and success of international cooperation in that regard. However, even though a long time has passed since Wolfgang Friedmann pointed out international law's gradual turn towards cooperation at different levels,[535] a duty to cooperate is not a commonplace occurrence yet.

---

533 We note also the argument made by Broude, holding that complexity is pervasive in all systems, and it is not unique to international law. As a result complexity in itself ought not be the dissuading factor leading a subject-matter to escape the domain of international law. Tomer Broude, 'Complexity Rules (or: Ruling Complexity), a Response to Jutta Brunnée' (Social Science Research Network 2017) SSRN Scholarly Paper ID 3075798 <https://papers.ssrn.com/abstract=3075798> accessed 25 October 2020.

534 Some authors focus on a 'carrot and stick' balance when introducing trade measures' support. See, for example, Tracey Epps and Andrew Green, *Reconciling Trade and Climate: How the WTO Can Help Address Climate Change* (Edward Elgar 2010); Andrew Green and Tracey Epps, 'Is There a Role for Trade Measures in Addressing Climate Change?' (2008) 15 31; Aaditya Mattoo and Arvind Subramanian, *A 'Greenprint' for International Cooperation on Climate Change* (The World Bank 2013) <http://elibrary.worldbank.org/doi/book/10.1596/1813-9450-6440> accessed 25 October 2020; Barrett and Stavins (n 530); Gabrielle Zoe Marceau, 'The Interface between the Trade Rules and Climate Change Actions' in Deok-Young Park (ed), *Legal Issues on Climate Change and International Trade Law* (Springer 2016). For extensive treatment of the topic, see, Thomas Cottier, Olga Nartova and Sadeq Z Bigdeli (eds), *International Trade Regulation and the Mitigation of Climate Change: World Trade Forum* (Cambridge University Press 2009); Tamiotti, World Trade Organization and United Nations Environment Programme (n 73).

535 Wolfgang Friedmann, *The Changing Structure of International Law* (Stevens & Sons 1964) 61–63.

Cooperation is almost always voluntary in international affairs, subject to the consent of a state as custodian of the sovereign authority. This comes out clearly in the Charter of the United Nations. While one of the purposes of the UN is to achieve international cooperation in solving economic, social, cultural, and humanitarian problems,[536] the key principles the organisation abides by are, *inter alia,* respect for sovereign equality and political independence of the member states.[537]

As a result of the above, duties of cooperation can mostly be found in limited constellations of consent-based regulatory frameworks (e.g. treaties), which address shared interests of both economic and non-economic nature. These duties arise due to the interdependent nature of the issues needing to be regulated, requiring reciprocity instead of wilful action by individual states. The legal regime of international trade is such an area. The trade regime is premised upon interdependence rather than independence of nations in their economic relations.[538] Thomas Cottier also highlighted that international trade rules make a reciprocal regime; one that is built around a *quid pro quo* exchange of commitments of economic interest for all the parties involved.[539] In the core of the multilateral trade rules, there is an obligation to negotiate in good faith, binding all the parties to engage in interaction without the constraints of reaching a final outcome.[540]

Duties of cooperation, when arising within treaty frameworks, are also circumscribed by the same. Such a duty tends to pertain only to the subject-matter that is of interest to the treaty. This holds true for the trade regime. The duty to negotiate and consult in the WTO law does not extend to fringe interactions which form the essence of 'trade and ...' issues, e.g. labour rights or animal welfare, unless it is formally extended by agreement. Similarly, while there is a duty to cooperate in the climate regime arising from the legal recognition of the problem as a common concern of humankind, it does not automatically extend to the legal realm of trade. This disconnect is a product of fragmentation, as was detailed in the first chapter. We recall the proposition that a constitutionalist frame is best suited to anticipate such fragmentation and respond to it based on existing and new meta-norms, i.e. legal principles that can guide separate rule systems to mesh and integrate.[541] This is the primary role of the

---

536 Article 1(3) Charter of the United Nations 1945 (1 UNTS XVI).

537 Article 2, ibid.

538 Donald McRae, *The Contribution of International Trade Law to the Development of International Law*, vol 260 (The Hague Academy of International Law 1994) 111.

539 Cottier, 'The Principle of Common Concern of Humankind' (n 7).

540 Cottier and Payosova (n 169) 15.

541 See Chapter 1 III D at pp. 27-28 above. Also, Ernst-Ulrich Petersmann, 'From Negative to Positive Integration in the WTO: Time for Mainstreaming Human Rights into WTO

Common Concern of Humankind doctrine. With respect to LCT diffusion and trade, the doctrine is an addition to the underlying framework of principles in the trade regime, helping to launch and sustain an expanded cooperation agenda therein.

It should also be recalled at this point that the principle of sustainable development is already a mainstay of the trade regime, providing a foundational basis for 'trade and …' integration.[542] However, even when the principle is given its fullest expression, it would suffice to create space for *ex post* legitimation and not serve as the basis for an *ex ante* demand. But making a demand that countries act *ex ante,* is the essence of a pre-existing duty to cooperate.[543] To clarify, the principle of sustainable development does not go so far as to put an actor under a strict positive responsibility to act in stopping climate change. Pursuant to the doctrine of Common Concern, the discourse is framed as such that it goes beyond the question of what states 'may' or 'could' do to prevent climate change. It rather points out what states 'must' do to that end.[544] For any such deliberation to take place to that effect at the multilateral stage, the essential precondition is having a duty to cooperate in place.

Leaving the defined boundaries of trade cooperation to outline how a state 'shall' or 'must' act would appear to go against the grain of the fundamental international law rule of coexistence, marked by the respect for sovereignty and political independence, as initially indicated. In response, we take the line of argument that understanding sovereignty as an exclusive power monopoly wielded by a government is an outdated approach. John Jackson correctly pointed out that if sovereignty is understood in terms of its core function, i.e. allocation of power, the changing fundamentals of world affairs do indeed require a departure from the traditional understanding.[545] Sovereignty-modern, as Jackson termed it, calls for a rebalancing of the power exclusivity of each state based on proportionality and subsidiarity, among other things.[546] This line of thought would challenge the exclusive dependency upon states'

Law' (2000) 37 Common Market L. Rev. 1363; Thomas Cottier and Panagiotis Delimatsis (eds), *The Prospects of International Trade Regulation: From Fragmentation to Coherence* (Cambridge University Press 2011).

542 Voigt (n 209).

543 See pp. 27-28 above.

544 Krista Nadakavukaren Schefer and Pablo Arnaiz, 'Duty to Protect, Climate Change and Trade' in Panagiotis Delimatsis (ed), *Research handbook on climate change and trade law* (Edward Elgar 2016).

545 John Howard Jackson, 'Sovereignty-Modern: A New Approach to an Outdated Concept', *Sovereignty, the WTO and changing fundamentals of international law* (Cambridge University Press 2006).

546 ibid 71–78.

consent in determining whether trade rules ought to be employed for climate protection. We can also consider the argument of Schefer and Arnaiz in the following terms:

> [S]ince the consequences of climate change on certain populations is expected to be serious enough to be of concern to the international community as a whole, states will have a duty to take any steps necessary to prevent realization of these threats to the extent possible, [...]. Given the inextricable connections between trade and climate change, as well as the likelihood of any mitigation and adaptation efforts affecting trade, the trade law system must be incorporated into any responsibility framework.[547]

However, recourse to the doctrine of Common Concern does not mean abandonment of the respect for sovereignty principle altogether. It rather necessitates updating our terms of understanding the notion. In areas marked by interdependence, a sovereign's goals of self-determination and public welfare inherently requires that the authority is exercised in cooperation.[548] Thomas Cottier holds:

> As the principle of Common Concern seeks to prevent or remedy threats to international peace, security and welfare in a broader sense, the purpose is in line with the original goals of sovereignty enabling to maintain law and order, provide peace and welfare, and prosperity in society. The principle of Common Concern of Humankind thus complements the same goals aspired by self-determination and enters the stage where these very goals cannot be secured by States alone but depend upon international cooperation. Common Concern helps us to reshape and understand the proper functions of contemporary modern sovereignty. We

---

547 Schefer and Arnaiz (n 544) 67–68.

548 Samantha Besson, 'Sovereignty in Conflict' (2004) 8 European Integration Online Papers <https://papers.ssrn.com/abstract=594942> accessed 25 October 2020; Franz Xaver Perrez, 'Efficiency of Cooperation: A Functional Analysis of Sovereignty' (1998) 15 Arizona Journal of International and Comparative Law 515; For a deeper take on the relation between Common Concern doctrine and pemanent sovereignty, see, Cottier, 'The Principle of Common Concern of Humankind' (n 7); Also, Alexander Beyleveld, 'Exploring the Recognition of New Common Concerns of Humankind: The Example of the Distribution of Income and Wealth within States' in Thomas Cottier (ed), *The Prospects of Common Concern of Humankind in International law* (Cambridge University Press 2021).

> can perceive it as a dialogue between the two concepts, influencing each other in shaping and coordinating their respective contours.[549]

Of course, despite the salience of the argument qualifying the exclusive nature of the notion of sovereignty, an unconditional responsibility to cooperate is not practical. As much as trade cooperation would be necessary, so would it be necessary to appropriately delimit its scope. The limits of the influence of the Common Concern doctrine upon the trade regime, as detailed earlier,[550] would come into play in this regard.

Over the past number of years, there have been many well-thought out propositions on the type of appropriate trade actions that would contribute to climate mitigation as well as the transfer of LCTs.[551] In comparison, very little work has been done on advancing a formal basis on which such propositions of positive actions could take root in the WTO law and practice.[552] Citing the example of fisheries subsidies negotiation, Margaret Young astutely suggested that the interaction between trade and climate regimes must be, *inter alia,* based on principles underlying the climate regime.[553] While it sounds like a lucrative proposition, it should be noted that regulation of fisheries subsidies is explicitly mandated to the WTO through the sustainable development goals (SDGs). No such mandate has so far been assigned to the WTO regarding climate change.[554]

The proposed doctrine of Common Concern can compel the undertaking of effective trade policy responses to the climate crisis. By so doing, it will serve

---

549 Cottier, 'The Principle of Common Concern of Humankind' (n 7) s 1.4.4.

550 See Chapter 1 VI at pp. 47-48 above.

551 See for example, Ricardo Melendez-Ortiz and Mahesh Sugathan, 'Enabling the Energy Transition and Scale-Up of Clean Energy Technologies: Options for the Global Trade System – Synthesis of the Policy Options' (2017) 51 933; James Bacchus, 'Global Rules for Mutually Supportive and Reinforcing Trade and Climate Regimes' (International Centre for Trade and Sustainable Development (ICTSD), World Economic Forum (WEF) 2017); Mattoo and Subramanian (n 534); Gary Clyde Hufbauer, Steve Charnovitz and Jisun Kim, *Global Warming and the World Trading System* (Peterson Institute for International Economics 2009).

552 Except, of course, the work done surrounding the doctrine of Common Concern by Thomas Cottier and others.

553 Margaret A Young, 'Climate Change Law and Regime Interaction' [2011] Carbon & Climate Law Review 12. However, one point is that unlike climate change the sustainable development goals (SDGs) explicitly mandates the WTO to deliver upon fisheries subsidies regulation.

554 Instead, as noted before, there are examples of conscious efforts by Members to keep the two regimes separated. See, Chapter 2 IV B (ii) at pp. 97–100.

as a convenient framework to mainstream the existing propositions. It would also enhance the legitimacy of the WTO in a constitutionalist legal order.[555] It is without any doubt that the states already have the obligation to resolve the common concern of climate change. What remains to be done still is an express and effective foregrounding of that obligation in the domain of trade law. The Common Concern doctrine is well-equipped to do that. The proposed doctrine will serve as the formal basis to grant an enhanced mandate to the WTO for working in the interface area of trade and climate change and to determine the terms of its deeper interaction with the climate governance institutions.

Before moving to the next point, we must admit that confining the discussion of Common Concern inspired cooperation only to that between states is limiting in a sense. We recognise that for the diffusion of LCT, cooperation must also influence other levels of governance, e.g. cities, and include actors other than the state, e.g. research collaboration between firms and universities. Nevertheless, international cooperation is a good starting point for the discussion. It is also influential to bring about broader cooperation.

B *Key Issues Regarding a Novel Duty to Cooperate*

Following up on the argument that the doctrine of Common Concern is well poised to be placed within the trade law domain to fill the absence of a duty towards positive cooperation, here we outline the key points of such an endeavour. To recap, as the legal paradigm of Common Concern demands for adequate preventive and remedial actions to be taken, the duty to cooperate arising therefrom obliges the involved parties to look for and adopt the best possible means of doing so. Put in the context of international trade regulation, the doctrine would demarcate in clear terms the reach of the exclusive policy autonomy of sovereign states.[556] A potential delineation of such manner has a twofold impact. On one hand, a well-defined domain of interdependent action in the trade regime serves as a better rallying point around which the governments can pursue meaningful mutual engagement in good faith to tackle the identified gaps in the trade and climate policy.[557] On the other hand, absence of any bearing of an issue to a known Common Concern serves to reinforce its

555 Cottier and Payosova (n 169).

556 Arguably, by the acceptance of climate change as a common concern already entails that with respect to the issue no one state has absolute policy autonomy (see chapter 1 pp 34-37). Express use of the notion in the trade field would assist the dialogue in clarifying the ambit of interdependent rule making.

557 The importance of such systemic change particularly involving the trade regime was one of the conclusions made in the previous chapter. See p. 76 above.

place squarely within the classical domain of sovereignty. This clear demarcation through the linkage with Common Concern limits the proposed duty to cooperate only to narrow, critically important areas.

Developing an enhanced cooperation agenda based on the doctrine of Common Concern would require three key steps, i.e. (i) recognition, (ii) coherent rules of action, and (iii) equity and differentiation. Formal recognition of the concept expedites the inclusion of the notion into the body of WTO law. The recognition must thereupon be followed by the creation of an institutional mandate and forum, making a shared understanding of the needs and related responses possible. Lastly, a balance must also be engrained in allocation and apportionment of responsibility between the WTO members, incorporating a standard of equitable differentiation. These three steps are elaborated hereunder.

(i) Incorporation through Recognition

To the extent concerted action in pursuance of a Common Concern is envisaged to take place at the WTO, it can only be possible through appropriate agenda-setting at the Ministerial level. An express recognition of the doctrine of Common Concern of Humankind, as well as establishment of a shared understanding of its consequences, creates a basis for the agenda-setting.[558] An example can be given of sustainable development. Recognition of sustainable development in the preamble of the Marrakesh agreement enabled the members to set the Doha Development Agenda, which, among others, integrated the notion of mutual supportiveness of the goals of free trade and environmental protection.[559] Not only would recognition serve the purpose of agenda-setting, but bringing Common Concern of Humankind into the folds of the treaty regime of international trade would also allow recourse to the principle for the purposes of interpreting the treaty obligations.[560]

At the end of the day, it is a consensus-building exercise that would be successful only if taken up by the willing state and non-state actors. Repeated claims made on the basis of Common Concern, and proposals for negotiation

558 Common Concern would serve the purpose of establishing an inclusive agenda. On this point, see again, Young (n 553) 153. The author notes – '[r]egime interaction during negotiation, implementation and adjudication will be informed by principles that encourage transparency and inclusivity. Such principles recognise that the full range of "interests"- of all those affected by climate change- needs to be incorporated in the meeting of regimes'.

559 Same is true for setting the fisheries subsidies negotiation agenda. 'Doha Work Programme: Ministerial Declaration' (n 468), Annex D, para 9.

560 See Chapter 1 V C at p. 45 and onwards.

that captures the varying interests of the members are therefore important. In the initial phase, already familiar language such as – "[r]ecognizing that climate change is a common concern of humankind, members shall, therefore, take steps to resolve the concern, namely …",[561] can start the process of claims and responses.

(ii) Coherent Rules of Action

Recognition of Common Concern must be followed by defining the perimeter of climate action in the trade regime. This requires a clear articulation of the shared goals, specification of the scope of activities, as well as limits of the incursion of trade rules into the climate domain. In broadest terms, the fundamental purpose of trade cooperation should be to pay due attention to the reality of climate change and the need to take appropriate actions, while taking into account the shared values and agreed goals in that regard. Also important is to set the general terms of interaction between the regimes. It means that within the scope of Common Concern, the climate protection imperative should receive primacy over impartial preservation of market access benefits and strict adherence to non-discrimination.[562]

A shared understanding of the objective further triggers the question of tasks apportionment along two dimensions of governance, horizontal and vertical, in accordance with the principle of subsidiarity.[563] Horizontal apportionment of tasks need to take place at the international level. Along this dimension, the issue would be the sharing of detailed rulemaking mandate between the trade and the climate regime at the global level. The vertical apportionment concerns the linkage between international and the lower levels of governance. Along that dimension, the principal task would be to create a complementary and interlocked system for sharing the governance function to

561 The language can build upon the expression as contained in the Preamble of the Paris Agreement. One further example is Article 275 of the Free Trade Agreement between the EU, Colombia and Peru. See p. 109 above.

562 Young (n 553) 152. The author notes – '[t]he negotiation of new international laws relating to climate change which have the possibility of interaction with existing laws from other regimes must be attendant to the possibilities and constraints of regime interaction'.

563 Isabelle Feichtner, 'Subsidiarity', *Max Planck Encyclopedia of Public International Law* (Online, Oxford University Press) <https://opil.ouplaw.com/view/10.1093/law:epil/9780199231690/law-9780199231690-e1477?print=pdf> accessed 25 October 2020. Subsidiarity is a principle of power allocation found frequently in domestic constitutional law. It is also a growing norm in international affairs. While scholars differ on the meaning of the notion, here it is used as a principle that sets the locus of action at a level of governance or a regime that is the most competent, effective, and proximate to the cause.

implement the rules that translate the climate responsibility into effective and adequate action.[564]

To the extent removal or reform of market barriers positively contribute to address the Common Concern of climate change, the notion of subsidiarity applied horizontally should dictate that the WTO is not absolved of responsibilities on that front.[565] Unlike the opposing view maintained by some members as noted in the previous chapter,[566] subject-matter expertise available at the WTO necessitates the finding that the organisation is the best platform to guide the power of international trade in addressing the climate change. For example, while conservation and management of marine fisheries resources are contributed to by different international organisations and treaty bodies, the work on regulation and removal of fisheries subsidies is mandated to the WTO.

Effective implementation of any outcome of international cooperation at the WTO would require support from other levels of governance. The essence of vertical subsidiarity in this regard is putting in place a shared and symbiotic relationship between international and domestic law. On one hand, rulemaking at the international level should ensure that ample options exist to suit a state's specific circumstances and interests. On the other hand, domestic actions should ensure that sufficient effort is made to meet the targets set at the global level.

(iii) Equity and Differentiation

In law, the role of equitable considerations is to imbue strict positivistic readings of black-letter rules with contextual considerations of an economic, moral, or developmental character.[567] In this sense, equity is present in different domestic legal systems,[568] as well as at the international level.[569] Equitable

---

564 Cottier and Hertig (n 117) 320–322. The authors note that 'transboundary environmental problems do not need to be regulated comprehensively on the global level. [...] International law may prescribe the goal to be reached in terms of CO2 reduction, while it is up to "lower" levels of governance to choose the means to reach that aim and to implement them'.

565 Robert Howse and Kalypso Nicolaidis, 'Enhancing WTO Legitimacy: Constitutionalization or Global Subsidiarity?' (2003) 16 Governance 73, 86–88.

566 See Chapter 2 IV B at pp. 98-99 above.

567 Cottier, 'The Principle of Common Concern of Humankind' (n 7) ss 1.3.2.1, & 1.5.3.

568 Thomas Cottier, 'Equity Revisited: An Introduction', *Equitable principles of maritime boundary delimitation: the quest for distributive justice in international law* (Cambridge University Press 2015) 9–13; Also, Thomas Cottier, 'Equity in International Law' in Thomas Cottier, Shaheeza Lalani and Clarence Siziba (eds), *Intergenerational Equity: Environmental and Cultural Concerns* (Brill Nijhoff 2019) <https://brill.com/view/title/39490> accessed 25 October 2020.

569 Cottier, 'Equity Revisited: An Introduction', ibid 22–24.

considerations and due regard to different socio-economic conditions remain at the heart of the special and differential treatment standards available under the WTO agreement.[570] While trade has led to growth, the benefit therefrom does not reach all within and between countries; meaning that the agenda of equity therein remains incomplete.

In this context, it is proposed that any new obligations which are the outcome of trade cooperation for LCT diffusion must balance the states' responsibilities of compliance with their ability to do so. Similarly, homework measures that are adopted in relation to the new cooperation arrangement should also be modulated in their application while taking due account of equitable considerations. This way, incorporation of equity plays a positive role in ensuring inclusivity and participation by all actors, which are themselves common attributes of multilateral climate actions.

A legal context is necessary for the implementation of equity, as in the absence thereof, the notion becomes ambiguous and hence difficult to put into action.[571] While the doctrine of Common Concern serves as the tool to broaden the ground for applying equity in trade law, the particular legal context is aptly supplied by the principle of common but differentiated responsibility (CBDR). CBDR is a long-standing and dynamic foundational norm of the climate regime, which apportions the burden of climate responsibility among countries having regard to their historic contribution to the problem, as well as different levels of ability to meet the demands.[572] Reflecting the change in the economic situation of the countries, the nature of the CBDR principle has also changed over time. Initially, under the Framework Convention (i.e. the UNFCCC), CBDR was reflected in a sharp division between the developed (listed in Annex-I) countries and others in terms of mitigation commitments, as well as commitments regarding financial and technological support.[573] The voluntary nature of the nationally determined contributions (NDCs) under the Paris Agreement largely dispenses with differentiation on the mitigation front, as all countries are equally obliged to commit.[574] With respect to support provisions, especially finance, differentiation can still be observed, but a specific reference

570 ibid 26.
571 ibid 31–34.
572 Bodansky, Brunnée and Rajamani (n 129) 27, 52.
573 ibid 28.
574 ibid 219–220, 223–224. The authors call it a model of 'bounded self-defferntiation'. The only exception is the obligation upon developed countries to provide financial support to developing countries for mitigation and adaptation. Article 4.5, read with Article 9.1, Paris Agreement (n 28).

to UNFCCC Annex-I is missing.[575] These dynamic developments should be taken into consideration at each stage of climate action in pursuance of the Common Concern doctrine, especially when such measures entail costs to other countries. Compliance with the CBDR is also necessary due to its position as a well-established guiding norm for climate action, which cannot be abandoned simply by switching action platforms at the international level.

Equity and differentiation are the safeguards to maintain a balanced agenda and to prevent the Common Concern doctrine from becoming a tool of value imperialism.[576] It should not, however, be automatically assumed that a lack of capacity to act, or pressing economic development priorities can altogether excuse governments from any compliance responsibility. Equitable considerations would rather necessitate identification of the capacity gaps and development of support systems for such WTO members.

II Cooperation Regarding Low-Carbon Technology Diffusion

This section portrays how the above-outlined trade cooperation agenda would shape the relationship between trade and LCT diffusion. The previous chapter showcased the differences in the conceptualisation, pursuit, and institutional frameworks regarding technology development and transfer between the climate and the trade regimes. While the soft law based climate regime has witnessed an incremental development in rulemaking, the stricter trade regime has fallen short of making any notable progress. It is proposed that the latter situation be changed by developing a new narrative of trade action, based on the framework of cooperation outlined above. The effort would be initiated by establishing a shared understanding of the key notions, and also by articulating the trade regime's role. The new narrative would be an improvement in terms of its prioritised focus on the diffusion of LCT s, also in terms of creating new opportunities to take empirically informed actions.

A *Outline of the Proposal*

The starting point of cooperation for LCT diffusion is a shared belief in the positive contribution of domestic trade policy measures to that effect. The next

575 Bodansky, Brunnée and Rajamani (n 129) 225–226.

576 Peter-Tobias Stoll explains that a doctrine such as Common Concern runs the risk of imposing liberal western values across the board. See, 'Comments: The Doctrinal Approach of Common concern' in Cottier (ed) *Prospects of Common Concern in International Law*, (Cambridge University Press 2021).

important point is an agreement among the WTO members endorsing that the deployment and diffusion of LCTs are better facilitated in the existence of an enabling policy environment domestically, as well as globally. Such an agreement is the first step to create a ground of shared understanding, as well as recognition of the relevant rules and principles of the climate regime. Though the creation of necessary policy environment is a domestic prerogative, a global consensus to do so enables the realisation of that target in a complementary, mutually beneficial, and least trade-distorting fashion. Towards this end, trade cooperation at the international level should establish the need to prevent the failure of the markets to adequately spread LCT. Appropriate trade-related measures can contribute to the growth of new technology markets, address the price competitiveness problem, change patterns of production in the manufacturing hubs, reduce consumption emission in the biggest markets, attract further investment in the key sectors, and boost technology outflows. Although a theoretically sound claim, no concrete steps have yet been taken to turn it into reality.

Operating under the responsibility to cooperate arising out of the doctrine of Common Concern, the role of the trade regime, therefore, would be to complement the progress made in the climate regime regarding clean technology diffusion. In this regard, it would be important to reflect the same spirit conveyed through the terms of the technology framework (TF) serving the Paris Agreement. The foundational principles enshrined in the TF are coherence, inclusiveness, a results-oriented approach, a transformational approach, and transparency.[577] Those should also guide cooperation in the trade regime. The framework identifies the promotion of diffusion and deployment of existing and emerging climate technologies as one of the factors identified for innovation promotion.[578] The TF also acknowledges the need for market regulation and an enabling policy environment. Furthermore, it is mentioned that the private sector should be made aware of future market opportunities and also be incentivised to participate.[579] With respect to the enabling environment and capacity building, the technology framework invites governments to take steps to enhance private sector involvement through policy interventions that create "favourable market conditions for climate technologies".[580] Considered together, the TF supplies the docking point for trade cooperation to feed into

577 Para 3, Technology framework under Article 10, paragraph 4, of the Paris Agreement (n 277).

578 Para 8(c) ibid.

579 See Chapter 2 II A (iii) at pp. 65-66 above.

580 ibid.

the LCT diffusion goals. Well-functioning markets, healthy competition, and appropriate protection of intellectual property – all contribute to realising an enabling regulatory environment for technology transfer. This includes market mediated transfers, coupled with necessary support mechanisms, which are useful and indispensable complements to the overall efforts to mitigate climate change.

While cooperation to create an enabling environment can be worthwhile even when it is not all-inclusive, broadest possible participation is the most desirable outcome nonetheless. Effective cooperation efforts must at least cover the top emitters,[581] the big markets,[582] and countries on the technology frontiers[583] – all culminating to indicate the special relevance of the G20 nations. Except for any poor, or vulnerable economy, countries belonging in these categories are well-integrated into the global trading system, which shows the potential of trade rules to modify their practices. Moreover, as many of these countries would be middle to high-income ones, they would be more amenable to regulation through trade policy preferences and restriction, compared to promises of financial or other forms of assistance.[584] The latter is nevertheless an important issue with regard countries specifically vulnerable to climate change impacts.[585] Ensuring participation by these economies in cooperation is indispensable to retain the legitimacy of the effort. Moreover, it is also important for these countries to have an equal voice in rule-setting.

The substantive content of the proposition can be presented in a simplified 'push-pull' interaction as depicted in Figure 3 below. The main message conveyed here is that trade cooperation for the diffusion of LCT principally involves putting together complementary measures that can be adopted and

581 According to the latest (2014) available data, the ten biggest greenhouse gas emitting countries and regions are, China, United States, European Union (28), India, Indonesia, Russia, Brazil, Japan, Canada, and Iran. Available at www.climatewatchdata.org, accessed 25 October 2020.

582 According to the latest (2017) available data, the ten biggest importing countries are, China, United States, Germany, Japan, France, South Korea, Italy, Netherlands, Mexico and Canada. Available at www.wits.worldbank.org, accessed 25 October 2020.

583 Countries that are at the technology frontier would vary depending on the field of innovation in question. However, as the patent concentration studies cited in the previous chapter showed, quite invariably these are mostly OECD countries with the exception of India, China and Brazil in select areas. For more, see Chapter 2 III A at pp. 77-80 above.

584 As the insights from the CDM projects also shows that some of these countries, e.g. India and China, are more receptive to market-mediated technology transfers in comparison to other developing countries.

585 It is difficult to group a category as such. It should nevertheless include, *inter alia*, lower income countries, especially coastal and small island states.

implemented by the parties to the technology-related transactions. From a macro perspective, measures to facilitate clean technology diffusion should primarily focus on two issues. First, in the countries where technologies originate (labelled 'Foreign'), appropriate incentives must be introduced to encourage their outflows to deserving destinations. This is a 'push factor' (number 1) as shown in the figure. Second, countries at the receiving end of the LCTs (labelled 'Home') must create policy arrangements that ease the domestic producers' access to cleaner technology solutions. This is a 'pull factor' (number 2), also a part of the domestic enabling environment at Home. The exact choice of pull measures may depend on the actual market situation and barriers prevalent therein. In addition to the two issues, process and production regulating measures like a carbon tax (number 3) adopted at the major destinations for the Home's exports (labelled Foreign) may further boost the demand for LCT in Home's export-oriented sectors. Side by side, appropriate assistance mechanisms must also be put in place to reflect differentiated responsibility and also to ensure that the trade policy measures in the foreign countries do not unreasonably affect the market access opportunities of the developing nations.

Certain caveats should be duly noted. First is the importance of complementarity. For successfully facilitated clean technology transactions, it is important

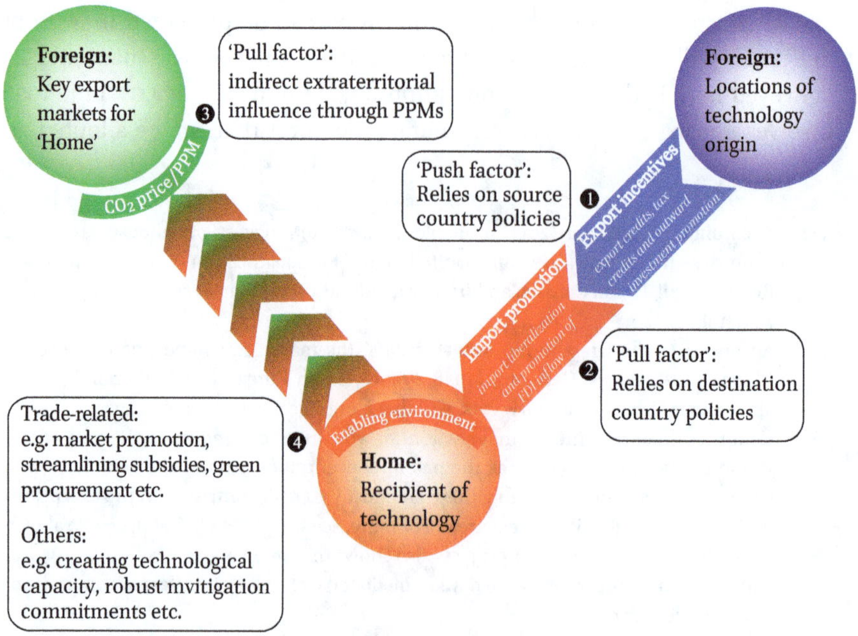

FIGURE 3 Trade-related aspects of clean technology diffusion

that the 'push' and 'pull' measures are complementary to each other. This goes back also to demonstrate the need for prior cooperation between the parties to establish mutual understanding and commitment to a shared goal. Second, cooperation itself is only the first step, demonstrating the political commitment. It must be followed up by practical measures that are implemented domestically. In the absence of domestic implementation, cooperation alone cannot bring diffusion of LCT s. That is the domain of homework obligations; another aspect of the Common Concern doctrine. Last, reforms of market regulations are but one facilitator for technology transfer. While focusing on the enabling environment and the trade rules, it must also be accepted that other measures beyond the domain of WTO laws are also as important for successful transfers of LCT s, e.g. domestic investment on education and training.

B *Identifying Actors and Respective Motivations*

The framework above also identifies that trade policy assistance for LCT transactions can arise from different directions– from actors whose motivation to so act may vary to a degree. Two such actors are those that are directly engaged in the commercial transaction leading to diffusion of technology, i.e. the supplier and the receiver. Irrespective of the exact nature of the private transactions (e.g. license agreement, export and import, foreign investment, or public-private partnership), trade policy measures exist that match the motivation of the respective ends. This apart, in cases where the technologies are sought to service export-oriented sectors, demand changes in the large enough consumption market (e.g. processing standard imposed by the EU) can further hasten the suppliers' choice of investment in new solutions.

Suppliers of LCT s: This category of actors would include, but would not exclusively be limited to the handful of locations at the technology frontier.[586] Firms are in need of innovation that suits their specific circumstances. Any other firm having the necessary solution can be a supplier of LCT. While the suppliers are undoubtedly motivated by the necessity of climate mitigation, but there also are the interests of accessing new markets and revenue growth. Policies that incentivise out-licensing, investment, technology cooperation, as well as trade, are most suited to further trigger the motivation of the suppliers.

Receivers of LCT s: In theory, LCT s are in demand all over the world to keep going 'green'. From a trade perspective, the primary focus of policy should be to influence sectors or locations that are significant sources of GHG emissions due to intensified production and export activities due to being a global

586 See n 583 above.

manufacturing hub (e.g. China), or specific export-oriented activities. For such locations to deploy LCTs, the action ought to make reasonable business sense. More specifically, in these locations, apart from climate change mitigation, the key driving motivation would be securing access to export markets in the long-term. Policy measures that result in a lower cost of the technologies, contribute to creating long-term demand for low-carbon products and secure the firms from competing with polluting alternatives will be appropriate for such regions.

Another equally important category of technology receivers is the poorer countries with development constraints and strong export dependency. These locations cannot, for obvious economic and capacity constraints, undertake too drastic a shift towards clean technologies. It is of utmost importance to make sure that the economic development opportunities of these countries achieved through trade are not unduly constrained. Thus any cooperation scheme at the multilateral level must incorporate support mechanisms that can adequately assist these regions to set out on a low-carbon growth trajectory.

Large consumption/importing markets: These are the large markets (e.g. the US or the EU) serving as export destinations for many countries. Changes in the consumption patterns and regulations in such regions are of utmost importance for reducing carbon leakage, as well as to establish full responsibility for emissions made. Such steps can also create an additional demand-pull that would encourage the suppliers to shift towards cleaner products and production. The focus should remain on the need to reflect changing consumer choices, as well as the shared and differentiated responsibility to address carbon emissions. As consumption regulation measures can easily take a pure protectionist bias, it is important that the Common Concern doctrine draws the limits for their application.

C *Identifying Relevant Measures*

There are different trade measures that suit particular situations and motivations of the actors and positively contribute to the LCT diffusion in line with the proposed narrative. These measures are themselves not new, but the emphasis on their potentially facilitative role for LCT diffusion is. In light of the foregoing paragraphs, it is contended that the respective position of a country or sectors therein would dictate the type of trade policy measure that should be deployed in any given situation. As a result, when thinking of relevant policy measures, it is prudent not to advocate for a fixed list of options. Instead, we argue that the form and nature of trade-related actions facilitating diffusion of low-carbon technology are context-dependent.[587]

587 For some indication, see, Traerup, Greersen and Kundsen (n 408) 5, 14–18.

Most of the trade policy measures facilitating clean technology diffusion can be put into either one of the following three categories, i.e. (i) market access reform, (ii) process and production regulation, and (iii) industry-level incentives. In a given circumstance, appropriate measures from one of these categories can potentially boost LCT transactions by positively influencing either the demand or the supply side of the transaction, as well as by boosting related consumption and production. These categories are covered below. Other beneficial measures not falling under any of these categories are mentioned thereafter.

(i) Easier Market Access for Low-Carbon Technology Products and Services

The dismantling of market access barriers is seemingly the least controversial avenue to augment the trade flow in LCT related goods and services. Unsurprisingly, liberalisation of environmental goods and services (EGS) is a long-standing Doha agenda.[588] Even so, many developing countries still maintain unbound, or very high bound rate tariff lines relevant to clean technologies.[589] For example, in South Asia, Bangladesh and Myanmar have no fixed upper limits (i.e. the bound rate of duty) on the rates of import tariffs applicable on solar PV cells (HS854140). In Pakistan, the bound rate of tariff for the same is 50% ad valorem.[590] Lower prices resulting from the removal of market access barriers provide dual benefits. It allows interested recipient firms better options and prices for cleaner technology solutions, as well as grants better market access to the relevant suppliers of technology.[591]

Though easy sounding, easing market access for LCT products has proven to be exceedingly difficult, if not impossible. The key reasons behind the failure to deliver on the Doha agenda on EGS and subsequent stalling of the plurilateral approach are disagreements regarding product coverage and negotiation method.[592] Scholars also contend that a large group of developing

588 See Chapter 2 IV B (ii) at p. 99 above.

589 David Ockwell and others (eds), 'The Role of Trade and Investment in Accelerating Clean Energy Diffusion: Private Sector Views from South-Asia', *Low-carbon technology transfer: from rhetoric to reality* (Routledge 2012) 275–277.

590 'Tariff Download Facility: WTO Tariff Data Base' <http://tariffdata.wto.org/Default.aspx> accessed 25 October 2020.

591 Melendez-Ortiz and Sugathan (n 551) 940–941.

592 Mark Wu, 'The WTO Environmental Goods Agreement: From Multilateralism to Plurilateralism' in Panagiotis Delimatsis (ed), *Research handbook on climate change and trade law* (Edward Elgar 2016) 285–289; Robert Howse and Petrus B van Bork, 'Options for Liberalising Trade in Environmental Goods in the Doha Round' (International Centre for Trade and Sustainable Development 2006) <https://www.files.ethz.ch/isn/92782/2006_07_Options_for_Liberalising_Trade_.pdf> accessed 25 October 2020; ICTSD (n 512).

and least-developed countries have no export interest in the products under negotiation.[593] As a result, on one hand, there is a perverse incentive for many members to free-ride without meaningful engagement;[594] and on the other hand, actively engaged members try to maximise benefits by including products of export interest that have very little to do with environmental benefit.[595]

When the Doha mandate was framed in the early 2000s, development and transfer of climate technology was not a top global priority as it is now. As a result, the negotiations did not focus on this aspect. Any future negotiation mandate should take account of the mutual benefits arising from climate technology diffusion, which may then make reaching a balanced outcome easier.

While services are an inseparable component for the deployment of LCTs, there has been no focused discussion on improving market access for the necessary services. The need for such improvement arises from the fact that the components part of the clean technologies are often vertically integrated with a range of services (e.g. design and engineering, construction, sale, maintenance and operation, training etc.).[596] The difficulty is that there is very little understanding of the extent of the services need in this regard.[597] Also, the current

593 Mark Wu, 'Why Developing Countries Won't Negotiate: The Case of the WTO Environmental Goods Agreement' (2014) 6 Trade, Law and Development [i]; Fahmida Khatun, 'Trade in Environmental Goods by Least Developed Countries: Issues for Negotiations' (2012) 13 South Asia Economic Journal 157.

594 Wu, ibid.

595 ICTSD (n 512).

596 For a broad overview of the relevant services, see, Ronald Steenblik and Massimo Gelosso Grosso, 'Trade in Services Related to Climate Change: An Exploratory Analysis', vol 2011/03 (2011) OECD Trade and Environment Working Papers 2011/03 <https://www.oecd-ilibrary.org/trade/trade-in-services-related-to-climate-change_5kgc5wtd9rzw-en> accessed 25 October 2020; For WTO focused discussion, Thomas L Brewer and Andreas Falke, 'International Transfers of Climate-Friendly Technologies: How the World Trade System Matters' in David Ockwell and Alexandra Mallett (eds), *Low-carbon technology transfer: from rhetoric to reality* (Routledge 2012) 297–298; Thomas L Brewer, 'International Technology Diffusion in a Sustainable Energy Trade Agreement: September 2012' in Gary C Hufbauer, Ricardo Melendez-Ortiz and Richard Samans (eds), *The Law and Economics of a Sustainable Energy Trade Agreement* (Cambridge University Press 2016) <https://www.cambridge.org/core/product/identifier/9781316137048%23AT-app-7/type/book_part> accessed 25 October 2020.

597 Neither the guidance documents of the technology needs assessments, nor the process of assessments itself have so far have made any indication in this regard. For some relevant discussion, see, Joachim Monkelbaan, 'Trade in Sustainable Energy Services: October 2013' in Gary C Hufbauer, Ricardo Melendez-Ortiz and Richard Samans (eds), *The Law and Economics of a Sustainable Energy Trade Agreement* (Cambridge University Press 2016) <https://www.cambridge.org/core/product/identifier/9781316137048%23CN-bp-3/type/book_part> accessed 25 October 2020; Olga Nartova, 'Assessment of GATS' Impact

services classification system does not allow sufficiently exclusive identification of the climate-related services to launch multilateral negotiations.[598]

The earlier mentioned success of the APEC countries in reducing tariffs on a list of environmental products[599] is an example that shows market access reform can be achieved among a smaller number of participants. While the APEC list is incomplete when it comes to climate technology related products,[600] it has successfully influenced some other preferential trade agreement (PTA) negotiations.[601] We assume that an exclusive focus on liberalising LCT or climate-related products and services based on the Common Concern narrative could be substantially easier to implement within smaller constellations.

It is also possible to explore non-reciprocal ways of easing market access. There is no prohibition against unilateral liberalisation of the domestic market for goods and services of relevance for the LCTs. Also, further examination should be made on whether preferential market access schemes like the GSP+ can introduce preconditions such as adequate emission reduction efforts by the candidate countries.

(ii) Regulation of Production Processes and Performances

Process and production measures, commonly known as PPMs, generally refer to government interventions to influence process and production across borders.[602] As a category, PPM is broad. It can include varied types of measures which, when deployed by a significantly large importing market, can trigger the uptake of LCTs by the exporting firms. This way, the PPMs allow the importing country to conditionally grant the benefit of its domestic market access, at the same time reflecting fundamental public policy concerns. Some of the prominent tools that fall into the PPM category are taxes, technical regulations, and other forms of preconditions that apply to products' intrinsic

on Climate Change Mitigation' in Thomas Cottier, Olga Nartova and Sadeq Z Bigdeli (eds), *International trade regulation and the mitigation of climate change: World Trade Forum* (Cambridge University Press 2009).

598 Mahesh Sugathan, 'Winds of Change and Rays of Hope How Can the Multilateral Trading System Facilitate Trade in Clean Energy Technologies and Services', *Clean Energy Technologies and the Trade System: Proposals and Analysis* (International Centre for Trade and Sustainable Development (ICTSD), World Economic Forum 2013); Also see, Monkelbaan, ibid; Nartova, ibid.

599 See p. 108 above.

600 Vossenaar (n 514).

601 Melendez-Ortiz and Sugathan (n 551). It was mentioned that some PTAs negotiated by Canada uses the APEC list as basis for tariff reduction.

602 Kateryna Holzer, *Carbon-Related Border Adjustment and WTO Law* (Edward Elgar 2014) 92–93.

characteristics or their production methods.[603] Compliance with the importing country's PPM would therefore enable an exporter to avoid financial costs (e.g. tax burden), or valuable benefits (e.g. licenses or permits for export). Relevant product characteristics related compliance requirements imposed by a PPM can include efficiency or performance standards (e.g. fuel efficiency of a car, or energy efficiency of consumer electronics).[604] Process requirements could be based on emission footprint standards, or specific processing requirements (e.g. low-emission aluminium smelting methods).

As part of the broader PPM category, technical regulations and standards pertaining to the reduction of GHG emissions can be considered as technologies in their own right. Mandatory technical regulations and certification are important not only to shape demand, but also to overcome the technical barriers by defining new markets for LCTs. Side by side, voluntary standards are increasingly becoming norms rather than exceptions guiding different aspects of sustainability in trading relations between businesses, as well as between businesses and consumers. Delimatsis points out that while so far the voluntary sustainability standards have been slow to incorporate climate change related criteria, such inclusion may prove to be controversial due to the added cost and possible negative impact on poverty reduction resulting from diversion of trade.[605] The author proposes for the standards schemes to be connected to climate finance mechanisms so that the producers and the suppliers along the value chain can reap benefit from the capacity-building supports.[606] This would further contribute to clean technology diffusion.

While the appeal of the PPMs regarding technology diffusion lies in the possibility to channel domestic demand and thereby triggering the need for corresponding technology in the production source countries, it leaves a WTO member open to a potential legal challenge. This is especially true for the measures that distinguish based on non-product related attributes (e.g. emission footprint), which according to the current WTO jurisprudence may be

603 For a detailed overview, see, Christiane R Conrad, *Processes and Production Methods (PPMs) in WTO Law: Interfacing Trade and Social Goals* (Cambridge University Press 2011) 21–56.

604 For a quick take on the relevance of standardization in different sectors of GHG emission, see, Jorge L Contreras, 'Standards and Related Intellectual Property Issues for Climate Change Technology' (Social Science Research Network 2012) SSRN Scholarly Paper ID 1756283 418–421 <https://papers.ssrn.com/abstract=1756283> accessed 25 October 2020.

605 Panagiotis Delimatsis, 'Sustainable Standard-Setting, Climate Change and the TBT Agreement' in Panagiotis Delimatsis (ed), *Research handbook on climate change and trade law* (Edward Elgar 2016) 159.

606 ibid 160.

considered as discriminatory.[607] Notwithstanding that, there is considerable leeway in finding such measures as compliant with the GATT 1994 and other covered agreements.[608] With respect to renewable energy, Thomas Cottier proposed that the use of non-product related PPM measures be matched with the related technology transfer support so that the development concerns can be addressed.[609]

The next chapter discusses some of these issues in the context of a proposed carbon pricing measure.

(iii) Promotion of Trade in Low-Carbon Technologies through Incentives

Regulation of domestic incentives is important for the diffusion of LCTs in two ways. First, governments can support the domestic commercial entities that enter into low-carbon technology related export or investment transactions with developing country firms by sharing the political or financial risks undertaken (e.g. through official export credit supports).[610] Such support measures might help to materialise LCT transactions which otherwise would not have taken place. Tax rebates schemes are often provided to domestic industries to be established in new locations. Incentives in equal terms can be provided to invest in low-carbon development across borders as well.[611] Second, the geographies seeking to attract new technologies can likewise devise specific incentives, e.g. feed-in tariffs (FITs), to attract foreign investments. With respect to incentivising low-carbon technology transfer to least-developed countries, more could be achieved within the framework of Article 66.2 of the TRIPS.

---

607 Conrad (n 603) 13; Erich Vranes, 'Carbon Taxes, PPMs and the GATT' in Panagiotis Delimatsis (ed), *Research handbook on climate change and trade law* (Edward Elgar 2016); Steve Charnovitz, 'The Law of Environmental PPMs in the WTO: Debunking the Myth of Illegality' (2002) 27 Yale Journal of International Law 59, 91.

608 Gabrielle Marceau, 'Do PPM Concerns Have a Future' in Denise Prévost, Iveta Alexovičová and Jens Hillebrand Pohl (eds), *Restoring trust in trade : liber amicorum in honour of Peter van den Bossche* (Hart 2019).

609 Thomas Cottier, 'Renewable Energy and Process and Production Methods' (International Centre for Trade and Sustainable Development (ICTSD), World Economic Forum (WEF) 2015) 5–6.

610 Michael Finus and others, 'International Cooperation: Agreements and Instruments', *Climate change 2014: mitigation of climate change: Working Group III contribution to the Fifth Assessment Report of the Intergovernmental Panel on Climate Change* (Cambridge University Press 2014) 1035–1036. Chapter 5 of the thesis discusses this option in greater detail.

611 Bernard M Hoekman, Keith E Maskus and Kamal Saggi, 'Transfer of Technology to Developing Countries: Unilateral and Multilateral Policy Options' (2005) 33 World Development 1587, 1593–1594.

Given the increased developing country interest in domestic supports, as well as the shared commitment to climate responses, it would be quite worthwhile to explore any opportunity to rejuvenate the non-actionable category of subsidies. As argued later, the resurrection of Article 8 *in toto* may not be the best way possible.[612] Instead, members should renegotiate the provision to allow measures of direct pertinence to resolve issues of Common Concern, including that of LCT diffusion. With respect to the agriculture sector, there is already scope for supporting farmers with climate-friendly means and methods. To the extent developing and least-developed countries would need access to better farming methods, additional support mechanisms could be developed. Again, the TRIPS Article 66.2 can be of utility for the LDC s in this regard.

Currently, there exist no prohibitions on encouragement of foreign investment, or on subsidisation of services export. While lack of regulation is not good news in itself, as it leaves the markets solely at the will of the parties, this can nonetheless be used as an opportunity to incentivise LCT related investment and services outflow.

Another area of regulation in this regard is to rationalise and reduce incentives that act against the diffusion of LCT s. Such are subsidies provided for fossil-fuel production and prices thereof, supports towards polluting electricity generation, as well as similar infrastructure and generation supports abroad.

(iv) Other Areas

Although market-mediated transfers account for a large part of LCT diffusion across countries, there are also some that due to inherent characteristics do not find themselves in private markets.[613] Non-market technologies are of a one-off type, i.e. not so frequently transacted as to sustain a private market domestically. For example, power plants, grid infrastructure, and transport management systems would fall within this category. Often governments are the providers of these. Hence public procurement policies can play a role in showing preference LCT s over others.

Apart from that, long-term policy signals are also important to induce technology diffusion. Trade policy, especially when committed through international legal instruments, plays a complementary part to assure the private actors in the market, as well as investors overseas, of a stable and facilitative business environment. Needless to say, other business environment indicators can also play a beneficial role. With respect to LCT, of special significance is

612 More on this in Chapter 5 III B below.

613 Boldt and others (n 55) 710.

ensuring that relevant and adequate educational and training opportunities are available to the domestic workforce. These aspects indeed merit a deeper discussion, but they remain beyond the scope of the study.

For the developing country firms moving closer to the technology frontier, access to cutting edge products and solutions can become growingly problematic. It is because the industry leaders may become reluctant to share their intellectual property (IP) due to concerns over competition. Research indeed suggests that there are some key pieces of technology that firms refuse to share.[614] In such cases, IPR related flexibilities like compulsory licensing can play a role. That apart, there is no general case to be made for deviation from the minimum IP protection standard secured under the TRIPS.[615] What is more important for technology transfer is a transparent and predictable legal system capable to protect the IPRs of the foreign holders. This is a contributing factor to building long-term trust and thereby boosting the inward flow of LCTs. However, it is also important that effective competition regulation is put in place so that concentrated market power does not result in abusive practices.

D *A New Balance*

Introducing a new narrative of trade and diffusion of LCT, especially one that calls for the undertaking of positive responsibility, requires striking a new and careful balance along several dimensions.

One factor is to delimit the domain of the Common Concern inspired narrative within the trade regime. Informed by the notion of horizontal subsidiarity, the operational mandate of the WTO with respect to clean technology diffusion has to be precisely drawn. With the helpful hint from the technology framework (TF) as agreed by parties in the Paris Agreement, the reach of the institutional intervention of WTO in this regard would go no further than necessary for trade rules to make a direct and positively beneficial contribution to clean technology diffusion.[616]

Another aspect of the balance concerns the implementation of specific trade policy measures through domestic actions. While good faith trade cooperation devolves upon all states as a shared responsibility, the principle of differentiation would suggest that actions following the outcome of cooperation

614 See for example the study of Watson and Byrne on the experience of the Chinese firms in Chapter 2 III B at p. 83 above.

615 This is extensively addressed in Chapter 2 III A above.

616 Although, there can theoretically be other Common Concern inspired mandates to tackle other aspects of climate change through trade related responses. Any such additional areas would also be delimited in the same fashion.

be conditioned upon the ability, as well as the availability of support. For the LDCs in particular, the homework responsibility should therefore be made conditional upon their receiving necessary support. That apart, the developing countries can be granted relatively more policy room to incentivise their domestic firms' adoption of LCTs. Such an approach would make it easier to find an agreement among stakeholders in different situations.

Furthermore, to put in place an economic policy environment conducive to the diffusion of LCTs, it is also important that there is a degree of complementarity between steps taken by different actors themselves, and also between the trade regime and others on the whole. For example, successful technology diffusion would be achieved when sectors or technologies incentivised from one side meet with complementary promotions from the other side. Similarly, incentivising growth of clean technology-based industries needs to be met with removal of support from the fossil-based energies and sectors. Overall, it should be kept in mind that trade measures would complement the TF and not supplant it.

E *Ensuring Compliance*

In theory, the proposed narrative for technology diffusion should be mutually beneficial and therefore should not draw any significant compliance challenges. However, if cooperation is not achieved, or if one or few significant polluters do not cooperate, the doctrine of Common Concern would call for, also legitimise, unilateral imposition of trade restrictions by the counterparts.[617] In cases where unilateral countermeasures are being considered, it must be made sure that the non-cooperation is wilful (based on *mala fides*) and not arising out of true capacity constraints. Also on the part of the countries taking measure, such a step must come subsequent to attempts at a conciliatory settlement between the parties. This point is elaborated at length in the last chapter of the book.

III Implementing the New Approach

A *Overcoming Political Inertia*

At the outset, it must be admitted that the key practical challenge to putting the proposed narrative into operation is overcoming the apparent political inertia in the multilateral trading system. The doctrine of Common Concern

617 Cottier, 'The Principle of Common Concern of Humankind' (n 7).

proposes to overcome this challenge by suggesting further responsibility be assumed by states. However, as discussed in the first chapter, this normative aspect of the doctrine requires more support in the form of affirmative state practice to achieve unquestionable legal salience. Though the initiation of state practice itself is hardly a matter for legal enquiry traditionally, legal scholars, as we also noted in the first chapter, highlight from time to time the dialectical process of the emergence of new legal norms through repeated practice.[618] What can nevertheless be said is that the important next step for the doctrine of Common Concern to overcome the political inertia is 'norm entrepreneurship', as termed by Finnemore and Sikkink.[619] It means that the interested state and non-state actors[620] need to take the vanguard position in putting the proposition into operation. Countries that take the lead in domestic trade-related climate action (e.g. the European Union), can be expected to do the same with respect to LCT diffusion. The accumulation of political will to engage with the proposed technology diffusion narrative can speed up if demands to that effect come from the non-state actors (e.g. the different citizens' movements).[621] The potential economic benefits of the proposed arrangement would also work to that effect. Importantly, the fundamental thrust behind the Common Concern based argument for LCT diffusion is that the benefits arising therefrom are shared by all irrespective of their geographic locations. This brings the proposed cooperation narrative to the domain of a positive-sum game.

For the willing political actors, operating under the precept of Common Concern as a basis of action can provide additional legitimacy support. Any such action taken would, in a reflexive fashion, accord legal salience to the doctrine, and through that to the proposed narrative of clean technology diffusion. In addition, engagement of the trade regime in relation to broader common interests will also contribute to the output legitimacy of the WTO. On the opposite side, outright refusals to engage in good faith discussions and consensus-building to facilitate LCT diffusion under the framework of Common Concern should be seen as unbecoming of the responsibilities of a sovereign actor and therefore illegitimate.

618 See Chapter 1 V C above.

619 Finnemore and Sikkink (n 199).

620 Bacchus terms it as 'the willing', James Bacchus, *The Willing World: Shaping and Sharing a Sustainable Global Prosperity* (Cambridge University Press 2018).

621 See, for example, 'Act Now' (*Extinction Rebellion*) <https://rebellion.global/about-us/> accessed 25 October 2020.

B *Tasks at the Multilateral Level*

The experience with the environmental goods negotiations at the WTO has aptly taught that even seemingly easy multilateral cooperation can be very fraught in practice. Nevertheless, for reasons outlined earlier,[622] cooperation is most beneficial when it takes place at the multilateral level. To reiterate in brief, only through multilateral cooperation is it possible to take full account of the varied stakeholder interests, potentially resulting in a truly shared understanding of LCT diffusion and the related parameters of coordination between the climate change and the trade regimes. On the same note, institutional coordination between the WTO and the UNFCCC at specific issue levels is impossible in the absence of a multilateral initiative. Compared to regional cooperation, multilateral engagement should be preferred by the developing countries, because otherwise, the standards of differential treatments may suffer the chance of being omitted out of any agreed outcome.[623]

First, the WTO members must recognise the need to act to prevent climate change, based on the doctrine of Common Concern. Such recognition, as noted earlier, is best done through a Ministerial declaration. The declaration should expressly mention that climate change is a common concern of humankind and therefore the members have a responsibility to adopt and implement necessary trade-related measures. It must further be noted that against the backdrop of a mutually supportive trade and environmental rules, the special situation of climate as a common concern begs for positive steps to be taken within the trade regime. Such actions should be complementary to the attainment of the goals embedded in the Paris Agreement. Noting the positive impact trade policy can have on various areas of climate action, the members shall cooperate to facilitate those outcomes while being aware of the special situation of the developing and least-developed members. The Hong Kong ministerial declaration on fisheries subsidies can be instructive in this regard.[624]

---

622 See section II at p. 127 above.

623 One can note the experience of the multilateral environmental agreements in this regard, which played a crucial role in mainstreaming the differentiated responsibility norm.

624 Annex D, 'Doha Work Programme: Ministerial Declaration' (n 470) para 9, holding "recall our commitment at Doha to enhancing the mutual supportiveness of trade and environment, note that there is broad agreement that the Group should strengthen disciplines on subsidies in the fisheries sector, including through the prohibition of certain forms of fisheries subsidies that contribute to overcapacity and over-fishing, and call on Participants promptly to undertake further detailed work to, inter alia, establish the nature and extent of those disciplines, including transparency and enforceability. Appropriate and effective special and differential treatment for developing and least-developed Members should be an integral part of the fisheries subsidies negotiations, taking into account the

The next step is to put in place operational rules that would provide the substantive content and extent of a member's responsibility to act to facilitate diffusion of LCTs. Within the WTO legal framework, substantive rulemaking can take different avenues (e.g. partial amendments of the existing rules, plurilateral or multilateral agreements, time-limited specific waivers, peace clauses etc.).[625] The best possible approach would be for the members to create a negotiation mandate and a platform to develop new rules facilitating the diffusion of climate technology. Until an agreement is reached and has become applicable for all members, possible illegality of any trade measures demonstrated to promote LCT diffusion within the Common Concern framework shall be waived.[626]

To specify the subject-matter of cooperation, it is possible to have an emission sector-focused approach (e.g. energy, transport, agriculture, industry, waste etc.), or a trade-issue specific one (i.e. liberalisation, PPMs, incentives, differential supports, and other issues). A sector-focused approach would allow dealing with the full spectrum of trade-related concerns across the different covered agreements pertaining to the chosen sector.[627] This would unlock more possible combinations while exchanging concessions and therefore may ease finding of an agreement. The attractiveness of the other option, i.e. a trade-issue focused agenda lies in its simplicity, as it will keep the negotiation agenda linear and thereby cut down on complexity. It would also have the advantage of familiarity, as the members' representatives and the institutional expertise are attuned to tackle the questions in a trade-issue specific manner. Moreover, as each of the trade-related questions neatly belong to specific covered agreements, subsequent integration of any outcome would be relatively easier.

---

importance of this sector to development priorities, poverty reduction, and livelihood and food security concerns;".

625 For a comparative discussion on each of the avenues in the context of clean energy technologies, see, Amelia Porges and Thomas L Brewer, 'Climate Change and a Renewable Energy Scale-Up: Responding to Challenges Posed to the WTO', *Clean Energy Technologies and the Trade System: Proposals and Analysis* (International Centre for Trade and Sustainable Development (ICTSD), World Economic Forum 2013).

626 Article IX:3 and IX:4, Marrakesh Agreement Establishing the World Trade Organization (n 226); Porges and Brewer, ibid 56–57.

627 For a similar proposition, see, Thomas Cottier and Donah Baracol-Pinhão, 'Environmental Goods and Services: The Environmental Area Initiative Approach and Climate Change' in Thomas Cottier, Olga Nartova and Sadeq Z Bigdeli (eds), *International trade regulation and the mitigation of climate change: World Trade Forum* (Cambridge University Press 2009).

A question may nevertheless arise regarding the method of integrating the substantive outcome with the covered agreements. Though this is a question that is better left to the nature of the ultimate outcome, a few observations are warranted here. Any negotiated reduction in tariffs can be appended to the GATT schedule of commitments or as a separate plurilateral agreement. Other issues like the PPM question can be resolved by agreeing to an interpretative understanding. Where the issue would be a shortcoming in one of the WTO covered agreements (e.g. the agreement on subsidies), amendment of the existing provisions or inclusion of new ones will be the solution. There may also be issues that may advance the ongoing work agenda at the WTO. One such is the discussion on a better classification of services to facilitate market access negotiation under the GATS. Progress in that regard can be finally subsumed in the agreement as well.

Furthermore, current coordination between the WTO and the UNFCCC secretariats needs to be deepened. With respect to LCT, upcoming work in the climate regime under the supervision of the technology executive committee (TEC) has elements that are of much relevance to the WTO. An understanding should be struck between the TEC on one hand and the WTO secretariat under the committee on trade and environment (CTE) leadership on the other. The understanding should cover mutual information and expertise sharing, coordination of tasks, as well as sub-delegation and co-working, if possible. In the same vein, the mandate of the working group on trade and technology transfer (WGTTT) should be reformulated with specific emphasis on trade-related climate technology diffusion issues. Recommendations by the WGTTT on ways to remove LCT diffusion obstacles can open new paths towards cooperation.

It is important that the development concerns find adequate attention in the process of negotiations. However, development should not be an excuse to shield the major emitters from making significant, effective commitments. This would be counterproductive. The focus should rather be on identifying the constraints that the countries face and the nature of assistance that could be provided to tackle those. Of course, the developing countries' responsibilities would be conditional upon the provision of the necessary support. With special regard to the LDC s, arguably, Article 66.2 of the TRIPS Agreement already supplies a robust platform for incentivising technology transfer. However, the performance of the developed countries' obligation under that provision could be better guided so that the climate-related technology needs are taken into special account. The language of this provision can be connected to the identified technology needs and the nationally appropriate mitigation actions (NAMA s) by the LDCs, which can then be advanced to the developed country parties for finance or other incentives. Comparable mechanisms should also be devised for developing countries in need of support.

While some of these tasks can arguably be undertaken under the current Doha negotiation mandate (e.g. goods and services market liberalisation), it would be optimal to draw up a new trade and climate negotiation agenda comprised of the proposals made here. As political feasibility is the wall between the optimal and the real, in all probability, a few of the prioritised issues must make the cut. Willing states should find in the Common Concern-based cooperation agenda a balanced approach worth investing in.

C *Incorporation in Preferential Trade Agreements* (PTAs)

The preferential trade agreements (PTA s) serve not only as labs for the willing states to try out new commitments with limited participation but they also pave the way for the inclusion of emerging issues, as well as their subsequent multilateralisation.[628] Outside the shadow of the WTO, the PTA s are the next best option to generate trade cooperation regarding diffusion of LCT s. The PTA s can serve as platforms for technology-related experience and information sharing, involve non-state actors, as well as test a range of market reform measures (e.g. removal of fossil fuel subsidies, or easing market access). Modern PTAs can hypothetically include commitments regarding facilitation of cross-border investments in LCT s- something beyond the reach of the WTO.

Benefits apart, PTA s have structural limitations as well. Issues of interest covered in the PTA s would tend to be narrowly tailored to the interests of the parties. This is a challenge to subsequent multilateralisation of the contents of such agreements. Also, some issues, e.g. institutional coordination, are inherently multilateral and cannot be addressed in a PTA setting. It should also be noted that apart from preferential market access, the PTA s cannot legiti mise any other actions in contravention of the WTO laws (e.g. export subsidies for LCT).

That being mentioned, the best examples of progress made through the PTA s so far are the agreements between liberal trade partners that are also willing to combat climate change. For instance, agreements signed by the European Union with its like-minded partners provide the best available examples of treaty language regarding trade and climate cooperation. The EU-Colombia-Peru agreement has already been mentioned for its formal

628 James Bacchus, 'On Making and Remaking Enabling Frameworks for Sustainable Development', *The willing world: shaping and sharing a sustainable global prosperity* (Cambridge University Press 2018) 374–376.

endorsement of climate change as a common concern of humankind by the parties.[629] The agreement between the EU and Singapore saw the parties be open to the possibility of "cooperation on trade-related aspects of the current and future international climate change regime, including ways to address adverse effects of trade on climate, as well as means to promote LCTs and energy efficiency".[630] The recently concluded Comprehensive Economic and Trade Agreement (CETA) between the EU and Canada also advances similar cooperation language.[631] The CETA provides an opportunity to consult with the non-state actors.[632] Such opportunities are ideal for advancing the narrative currently proposed. As the forerunners, these countries should explore ways of further strengthening their PTA commitments with respect to climate action.

D *Domestic Actions*

As the narrative has demonstrated, the efforts ultimately boil down to facilitative trade measures taken for climate technology diffusion at the domestic and sub-state levels. There is a significant difference between such actions taken against the backdrop of effective international cooperation, and otherwise. In the first scenario, a large part of the domestic action is an implementation of the agreed international arrangement, the terms of which are determined by the nature of the actor, the action in question, and the particularities of the domestic legal system. Depending on those factors, actions can vary from liberalisation to export promotion, or from improvement of the business environment for the relevant industries to the adoption of PPMs. In the second situation, i.e. in the absence of a legitimising background of an international legal framework, a duty to act in response to the common concern of climate change nevertheless exists. But as it is not woven into the structure of trade law, any trade measure taken in pursuance of common concern may be difficult to justify. Therefore, in the absence of cooperation at the international

629 See Chapter 2 IV D (ii) at p. 109 above.

630 Article 12.10 (f), EU – Singapore free trade agreement.

631 The parties envisage cooperation to extend on "trade-related aspects of the current and future international climate change regime, as well as domestic climate policies and programmes relating to mitigation and adaptation, including issues relating to carbon markets, ways to address adverse effects of trade on climate, as well as means to promote energy efficiency and the development and deployment of low-carbon and other climate-friendly technologies;", Art 24.12, sub 1(e), Comprehensive Economic and Trade Agreement (CETA). In 2018, the CETA joint committee issued a recommendation to cooperate towards promotion of the objectives of the Paris Agreement.

632 Articles 24.7 and 24.12, sub 3, ibid.

level, domestic actions, probably carried out only by the willing parties, would put those parties under a disproportionate burden.

As a last resort, the Common Concern doctrine is open to the possibility of unilateral countermeasures to elicit adequate actions from the non-compliant trading partners. It would be important to pay due regard to the expression 'last resort' before one summarily dismisses the proposition. We echo an earlier statement that this option is not proposed as a response against capacity-constrained actors, or those that must prioritise economic development over everything else. Putting aside the reasonable causes of variable compliance, one would see the kernel of realism that is embedded in this proposition. It is important that the opportunity to impose trade-related countermeasures exists against the blatant dismissal of the necessity of action, or blunt denials of the facts on climate change. While previously such propositions were labelled as yet another developed country ploy, it should be noted that with the change of that traditional narrative, the developed countries (e.g. the United States) would also find themselves in the crosshairs.[633]

IV Conclusion

This chapter has outlined a new trade cooperation narrative to guide the reform of the WTO rules and domestic trade policies for the benefit of LCT diffusion. We portrayed here that trade measures have not only restrictive but also facilitative aspects, which can be put to use for the diffusion of clean technology. Furthermore, the deployment of trade measures need not necessarily affect climate commitments. The regimes can continue to retain their respective structural and operational uniqueness. Nevertheless, the same values of climate action can be animated in both systems. The Common Concern of Humankind doctrine can guide the trade regime in such a way that it contributes to the fulfilment of climate targets.

At the heart of the narrative is a responsibility to effectively cooperate within the trade regime, founded upon the doctrine of Common Concern. The contributory and complementary role of trade policy measures is often overlooked in the climate literature as the latter tend to highlight the use of trade tools only as a vehicle for delivering threats of sanctions. This chapter advanced that the Common Concern doctrine based cooperation framework can be used to drive forward a novel, empirically informed, and dedicated narrative for the

633 Mattoo and Subramanian (n 534) 21–24; Simon (n 528).

diffusion of LCTs. To implement that in practice, the chapter has outlined a 'push-pull' framework, also identified the relevant sets of actors and measures therein. While cooperation should ideally take place in a multilateral setting, it is also the most difficult to do so at that level. Easier, in comparison, is cooperation among a smaller constellation of actors, e.g. in a PTA setting. The chapter suggests that more and stronger steps be taken along those avenues.

Appropriate domestic measures are what eventually carry the day. Therefore, the chapter further suggests that given the available policy options and the particular situation of a country, the cooperative outcome must further be implemented through suitable actions at different levels of domestic governance. However, keeping in mind the tenets of equity and differentiated responsibility, due care must be taken to account for the special situations of developing and least-developed countries. While this would not exempt the countries from adopting necessary measures, respective actions must be met with adequate support.

CHAPTER 4

Assisting the Diffusion of Low-Carbon Technology through Emission Pricing

This is the first of the two chapters that take the discussions to the level of domestic trade policy measures for low-carbon technology (LCT) diffusion. Following the outlines of the proposed trade cooperation narrative laid out in the previous chapter, the goal here is twofold. One is to take the application of the narrative a step further by looking into a particular facilitative trade policy action in the backdrop of the existing framework of rules. Such an exercise would contribute by highlighting the bottlenecks where climate mitigation motivated measures may come to conflict with trade rules. The other goal is to identify the ways the proposed doctrine of Common Concern can ease or tackle those challenges.

In substantive terms, the present chapter would call for pricing of GHG emissions domestically and also for imposing similar regulation upon imports (i.e. border adjustment). It would also propose that additional revenue gained from carbon pricing of imports be reverted to the production sources, the developing countries in particular, as technology upgradation support. The driving hypothesis here is that through the pricing of GHG emissions, it is possible to create a business environment that renders low-emission production and processing lucrative. To establish that hypothesis, the first section supplies a factual background to carbon pricing, as well as describes the key components of the proposed pricing approach. Thereafter, the second and the third section discuss the thorny issues with respect to WTO rules in this regard. The following section introduces a counterfactual position, proposing a harmonisation endeavour under the rubric of Common Concern of Humankind. The concluding part sums up the analysis and the key findings therefrom.

I Pricing Emission using Taxes and Tariffs: A Brief Introduction

The two-most-debated means of putting a price on GHG emissions are either imposition of a tax, or establishment of an emission permit trading system.[634]

634 Ian WH Parry and others (eds), *Fiscal Policy to Mitigate Climate Change: A Guide to Policymakers* (International Monetary Fund 2012) 2.

Due to various challenges attached to the global implementation of a cap and trade system,[635] carbon pricing through taxation is relatively less complicated and more effective.[636] In addition, under specific circumstances, carbon tariffs, a less-discussed policy option, can also be as efficiently deployable as the taxation based approach.

The factor common to carbon taxes and tariffs is that both of these are appropriate tools to impose a price on GHG emissions (i.e. CO_2 or CO_2 equivalent) embedded in imports. With respect to taxation, the process is known as 'border tax adjustment' (BTA), a general term denoting the act of adjusting the taxes on imports as equivalent to the domestic standards.[637] It means that untaxed imports coming in from overseas will face an additional tax burden, like a tariff; and domestic products will be relieved from the same when bound for export, like a subsidy.[638] Relevant rules regulating the application of import BTA is found in the GATT, while the same for export adjustment is found in the SCM agreement. For this chapter, the focus would be on import adjustment. Export exemptions are not discussed because those are motivated solely by industrial competitiveness concerns and not that of climate mitigation. Carbon tariffs, a novel idea, seeks to mimic the effect of carbon pricing of imports through a variable duty. Details are provided in the following paragraphs.

A *Rationale behind Carbon Pricing for Technology Diffusion*

The choice between taxes or tariffs as the best applicable option will depend on contextual factors, as explained below. Irrespective of the choice, the common rationale in both cases is that imposing an effective price rate on carbon emissions in the export destinations can create a strong 'demand-pull' among

635 Such challenges include the difficulty in agreeing on a global emission cap and distribution of the permits across countries, domestic administration and allocation challenges, opportunities for corruption etc. See, Richard N Cooper, 'The Case for Pricing Greenhouse Gas Emissions' in Peter C Cramton, David JC MacKay and Axel Ockenfels (eds), *Global carbon pricing: the path to climate cooperation* (MIT Press 2017); William Nordhaus, 'Climate Clubs and Carbon Pricing' in Peter C Cramton, David JC MacKay and Axel Ockenfels (eds), *Global carbon pricing: the path to climate cooperation* (MIT Press 2017) 119.

636 Martin L Weitzman, 'How a Minimum Carbon-Price Commitment Might Help to Internalize the Global Warming Externality' in Peter C Cramton, David JC MacKay and Axel Ockenfels (eds), *Global carbon pricing: the path to climate cooperation* (MIT Press 2017) 129–130.

637 Timothy M Todd, 'What Is A Border Adjustment Tax?' *Forbes* (17 January 2017) <https://www.forbes.com/sites/timtodd/2017/01/17/what-is-a-border-adjustment-tax/#4c7de2c-bc1b9> accessed 25 October 2020.

638 For details, see, Holzer (n 602) 42–62.

export-oriented firms towards emission reduction through clean technology upgrades.[639]

While carbon taxes are widely regarded as the most viable economic policy tool to mitigate emission,[640] a carbon tariff is a relatively new idea. Carbon taxes are so called because they are most often designed as a rate imposed on per-unit of carbon dioxide (CO_2) emission. The tax can also be similarly imposed on emissions of other greenhouse gases (e.g. NO_2, CH_4, and other Kyoto Protocol gases) by converting those in CO_2 equivalent terms. When imposed, the impact of a carbon tax is expected to pass along the supply chain influencing the final price of the output.[641] A carbon tariff can hypothetically follow the same method of rate calculation as that of the tax. But as the term 'tariff' suggests, unlike a tax, it would be imposed only upon imports. Tariffs can be an appropriate tool to implement carbon pricing when discharging responsibility for import consumption is the regulator's only intent. The same would be the case if the regulator seeks to curb emissions from a specific industry which is domestically absent, for example, production of cement or aluminium. The main point here is that unlike a tax system, which requires a pre-existing domestic base to be adjustable on imports, tariffs do not face any such preconditions. Tariffs would also make better sense in geographies where domestic sources of emission are already minimised, or non-existent. For example, Bhutan has a negative emission profile and a very limited domestic tax base.

Like any other environmental taxation, internalisation of the external costs (i.e. cost to the climate) into the price is the fundamental motivation behind a carbon tax.[642] The same can also be said about carbon

---

639 See Figure 3 at p. 130 and related explanation.

640 International Monetary Fund (IMF), 'Fiscal Monitor: How to Mitigate Climate Change' (IMF 2019) 3–4; Victor Gasper and others, 'Fiscal Policies to Curb Climate Change – IMF Blog' (*IMFBlog*, 10 October 2019) <https://blogs.imf.org/2019/10/10/fiscal-policies-to-curb-climate-change/> accessed 25 October 2020; Leslie Hook, 'Surge in US Economists' Support for Carbon Tax to Tackle Emissions' *Financial Times* (17 February 2019) <https://www.ft.com/content/fa0815fe-3299-11e9-bd3a-8b2a211d90d5> accessed 25 October 2020; 'How to Design Carbon Taxes' [2018] *The Economist* <https://www.economist.com/finance-and-economics/2018/08/18/how-to-design-carbon-taxes> accessed 25 October 2020. It should also be taken into account that the 2018 Nobel Prize in economics was awarded partially to Willian Nordhaus for his trendsetting work on carbon pricing.

641 Cooper (n 635) 94.

642 Janet E Milne and Mikael Skou Andersen, 'Introduction to Environmental Taxation Concepts and Research' in Janet E Milne and Mikael Skou Andersen (eds), *Handbook of research on environmental taxation* (Edward Elgar 2012) 15–19; OECD, *Environmentally Related Taxes in OECD Countries: Issues and Strategies* (OECD Publishing 2001) 21–22.

tariffs.[643] From an economic point of view, carbon pricing policies are more efficient in curbing GHG emissions than alternative regulatory approaches.[644] Ideally, an economy-wide implemented carbon price would be most effective at least cost, as it would allow mitigation activities to be undertaken where they are cheapest (upstream or downstream supply chain), without being tied to a specific segment or technology, as a regulation may suggest.[645] A carbon tax or tariff can therefore act as additional catalysts to new technology deployment and diffusion all across the economy, as cheaper ways of mitigating emission at all levels of energy use become attractive.[646] Carbon pricing adjusts the cost of carbon-based energy, thereby making the substitutes relatively more attractive.[647]

Compared to a tax based approach, a tariff scheme can be lucrative due to the strategic ease in initial adoption. From a legal point of view, the structure of the WTO laws suggests different sets of rules for tariffs and taxes. In that regard, as detailed later, there is arguably more policy room to legitimise a tariff than a tax.[648] Also, the WTO is better placed, in terms of jurisdiction, to manage tariffs rather than handling tax cooperation.

What also builds a case for adopting carbon pricing policies is the surprising scale of underutilisation of the approach even among the developed countries. Except for a few jurisdictions and limited instances of taxes on fuel and road transports, the bulk of emissions from the OECD countries is not priced. One recent report highlights that 60% of all OECD emissions resulting from energy use still remain outside any pricing scheme.[649] Moreover, 90% of all OECD emission is taxed at a rate that is bellow 'effective'.[650] The result of inaction

643 Thomas Cottier, Olga Nartova and Anirudh Shingal, 'The Potential of Tariff Policy for Climate Change Mitigation: Legal and Economic Analysis' (2014) 48 Journal of World Trade 1007; Holzer (n 602) 205–207.

644 Jean-Philippe Barde and Olivier Godard, 'Economic Principles of Environmental Fiscal Reform' in Janet E Milne and Mikael Skou Andersen (eds), *Handbook of research on environmental taxation* (Edward Elgar 2012) 35–40; OECD, *Environmentally Related Taxes in OECD Countries* (n 642) 22–23.

645 Alan Krupnick and Ian Parry, 'What Is the Best Policy Instrument for Reducing CO2 Emissions?' in Ian WH Parry, Ruud A de Mooij and Michael Keen (eds), *Fiscal policy to mitigate climate change: a guide to policymakers* (International Monetary Fund 2012) 3–13.

646 Tom Tietenberg, 'Carbon Pricing: Lessons Derived from Experience' in Ian WH Parry, Ruud A de Mooij and Michael Keen (eds), *Fiscal policy to mitigate climate change: a guide to policymakers* (International Monetary Fund 2012) 165–166.

647 OECD, *Effective Carbon Rates* (OECD Publishing 2016) 28–29 <http://www.oecd-ilibrary.org/taxation/effective-carbon-rates_9789264260115-en> accessed 25 October 2020.

648 See section II below.

649 OECD, *Effective Carbon Rates* (n 647) 50–51.

650 ibid.

is an exponential rise in future costs of implementation, contributing to the growing possibility of failure to limit the global temperature rise within the Paris Agreement target.[651]

In relation to domestic implementation, bringing imports also under the coverage of carbon tax (i.e. border adjustment) enables a country to influence the production processes of the source countries to shift towards less emitting modes.[652] This way, an import adjusted carbon tax can create an opportunity for greater uptake of LCTs globally.[653] Facing a growing scale of unpriced emission destined to the developed country,[654] consumption responsibility, as well as the principle of polluter pays,[655] can be put into effect within the broader Common Concern framework. Price put on carbon emission would also further attainment of the SDG of sustainable production and consumption.[656]

B *Design Considerations for an Effective and Equitable Measure*

This part discusses key design issues that relate to carbon pricing with trade and technology diffusion aspects. Design characteristics of the pricing measures play a strong role in determining the extent to which least-cost mitigation and technology diffusion can be expected as a result. A range of factors deserves consideration to this effect, including the subscribed policy goals of the instrument, optimality considerations, and also political feasibility concerns.[657] A carbon pricing program has to make initial policy decisions about

---

651 Valentina Bosetti and others, 'Emissions Pricing to Stabilize Global Climate' in Ian WH Parry, Ruud A de Mooij and Michael Keen (eds), *Fiscal policy to mitigate climate change: a guide to policymakers* (International Monetary Fund 2012) 59–62.

652 OECD, *Environmentally Related Taxes in OECD Countries* (n 642) 74–75; However, there is a view that adjustment of imports only makes the approach 'non-neutral. Reinhard Quick, 'Guest Post: A Carbon Border Tax or A Climate Tariff?' (*International Economic Law and Policy Blog*, 2 October 2019) <https://ielp.worldtradelaw.net/2019/10/guest-post-a-carbon-border-tax-or-a-climate-tariff.html> accessed 25 October 2020. In contrast, upholding neutrality would mean exempting the carbon intensive exports from the coverage of the scheme. Gabriel Weil, 'Incentive Compatible Climate Change Mitigation: Moving beyond the Pledge and Review Model' (2017) 42 William & Mary Environmental Law and Policy Review 923, 944–946.

653 Holzer (n 602) 55–56; Ian Parry, Rick van der Ploeg and Roberton Williams, 'How to Design a Carbon Tax' in Ian WH Parry, Ruud A de Mooij and Michael Keen (eds), *Fiscal policy to mitigate climate change: a guide to policymakers* (International Monetary Fund 2012) 35–36.

654 Fernández-Amador, Francois and Tomberger (n 81).

655 OECD, *Effective Carbon Rates* (n 647) 29–30.

656 Goal 12, United Nations General Assembly (n 210).

657 Parry, van der Ploeg and Williams (n 653) 8.

the coverage, level of price imposition, administrative, and monitoring efficiency, as well as revenue utilisation priorities.[658]

(i) Specifying a Tax Base

Determination of the tax base as well as an effective tax rate ensures the adequate coverage and strength of the program. From an optimality point of view, covering almost all the emission sources with a common rate of tax is ideal. Especially with regard to taxing CO_2 emissions, a uniform rate changes relative prices of the energy and therefore allows users to substitute between sources and move towards cleaner sources as necessary, combining with use efficiency and reduction of demand.[659] However, practically, a uniform carbon price is difficult to implement politically as there may be strong commercial, social, or developmental interest to exempt some economic sectors (e.g. agriculture, or small enterprises), or class of population (e.g. low-income households).[660] Therefore, it is pragmatic to initiate a pricing program that covers one gas, preferably CO_2, in priority sectors, and gradually expands thereupon.[661]

(ii) Determining Coverage of the Pricing Scheme

Policy considerations of exempting select sectors, or activities from tax coverage, and administrative ease of implementation may dictate the point in the energy supply chain where a CO_2 the tax will be levied. As the figure (Figure 4) in the next page shows, a carbon tax can be imposed at an upstream position (e.g. for coal, at the mouth of the mine; for petroleum, at the refineries; or at the border), or at different downstream stages (e.g. distribution levels, or at the point of use).[662] The more upstream a tax is imposed, the wider becomes its coverage. Cooper argues that taxing fossil fuels at the upstream, coupled with

658 ibid 27–28.

659 ibid 29–31.

660 An appropriate example of the political challenge of implementing a carbon price is the 'gilet jaune' movement in France, which was triggered by climate motivated fuel tax that especially hurt the poorest sections of the population. 'Who Are the "Gilets Jaunes"?' *BBC News* (6 December 2018) <https://www.bbc.com/news/world-europe-46424267> accessed 19 May 2020; Cristina Abellan Matamoros, 'What Are the Gilets Jaunes so Upset About?' (*euronews*, 16 November 2018) <https://www.euronews.com/2018/11/16/what-s-all-the-fuss-about-the-french-fuel-tax-hikes-euronews-answers> accessed 19 May 2020; See also, Partnership for Market Readiness (PMR), *Carbon Tax Guide: A Handbook for Policy Makers* (World Bank 2017) 75–79.

661 Tietenberg (n 646) 159.

662 Partnership for Market Readiness (PMR) (n 660) 79–81.

rebates for any downstream mitigation is an optimal method.[663] In practice so far, however, there has been no such program and a downstream approach is most commonly found.[664] Downstream taxes focusing on industry-specific activities (e.g. steel, or aluminium industries) would be easier to implement compared to an economy-wide upstream tax, which may become difficult to monitor.[665]

(iii) Carbon Footprint Calculation

The imposition of a carbon price on imports, either through border adjustment or tariffs, would require calculation of a partial or complete carbon footprint of the product in question.[666] Carbon footprint calculation requires establishing 'system boundary', i.e. clear designation of the scope of activities regarding which the emissions are to be calculated.[667] When the system boundary comprises of one firm (i.e. a site footprint) the emission footprint is partial, but easy to compute.[668] In contrast, a complete carbon footprint of a product would require the system boundary to cover the whole lifecycle of the product.[669] Such calculation would quickly become prohibitively complex, as it would span across activities of many firms in different jurisdictions.[670] Therefore, at the initial stage, carbon pricing of imports should attempt to approximate a products' share of the site footprint of the exporter. Even in that situation, the impact of a carbon price can be particularly burdensome to the developing and least-developed countries, as their energy system depends on fossil fuel to a relatively larger degree. These concerns, as well as technology support need, must be addressed through recycling the additional revenue as explained later.

663 Cooper (n 635).

664 Tietenberg (n 646) 159–160.

665 Parry, van der Ploeg and Williams (n 653) 36.

666 Lidija Čuček, Jiří Jaromír Klemeš and Zdravko Kravanja, 'Chapter 5 – Overview of Environmental Footprints' in Jiří Jaromír Klemeš (ed), *Assessing and Measuring Environmental Impact and Sustainability* (Butterworth-Heinemann 2015) 159–161.

667 Robin Kent, 'Chapter 9 – Carbon Footprinting' in Robin Kent (ed), *Energy Management in Plastics Processing (Third Edition)* (Elsevier 2018) 388–389 <http://www.sciencedirect.com/science/Article/pii/B978008102507950009X> accessed 25 October 2020.

668 ibid 390–397.

669 ibid 398–399.

670 The computational difficulty led William Nordhaus to propose a single-rate enforcement tariff. See, William Nordhaus, *The Climate Casino: Risk, Uncertainty, and Economics for a Warming World* (Yale University Press 2013) 254–257. It is to be noted that Nordhaus' proposition is an enforcement step, recourse to which is open only after the failure of cooperative efforts to establish a carbon price floor.

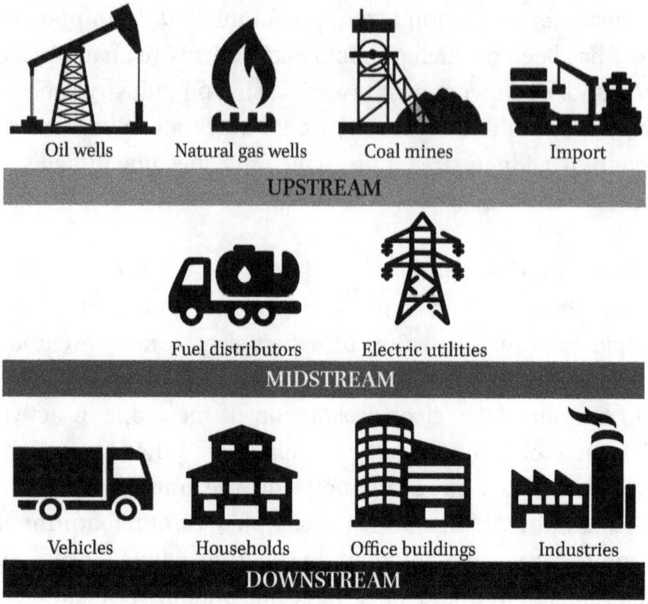

FIGURE 4 Potential stages for carbon pricing in an economy. Graphic adapted from Partnership for Market Readiness (PMR) (n 662) 80

(iv) Fixing Emission Price

It is important to fix a price rate for carbon emissions that is at least high enough to induce a behavioural change of the actors towards abatement (Box 3). A related concern is generation of revenue at a scale adequate to support the sectors and communities most affected financially due to emission pricing. The band within which an optimal price can be found is limited at the upper range by the marginal cost of emitting one extra ton of CO_2 to the atmosphere[671] and at the lower ranges by political viability. What should also be noted regarding the rate of carbon pricing is that it needs to move gradually upwards, as the risk to climate increases with time. As a result, the more global inaction worsens the climate risk, the sharper would be the upward movement of carbon pricing over time.[672] According to the OECD, attaining the ambitious 1.5°C target of the Paris Agreement would require a carbon price of EUR50 per ton imposed today. The rate increases towards hundreds of euros by 2050.[673] Other economists also suggest prices ranging from USD25 to USD100 per ton of

671 OECD, *Effective Carbon Rates* (n 647) 31.

672 Bosetti and others (n 651).

673 OECD, *Effective Carbon Rates* (n 647) 31.

carbon emission.[674] A recent IMF report called for the immediate imposition of a tax, which would gradually rise to USD75 per ton by 2030.[675]

Box 3: Carbon Pricing in Practice
Examples of Carbon Pricing in Different Jurisdictions[676]
The **British Columbia carbon tax program** is one of the forerunners in introducing a carbon tax. The tax is applied and collected at the wholesale level on different fuels. The general rate is $10 per tonne of CO2 equivalent emission, but the actual applicable rate varies depending on fuels. Introduced in 2008, the tax raised an estimated amount of $1849 million over the first three years – an amount that was earmarked to reduce the individual and corporate income tax rates. The tax does not apply on biodiesel, ethanol, or exported fuels.

A carbon tax has been in place in Sweden since 1991. While initially the rate was EUR 24 for per ton of CO_2 emitted, by 2019 it has gradually increased to EUR 114. The industries within the coverage of the EU emission trading scheme (ETS) are exempted from the tax. The revenue generated is not earmarked, although according to the government, it may be spent for purposes related to the tax, e.g. addressing distributional impacts, or financing climate-related projects.

In Switzerland, a **CO_2 levy** is in place since 2008. It is imposed on all fossil-based fuels, and oils used for heating purposes. The current rate of levy (as of January 2018) is CHF 96 per ton of CO_2 emission. A major

674 Joseph E Stiglitz, 'Overcoming the Copenhagen Failure with Flexible Commitments' in Peter C Cramton, David JC MacKay and Axel Ockenfels (eds), *Global carbon pricing: the path to climate cooperation* (MIT Press 2017) 102; Nordhaus, 'Climate Clubs and Carbon Pricing' (n 635) 120–121.

675 Gasper and others (n 640). See for greater details, International Monetary Fund (IMF) (n 640).

676 Sources of the examples are, OECD, 'Database on Policy Instruments for the Environment' <https://pinedatabase.oecd.org/#> accessed 25 October 2020; Partnership for Market Readiness (PMR) (n 660); 'Sweden's Carbon Tax' (*Government offices of Sweden*, January 2019) <https://www.government.se/government-policy/taxes-and-tariffs/swedens-carbon-tax/> accessed 25 October 2020; 'CO2 Levy' (*Federal Office for the Environment (FOEN*), 2018) <https://www.bafu.admin.ch/bafu/en/home/topics/climate/info-specialists/climate-policy/co2-levy.html> accessed 25 October 2020; Ivetta Gerasimchuk and others, 'Stories from G20 Countries: Shifting Public Money out of Fossil Fuels' (International Institute for Sustanianable Development 2018) <https://www.iisd.org/sites/default/files/publications/stories-g20-shifting-public-money-out-fossil-fuels-en.pdf> accessed 25 October 2020.

portion (two-thirds) of the revenue is allocated for redistribution purposes. The rest is spent on supporting energy-efficient building renovations, and to replenish a technology fund.

A **petroleum and coal tax** is in place in Japan since 1978. In 2012, the rates were increased as a special response measure to global warming. Under the present scheme, coal and natural gas are taxed at EUR 11.3 and EUR 15.4 per ton. The tax, however, exempts certain sectors (e.g. agriculture, forestry, and fisheries), as well as specific industries (e.g. coal imported for steel and iron manufacture). The revenue generated is earmarked to improve energy supply and demand structure. It is also spent to introduce alternative energy sources.

In India, a **clean energy cess** was put in place in 2010. It was a fixed tax imposed on coal, lignite, and peat mined in India, although the rate increased over time. Initially earmarked to replenish the National Clean Energy Fund created the same year, subsequent budgetary crisis saw the fund being diverted elsewhere. The tax was collected as excise duty. In 2017 the clean energy cess was replaced with a goods and services tax (GST) at the same rate.

A **carbon dioxide vehicle emissions tax** has been introduced in South Africa in 2010. Initially applying on new passenger vehicles, from 2011 the tax was also extended to double cabs. The tax charges for grams of CO_2 emission per kilometre, beyond a fixed threshold. For double cabs, the rate is EUR7.79 per gCO_2/km. For new passenger vehicles, the rate is EUR 6.36 gCO_2/km.

(v) Revenue Utilisation

Revenue generated from carbon pricing can be substantial, allowing for investments to meet specific policy goals, which can include, among others, addressing the barriers to adoption of LCTs. It is suggested that an appropriately measured carbon tax (e.g. about USD25 per ton) can generate 1 per cent of the GDP in terms of additional revenue, or even more depending on the carbon intensity of the economy.[677] Available studies mostly suggest utilisation of the

677 Parry, van der Ploeg and Williams (n 653) 32; Ian WH Parry, 'Reflections on the International Coordination of Carbon Pricing' in Peter C Cramton, David JC MacKay and Axel Ockenfels (eds), *Global carbon pricing: the path to climate cooperation* (MIT Press 2017) 20; Ian WH Parry, Chandara Veung and Dirk Heine, *How Much Carbon Pricing Is in Countries' Own Interests? The Critical Role of Co-Benefits* (International Monetary Fund 2014) 20.

revenue from carbon pricing either to readjust the tax burdens[678] or to invest in climate technologies and addressing market barriers.[679] The information box above supplying a snapshot of actual practice also corroborate such suggestion.[680] We however argue that imposition of taxes and tariffs on imports originating from developing countries would be justified and equitable only if commensurate efforts are made to make necessary technologies available to those countries. Therefore, when a carbon pricing scheme is extended to cover imports, the related plans of revenue utilisation should also include the needs of the developing countries. One way of doing it would be to channel a part of the revenue income from carbon pricing through a new, or an established financial mechanism for LCT adoption support in developing countries. As shown below, this is a chief part of the carbon pricing measure proposed in this chapter.

C *The Need for International Cooperation*

It is broadly agreed that global cooperation to settle a carbon price floor is the most effective means to ramp up mitigation efforts in addition to the nationally determined contributions (NDC s) under the Paris Agreement. Given the weak ambition regarding the latter, there is high confidence that in the absence of such cooperation, meeting the Paris target would be impossible. This indicates how important cooperation is in terms of implementing a carbon price.[681] To explain further, the need for cooperation on carbon pricing arises first and foremost from the looming failure of the Paris arrangement to deliver the necessary scale and ambition of climate mitigation. Second, unilateral pricing of emission may affect the competitiveness of domestic products vis a vis imports. While border adjustments can address the competitiveness concern, a neutral approach to BTA s would call for exempting domestic exporters from coverage, resulting yet again in emission leakage. International cooperation leading to an agreed minimum carbon price, coupled with tools of enforcement would be the best way to address the competitiveness and leakage concerns.[682]

678 International Monetary Fund (IMF) (n 640) 16–17.

679 ibid 19–22.

680 There are many instances worldwide where carbon tax revenue is used domestically for technology upgrade, climate finance, or energy efficiency. See, Partnership for Market Readiness (PMR) (n 660) 126; David Klenert and others, 'Making Carbon Pricing Work for Citizens' (2018) 8 Nature Climate Change 669; Holzer (n 602) 236–238.

681 Peter C Cramton, David JC MacKay and Axel Ockenfels (eds), *Global Carbon Pricing: The Path to Climate Cooperation* (MIT Press 2017) 1–5.

682 Chapter 2, Parry and others (n 634) 43.

The biggest challenge against a multilateral agreement on carbon pricing is the difference in needs and capacities between countries. As a result, a uniform pricing-for-all strategy, only on its own would be inimical to the reciprocal building of trust among the partners over the long-term.[683] Therefore, in addition to a global commitment to carbon pricing, need-specific support has to be made available, as indicated before,[684] by deploying a portion of the revenue generated by the pricing schemes. With respect to a global approach, it may also be required that a new platform is developed.[685] While the WTO ticks many of the boxes of an ideal cooperation platform for carbon pricing, the subject-matter jurisdiction of the institution currently does not cover international taxation.

Instead of immediately taking on the challenges of a multilateral agreement, smaller, club-based approaches are an alternative for building cooperation from bottom up. Nordhaus is one of the proponents of the club approach.[686] Cooperation on a global scale is difficult because an increase in the number of parties lead to a gradual erosion of trust. In contrast, among like-minded club members, cooperation is comparatively easier to achieve. Nordhaus' suggestion therefore involves parties with significant overlaps of interests forming clubs, where an agreed carbon price floor would be established.[687] Existing preferential agreements between trading partners can serve as initial platforms for building such clubs. Use of trade agreement would further enable the opportunity to enforce the commitments through punitive tariffs.[688]

There are significant complementarities between the Common Concern based LCT diffusion agenda and existing calls for cooperation regarding carbon pricing. It should not be surprising as both share the same goal to resolve the climate-related collective action challenge. The doctrine of Common Concern of Humankind can lend a legal character to the already existing insight, thereby strengthening this complementarity. We return to this point in the concluding section.

---

683 Elinor Ostrom, *A Polycentric Approach for Coping with Climate Change* (The World Bank 2009).

684 See pp. 144, 148 above.

685 Weitzman (n 636) 131.

686 William Nordhaus, 'Climate Clubs: Overcoming Free-Riding in International Climate Policy' (2015) 105 American Economic Review 1339.

687 Nordhaus, 'Climate Clubs and Carbon Pricing' (n 635).

688 See chapter 21 in, Nordhaus, *The Climate Casino: Risk, Uncertainty, and Economics for a Warming World* (n 670). Chapter 6 of this volume addresses issues regarding the position and utility of trade sanctions in the proposed technology diffusion narrative.

D *The Measure Proposed*

We propose a carbon pricing measure that is designed to address the Common Concern of low-carbon technology diffusion. It is comprised of two principal parts. The first part is that of introducing a carbon price preferably through a tax, or a tariff scheme, as appropriate. Second, in deserving situations, the revenue generated from carbon pricing of imports should be recycled as clean technology diffusion support back to the product origin countries. While the latter proposition is not novel,[689] it remains unexplored in literature and practice. Not only is technology support essential for a carbon pricing scheme to address the problem of low-carbon technology diffusion, but it may also further enhance the justifiability of any possible WTO legal inconsistency suffered by the measure.

Generally, taxation approach would stand out as the most familiar way of implementing a carbon price. That being said, it is equally true that the approach will make little sense in case a domestic tax base is absent. In the latter situation, only a tariff-based scheme makes sense. However, adoption of a tariff-based approach is novel and may bring forward a few technical hurdles.

With respect to the taxation approach, an appropriate method of border adjustment can be an information intensive process. As hinted before, complexities can arise as domestically a carbon tax can be levied in different levels (i.e. upstream, or downstream), but the imports only come under its purview at the product stage. The easiest method would be to require the foreign producer to assess its site carbon footprint,[690] which can then be used to determine emission per unit of output.[691,692] Any approximation attempt should abide by the

---

689 There is one earlier example of such a proposition being made. See, Aaron Cosbey and others, 'A Guide for the Concerned. Guidance on the Elaboration and Implementation of Border Carbon Adjustment' (Entwined 2012) Policy report paras 82–85 <http://www.ssrn.com/abstract=2178312> accessed 25 October 2020. The authors mention that use of the BTA revenue for technology transfer moves the trade regime closer to the CBDR principle (para 84).

690 The methodology for site footprinting are less complex. Also there are several compatible standards available at the public domain. For more, see Tao Gao, Qing Liu and Jianping Wang, 'A Comparative Study of Carbon Footprint and Assessment Standards' [2013] International Journal of Low-Carbon Technologies < https://academic.oup.com/ijlct/article/9/3/237/812115 > accessed 25 October 2020.

691 Simplistically for example, the general formula would be the approximate net emission multiplied by the carbon price and divided by the total amount of widgets produced at a particular calculation period.

692 A comparable real example is the way the US superfund tax on petroleum was proposed to be applied on imports. Products derived from the domestically taxed substances, which contained the taxed chemical of a volume of more than 50% of its material weight was brought within the measure's coverage. *United States – Taxes on Petroleum and Certain*

constraint that the proposed burden should never be greater upon the imports, when compared to the domestic counterparts.

As tariffs are a relatively less granular tool when it comes to reflecting a carbon price, one should not expect a price approximation closely related to a product's actual emission footprint. A carbon tariff would call for additional product classification beyond the six digits of the harmonised system (HS).[693] An additional two digits can be added to further categorise products in different bands of emission profiles, which should then be matched to varying levels of tariffs. This can be particularly useful with respect to products that are not complicated, but emission-intensive (e.g. metals like aluminium and steel). To illustrate, research suggests that for each kilogram of primary aluminium production, emission of greenhouse gases can range from 5.92 $KgCO_2eq$ to 41.10 $KgCO_2eq$, to which subsequent operation add a fraction more.[694] A member seeking to regulate emission therefrom can choose the relevant tariff lines (HS codes 7601–16) and further classify it at 8 or 10 digits HS level into several bands of increasing emission intensity. While the lowest category can be allowed zero tariffs, the maximum emission footprint could be imposed tariff at the bound level.

Most importantly, irrespective of whichever approach is used, it is of utmost importance that the benefit of the revenue generated through the introduced scheme is shared with the developing and the least-developed countries. To that effect, it is proposed that the bulk of the import revenue from carbon pricing accruing to a developed country should be used to support technology upgradation by the developing country firms. It is possible to envisage channelling of such revenue through the established funds (e.g. the Green Climate Fund (GCF)) by creating a new window of technology support granted to the

Imported Substances [1987] GATT Panel L/6175-34S/136 2–3. There are earlier US examples of similar cooperation with respect to Superfunds. In current respect sharing of information such as the energy source, used processing methods, and efficiency technologies in place would be relevant.

693 'Harmonized Commodity Description and Coding Systems (HS)' (*UN Trade Statistics*) <https://unstats.un.org/unsd/tradekb/Knowledgebase/50018/Harmonized-Commodity-Description-and-Coding-Systems-HS> accessed 25 October 2020. According to the UNTS, 'The Harmonized System is an international nomenclature for the classification of products. It allows participating countries to classify traded goods on a common basis for customs purposes. At the international level, the Harmonized System (HS) for classifying goods is a six-digit code system'.

694 Meenu Gautam, Bhanu Pandey and Madhoolika Agrawal, 'Carbon Footprint of Aluminum Production', *Environmental Carbon Footprints* (Elsevier 2018) 210–211 <https://linkinghub.elsevier.com/retrieve/pii/B9780128128497000088> accessed 25 October 2020.

trade exposed sectors of the developing countries.[695] The developing countries should also follow suite wherever possible. Revenue utilisation from the earlier CDM projects will serve as a lesson in this regard. In case such a scheme cannot be put into action, bilaterally arranged revenue returns will be the next best solution. Support from the carbon pricing revenue should focus on the countries that are eligible to obtain technological assistance under the UNFCCC technology mechanism (TM) and the Paris technology framework (TF). Apart from ensuring LCT diffusion to the developing and least-developed export origins, such recycling schemes would contribute to the legitimacy enhancement of the carbon pricing measure by making equitable considerations and implementing the differentiated aspect of climate responsibility.[696] It would also play an important role in bolstering justifiability of the measure with respect to the WTO laws, as explained later in this chapter.

II WTO Eligibility of a Carbon Pricing Measure

Although regulation of GHG emission through taxes or tariffs are guided by the same purpose, treatment of these measures under the WTO laws could become significantly different from each other. In scholarly literature, WTO compatibility of carbon taxes has dominated the attention,[697] whereas little examination

695 Peter C Cramton and others, 'Price Carbon – I Will If You Will' in Peter C Cramton and others (eds), *Global carbon pricing: the path to climate cooperation* (MIT Press 2017). Authors therein suggested contribution of revenue to the GCF. Similar suggestion was made by Scott and Rajamani in the context of utilising the revenue of the EU Aviation Emission Trading Scheme. Also J Scott and L Rajamani, 'EU Climate Change Unilateralism' (2012) 23 European Journal of International Law 469.

696 Stiglitz (n 674).

697 A large body of literature already exists on the issues of border adjustment of a carbon tax. To indicate a few, Hufbauer, Charnovitz and Kim (n 551) chs 1, and 2; Robert Howse and Antonia Eliason, 'Domestic and International Strategies to Address Climate Change: An Overview of the WTO Legal Issues' in Thomas Cottier, Olga Nartova and Sadeq Z Bigdeli (eds), *International trade regulation and the mitigation of climate change: World Trade Forum* (Cambridge University Press 2009) 60–69; Henrik Horn and Petros C Mavroidis, 'Climate Change and the WTO: Legal Issues Concerning Border Tax Adjustments' (2010) 53 Japanese YB Int'l L 19; Joost Pauwelyn, 'Carbon Leakage Measures and Border Tax Adjustments under WTO Law' in Geert Van Calster and Denise Prevost (eds), *Research handbook on environment, health and the WTO* (Edward Elgar 2013); Holzer (n 602); Joel P Trachtman, 'WTO Law Constraints on Border Tax Adjustment and Tax Credit Mechanisms to Reduce the Competitive Effects of Carbon Taxes' (Resources for the future (RFF) 2016); John S Odell, 'Our Alarming Climate Crisis Demands Border Adjustments Now' (ICTSD 2018) Think Piece. Nordhaus indicated the complexity in calculation of carbon footprint and suggests use of tariffs instead. Nordhaus, 'Climate Clubs and Carbon Pricing' (n 635); Also, Cottier, Nartova and Shingal (n 643).

has been made on the tariff opportunity.[698] Practically, however, any exporting country challenging the carbon pricing measure by an importing country can argue that such actions are ineligible; in other words, outright inconceivable within the framework of WTO. If not so, a complainant can still argue that such measures result in discriminatory treatment of their products in a market. In response, any party taking a carbon pricing measure will need to argue that such measures are possible and do not result in discrimination. If found discriminatory, a respondent can further argue that such discrimination has a legitimate policy grounding and hence it is justifiable under the WTO law. As these arguments are unpacked step by step, the present section will tackle the eligibility aspect, i.e. whether or not the proposed pricing measure is outright incompatible with the existing framework of trade rules. Later discussions will address the aspects of discriminatory impact and potential legitimacy of the measure. These sections are interrelated without any doubt.

Due to the intended impact of a carbon pricing measure on how imports are produced abroad, in trade law terms they are known as 'process and production measures' (PPM s).[699] With regard to the PPM s, the thorny and yet to be decided question is that whether the reach of domestic trade policy can extend so far as to dictate production methods despite the fact that such conditions do not influence the physical properties of the product. Carbon pricing falls in this category of non-product related PPM s, commonly known as NPR-PPMs. The place of this category of measures under WTO laws continues to be controversial.

A *Eligibility of Carbon Taxes*

The relevant law that determines border adjustability of domestic taxes is Article II:2(a) of the General Agreement on Tariffs and Trade (GATT).[700] A plain reading of the provision shows that an equivalent charge can be imposed on imports when there is a domestic tax on products similar to the imported good, or on an input the import is produced from. The standard of required equivalence is informed by the national treatment provision as found in Article III:2

---

698 The only serious assessment of this option is made by Thomas Cottier, Olga Nartova, and Anirudh Shingal in a journal contribution. See, Cottier, Nartova and Shingal (n 643).

699 See a brief refresher on the concept, see Chapter 3 II C (ii) at pp. 135-136 above.

700 It provides that "Nothing in this Article shall prevent any contracting party from imposing at any time on the importation of any product: (a) a charge equivalent to an internal tax imposed consistently with the provisions of paragraph 2 of Article III in respect of the like domestic product or in respect of an Article from which the imported product has been manufactured or produced in whole or in part;".

of the GATT.[701] In essence, Article II:2(a) reflects the destination principle of taxation.[702]

The only trade dispute where the decision sheds some light on Article II:2(a) is the *India – Additional duties*.[703] There the Appellate Body (AB) had the opportunity to clarify the exception the provision forms to the general prohibition against subjecting imports to any fiscal burden other than 'ordinary customs duties' (OCDs) and 'other duties and charges' (ODCs) at the border.[704] It was also explained that the standard of non-discrimination in Article III:2 is the metric that informs the measurement of 'equivalence' between the border charge and internal tax, as mentioned earlier.[705] Also, the comparison between the charge and the tax from a national treatment point of view is an integral part of Article II:2(a); so much so that a separate claim of breach is not required with respect to Article III:2.[706]

The imposition of a charge equivalent to a domestic carbon tax upon imports can be challenged because of the ambiguity in characterisation of the tax itself.[707] As the explanation above shows, border adjustments are allowed regarding taxes imposed "in respect of an article from which the imported product had been manufactured or produced in whole or in part".[708] Kateryna Holzer identifies that it is conceptually problematic to consider that GHG emission, upon which tax is based, is an 'article' from which the product is manufactured.[709] Moreover, the legal provision entrusted with the maintainance of

701 For more on the national treatment standard, see section III below.

702 It is '[a] regime of international taxation according to which consumption taxes are levied where products are consumed. The rates of VAT and excise applied are those of the country of final consumption, and the entire revenue accrues to that country's budget. This system ensures production neutrality, since indirect taxes do not discriminate between foreign and domestic producers, and exports are exempt from domestic taxation. The disadvantage is the need for monitoring of cross-border trade flows'. 'Destination Principle of Taxation – Oxford Reference' < https://www.oxfordreference.com/view/10.1093/oi/authority.20110810104737666#:~:text=A%20regime%20of%20international%20taxation,accrues%20to%20that%20country's%20budget.&text=See%20also%20origin%20principle%20of%20taxation. > accessed 25 October 2020.

703 *India – Additional and Extra-Additional Duties on Imports from the United States* [2008] Appellate Body Report WT/DS360/AB/R, DSR 2008:XX 8223.

704 ibid 153.

705 ibid 170, 172, 175.

706 ibid 180.

707 Holzer (n 602) 99–100.

708 Article II:2(a), General Agreement on Tariffs and Trade; Hufbauer and others noted that the french version of the provision is even more restrictive in its wording. Hufbauer, Charnovitz and Kim (n 551) 68.

709 Holzer (n 602) 100–101. The author points out that '[a] carbon tax is levied not on an input but on emissions released in the production process'. She also pointed out that Article

equivalence between the import charge and domestic tax, only covers "internal taxes or other internal charges [...] applied, directly or indirectly, to like domestic products".[710] This prompted Frieder Roessler to hold that border adjustments apply to those domestic taxes that are imposed on products, and not to the taxes that tackle negative externalities but are borne by the producers (e.g. energy tax).[711]

On the contrary, the view proffered here is that a carbon tax does indeed apply to a product, directly or indirectly. As a result, it comes under the purview of the GATT Article III:2,[712] and also thereby allow border adjustment. When a tax is considerable as applied to a product is a decision to be made based on evidence. As long as the tax burden is shifted to the final consumer through price, it should be considered as applied to the product. As one Panel explained that the requirement for a tax to be within the scope of the GATT Article III:2 is the existence of some connection between a product and the tax, even if indirect.[713] Also as explained earlier, the choice of imposing a carbon tax in a specific stage of energy production and use is itself a function of administrative expedience. In all cases, the burden can be reasonably expected down to the final consumer. Joost Pauwelyn also held the view that an upstream tax can nonetheless be considered as applied to a product where there is a close enough nexus between the tax and the product for the destination principle to be applicable.[714]

Further support to such a conclusion can be drawn from the rules under the WTO Agreement on Subsidies and Countervailing Measures (ASCM),[715] which regulates the extent to which an analogue export adjustment is possible. Given the assumption that the nature and limits of border adjustment regarding imports and exports must be at par, the argument would be that if duties like carbon taxes are allowed to be withdrawn from exports under WTO rules, the

---

III:2, which also conditions the subject-matter scope of taxes adjustable at the border include, among others, those that are "applied indirectly" to products.

710 First sentence, Article III:2, General Agreement on Tariffs and Trade (n 426).

711 Frieder Roessler, 'India – Additional and Extra-Additional Duties on Imports from the United States' (2010) 9 World Trade Review 265, 271.

712 It should be noted that the subject-matter scope of Article III:2 has been read to be wide enough so as to prevent any possibility of discrimination of imports through taxation. *Japan – Taxes on Alcoholic Beverages* [1996] Appellate Body Report WT/DS8/AB/R; WT/DS10/AB/R; WT/DS11/AB/R, DSR 1996:I 97 17–20.

713 *Mexico – Tax Measures on Soft Drinks and Other Beverages* [2006] Panel Report WT/DS308/R, DSR 2006:1 43 [8.40, 8.42].

714 Pauwelyn, 'Carbon Leakage Measures and Border Tax Adjustments under WTO Law' (n 697) 476–480.

715 Agreement on Subsidies and Countervailing Measures (n 434).

same should be allowed to be applied on similar imports. Dealing with indirect taxes, paragraph (g) in Annex I of the ASCM indicates that such taxes can be withdrawn from exports up to the extent to which they applied on like products destined for domestic consumption. Indirect taxes, as understood in the ASCM, cover "all taxes other than direct taxes and import charges".[716] Based on the same arguments that carbon tax is considerable as applied to a product, there is a strong probability that a carbon tax would be deemed as an indirect tax under the paragraph (g) and therefore be found as adjustable regarding exports.[717] To retain a consistent scope of border adjustments, they should also be adjustable regarding imports.

Lastly, from a natural science perspective, it is possible to consider the tax as one on certain types of energy sources that serve as input in the product. David Stern points at the laws of thermodynamics which imply that any production would require a minimum amount of energy to "carry out the transformation of matter".[718] Moreover, like tangible matters used as input in the production process, energy is also a non-reproducible factor of production. Both are consumed during production, releasing waste in the end.[719] The energy sources (e.g. coal, or petroleum) that are taxed under carbon pricing are tangible and fall within the domain of goods. So also does electricity, irrespective of the absence of physical dimension.[720] Put together, an argument that fossil-based energy sources or electricity produced therefrom are Articles from which a product is made is indeed conceptually a valid one.

In conclusion, despite the divisive views, there are strong arguments on behalf of the position that carbon taxes are eligible for border adjustments under the WTO laws, so long as the like domestic products are also effectively brought under its coverage. Of course, a clear decision to that effect passed down in a dispute would be most welcome, but such may not occur any time soon. Nevertheless, there exist very sound reasons as shown above to construe that energy sources are very much akin to the other material inputs used in production. So,

716 Footnote 58, ibid.

717 Coppens, *WTO Disciplines on Subsidies and Countervailing Measures* (n 440) 516–518.

718 David Stern, 'Stochastic Trend: Energy as a Factor of Production' (*Stochastic Trend*, 18 April 2010) <http://stochastictrend.blogspot.com/2010/04/energy-as-factor-of-production.html> accessed 25 October 2020.

719 ibid.

720 *Canada – Certain Measures Affecting the Renewable Energy Generation Sector / Canada – Measures Relating to the Feed-in Tariff Program* (n 4) para 7.11; Thomas Cottier and others, 'Energy in WTO Law and Policy' in Thomas Cottier and Panagiotis Delimatsis (eds), *The prospects of international trade regulation: from fragmentation to coherence* (Cambridge University Press 2011) 215.

like taxes on input materials, energy taxes and other comparable forms of carbon pricing should also be adjustable at the border. If none of these arguments is found as salient enough, one can turn to the next alternative, i.e. imposition of a carbon tariff. Eligibility of this option is discussed next.

B *Eligibility of Carbon Tariffs*

Although it is arguably easier to implement carbon pricing for imports through a tariff scheme, the technicalities involved nevertheless call for close attention. Tariffs, also known as ordinary customs duties (OCD s), are legitimate levies applicable upon products in connection with importation.[721] Tariffs are administered following a harmonised system (HS) of product classification,[722] and organised into schedules.[723] Schedules are the basis on which tariff negotiations are carried out to bring down the overall level of restrictions.[724] Successful tariff negotiations result in bound rates of duties that members do not exceed. However, tariff actually applied (i.e. the applied rate) by a WTO member can, and often do, go much below the bound rate, as long as all similar imports from all origin are treated in the same fashion.

With respect to the simulation of a carbon pricing measure using tariffs as detailed earlier, a member would need to modulate the applied rates within the sub-classes of a six-digit HS code.[725] This entails that the lowest band of tariff, possibly zero, would be imposed on the sub-group with the smallest carbon footprint in a class of products. Then it would be required that the applied rate is increased step-by-step for product sub-groups with higher footprints. Eventually, the highest applicable rate may even go beyond the bound rates. This is especially true for the developed countries whose duties are already bound at very low levels with little or no room between those and the rates applied. From the legal point of view, this will require in many cases deconsolidation of the tariff commitments. As Thomas Cottier and others have already shown, consolidated tariff lines are not irreversible, and there are lawful ways to reach deconsolidation.[726] Modifying a member's schedule of concessions to

---

721 Paragraphs (a) and (b), Article II:1, General Agreement on Tariffs and Trade (n 426).

722 According to the World Customs Organization, the HS system covers 5000 product groups in 6-digit codes. The HS codes are used for 98% of international trade transactions. See, 'What Is the Harmonized System (HS)?' (*World Customs Organization* (WCO)) <http://www.wcoomd.org/en/topics/nomenclature/overview/what-is-the-harmonized-system.aspx> accessed 25 October 2020.

723 Article II, General Agreement on Tariffs and Trade (n 426).

724 Article XXVIIIbis, ibid.

725 See p. 151 above.

726 Cottier, Nartova and Shingal (n 643) 1022–1023.

deconsolidate tariffs is a multi-party exercise of rebalancing interests through exchanges of concessions among them and subsequent multilateralisation of the outcome.[727] However, if such a negotiated settlement cannot be attained, applied carbon tariff beyond bound rates will fall foul of the GATT Article II:1(b) with or without drawing similar withdrawal of concessions from other parties.

Another issue is that while over time the price of GHG emission moves upwards, a tariff rate is expected to move in the opposite direction. It is recognised by the WTO members that tariffs are an obstacle that should be reduced over time.[728] Although initially it may not be a manifest conflict, if a tariff scheme is carried out over the long-term, the outcome will not be in line with the spirit of the organisation anymore.

In conclusion, the tariff approach offers an attractive, viable, possibly even easier alternative option to engage in carbon pricing over the short or medium-term. In terms of efficiency, tariffs may not be as robust a tool as tax, but they will indeed be easier to implement due to lesser complexity. However, deconsolidation of tariff lines and determination of appropriate tariff rates could nonetheless pose some technical challenge. In cases where the tariffs will go beyond the bound rates of duty, it can draw challenge and retaliation from other partners. Such problems can be resolved through appropriate consultation. We will come back to this point in the end.

III Discriminatory Impact of Carbon Pricing

The non-discrimination principle in the GATT and the other WTO covered agreements form the essential bulwark to preserve the equal economic freedom of the members. At the heart of the non-discrimination rule lies a time-tested insight – that unfettered markets are in most cases the best approach for the allocation of global resources through cross-border trade.[729] The commitment to non-discrimination preserves this position by ensuring that

727 Article XXVIII, General Agreement on Tariffs and Trade (n 426).

728 Article XXVIIIbis: 1, ibid.

729 The preamble to the GATT described the contracting parties' goal as achieving growth, expansion of trade and resource utilization by reducing trade barriers and discriminatory practices. See, Preamble, ibid. Advent of the WTO sought to build a viable multilateral system on that core, while further qualifying the nature of growth – by express subscription to the notions of optimality of resource usage, sustainable development, environmental protection and differentiation. See, Recital 4, Preamble, Marrakesh Agreement Establishing the World Trade Organization (n 226).

equal terms of competition prevail for any products in every market within the members' jurisdiction. In legal terms, this commitment results in two distinct obligations. One, known as the 'most-favoured nations' (MFN) obligation, compels the WTO members to accord imports the same opportunity to compete in the domestic market as other imports belonging to the same category.[730] The other, known as 'national treatment' (NT) obliges members to accord to imports at least as favourable treatment as provided to comparable domestic products with respect to fiscal and non-fiscal measures.[731] As well known, however, deviation from the non-discrimination commitment is permitted to, *inter alia*, meet specific policy goals in line with the general exception clause in the GATT.[732]

In case a complainant challenges the trade aspects of a carbon pricing measure, it will be on the basis of the argument that despite different emission profiles, the final products are the same. Therefore, putting a carbon price either through tax or a tariff influences the market price of the product and takes the competitive edge away to the detriment of the complainant's economic interest. This argument can be fashioned as an MFN violation claim to challenge both tax and tariff-based approaches, indicating different pricing of similar imports. The tax-based approach can face an additional challenge of NT violation, indicating detrimental tax burden upon imports *vis a vis* domestic products. Below, it is shown that the claims of discriminatory carbon pricing can be responded to on merits by arguing either that emission profile of a product is a significant criterion capable of outweighing other similarities between products, or a difference in the imposed fiscal charges between such products is not discriminatory at all. It can be further argued that even if considered discriminatory *prima facie*, it is possible to save a revenue recycled carbon pricing policy under the GATT exception clauses.

The current section explores the extent of the above arguments in the context of the present-day understanding of the non-discrimination obligation in GATT, as well as the provisions for legitimising the exceptions therefrom. The goal is to flag the contentious questions, which will be taken up for further examination in relation to the doctrine of Common Concern.

A *Product Comparability: The Test of 'Likeness'*

As the first step of non-discrimination analysis in the context of a dispute, the test of likeness establishes the comparability between the alleged

730 Article I:1, General Agreement on Tariffs and Trade (n 426).
731 Article III:2, ibid.
732 Article XX, ibid.

discriminated product or a category thereof and the product or group that is beneficially treated.[733] With respect to the carbon pricing proposal, such comparability question could, for example, very simplistically be like whether aluminium billets (HS 760120) smelted using geothermal energy is comparable to the same smelted using fossil fuels. Depending on the nature of the claim, determination of the scope of comparability between products would be of utmost importance.

It is important to start by recounting the concept of likeness. Under both Articles I and III of GATT, the test of likeness is essentially the same, that is, a case-specific[734] exercise of comparing a range of attributes of the products under inspection,[735] to determine how closely they actually or may potentially compete in a given market.[736] The required closeness of the competitive relationship between products to satisfy the test depends on the legal context in which the analysis takes place.[737] Moreover, the level of closeness would also later inform the discrimination analysis, to decide as to the level of intervention that may amount to a disruption of the competitive relationship.[738] The range of product attributes that would generally merit attention during a likeness analysis are grouped into four categories, namely – (i) physical properties, (ii) end uses, (iii) consumer perception, and (iv) tariff classification.[739] A Panel is free to be guided by the factual context while giving weight to the evidence considered across all the categories.

---

733 Reference to 'likeness' here refers to the product comparison standard in relation to a non-discrimination analysis especially under the GATT. It is a general reference to 'like products' under Article I and 'like products' and 'directly competitive and substitutable' (DCS) products in Article III:2 and the related *Ad* Note. The differences in the standard of comparison in these terms are further clarified during analysis.

734 *Japan – Taxes on Alcoholic Beverages* (n 712) 21–22; *European Communities – Measures Affecting Asbestos and Asbestos Containing Products* [2001] Appellate Body Report WT/DS135/AB/R, DSR 2001:VII 3243 [99].

735 *European Communities – Measures Affecting Asbestos and Asbestos Containing Products*, ibid para 103.

736 ibid paras 102–3, 109.

737 'The concept of "likeness" is a relative one that evokes the image of an accordion. The accordion of "likeness" stretches and squeezes in different places as different provisions of the WTO Agreement are applied'. *Japan – Taxes on Alcoholic Beverages* (n 712). It is especially important with respect to Article III:2. When the competing products are very close, there is no room for even a minimum tax difference under the first sentence of Article III:2. In case the products compared are 'directly competitive and substitutable' the standard allows some room for a tax to vary.

738 ibid.

739 *European Communities – Measures Affecting Asbestos and Asbestos Containing Products* (n 734) para 101.

With respect to the general categories of product attributes considered during the likeness analysis, it should be kept in mind that those were never meant to form a conceptual straightjacket. Nevertheless, the practice of considering the four categories of attributes is a well-reasoned interpretative outcome, proven through the test of time.[740] Characteristic to the early Appellate Body (AB) judgments, the likeness test was developed following the Vienna Convention step by step;[741] first approaching the literal meaning, then the context, and later drawing upon subsequent practice of the parties.[742] While following of these exact four categories are not a binding rule, it is advisable as per dictates of efficiency, cohesion, and formality. However, these fourfold categories, are not immune to evolution over time when circumstances require. The AB itself was clear on this point when holding the following:

> These criteria are, it is well to bear in mind, simply tools to assist in the task of sorting and examining the relevant evidence. They are neither a treaty-mandated nor a closed list of criteria that will determine the legal characterization of products. More important, the adoption of a particular framework to aid in the examination of evidence does not dissolve the duty or the need to examine, in each case, *all of the pertinent evidence*. […] Accordingly, whether the Border Tax Adjustments framework is adopted or not, it is important under Article III:4 to take account of evidence which indicates whether, and to what extent, the products involved are – or could be – in a competitive relationship in the marketplace.[743]

740 *Japan – Customs Duties, Taxes and Labelling Practices on Imported Wines and Alcoholic Beverages* [1987] GATT Panel BISD 34S/83 [5.5]; *European Communities – Measures Affecting Asbestos and Asbestos Containing Products* (n 734) paras 91–92.

741 *United States – Standards for Reformulated and Conventional Gasoline* [1996] Panel Report WT/DS2/R, DSR 1996:I 29 [6.8].

742 The evidence of subsequent practice comprises solely of the GATT era report on Border Tax Adjustments. GATT, 'Report by the Working Party on Border Tax Adjustments' (1970) L/3464. Especially this excerpt from pargraph 18 of has been the key foundation of interpreting 'like product'. "[…] problems arising from the interpretation of the term should be examined on a case-by-case basis. This would allow a fair assessment in each case of the different elements that constitute a 'similar' product. Some criteria were suggested for determining, on a case-by-case basis, whether a product is 'similar'; the product's end-uses in a given market; consumers tastes and habits, which change from country to country; the product's properties, nature and quality."

743 *European Communities – Measures Affecting Asbestos and Asbestos Containing Products* (n 734) paras 101, 102 [emphasis supplied].

So there is no legal obstacle in considering the emission profiles during a likeness analysis, provided that the emission footprints have a bearing on the closeness of the competitive relationship between and among products. On this latter issue, at least two arguments are possible to show that emission footprint may impact how closely products compete in a market. For one, given the impending hazard of climate change, it can be assumed that consumers would indeed prefer the product that contributes less to emission. Another argument, drawing analogically from the AB position in the *Canada – Renewable Energy* dispute, is that products with differing emission footprints may belong to different markets. We elaborate upon these two arguments below.

The argument that the products' emission profile would influence consumer choice is plausible but only occasionally salient. The proponents of this argument indicate that in *EC – Asbestos* the AB found consumer preference for health-risk-free product to be likely even in the absence of evidence.[744] By extension, therefore, it could be said that if evidence of the risk of unmitigated emission and related consumer preference is submitted, it would be positively assessed by a dispute settlement Panel.[745] However, the issue that arises is that when actual evidence is looked at, this intuitive presumption may not hold. Except for some developed countries, final consumers may not always act as price averse.[746] Had they been so, the situation of free-riding would not arise in the first place.[747] Moreover, in situations where consumers' preferences are prone to external influence,[748] a Panel or AB would be cautious so as not to put such weight to this factor that fully diminishes other similarities between the compared product groups. Especially when the product compared is an input (going to firms), price-sensitivity of the consumers is more manifest than in a similar situation involving a final product (going to individual consumers).

744 ibid 123, 130, 139, 145.

745 The argument could be further refined holding that there is a latent consumer demand in the market that is masked by the availability of similar products with higher carbon footprints. ibid 123; *Korea – Taxes on Alcoholic Beverages* [1999] Appellate Body Report WT/DS75/AB/R, WT/DS84/AB/R, DSR 1999:I 3 [115].

746 With respect to environment friendly (green) products in general, research finds that consumers do not act as green as they say. For a general survey, see, Jonas Lehmann and Yossi Sheffi, 'Consumers' (Not so) Green Purchase Behavior' Draft Paper 26, 3 (2019) <https://sheffi.mit.edu/sites/sheffi.mit.edu/files/2019-08/Consumers%27%20%28not%20so%29%20Green%20Purchase%20Behavior.pdf> accessed 25 October 2020.

747 The fundamental tenet of environmental economics is the assumption that price responsive behaviour of the consumers give rise to free-riding.

748 Holzer (n 602) 113.

The argument that products with different emission profiles could be considered to exist in different markets and therefore are non-competitive is one that is made drawing analogical support from the AB decision in the *Canada – Renewable Energy*[749] dispute. The AB in that dispute held (albeit on a different context) that the market for electricity produced from renewable sources is not the same as that produced from fossil fuels, when the inherent differences in costs, supply, and demand characteristics, and underlying policy intents are taken into due consideration.[750] Some scholars raised the question whether, by analogy, it is possible to argue that maybe products differing in emission footprint also do not belong in the same market.[751] But the challenge is that unlike the electricity scenario there is no single sharp distinction here, as products would be made from various (often mixed) electricity sources and would have a varying emission portfolio, making one clear distinction difficult to find. An analogy as such can lead to an outcome where there are as many markets as there are product groups of a distinct emission footprint, which is unreasonable. However, if the comparison is between products exclusively made from renewable electricity (i.e. zero carbon footprint) and those having some carbon footprint, there may be some plausibility that the argument will hold water.

So, although a product's physical properties have been merited as a key category of consideration, it does not rule out the opportunity to consider the non-physical attributes (NPA) as well.[752] But the extent to which emission footprint as an NPA will set products competitively apart from one another is difficult to determine. For reasons detailed above, a finding that products differing on emission footprint do not compete at all in a given market would be highly implausible. Also, the carbon price measure itself is adopted assuming a competition between such products, which the measure sets out to modify through

749 *Canada – Certain Measures Affecting the Renewable Energy Generation Sector / Canada – Measures Relating to the Feed-in Tariff Program* (n 500).

750 For details, see p. 218 below.

751 Steve Charnovitz, 'Border Tax Equalization' in Jagdish N Bhagwati, Pravin Krishna and Arvind Panagariya (eds), *The world trade system: trends and challenges* (The MIT Press 2016) 40; Cottier, 'Renewable Energy and Process and Production Methods' (n 609) 3. Cottier, however, remains critical of the AB view. It should also be noted that the Panel in the dispute did not take this view either.

752 It is also worth highlighting that the key source of interpretation, i.e. the border tax adjustment report, talks about products properties in general and not 'physical' properties. In the *Brazil – Taxation* dispute, Panel's likeness analysis focuses on the BTA expression rather than the *Asbestos* criteria. *Brazil – Certain Measures Concerning Taxation and Charges* [2017] Panel Report WT/DS472/R; WT/DS/497/R [7.122].

corrective intervention. Much would depend on the magnitude of the difference in emission footprints between products. Going back to the aluminium example, there is plausibility in the argument that aluminium from geothermal smelters and that from coal smelters are not 'like product' under the first sentence of Article III:2. But it is difficult to decide when fossil fuel and coal smelted aluminium is considered.

The ultimate finding in a dispute would indeed depend upon the way a Panel exercises its discretion in attaching relative weight to the differing non-physical properties vis a vis the possible similarity in other categories. Here lies another challenge. If argued that any non-physical properties should be given weight against similarity in other categories, it would reduce the value of likeness determination as a vanguard against protectionism. One probably could think of some criteria that would guide the discretion of the tribunal while making an assessment. It is not difficult to see the role of Common Concern in that respect. We will return to this issue in a later part.

B *Standard of Discrimination: Change in Conditions of Competition*

In case products varying in emission footprints are found to be in a close enough competitive relationship, the question then arises whether subjecting those products to different financial burdens can be considered as discriminatory. As already indicated, whether a claim of MFN or and NT violation or both is raised depends on the adoption of tax or tariff approach in pricing. The claim regarding MFN would, in essence, be that there are some products that face a lower tax burden or custom duty in the respondent's market compared to the claimant's products. With respect to the tax based pricing approach, an additional national treatment (NT) violation claim could be lodged when claimant's products face a higher tax amount vis a vis some comparable do mestic products.

With respect to the legal analysis of finding discrimination, Articles I and III:2 of GATT show some similarities, also differences. Although 'discrimination' is not a term used in this provision, there is certainly a homogenous understanding of this notion that finds expression through the treaty terms. Under both provisions, a determination of any measure falling within its clutches as discriminatory entail answering whether the effect thereof is translated into loss of competitive opportunity for the complainant's products.[753] However,

753 *United States – Measures Concerning the Importation, Marketing and Sale of Tuna and Tuna Products* [2012] Appellate Body Report WT/DS381/AB/R, DSR 2012:IV 1837 [7.278]; *European Communities – Measures Prohibiting the Importation and Marketing of Seal Products* [2014] Appellate Body Report WT/DS400/AB/R, WT/DS401/AB/R, DSR 2014:I 7

given the differences in terms of scope and subject-matter focus of the two provisions, the factors that are probative of discrimination in the respective legal settings indeed differ. This point is elaborated in the next paragraph. Another feature that is common in both instances is that the legal analysis of finding discrimination is independent of subjective intent. It is 'value-neutral' in the sense that the effect in the market in terms of competition between products, proven empirically, is the sole determiner of the existence of discrimination.[754]

As mentioned above, despite the same goals, analyses under Articles I and III go through distinct legal sequences. It is because the analysis of discrimination under respective provisions follows closely the structure and the wording therein. Under the MFN provision,[755] the analysis involves determining whether the challenged measure grants an 'advantage', i.e. one that competitively favours products in the market. If so, not extending the same 'immediately and unconditionally' to all products would amount to discrimination. Whereas regarding a claim of internal taxation related NT breach under Article III:2, finding of discrimination follows a very different structure. Under this provision, the degree of similarity between two compared product groups determine the magnitude of difference in fiscal burden that may be considered discriminatory. If products are so close as to be considered 'like' under the first sentence,[756] tax burdens upon them have to be the same. If products are not 'like' but nevertheless 'competitive and substitutable' with each other, the analysis will be covered by the second sentence of the provision,[757] where existence of a *de*

[5.88]; Peter Van den Bossche and Werner Zdouc, *The Law and Policy of the World Trade Organization: Text, Cases and Materials* (Fourth edition, Cambridge University Press 2017) 308–309, 344–345.

754 Intent based argument, i.e. a measure is not discriminatory if not pursued with a protectionist intent, has long before rejected by the Appellate Body for good reasons. See *Japan – Taxes on Alcoholic Beverages* (n 712) para 119.

755 The relevant part of the text of the provision (GATT Article I) provides that "[…] any advantage, favour, privilege or immunity granted by any contracting party to any product originating in or destined for any other country shall be accorded immediately and unconditionally to the like product originating in or destined for the territories of all other contracting parties."

756 It provides that "The products of the territory of any contracting party imported into the territory of any other contracting party shall not be subject, directly or indirectly, to internal taxes or other internal charges of any kind in excess of those applied, directly or indirectly, to like domestic products."

757 The second sentence of Article III:2 of GATT provides that "[…] no contracting party shall otherwise apply internal taxes or other internal charges to imported or domestic products in a manner contrary to the principles set forth in paragraph 1." The reference to

minimis level of tax difference would not matter. Any greater level of difference would be found discriminatory if it is maintained 'so as to afford protection to domestic production' (SATAP test, in short).[758] Finding on the latter is decided upon based on the design, structure, and operation of the measure as well as the actual amount of tax differential.

(i) The Possible Outcome under National Treatment Obligation

Without a doubt, a carbon tax will impose a differential burden upon products, both domestic and foreign. The question whether such differential tax burden would be considered a breach of Article III:2 or not, irrespective of being origin neutral, depends upon contextual factors. One issue would be how the comparable product groups are drawn. Another question would be how closely competitive the products are considered to be.

According to the Panel in *Argentina – Hides and Leather*, a comparison of the tax burden for the purpose of discrimination would take into account actual and not the nominal burden.[759] The Panel argued that otherwise, a member would be able to shift the tax bases and impose the same nominal rate with different outcomes between imports and domestic products. This finding disadvantages a carbon tax even when it applies a uniform rate of emission price. The problem is that the tax is imposed on products with respect to their negative emission externality, which is not a traditional product attribute.[760] This leads to the difficulty in arguing that different final tax burdens are non-discriminatory. To illustrate the point, had the uniform rate been based upon the presence of any trace element (e.g. mercury) in the product in a varying degree, the actual fiscal burden would not be discriminatory despite the amount being different from one to another. In this illustration, the tax can easily be characterised as a tax on the ingredient itself, applied in a uniform manner. But the same argument is not easy to apply with respect to embedded emissions by considering the tax as that on the emission externality. It is because the

---

'competitive and substitutable' products come from the explanatory note of the provision. This was understood as covering a wider scope of products that compete with each other, but are not 'like' under the narrow sense of the term in the first sentence. Van den Bossche and Zdouc (n 753) 366–370.

758 This standard arises from Article III:1 that is referred in the second sentence (see footnote above). The provision maintains that differential treatment "should not be applied to imported or domestic products so as to afford protection to domestic production."

759 *Argentina – Measures Affecting the Export of Bovine Hides and the Import of Finished Leather* [2001] Panel Report WT/DS155/R, DSR 2001:V 1779 [11.182]; Holzer (n 604) 123; Van den Bossche and Zdouc (n 753) 364.

760 For an alternative, wider understanding of 'product', see p. 190-191 below.

emission has not crossed the border with the product, unlike an incorporated ingredient. However, if one conceptualises a manufactured product to be composed of not only what it physically embodies, but also of the externality it imposes, there would be an opportunity to characterise a uniformly applied carbon tax as not discriminatory. We return to this argument in the following section.

Nevertheless, one fact that may lead one to be optimistic about implementing a carbon tax without drawing a challenge is that so far, none of the tax measures successfully challenged at the WTO is a transparent single-rate tax applied equally upon domestic production and imports. The WTO disputes involving taxation of alcoholic beverages are the best analogues. In all those disputes, the challenged tax rates were such that are designed in a tiered fashion, effectively putting most of domestic production on a lower bracket than the imported ones. One may hope that a transparent carbon price, applied even-handedly, would not even draw a challenge. A case on point, as mentioned by Pauwelyn, is the excise tax on ozone-depleting chemicals in the US, which has remained in place for more than a decade without being challenged.[761]

Following the discussion above, it is clear that regarding an assessment of the breach of NT obligation, the methods of drawing up the compared product groups, as well as the level of comparison would play an important role in finding discrimination. While comparing the final tax burden on products may allow for easier finding of discrimination, if the tax rates are compared, it could be found that despite different final burden, the measure itself does not discriminate. In contrast, if only the imported highly taxed products are compared with any available low taxed domestic products, finding of discrimination will be easy.[762] It is however assumed here that the comparison will be between the general incidences of taxation upon all domestic against all complainants' imports.[763] As the issue itself is not yet fully resolved, we attempt to find and weigh analogical support from the existing jurisprudence in the following paragraphs.

761 Sections 4681 and 4682, United States Internal Revenue Code; Pauwelyn, 'Carbon Leakage Measures and Border Tax Adjustments under WTO Law' (n 697) 493.

762 This is what Ehring termed as a 'diagonal' test. Lothar Ehring, 'De Facto Discrimination in World Trade Law' (2002) 36 Journal of World Trade 921, 924, 926.

763 Ehring argued that taxation 'in excess' should require further proof of asymmetric detrimental impact on imports, i.e. the benefit of differentiated taxation is reaped by a relatively larger proportion of domestic industries than the foreign. However, such a requirement may raise predictability concerns as the asymmetric impact on the complainant would depend on the distribution of its industries across the high and low taxed categories. See ibid.

If the carbon tax is covered under the first sentence of Article III:2, there would be a very slim chance for it to be found non-discriminatory, unless it is agreed that an even-handed application of emission-based tax rate would not be discriminatory despite the varying final burden of tax.[764] Otherwise according to the existing jurisprudence, any difference of tax burden would be considered 'in excess' and therefore discriminatory.

However, if the measure falls under the second sentence of the provision because the compared products are rather considered as directly competitive and substitutable, it would have slightly better chances to pass the discrimination assessment. The provision requires competitive and substitutable products to be 'similarly taxed', allowing differentiation below a *de minimis* threshold. Moreover, the dissimilar taxation would be discriminatory only when it is undertaken "so as to afford protection" (SATAP) to domestic production.[765]

The existence of the SATAP requirement may allow for further flexibility. It ought to be noted that in a GATT-era approach to the interpretation of 'likeness' the phrase "so as to afford protection" was understood as bringing consideration of the policy objective into play.[766] Under the WTO jurisprudence, that approach was rejected very early on,[767] as well as the express influence of the SATAP standard was limited only to the second sentence of Article III:2. According to the Appellate Body (AB), the proof of the SATAP requirement required establishment of the protective application of a measure.[768] It entails an overall assessment of the design, structure, and application of the measure with a view to objectively ascertain the true purpose.[769] If no protective

764 This argument is made later in the chapter in light of the doctrine of Common Concern. See section IV B at p. 192 and onwards.

765 *Japan – Taxes on Alcoholic Beverages* (n 712) 116.

766 *United States – Measures Affecting Alcoholic and Malt Beverages* [1992] GATT Panel DS 23/R-39S/206 [5.23–5.26]. This is the 'aim and effects' approach. See for details, Robert E Hudec, 'GATT/WTO Constraints on National Regulation: Requiem for an "Aim and Effects" Test' (1998) 32 The International Lawyer 32, 626–635.

767 *Japan – Taxes on Alcoholic Beverages* [1996] Panel Report WT/DS8/R; WT/DS10/R; WT/DS11/R, DSR 1996:I 125 [6.16–6.17, 6.33]; Van den Bossche and Zdouc (n 753) 362.

768 *Japan – Taxes on Alcoholic Beverages* (n 715) 18. According to the AB, '[a]lthough it is true that the aim of a measure may not be easily ascertained, nevertheless its protective application can most often be discerned from the design, the architecture, and the revealing structures of a measure'. See Hudec's critique of the point, Hudec (n 766) 631–632.

769 *United States – Section 337 of the Tariff Act of 1930* [1989] GATT Panel BISD 36S/345 [5.2.2]; *Philippines – Taxes on Distilled Spirits* [2012] Appellate Body Report WT/DS396/AB/R, WT/DS403/AB/R, DSR 2012:VIII 4163 [250]; *Japan – Taxes on Alcoholic Beverages* (n 712) 29.

application is found, dissimilar taxation of directly competitive and substitutable products do not breach NT commitment.[770]

As the SATAP requirement closely examines a measure in terms of its operation, it may serve to show a carbon-tax as non-discriminatory, especially in circumstances where the additional financial burden due to the taxation falls evenly between domestic and foreign products. However, it is not conclusive as facts will differ in every case.[771] The SATAP analysis, in essence, would look at whether the foreign producers predominantly bear the high tax burden or not.[772] Therefore, if the tax is introduced in a sector where the foreign products are more polluting in nature, it would surely be considered as discriminatory under the current standard.

(ii) The Possible Outcome under the Most-favoured Nation Obligation

Not much examination is required to hold that in many cases a carbon price measure would be found to be breaching the most-favoured nation obligation. Establishing a breach of Article I of the GATT requires four preconditions to be fulfilled– (i) the measure should fall within the described scope of the provision, (ii) the products under consideration should be 'like', (iii) the measure in question should be granting an advantage, (iii) the advantage should be shown as not granted to all like imports, immediately and unconditionally.[773] A tax measure falls within the scope of the MFN provision without any doubt. The related question of 'likeness' between products have already been addressed, showing that there will unavoidably be products that are in a competitive relationship in the market facing different tax or tariff burden due to variation in their carbon footprints. The only remaining question is whether the benefit of a lesser tax burden on some imports compared to others will be considered an 'advantage' within the meaning of the GATT Article I.

In the context of the open-ended wording as "*any* advantage, favour, privilege or immunity" as used in Article I, the term advantage has been given a wider interpretation. It was held that any measure providing favourable competitive opportunity to some product or affecting the competition between

770 Van den Bossche and Zdouc (n 753) 374.

771 *Korea – Taxes on Alcoholic Beverages* (n 745) para 137.

772 *Chile – Taxes on Alcoholic Beverages* [2000] Panel Report WT/DS87/R, WT/DS110/R, DSR 2000:I 303 [7.158]. The panel therein found that 95% of the foreign products fell under the highest tax brackets under the disputed measure.

773 *European Communities – Measures Prohibiting the Importation and Marketing of Seal Products* (n 753) para 5.57.

products would be considered an advantage.[774] Similarly granting of favourable marketing opportunity was also found to be an 'advantage'.[775] Tariff differentiation among like products was also deemed as advantageous.[776] As a result, provided that products with different embedded emissions are considered to be 'like', different tax or tariff burdens would surely be seen as affecting their competitive relationship and according advantage to the products that face lower fiscal burden. Such benefit, when not extended to all other polluting products, would constitute a breach of the MFN obligation.

C *Justifying the Pricing Measures*

A carbon pricing measure that fails to meet the non-discrimination standard can yet be potentially saved under the general exception clause. The GATT Article XX is best understood as the balancing scale maintaining an equilibrium between one member's policy-driven market interventions and others' benefits guaranteed under the trade legal regime.[777] As a result, Article XX serves as the prominent, if not the only avenue that allows harmonisation of trade commitments with other global concerns.[778] The requisite conditions for compliance with Article XX come in two tiers.[779] First, the policy intent of the carbon pricing measure must be brought within the coverage of one of the sub-paragraphs (a) to (j). This is known as provisional justification. For the purposes of this chapter, the policy intent should be taken to be diffusion of low-carbon technology and thereby contribution to enhanced emission mitigation. Second, the opening sentence of Article XX, (i.e. the *Chapeau*) requires fair implementation of any exceptional measure that is found as provisionally justifiable.

---

774 *European Communities – Regime for the Importation, Sale and Distribution of Bananas* [1997] Panel Report WT/DS27/R, DSR 1997:II; DSR 1997:III 7.239.

775 *United States – Certain Measures Affecting Import of Poultry from China* [2010] Panel Report WT/DS392/R, DSR 2010:V 1909 [7.417]; *United States – Measures Concerning the Importation, Marketing and Sale of Tuna and Tuna Products* (n 753) paras 237–240.

776 *European Communities – Conditions for the Granting of Tariff Preferences to Developing Countries* [2004] Panel Report WT/DS246/R, DSR 2004:III 1009 [7.58–7.60].

777 *European Communities – Measures Prohibiting the Importation and Marketing of Seal Products* (n 753) para 5.301.

778 *United States – Import Prohibition of Certain Shrimp and Shrimp Products* (n 94).

779 *United States – Standards for Reformulated and Conventional Gasoline* (n 93) 22; *United States – Import Prohibition of Certain Shrimp and Shrimp Products* (n 94) 119–121; *Brazil – Measures Affecting Imports of Retreaded Tyres* [2007] Appellate Body Report WT/DS332/AB/R, DSR 2007:IV 1527 [139]; *United States – Measures Affecting the Cross Border Supply of Gambling and Betting Services* [2005] Appellate Body Report WT/DS285/AB/R, DSR 2005:XII, p. 5663 (Corr.1, DSR 2006:XII, 5475) [292]; Van den Bossche and Zdouc (n 753) 554–556, 606–607.

With regard to provisional justification analysis, the policy intent mentioned above can potentially find cover under the sub-paragraphs (g),[780] or (b),[781] or even somewhat arguably under the subparagraph (a).[782] The legal requirement for a measure to find refuge under these provisions is generally twofold. First, a preliminary analysis will take place to ensure that the measure is structurally suited to contribute to the relevant policy goal.[783] There is a unanimity of scholarly opinion that a measure designed to tackle climate change will not fail at this stage.[784] We, therefore, do not dwell on this question. Second, the preliminary analysis is followed by a closer examination of the relationship between the measure and the policy goal, stringency of which is guided by the language of the specific provision (i.e. 'relating to' or 'necessary'). In addition, the wording of the subparagraph (g)[785] demands even-handed application, i.e. that the disputed measure is also implemented domestically. This section will briefly focus on the challenges possibly arising with respect to the relationship analysis part of the provisional justification assessment.

With respect to the low-carbon technology diffusion aspect of the carbon pricing measure, the Chapeau analysis takes special importance, as it dictates attention to be paid to the prevailing differences in situations between countries.[786] This is the only opportunity to introduce the equitable considerations and respect for the CBDR principle in implementation of the carbon pricing measure. This bears central importance, as detailed hereunder, not only to ensure that clean technology diffusion takes place, but also to justify a carbon pricing measure facing scrutiny at the WTO.

780 The text provides: "(g) *relating to* the conservation of exhaustible natural resources if such measures are made effective *in conjunction with* restrictions on domestic production or consumption;" [emphasis supplied].

781 The text provides: "(b) *necessary* to protect human, animal or plant life or health;" [emphasis supplied].

782 The text provides: "(a) *necessary* to protect public morals;" [emphasis supplied].

783 With respect to XX(g) this requires determination that the measure involves 'conservation of exhaustible natural resources. With respect to XX(a) and XX(b), it entails analysis of the design of the measure in question to service public morals and protection of human, animal, plant life or health. Van den Bossche and Zdouc (n 753) 558–559, 574, 579.

784 Marceau, 'The Interface between the Trade Rules and Climate Change Actions' (n 534) 13–15; Trachtman (n 697) 17; Holzer (n 602).

785 See, n 780 above.

786 The chapeau of Article XX allows an GATT inconsistent measure to be maintained '[s]ubject to the requirement that such measures are not applied in a manner which would constitute a means of arbitrary or unjustifiable discrimination between countries where the same conditions prevail, or a disguised restriction on international trade [...]'. General Agreement on Tariffs and Trade (n 426).

(i) Provisional Justification under Article xx(g): the 'Relating to' Standard

Among the 'related to' and the 'necessity' standards used to designate the required relationship between a measure and policy goals, the former, used in subparagraph (g) is the comparatively less stringent one. Test under the 'relating to' standard requires establishing a "close and genuine relationship of ends and means" between the policy goal and the measure itself.[787] As a stable climate is considerable as an exhaustible natural resource,[788] and a carbon pricing measure directly contributes to the mitigation of its worsening by reducing emission, as well as increasing demands for clean technologies, a close relationship between the pricing measure and conservation of the climatic conditions clearly exists.

As aforementioned, the subparagraph (g) also calls for even-handed application of the measure, which is easier to fulfil with respect to a carbon tax, but may pose a problem regarding a carbon tariff. A carbon tax that is applied domestically and also adjusted at the border is even-handed in effect. Whereas, a carbon tariff is by definition applicable only on imports. In cases where products or processes similar to those subjected to a carbon tariff exist domestically without being subjected to any comparable regulation, the even-handedness requirement will not be met.

(ii) Provisional Justification under Article xx(a) and (b): the 'Necessity' Standard

With respect to the necessity standard under sub-paragraphs (a) and (b), we note that whether the pricing of emission to facilitate technology diffusion and climate mitigation would be considered 'necessary' or not will be determined by 'weighing and balancing' all the relevant factors.[789] Under this approach of necessity determination, the apparent trade restrictiveness of a measure would be balanced against the extent to which the measure is apt to make a material contribution over time to the policy goal as well as the importance of

787 *United States – Import Prohibition of Certain Shrimp and Shrimp Products* (n 94) para 136.

788 Current jurisprudence concur that any resources, including the renewable ones, can be 'exhaustible' within the meaning of the provision. See, *United States – Standards for Reformulated and Conventional Gasoline* (n 741) para 6.37; *United States – Import Prohibition of Certain Shrimp and Shrimp Products* (n 94) paras 130–134; *United States – Measures Concerning the Importation, Marketing and Sale of Tuna and Tuna Products – Recourse to Article 21.5 of the DSU by Mexico* [2015] Panel Report WT/DS381/RW [7.512].

789 *Korea – Measures Affecting Imports of Fresh, Chilled and Frozen Beef* [2001] Appellate Body Report WT/DS161/AB/R, WT/DS169/AB/R, DSR 2001:I 5 [159–162].

the policy goal itself.[790] Overall, it remains a holistic exercise of qualitative and quantitative analysis of three categories of factors,[791] i.e. (i) relative importance of the goal, (ii) potential contribution of the measure to the goal, (iii) trade distortive impact and reasonable availability of less distorting alternatives.[792]

With respect to the assessment of the contribution of the carbon pricing measure to the policy objective, it is submitted that when applied to the specific situation under the subparagraph (a), a key challenge will be to establish the moral unacceptability of excessive greenhouse gas emission among the domestic population. Public morality, taken as the standard of right and wrong,[793] is understood as varying amongst the WTO members.[794] Therefore, the outcome will differ from case to case, subject to clear proof of the domestic moral rejection of an emission intensive lifestyle. In comparison, under the subparagraph (b), the contribution of carbon pricing to the protection of life, and health can be easily established through use of the available scientific evidence linking reduction of GHG emission to the safeguarding of ecosystems, livelihoods, and communities in the long-term.

With respect to the other factors playing a role in the necessity analysis under the subparagraphs (a) and (b), the nature of legal relationship between the WTO laws and the climate rules, especially the UN Framework Convention (UNFCCC), and the recent Paris Agreement will require determination. As almost all the WTO members are also part of the climate instruments, the latter would, in all probability, exert influence as a rule "applicable in the relation between parties".[795] While the Paris Agreement commitment to 1.5°C temperature

---

790 *European Communities – Measures Prohibiting the Importation and Marketing of Seal Products* (n 753) para 5.209. In both disputes, it was recognised by the Appellate Body that it is possible to qualitatively assess what a measure is apt to contribute in the long run.

791 ibid 5.214–5.215.

792 *Korea – Measures Affecting Imports of Fresh, Chilled and Frozen Beef* (n 789) para 164; *European Communities – Measures Prohibiting the Importation and Marketing of Seal Products* [2014] Panel Report WT/DS400/R, WT/DS401/R, DSR 2014:II 365 [7.630]; *United States – Measures Affecting the Cross Border Supply of Gambling and Betting Services* (n 779) paras 309–311.

793 *United States – Measures Affecting the Cross Border Supply of Gambling and Betting Services* [2005] Panel Report WT/DS285/R, DSR 2005:IX 5797 [6.465]; *China – Measures Affecting Trading Rights and Distribution Services for Certain Publications and Audiovisual Entertainment Products* [2014] Panel Report WT/DS363/R and Corr.1, DSR 2010:II 261 [7.759]; *European Communities – Measures Prohibiting the Importation and Marketing of Seal Products* ibid paras 7.410, 7.631–7.632.

794 *European Communities – Measures Prohibiting the Importation and Marketing of Seal Products* (n 753) para 5.199.

795 Article 31(3)(C), Vienna Convention on the Law of Treaties 1155 UNTS 331 (1969); *European Communities – Measures Affecting the Approval and Marketing of Biotech Products* [2006]

limitation will serve to showcase the importance for climate mitigation and diffusion of low-carbon technology, the fact that under the Paris Agreement commitments are voluntary could work against the necessity determination. On the one hand, a complainant could argue that a strict carbon pricing measure imposed by the respondent would restrict the independence granted to a member under the Paris rules. On the other hand, the respondent can rebut holding that the voluntariness of commitment under Paris is available to both the parties. Therefore, the respondent would be entitled to the policy space to introduce carbon pricing as long as there is a sufficient nexus between the measure and the policy goal, despite an indirect extraterritorial impact.[796]

Lastly, the assessment of the lesser trade-restrictive alternatives could also be challenging. Emission mitigation can be pursued in different forms, including ways that do or do not impact the market (e.g. a trade-restrictive carbon tax, against trade neutral afforestation). The Paris Climate Agreement leaves the parties to determine the appropriate means of mitigation, also providing opportunities to develop cooperation based market measures for the purposes of mitigation.[797] Although a complainant can always show alternative means of emission reduction, it is not clear whether different means should be considered as alternates to each other, given the fact that the more emission is reduced the better it is for the planet in the long run.

(iii) Differentiation and Article XX Chapeau

As the final step of the justification analysis, the Chapeau ensures that the manner of implementation of a measure does not add to the existing inconsistency that has been found to be provisionally justifiable. Purposed to prevent misuse of the Article XX carve-outs,[798] the wording of the Chapeau, among other things, forbids a measure to be applied a way that causes "arbitrary or unjustifiable discrimination between countries where the same conditions prevail". Past history shows that disputed measures often fail to

---

Panel Report WT/DS292/R / WT/DS293/R / Add.1 to Add.9 and Corr.1, DSR 2006:III 847. See in particular the paragraph 7.68 and footnote 243 of the Panel Report. In the mentioned footnote, the Panel notes that "[...] it would be incongruous to allow the interpretation of a treaty to be affected by rules of international law which are not applicable in the relations between all parties to the treaty, but not by a subsequent practice which does not establish the agreement of all parties to the treaty regarding the meaning of that treaty". The report has not been appealed.

796 For a concise overview on the extraterritorial aspects of the argument, see Chapter 6, below.

797 Articles 4 & 6 respectively, Paris Agreement (n 28).

798 *United States – Standards for Reformulated and Conventional Gasoline* (n 93) 22.

pass this test.[799] As this requirement is to avoid arbitrariness in application of a measure to similar countries, it logically follows that in case the countries are differently situated, the implementation of a measure with respect to them must vary as well. Countries upon which the same trade-restrictive measure would apply will face very different impact, in case prevailing conditions therein are not same. This absence of consideration of the different conditions results in further discrimination that may be 'unjustifiable or arbitrary'.[800] In the context of the present measure seeking to spread climate technologies, the question arises that whether the principle of CBDR, as found in the climate regime, would inform the WTO rules to such an extent that a member would be required to modulate the application of carbon pricing. We focus on this question below.[801]

Deciding whether 'same conditions prevail' is partially an interpretative exercise, which according to the AB is better fulfilled by understanding the conditions in the context of the specific policy objectives.[802] So far there has been no dispute where it has been found that prevailing conditions between countries are different. With respect to a carbon pricing measure, however, the matters may not be the same. The policy goal pursued by the imposition of a carbon price is mitigation of GHG emissions, also diffusion of low-carbon technology. Given that both the trade and climate treaty regimes have widespread membership and almost all WTO members are signatory to the Paris Agreement; following Article 31(3)(c) of the Vienna Convention,[803] interpretation of whether 'same conditions prevail' between countries in the context of climate mitigation goal, would be influenced by the CBDR principle. As a result, implementation of GATT inconsistent trade measures to address climate change must vary between countries, as same conditions do not prevail among all.

However, the nature and degree of differentiation could give rise to some complexities. We recall that the standard of differentiation dictated by the

799 Namely, *US – Gasoline* (DS2), *US – Shrimp* (DS58), *US – Gambling* (DS285), *Brazil – Retreaded Tyres* (DS332), and recently *EC – Seals* (DS400, DS401).

800 *United States – Import Prohibition of Certain Shrimp and Shrimp Products* (n 94) paras 165, 177.

801 We do not venture into interpretation of 'disguised restriction on international trade', although it is accepted that it could also be useful. For what the phrase may come to mean, see, Lorand Bartels, 'The Chapeau of the General Exceptions in the WTO GATT and GATS Agreements: A Reconstruction' (2015) 109 American Journal of International Law 95, 123.

802 *European Communities – Measures Prohibiting the Importation and Marketing of Seal Products* (n 753) para 5.299–5.303.

803 Vienna Convention on the Law of Treaties (n 795).

CBDR principle has evolved over time from a strict dichotomy between developed and developing countries to an approach of varying flexibility depending upon context.[804] Especially in the context of the Paris Agreement, one area in which the CBDR has been watered down is mitigation commitments, as all countries, irrespective of development status, are required to voluntarily undertake, implement and ambitiously revise respective mitigation contribution (the NDCs).[805] One key exception is that the developing countries 'shall' be provided support to implement ambitious targets.[806] Such support will come in the form of financial assistance, technology transfer, and support for capacity building. With regard to financial support, the classic dichotomous CBDR principle is at play putting the developed countries under strict obligation to support developing ones.[807] The obligation is slightly qualified with regard to capacity building.[808] Whereas with regard to technology transfer, the relevant provision holds that support "shall be provided to developing countries", but omits the subject from whom it would be coming.[809] To sum these all up in the present context, the only possible conclusion is that to the extent carbon pricing implemented by a developed country imposes upon developing WTO members additional mitigation responsibility, related financial, technological, and capacity building support must be forthcoming.[810] Otherwise, the carbon pricing measure shall be considered as unjustifiably discriminatory.

Hence, the revenue recycling aspect of the proposed carbon pricing measure has a role and value beyond that of implementing the Common Concern doctrine based low-carbon technology diffusion narrative. Not only would it facilitate diffusion of LCTs, it would also justify the carbon pricing measure, if it is found to be primarily inconsistent with the non-discrimination rules. Support extended from the developed to the developing countries in the context of a carbon pricing measure would modulate its impact as per dictates of the

804 See pp. 126-127 above. For greater details on the evolution of CBDR, see, Lavanya Rajamani, 'Ambition and Differentiation in the 2015 Paris Agreement: Interpretative Possibilities and Underlying Politics' (2016) 65 International and Comparative Law Quarterly 493.

805 ibid 20–21. On the whole, Article 4 of the Paris Agreement imposes similar standard of commitment upon developed and developing countries.

806 Article 4.5, Paris Agreement (n 28).

807 Paragraph 1 and 3 of Article 9, ibid. It is provided that the '[d]eveloped country Parties shall provide financial resources to developing country parties […]'. Also, 'developed country parties should continue to take the lead in mobilizing climate finance […]'.

808 Article 11.3, ibid.

809 Article 10.6, ibid.

810 Cosbey and others (n 689) 5; For the necessity of incorporating the CBDR principle in the context of the EU-ETS, Scott and Rajamani (n 695).

Chapeau. Moreover, this assistance function would also square the trade measure off with the fundamental climate law principle of differentiation.

However, the above path in which the CBDR principle enters the domain of trade rules raises a thorny question. As we see, due to the nature of the order of legal analysis, the requirement of adjusting a measure with the developing country situations comes into play only when the measure in question is considered discriminatory, and the recourse to the general exception clause is taken. Otherwise, i.e. in cases where a carbon pricing measure is found as not discriminatory, the scope of making a demand for equitable application vanishes. We discuss this issue, among others, in the next section.

The analysis of the discriminatory effect of carbon pricing under the WTO law reveals that its application on imports will probably be considered as discriminatory. However, it is possible that in some instances a tax measure may be found as not discriminatory, provided that the products under consideration are not fully alike, yet competitive, and the difference in tax rates are found as not applied to protect domestic production. As the last resort, the measure proposed may find refuge under the GATT Article XX, more confidently so when the revenue recycling aspect to ensure technology diffusion is appropriately implemented. The latter will ensure that the impact of the measure is modulated in accordance with the different prevailing situations in the countries. Of course, most of these WTO inconsistency issues can be resolved through cooperation. Of special importance in this regard would be multilaterally agreeing on a carbon price floor,[811] and mutual recognition arrangements to encourage domestic implementation of pricing schemes.[812]

IV Alternate Reading Aided by Common Concern

The final part of this chapter is intended to serve as a counterfactual reading of the WTO consistency of the proposed carbon pricing approach in a scenario where the doctrine of Common Concern is in the place of a full-fledged legal principle. Based upon the doctrine, we revisit the legal analysis presented in the previous part, now with the purpose of finding a frame that allows the trade rules to be understood in a fashion that does not put them at loggerheads with the efforts to price carbon emission. Any possibly harmonising reading should be taken as an example of the utility of the doctrine.

811 See as discussed in section I C at pp. 159-160 above.

812 Trachtman (n 697) 29.

Before heading further, it is important to note the ways Common Concern can build an inroad to the domain of trade rules. We recall that the exact legal status of the notion is difficult to pin down as it continues to mature. However, even in the absence of cooperative trade rulemaking along the lines depicted in Chapter 3 before, the common concern of humankind remains a foundational legal notion with relation to climate change. As a result, the traditionally agreed meaning of the notion can already influence the evaluation of climate motivated trade measures. What is also plausible is that it will eventually grow out of the treaty boundaries and become a self-standing notion, with a potential claim to become a part of customary law like sustainable development. Like the latter notion, Common Concern also has the legal structure of a principle, i.e. a propositional nature that is adaptable to various emerging circumstances, including the current one (i.e. trade rules). When applicable, it can be assumed that Common Concern, like sustainable development, will supply 'color, texture, and shading' to the provisions of the WTO law.[813] In so doing, it will carry the agenda of sustainable development further.[814] The notion should be readily available to take recourse to as a terminological or formal context of any WTO legal provision,[815] especially in cases where members' deployment of climate protection motivated trade measures are in question. Although use of the doctrine as a further context in line with Article 31(3)(c) of the Vienna Convention requires identical membership to both treaty regimes,[816] the answer in this specific case would indeed be affirmative.[817]

Following paragraphs retrace the previously presented analysis and looks at the role of the Common Concern doctrine in influencing the outcome.

A Regarding the Test of 'Likeness'

It was shown earlier that a key issue with respect to the likeness analysis regarding a carbon pricing measure was the uncertainty of the relevance and

813 *United States – Import Prohibition of Certain Shrimp and Shrimp Products* (n 94) para 153.

814 The relationship between the Common Concern doctrine and the principle of Sustainable Development has been elaborated at the outset. See Chapter 1 VI A at p. 48 above.

815 Under Article 31(1) of the Vienna Convention, while exploring meaning of a treaty term, or under Article 31(3)(c) as an applicable norm modifying parties obligations.

816 *European Communities – Measures Affecting the Approval and Marketing of Biotech Products* (n 795) para 7.71–7.72; *European Communities and Certain Member States – Measures Affecting Trade in Large Civil Aircraft* [2011] Appellate Body Report WT/DS316/AB/R, DSR 2011:I 7 [844–845]; Graham Cook, *A Digest of WTO Jurisprudence on Public International Law Concepts and Principles* (Cambridge University Press 2015) s 4.2.2.

817 Almost all WTO Members are also Members of the UNFCCC, as well as the Paris Agreement. However, the United States has declared to opt out of the later.

influence of non-product related attributes in finding likeness between products. We also found that the likeness test is a well-developed and very fine-grained exercise of judicial discretion. To expect that recourse to the doctrine of Common Concern would outright lead to finding products' differing only on account of emission footprints to be 'unlike', would be unreasonable. Nevertheless, in ways mentioned below, the doctrine can bring valuable contributions to make the discretionary judgment more informed.

The key contribution of the doctrine can be in opening the opportunity to consider differences in non-physical product attributes in a likeness test. Common Concern can assist to assign a wider meaning to the term 'product' in the references to 'like product' in the non-discrimination obligation. Product is a generic term, the meaning of which ought to adapt over the changing course of time.[818] Literally, it means "[t]hing produced by an action, operation, or natural process; a result, a consequence; spec. that which is produced commercially for sale"[819] – meaning that it cannot exist independent of any process that produces it, i.e. production. This attachment of a product with production process distinguishes it from other similar terms, like 'material', or 'element', and must be given appropriate attention during interpretation of the term. It finds a reasonable accommodation when a product is understood essentially as anything that has been worked upon and made ready for the market, in the process of which resources morph and produce positive (e.g. price) and negative (e.g. emissions, and waste) externalities. Therefore, a comparison between products should also be a comparison between their production externalities as inherent characteristics of the product itself. Since the issuance of the working party report on border adjustment in 1970, which supplied the core aspects of the likeness criteria,[820] much in this world has changed. The whole climate legal regime has since come into existence, underscored by the common concern principle, and highlighting the unavoidable necessity of altering polluting production processes. The doctrine of Common Concern would, therefore, dictate that likeness analysis of products take account of production externalities in the same way as any other product attributes. This understanding of the term 'product', assisted by the doctrine of Common Concern would also be in line with the WTO goals of sustainable development and optimal resource usage.

818 Gabrielle Marceau, 'Evolutive Interpretation by the WTO Adjudicator' (2018) 21 Journal of International Economic Law 791, 803–805.

819 *The New Shorter Oxford English Dictionary on Historical Principles*, vol 2 ([Repr], Clarendon Press 1993).

820 See (n 742) above.

The impact of such a broader understanding of the notion of a product can influence the likeness analysis through two of the established categories of assessment. First, assessment of a product's properties for the purpose of likeness determination should also take account of non-physical properties, most importantly, their emission profiles. Second, it would also require the dispute settlement Panels to make a cautious assessment of consumer preference in a given market. In situations where product prices do not reflect important non-physical qualities, consumer preference for the lower-priced product should be taken as a distortion that hides the real choice a consumer would have made, had the price been adjusted to reflect the true cost. The Common Concern doctrine would encourage a Panel to make this analysis. It is also relevant since sustainable consumption is also enshrined as an SDG.[821]

However, not all non-physical attributes (NPAs) should be given the same footing in likeness test, and the doctrine can serve as the metric as to which attributes make the cut, and those that would not. The Common Concern doctrine can further come into play in determining the weight to be attached to emission footprints of compared products. Recalling that the test is to determine the extent of competition between two products in the market, depending on the circumstances, for example, the amount of emission involved or the magnitude of the difference of carbon footprints among products, this attribute could be assigned appropriate weight directly so as to tip the balance with other characteristics displaying similarities between the products.

Overall, the doctrine of Common Concern can indeed guide the Panels' exercise of discretion as they weigh and balance all the relevant product attributes. As mentioned before, it should not be taken as a binary approach, meaning that products differing in emission footprints will automatically be considered unlike. Truncating the analysis at this stage would have the effect of precluding the requirement of differential adjustment of the measure through revenue recycling, as noted earlier. However, there remains a possibility that substantially large difference in emission footprints among the compared products in a market where consumers are proven to be sensitive towards carbon emissions may culminate in a finding of the absence of likeness. In other circumstances, different emission footprint may nevertheless set products competitively apart, but not exactly unlike.[822]

821 Goal 12, United Nations General Assembly (n 210) 22–23.

822 For example, finding products as 'directly competitive and substitutable' and not 'like' under Article III:2, due to difference in emission footprints.

B Regarding the Legal Standard of Discrimination

Recalling earlier analysis, we found that the main challenge with respect to the legal standard of discrimination and carbon pricing is that the current standard is most likely to find differential fiscal burdens upon competing products to be discriminatory. It is because when two products are considered alike, the price differential resulting from variable tax or tariffs would be considered as depriving one product of equal opportunity to compete against the other. Here we point out the fact that such a comparison between the products has never taken into account the possibility of pre-existing distortions in the market. This point is salient because for measures like carbon pricing, the economic and policy intuition (the environmentalist approach) that drives it assume such distortion and therefore attempts to cure it and bring back a level playing field. As a result, while both the carbon pricing measures and the legal standard of discrimination are geared to create equal terms of competition in the market, different treatment of the initial market conditions in the respective approaches put these two in apparent conflict.[823]

Therefore, we hold that a key reason for finding carbon pricing as discriminatory under the WTO laws is the fundamental difference between the WTO and the environmentalist intuitional thinking about how markets work. Under the WTO law, the principle assumption about the markets would appear to be that those are not distorted, in the backdrop of which a carbon tax or tariff induced differences in fiscal burden appear as distortive. In contrast, from an environmentalist perspective, a carbon price is the response to an already distorted market, where the intervening fiscal measure restores equity. Like the blind men inspecting an elephant, although these two views contradict each other, none are wrong. While the rules of trade cover the whole universe of cross border transactions, the environmental regime spills into the trade regime when there is a market failure (due to negative externalities). Differential tax burdens in an undistorted market are discriminatory, but the same is not true when there would be a market failure. The doctrine of Common Concern can be of particular utility to flag situations of pervasive market failure, which lead to destabilisation and massive loss of global welfare. The doctrine would also indicate that a legal assessment of discrimination with regard to any corrective fiscal interventions like carbon pricing in such a market should be more informed of the nuances involved. An informed approach in this regard would help to harmonise the divergent trade

823 Jagdish N Bhagwati, 'Reflections on Climate Change and Trade' [2008] Brookings Trade Forum 171, 171.

and environmental intuitions into a common understanding of the product markets.

The harmonised approach can be built upon acceptance that while in an undistorted market any differential intervention can discriminate against complainant's products, if a market is distorted, some differential treatment may be warranted to keep equal terms of competition. So, application of the legal standard of non-discrimination in any specific case, a distinction ought to be made between government interventions in undistorted markets and the situations of market failure. A beneficial parallel in this regard can be drawn with the Appellate Body decision in the dispute *Canada – Renewable Energy*, where the AB opined that the important imperatives of avoiding negative externalities can prompt the government to intervene in the market, which is not illegal *per se.*[824] Also to be noted is the already existing understanding that private markets do not guarantee efficient production of global public goods (GPG s).[825] So, in any dispute challenging government intervention, the fact that the situation in question is classifiable as a Common Concern should make a Panel aware of the possibility of the existence of a market failure. Combined with the proposed likeness analysis that takes into account the negative production externalities of any product, any Panel would have adequate information on the existence and extent of the distortions in a market arising from such unpriced externalities and affecting the competition between products. Based upon that, the fiscal interventions should not be termed discriminatory as long as they address that preexisting distortive competition gap between the products.

It should be clear that following this harmonised approach in the analysis of discrimination would not really require a deviation from the current legal standards. It would rather call for a more informed implementation of the same. The doctrine of Common Concern would aid the fact-based exercise of ensuring equal opportunities to compete between products. From a technical point of view, it would mean that a Panel should take into account the prior market conditions to construe what may amount to an advantage or excess taxation under Article I, and dissimilar taxation with protectionist motive under Article III:2. In each case, a recognised Common Concern of Humankind doctrine will indicate the possibility of the existence of market distortions and inform a dispute settlement Panel to take that into account.

---

824 *Canada – Certain Measures Affecting the Renewable Energy Generation Sector / Canada – Measures Relating to the Feed-in Tariff Program* (n 500) para 5.175, 5.177, 5.190.

825 Nordhaus, 'Climate Clubs and Carbon Pricing' (n 635) 111.

Although the approach above aided by the Common Concern doctrine may save the carbon pricing component of the proposed climate technology diffusion measure from being seen as discriminatory, this, along with finding that the products compared as 'unlike' due to variation in emission footprints, may admittedly exacerbate the existing challenge of accommodating the revenue sharing component of the measure within the WTO law. The support component of the proposed measure, as our earlier analysis has shown, only comes in play at the very last stage of the justification analysis to save a carbon pricing measure from being labelled as unjustifiably discriminatory. It follows that any pricing measure that is not considered discriminatory in the first place, gets absolved from the requirement of making implementational adjustment taking the CBDR principle into account.

To resolve this dilemma, fuller implementation of the Common Concern doctrine is called for. We remind that attention to equity is an essential part of the earlier outlined technology diffusion narrative, which is carried out by following the CBDR principle during the implementation of actual measures.[826] Therefore, while following the harmonised approach, a carbon pricing measure should be found non-discriminatory only when the application of the measure is adjusted to the varying responsibilities of the impacted countries. To make sure that it is the case, the proposed revenue recycling component of a carbon pricing measure remains relevant.

C *Regarding the General Exception*

The legitimate policy objectives endorsed under Article XX are wide enough to accommodate the climate mitigation goal. Common Concern is not essential, but a useful tool nevertheless, to underscore the importance of the LCT diffusion as an objective. The doctrine, arising in the climate context and the consequent responsibility to act would indicate a substantial linkage between a carbon pricing measure and the need for conservation of a stable climate. This would contribute to meet the 'relating to' requirement under the Article XX(g) of GATT, as previously discussed. In a similar fashion, with regard to 'necessity' analysis under subparagraphs (b), or (a), Common Concern can contribute to the 'weighing and balancing' exercise attaching further weight to the need for immediate and accelerated mitigation of carbon emission. It is important to note that although the Paris Agreement allows flexibility in terms of the nature and sectors in which mitigation commitments are undertaken, the doctrine does indeed highlight the necessity that such actions taken in an

826 See Chapter 3 I B (iii) at p. 125 above.

adequate scale. Therefore, even though there may be less trade-restrictive options to reduce emission, the flexibility granted to a member taking mitigation action under the Paris Agreement, combined with the urgency of doing so, as highlighted by the Common Concern doctrine, the need for carbon pricing cannot be downplayed.

The requirement of compliance with the Chapeau will need to be met by tuning the impact of the carbon pricing with respective economic development reality existing in each country. This is also demanded not only by the Common Concern doctrine, but also by the principles of equity and CBDR. However, Common Concern also dictates that mitigation remains of utmost importance. As a result, the fairness is reached through adjustment supports. Therefore, the doctrine would call for the adverse impacts of carbon pricing to be adjusted through financial and technological assistance and not through blanket exemptions from mitigation obligations.

V Conclusion

Carbon pricing plays an important role in resolving the crisis of ambition and cooperation challenge surrounding climate mitigation. Within the proposed Common Concern inspired narrative, an appropriate level of carbon tax or tariff can contribute to emission mitigation and technology diffusion in a mutually beneficial solution, provided that part of the revenue generated by pricing schemes in the developed countries is deployed for additional support to the developing countries. This chapter pointed out that a doctrine of Common Concern can tackle some of the lingering WTO consistency issues involving an emission pricing effort.

Cooperation is a useful and important prior step regarding carbon pricing. The chapter helps understand the nature and extent the cooperation problem related to emission pricing, which in its turn informs the appropriate responses thereof. Agreement on a carbon price floor, as indicated by many, is the least difficult target to be achieved through cooperation. While a multilateral or club type agreement on carbon pricing can pre-empt subsequent challenge under the WTO law. Appropriate forum in this regard remains wanting.

The domestic level is where the actual pricing takes place, with or without any agreement on a carbon price floor. In the absence of agreement, not only do countries remain free to adopt their own price rates, they can also challenge others' measures as discriminatory. Unilateral pricing is attractive as it can ensure responsible consumption, as well as address competitiveness concerns for some domestic manufacturers. Among the alternate options of tariffs or taxes, the latter may be a reasonable approach in most circumstances. It is important the pricing measures are somehow linked to a revenue sharing process, through which the developing countries can obtain assistance for access to necessary emission reduction technologies. Recycling of revenue, as the chapter proposed, makes sure that technology diffusion takes place. It also fends off challenges of discrimination under the WTO legal standard.

While under the current trade regulation framework, it is possible to challenge a carbon pricing measure as discriminatory, access to a legal notion such as Common Concern of Humankind can address some of those by promoting a more informed reading of the non-discrimination commitment. The current chapter also puts forth a proposition regarding a further nuanced understanding of the concepts like 'products' and 'markets' to facilitate such a reading.

In the end, recognition and agreement among all the stakeholders on matters of Common Concern of Humankind are of paramount importance. The international legal landscape of climate regulation is but a sum total of the aspirations of the countries. When most countries fail to signal a willingness to formulate and implement an effective mitigation agenda, the international legal landscape merely holds a mirror to that fact. It is not surprising that there are gaps and disconnects between trade and climate laws. So much so that a truly climate mitigation motivated trade measure will find difficulty in being compliant with the trade rules. The doctrine of Common Concern ventures to plug such gaps. The proposed meaning to this notion, when collectively supported, can build the bridges and find the new perspectives to generate the necessary harmonisation between the two rule systems.

CHAPTER 5

Encouraging Technology Export through Public Financial Support

This chapter supplies the second of the two case studies that test out Common Concern inspired trade measures in practice. This study zooms in to the issue of access to finance – one of the key obstacles for the private sector to acquire emission reducing technologies. Within that perimeter, the current chapter focuses on the relationship of potential support measures with the Subsidies Agreement of the WTO – especially, the control it would exercise on potential enhancement of such measures. While the argument of boosting climate finance is considered as a virtuous one on the whole, the opaque issue is whether the cause would also justify unregulated public finance of private transactions in low-carbon technologies (LCT), particularly when involving developing country partners. This issue is explored in detail here.

The chapter begins with an outline of the need for additional public finance for technology outflows and proposes the enhancement of export promotion support as a positive contributor. The approaches thereof, i.e. supply of financial credit in better terms, or sharing of destination-specific risks are then examined in the backdrop of the trade regulation – the Agreement on Subsidies and Countervailing Measures (ASCM, or the SCM agreement), to be specific. Then the lens of Common Concern of Humankind is brought into play to identify areas of further development. The chapter explains that the promotion of clean technology exports and investments could be mutually beneficial for all parties involved. To that effect, the Common Concern doctrine can facilitate an accommodating understanding of the subsidies regulation, as well as indicate the pertinent areas of new rule-making. This conclusion however remains subject to one important caveat. While markets often lack public support boosting trade or investment flows in the LCTs, it may enjoy the same in the sectors that are harmful to the climate. A successful paradigm of financial assistance in the light of resolving the common concern of humankind should also include a parallel focus on the withdrawal of counterproductive supports existing on the market.

 | DOI:10.1163/9789004446090_007

I Prospects and Challenges of Public Financial Support

We earlier noted how inadequate finance limits the success of the formal regulatory arrangements on technology transfer in the climate regime.[827] In the technology needs assessment (TNA) reports, most developing countries identify non-availability of finance as the biggest problem.[828] This is the context against which the need for augmentation of public financial support in this area must be assessed.

Despite its crucial importance, public share of total climate finance is not only minuscule, but its flow is also limited largely within developed countries. While the global total climate finance stood at somewhere between USD 456 and 681 billion in 2016,[829] only about a third or even less of that amount (USD 157 billion) has travelled from the public and private sources in the developed countries to the developing destinations.[830] Of the global total climate finance reported above, private financial flows, especially investment in renewable energy (USD 217 billion) and energy efficiency improvements (USD 224

827 See Chapter 2 II B at p. 67 and onwards.

828 See Chapter 2 III C at p. 85 above.

829 These numbers tend to vary largely due to disagreement on what counts towards climate finance and difference in approaches towards finding an aggregate number. This estimate is taken from the last biennial report (2018) prepared by the UNFCCC standing committee on finance. See UNFCCC, 'UNFCCC Standing Committee on Finance: 2018 Biennial Assessment and Overview of Climate Finance Flows Technical Report' (United Nations Climate Change Secretariat 2019) 55–58; For earlier estimates, see Sujata Gupta and others, 'Cross-Cutting Investment and Finance Issues', *Climate change 2014: mitigation of climate change: Working Group III contribution to the Fifth Assessment Report of the Intergovernmental Panel on Climate Change* (Cambridge University Press 2014) 1213–1214.

830 UNFCCC, 'UNFCCC Standing Committee on Finance: 2018 Biennial Assessment and Overview of Climate Finance Flows Technical Report' ibid 70. This is a very rough estimate. Detailed data, especially those of the private financial flows, do not exist. Similar numbers are reported in the IPCC fifth assessment report, Gupta and others (n 832) 1234. This should not be confused with the 100 billion goal committed to in the Copenhagen Accord. For different takes on the latter, see OECD and Climate Policy Initiative, 'Climate Finance in 2013–14 and the USD 100 Billion Goal' (Organization for Economic Cooperation and Development (OECD) 2015) <https://www.oecd.org/environment/cc/OECD-CPI-Climate-Finance-Report.pdf> accessed 25 October 2020; Climate Change Finance Unit, Ministry of Finance, Government of India, 'Climate Change Finance, Analysis of a Recent OECD Report: Some Credible Facts Needed' <https://dea.gov.in/sites/default/files/ClimateChangeOEFDReport_0.pdf> accessed 25 October 2020; Mariama Williams, 'The State of Play of Climate Finance – UNFCCC Funds and the $100 Billion Question' (South Centre 2019) 21 <https://www.southcentre.int/wp-content/uploads/2019/12/CPB21_The-State-of-Play-of-Climate-Finance-UNFCCC-Funds-and-the-100-Billion-Question_EN-1.pdf> accessed 25 October 2020.

billion) account for the lion's share. One estimate shows that public financial flows, comprised chiefly of finance through multilateral development banks, amounted to 34% of the total flow of climate finance in 2015 and 2016.[831] The same report also indicates that almost 80% of the total volume of climate finance is domestically raised and spent,[832] meaning that a relatively very small portion of that total flows to the developing countries. To illustrate, private foreign direct investment (FDI) flow to renewable energy projects in developing countries was USD 1.5 billion in 2016,[833] whereas in the same year, the total amount of funds spent globally on energy access stood at USD 19.4 billion.[834]

Therefore, there is a strong case for improving public financial support, especially by the developed countries, for activities that result in the diffusion of LCTs to developing countries. Such support will be counted towards the fulfilment of the existing commitment of amassing USD 100 billion in new and additional finance.[835] This would also be helpful in leveraging, as well as channelling private financial flows in the form of trade and investment transactions to locations that are otherwise unattractive in market terms. Domestically, such support can also open limited opportunities for green industrial policy. These issues are detailed below.

A *The Problem and Potential of Public Finance*

Public financial resources can be employed to cure the existing disincentives that prevent LCT spreading transactions from taking place. In cases where such transactions involve developed and developing country partners, public financial institutions of the developed country can be involved in ways that resolve the challenges of access to finance and other risk factors that would otherwise dissuade a private business entity. Such involvement corrects financial market failures and promises to augment the scale of transactions taking place.

Unaffordable prices and lack of adequate access to finance have already been highlighted as key barriers to low-carbon technology diffusion to developing countries.[836] These issues divert crucial energy infrastructure investments to high-carbon options with disastrous impacts over the long-run. For

831 Barbara K Buchner and others, 'Global Landscape of Climate Finance 2017' (Climate Policy Initiative 2017) 4.

832 ibid 13.

833 UNFCCC, 'UNFCCC Standing Committee on Finance: 2018 Biennial Assessment and Overview of Climate Finance Flows Technical Report' (n 832) 70.

834 Buchner and others (n 831) 7.

835 This is the goal 13.a of the Sustainable Development Goals (SDGs). See United Nations General Assembly (n 210).

836 See Chapter 2 III C at p. 85 and onwards.

example, the fifth IPCC assessment report predicted 78% of the upcoming investments in fossil fuel power plants to be taking place in non-OECD countries due to their relatively lower cost.[837] While ideally the developing countries are deserving destinations for low-carbon investment, most, except maybe a few, are considered relatively high-risk countries for investment in general.[838] This drives up the cost of capital, also the rate of return on investment desired by private investors.[839]

In more detail, challenges to the enhancement of trade and investment flow to developing countries involve investment risks, insufficient returns, inadequate market size, difficulty to raise longer-term capital, capacity, and human resource constraints.[840] The investment risks are manifested as risks due to the novelty of the technology, as well as risks arising from a specific locale – i.e. political and financial instability, rule of law problems etc.[841] Combination of these different risks makes it difficult for a foreign investor in LCT find a suitable financial proposition for their lenders and equity partners. Moreover, raising fund from the developing country financial markets are also challenging because of the absence of a deep market that can ensure an adequate supply of funds over the long term. All of these factors contribute to a market failure – where inadequate financial flows lead the developing countries to a higher-carbon trajectory.

In a global financial landscape highlighted by the growing clout of private financial services, the role of public financial support in addressing the above risks are complementary in nature. Public financial engagement in the clean technology sectors can leverage the flows of private finance by sharing risks. Because public engagement decreases the volatility of the sectors, the rate of returns on investment in those sectors increase, which can then help crowd-in private investors as well.[842] In parallel, allocation of public funds to the relatively risky ventures also leaves the traditional investment opportunities open

---

837 Gupta and others (n 829) 1217, 1236.

838 See generally, 'Country Risk Classification – OECD' <https://www.oecd.org/trade/topics/export-credits/arrangement-and-sector-understandings/financing-terms-and-conditions/country-risk-classification/> accessed 25 October 2020; Also, 'Sovereign Risk Indicators – S&P Global Ratings' <https://www.spratings.com/sri/> accessed 25 October 2020.

839 Gupta and others (n 829) 1236.

840 ibid 1224–1226; For a different classification, see, Martin Stadelmann, Paula Castro and Axel Michaelowa, 'Mobilising Private Finance for Low-Carbon Development' (Climate Strategies 2011).

841 Stadelmann, Castro and Michaelowa, ibid 6; Gupta and others (n 829) 1225.

842 Stadelmann, Castro and Michaelowa (n 840).

for private financing enterprises.[843] Overall, when such measures are taken by developed country governments, they are on one hand helpful in sharing and thereby reducing the risks faced by their exporters of and investors in low-carbon technologies. This additionally plays a role in reducing those countries' emission footprint from import consumption, a matter that remains so far unaddressed.[844] Side by side, such measures can also provide the developing country markets with much-needed technology and also access to additional finance.

B *Possible Avenues of Public Support*

Following above, it is submitted that the appropriate public policy option to support private trade and investment transactions depend very much on the nature of the prevailing obstacles and the existing policy environment. Public financial support for LCT diffusion can take place in various ways. Development assistance is one of the channels where financial assistance takes place in non-market terms. Financial incentives can also potentially be supplied by providing tax credits. Exporters of LCT s or domestic investors investing in clean technology sectors abroad can be provided tax relief based on the evidence of successful technology diffusion.[845] Two other options deal with addressing the financial constraints of the private actors engaged in clean technology related transactions. One way is to make necessary financial resources available to the relevant exporters, investors and related institutions at prevailing market rates, or even in better terms. The other option is for the government to help reduce the businesses' exposure to risks arising from the transactions.[846] Both of these options contribute to lowering of the overall cost faced by the private firms in

---

843 John Ward and others, 'Catalysing Low-Carbon Growth in Developing Economies: Public Finance Mechanisms to Scale up Private Sector Investment in Climate Solutions' (UNEP and Partners 2009); Stadelmann, Castro and Michaelowa (n 840); Karsten Neuhoff, 'International Support for Low-Carbon Growth in Developing Countries', *Climate policy after Copenhagen : the role of carbon pricing* (Cambridge University Press 2011).

844 See pp. 20, & 153 above.

845 Hoekman, Maskus and Saggi (n 611); Bernard Hoekman, Keith E Maskus and Kamal Saggi, 'Transfer of Technology to Developing Countries: Unilateral and Multilateral Policy Options' [2004] World Bank Policy Research Working Paper. It was proposed that as regional governments offer tax credits for companies to stay in technology poor areas, the central government can provide similar credits upon transfer of technology by a company abroad.

846 Traerup, Greersen and Kundsen (n 408) 16. In this recent synthesis of climate regime processes relevant to technology development and transfer, the authors highlight the potential of low interest credits, credit guarantees, improvement of access to international funds and other forms of incentives to get rid of technology diffusion barriers.

doing business. Export promotion tools like the supply of credits, credit guarantees, and insurances fall within these categories. This is where the chapter's focus would remain.

Public financial supports, like export credits, are the mainstays of global finance, especially in the post-financial crisis era. Export credit activities include financial supports provided at specific fixed rates, or floating rates, as well as liquidity support like extension of grants.[847] Instead of the actual supply of credits, the governments may also provide guarantees against default, thereby easing the businesses' opportunity to obtain finance from the private market. Governments may as well insure an exporter or investor against incurring risks abroad. One study gave the example of the Overseas Private Investment Corporation (OPIC) in the United States, which insures outward renewable energy investments against host government actions.[848]

These support measures are generally made available by countries to domestic exporters and investors irrespective of the nature of the transactions. Guided by a nationalist commercial motive, these work to enhance the comparative advantage of the domestic exporters. As a result, while there are instances of public agencies extensively supporting clean technology exports,[849] same is also true for other areas, including some polluting ones. For example, between 2010 and 2016, two major Chinese public finance institutions spent approximately USD 160 billion in energy finance – 80% of which went in building power plants abroad. Most (90%) of those power plants were of fossil-fuelled type.[850]

Investment promotion is one of the key ways by which public support can facilitate technology outflow. While much of the existing literature approaches

---

847 See for example, 'Our Solutions' (*Export Finance Australia*) <https://www.exportfinance.gov.au/about-us/our-solutions/> accessed 25 October 2020. Also, 'EDC Solutions' (*Export Development Canada*) <https://www.edc.ca/en/solutions.html> accessed 25 October 2020.

848 UN Environment Inquiry and Columbia Center on Sustainable Investment, 'Green Foreign Direct Investment in Developing Countries' (United Nations Environment Programme (UNEP) 2017) 25 < http://unepinquiry.org/wp-content/uploads/2017/10/Green_Foreign_Direct_Investment_in_Developing_Countries.pdf .> accessed 25 October 2020.

849 R Jachnik and others, 'Tracking Climate-Related Export Credits: Existing Official Reporting Practices, Illustration of Methodological Options and Implications through Project Examples' [2017] Working document prepared for the Research Collaborative on Tracking Private Climate Finance 8–16.

850 UN Environment Inquiry and Columbia Center on Sustainable Investment (n 848) 26. Chinese investment also tends to crowd out private firms. See Hong Ru, 'Government Credit, a Double-Edged Sword: Evidence from the China Development Bank' (2018) 73 The Journal of Finance 275.

the issue of green investment promotion from a host-state perspective,[851] home country incentives find only occasional limelight.[852] From the perspective of fostering outwards foreign direct investment (OFDI), the measures such as those mentioned above will allow home country firms to take benefit of advantages in other destinations, achieve further specialisation, and bring back revenue, as well as tangible and intangible skills.[853] It can be expected that financial incentives will encourage the domestic firms to furnish better technologies to their subsidiaries, and also search for suitable partners abroad. It should, however, be kept in mind that financial incentives are not the sole determiner for investment outflows. Investment outflow is influenced by various factors, which are not only comprised of those of the home country but also of host country characteristics, e.g. including macroeconomic stability, availability of desirable skills or factors, robust infrastructure etc. Therefore it is important to make sure that the incentives are open-ended so that the domestic firms can combine them with respect to their chosen country of investment.

In addition to triggering of greenfield investment in LCT sectors across borders, public finance can support domestic exporters in one-off technology transactions as well. Export credits will bridge the finance gap between the seller and the buyer; by allowing the buyer flexibility in terms of payment, and enabling the seller opportunity to recoup the investment in time.[854] Credits, guarantees, and insurances would enable exporters of clean technology to expand supply to newer markets, including those in the low-income economies.

C *The Promise and Challenge of the Export Credit Agencies* (ECAs)

Public financing of export is generally done either through export credit agencies (ECAs), or specially instituted banks (e.g. Export Import Banks).[855] The

851 For example, UNCTAD, 'Promoting Low-Carbon Investment' (United Nations 2013) Series A, number 7; Martin Dietrich Brauch and Aaron Cosbey, *Vehicles, Availability, and Governance of International Public Finance for Climate-Friendly Investment* (International Institute for Sustainable Development 2012); Ravindra Ratnayake, Marc Proksch and Mia Mikić, *Climate-Smart Trade and Investment in Asia and the Pacific: Towards a Triple-Win Outcome* (ESCAP 2011).

852 Karl P Sauvant and others, 'Trends in FDI, Home Country Measures and Competitive Neutrality' in Andrea K Bjorklund (ed), *Yearbook on International Investment Law and Policy* (Oxford University Press 2012).

853 Jan Knoerich, 'How Does Outward Foreign Direct Investment Contribute to Economic Development in Less Advanced Home Countries?' (2017) 45 Oxford Development Studies 443.

854 Marc Auboin, 'Improving the Availability of Trade Finance in Developing Countries: An Assessment of Remaining Gaps' (WTO 2015) Staff Working Paper ERSD-2015-06 3.

855 Here we use the term export credit agency (ECA) to cover both.

general rationale behind such engagement is not to compete with the sphere of commercial lending, rather complementing it to secure additional export growth.[856] Prior to the financial crisis, this motivation was becoming growingly questionable due to expansions in depth and coverage of private finance.[857] However, since the crisis, the slowing of commercial lending activities has led to widespread calls for stepping up public financing to maintain trade transactions at 'business as usual' levels. The crisis has even prompted the WTO to encourage increased ECA activity, despite the possibility of triggering member states' behaviour verging on illegal subsidisation.[858]

Technically speaking, there are no binding international law controlling the actions of the ECAs, although they are entities established by the states. There is however a soft law framework in the form of the OECD Arrangement on Officially Supported Export Credits (hereafter 'the arrangement', Box 4). The arrangement has a unique and special relationship with the SCM agreement.[859] Compliance with the arrangement provisions is required from the participants thereof, which is limited to the OECD member countries.[860] Some of the arrangement provisions are also indispensable for all the WTO members seeking to engage in the export promotion activities, as will be detailed later. Apart from the arrangement, there are other, less detailed alternative platforms that work to coordinate the activities of the ECAs. Such platforms include the Berne Union[861] and the International Working Group (IWG) on

856 Jian-Ye Wang and others, *Officially Supported Export Credits in a Changing World* (International Monetary Fund 2005) 5.

857 ibid 10–13.

858 Auboin (n 854).

859 In the broader context of international attempts at disciplining artificial supports to the exports, this relationship go far back – even before the currently existing organizations (i.e. OECD and the WTO). A list of prohibited subsidies was agreed at the Organization for European Economic Cooperation (OEEC), and was later inherited by the OECD. The list was later appended to the GATT Tokyo Round (1973–1979) Subsidies Code. Meanwhile, as the OECD arrangement came to being (see box above), an exception was introduced to the list. The WTO subsidies agreement inherited that list. Andrew M Moravcsik, 'Disciplining Trade Finance: The OECD Export Credit arrangement' (1989) 43 International Organization 173; Dominic Coppens, 'Rationale for Disciplining Export Credit Support: Historical Context', *WTO disciplines on subsidies and countervailing measures : balancing policy space and legal constraints* (Cambridge University Press 2014) 349–355.

860 Current participants are Australia, Canada, the European Union, Japan, Korea, New Zealand, Norway, Switzerland, Turkey, and the United States. OECD, 'Export Credits' <https://www.oecd.org/trade/topics/export-credits/> accessed 25 October 2020.

861 The Berne Union is a network of 85 export credit agencies, most of which are government linked. 'Berne Union – About the Berne Union' <https://www.berneunion.org/Stub/Display/8> accessed 25 October 2020.

export credits.[862] Unlike the arrangement, WTO rules do not take account of these emerging platforms, although the latter often bring more developing country participation.

Box 4: The OECD Arrangement
Arrangement on Officially Supported Export Credits
The OECD arrangement is, as Wang and others have put, a "gentlemen's agreement among its participants; it is not an OECD act".[863] It is an evolving document[864] that lays down the general terms of official finance for the participating countries. According to its provisions, official support can either be financing support (i.e. direct credit, or interest rate support), or pure cover (i.e. insurance, or guarantee). The arrangement also welcomes compliance by non-participants.

The goal of the arrangement is to prevent participants from competing in a race to the bottom regarding offered terms of export credit.[865] To achieve that, the arrangement suggests rules on maximum repayment terms, down payment limits, minimum interest rates to be charged for fixed-rate finance (CIRR),[866] and minimum premium rates for risk finance (MPR)[867]. The arrangement also accepts the possibility of financing at floating rates, which may in some cases dip below the CIRR, depending on the market situation.[868] Compliance with the provisions

862 The International Working Group (IWG) on Export Credits was established on a joint initiative by the United States and China. Its aim is to develop rules that cover not only OECD countries but also emerging countries like the BRICS.

863 Wang and others (n 856) 31.

864 The version in effect at the time of writing this chapter is the one dated 1 January, 2018.

865 Article 1, OECD, 'arrangement on Officially Supported Export Credits' (OECD 2018) TAD/PG(2018)1.

866 These rates are known as 'commercial interest reference rates' (CIRR). The CIRR s are generally set in the participants' currencies, as 100 basis points (1%) above a chosen base rate. The latter is derived from the yield of 3, 5, or 7 years government bonds issued by a participant. Overall, it ensures that while lending in its own currency, the government does not incur costs that cannot be recuperated. See Articles 19–22, ibid.

867 The participants are required to charge the minimum premium rates (MPR s) as a return for the risk coverage. The MPR s are determined taking into account several factors – (i) country risk classification, (ii) time at risk ('risk horizon'), (iii) buyer risk category, (iv) the percentage of political and commercial risk cover, (v) applied techniques of country risk mitigation, and (vi) applied buyer credit risk enhancements. See Articles 24–27 & Annex IX, ibid.

868 It is to be noted however that with respect to floating rate finance scheme the short-term market rate will be applicable. The recipient institution are proscribed from the choice of option between the market rate and the CIRR. Article 22, ibid.

of the arrangement is ensured through 'matching'[869] – a measure that allows a competitor to match the terms offered by a participant or a non-participant, despite those terms being in breach of the agreed rules.

Among the sector-specific special rules (termed 'understanding') that are appended to the arrangement, one set deals with renewable energy, climate mitigation and adaptation, and water projects.[870] Special minimum interest rates apply to the designated activities falling within the scope of the understanding. The scope of the designated activities leaves out many of the low-carbon technologies, while including fossil fuel-based power plants incorporating carbon capture technology.

The portrayal of the ECAs as climate benefactors can also be challenging due to the phenomenon described by an early report by the World Resources Institute (WRI) as 'policy perversity'.[871] While the countries commit to climate mitigation, their ECAs are run with the sole motivation of the promotion of domestic interests in commercial terms. As a result, not only is there an absence of climate, or environmental protection motivation, in real terms, a large portion of the ECA finance goes to polluting sectors. The WRI report indicated that fossil fuel power generation, oil, and gas sectors account for 40% of the public finance flowing from the developed to the developing countries.[872] The earlier example of massive Chinese financial support for building coal-fired power plants abroad should also be recalled.[873] In 2013, USD 1391 million of OECD export finance went to renewable electricity generation sector in the middle and low-income countries.[874] The same figure for fossil fuel power plants that year was USD 2464 million.[875]

Another issue with the current track record of the ECAs is the absence of transparency. The transactions and terms offered by the ECAs are often kept confidential. The participants to the arrangement report their activities to the OECD, but detailed information is either not reported or not regularly published by the organisation. In addition to business confidentiality, additional

869 Article 18, ibid.
870 Annex IV, ibid.
871 Crescencia Maurer and Ruchi Bhandari, 'Climate Notes: The Climate of Export Credit Agencies' (World Resources Institute 2000).
872 ibid 5–7.
873 See note 850 above.
874 OECD, 'Statistics on Arrangement Official Export Credit Support for Electric Power Generation Projects' TAD/ECG(2015)10/FINAL 6.
875 ibid.

reasons behind such non-transparency could possibly be a desire to hide non-popular supports, as well as to be immune from export subsidisation claims.[876]

In addition, despite the ECAs putative role as financiers of ventures that are conventionally deemed as risky, relatively very little goes to support transactions involving partners from low-income countries. According to the OECD, in 2015, about 5% of the overall official non-ODA finance support went to LDCs and low-income countries.[877] The aforementioned transparency problem also makes it difficult to determine how much of it can actually be considered to be in support of climate mitigation. According to the available figures on the OECD arrangement, much of the financial support for electricity generation projects goes to fossil fuel projects.[878]

D *The Proposed Measure*

Simply put, we propose that the ECAs should prioritise financing transactions that enable the diffusion of climate technologies. Within that context, supports in better than market terms must be extended to trade or investment transactions involving developing or least-developed country partners – transactions which would not otherwise materialise due to capital market failures in the technology destination regions. It is also proposed that the minimum interest rates currently applicable under the OECD arrangement be relaxed to the extent commercially viable, when the transaction tangibly benefits developing countries' clean technology access. To a degree, downward competition in offered terms of finance among the developed country ECAs regarding climate technologies can be desirable.

As the proposal made above is a part of the earlier detailed technology diffusion narrative,[879] the goal here is to create win-win consequences for the involved parties. The proposed measure will benefit the suppliers of LCTs by enabling business growth and market access. Similarly, it would help partially address the developing and least-developed country firms' problems of

---

876 Thomas Wenidoppler, 'ECAs Go to Market: A Critical Review of Transparency and Sustainability at Seven Export Credit Agencies in Central and Eastern Europe' (Finance and Trade Watch, CEE Bankwatch Network 2017).

877 OECD, 'Non-ODA Flows to Developing Countries: Export Credits' <http://www.oecd.org/dac/stats/beyond-oda-export-credits.htm> accessed 25 October 2020.

878 OECD, 'Statistics on Arrangement Official Export Credit Support for Electric Power Generation Projects' (n 874). On a further detailed level, the numbers on fossil fuel based electricity generation is dominated by support coming from Germany, Japan, Korea, and the United States; whereas, the same for renewables is contributed to a large extent by Germany and Denmark.

879 See Chapter 3 II A above.

technology affordability and finance. Mechanisms as such can also cater to the additional growth in LCT demand resulting from the proposed carbon pricing measure in the foregoing chapter.[880] The revenue recycling component of the pricing measure discussed in that connection can also serve as the source of finance to offer better credit terms to the developing countries. To the extent the LDCs are at the receiving end of the publicly supported technology transactions, the activities could be reported by the developed countries as partial fulfilment of their obligation to transfer technology under the TRIPS Article 66.2.

However, for such a proposition to be successful, it is important that the public financial supports are undertaken in a complementary manner. First of all, support for export and outward investments regarding LCTs must take place in conjunction with withdrawal from counterproductive engagements (e.g. financing coal power plants, or subsidising fossil fuels). Second, financial incentives for the facilitation of LCT transactions are supply-side solutions. For it to work, there must be effective demand in the receiving sector, itself depending upon an effective carbon price implemented domestically (e.g. possibly through a tax as discussed in the previous case study). Furthermore, countries seeking low-carbon technologies must also work to create an overall enabling regulatory environment by, among others, gradually reducing risks to foreign investments. This involves improvement of rule of law institutions, political stability, development of endogenous capacity, and improvement of adaptive skills.[881]

To sum up this section, increasing public financial support would play a direct and positive role to boost exports of and outward investments in LCT sectors. Such supports can be extended in the form of supplying credits, grants, and risk-sharing measures. Although these tools are useful in practice, a key challenge is that the export credit agencies (ECAs) that are in charge of deploying them, do not generally operate under a climate protection mandate. Moreover, the practice of official export credits does not have any applicable international law. While there is the non-binding OECD arrangement, its participants are mainly developed countries. Also, its coverage of climate-related projects falls short of including all forms of LCT transactions. Therefore, as a part of the homework obligation under the doctrine of Common Concern of Humankind, developed country governments, as well as other technology leaders need to provide public financial incentives to promote LCT transactions with the developing countries. Such efforts are beneficial for all the parties

880 See Chapter 4 I D above.

881 UNFCCC, 'UNFCCC Standing Committee on Finance: 2018 Biennial Assessment and Overview of Climate Finance Flows Technical Report' (n 829) 12, 100.

involved. However, in addition to enhancing the volume of transactions in low-carbon technologies, complementary actions are also required, including withdrawal of supports running counter to the motive of climate protection.

Next, the compatibility of the proposed measure and its challenges with respect to the WTO Agreement on Subsidies and Countervailing Measures (ASCM) are assessed below.

II ECA Activities and the WTO Subsidies Agreement

Although increasing export credit supports for clean technology diffusion are often prescribed, its relationship with the WTO laws, especially the SCM agreement is less looked into.[882] Financial assistance, provided by the government to its firms through the ECAs, can indeed boost low-carbon technology transactions. But the possibility of effectively doing so without breaching the provisions of the SCM agreement is questionable. Lack of experts' attention to this issue can either be due to a tacit understanding of the unresolved relationship between export credits and subsidies, or possibly be due to a recent paucity in actual trade disputes brought by members in this regard.[883]

WTO law, in particular, the SCM agreement, also the earlier GATT Articles VI and XVI, are attracted in situations where a government financial support has potentially trade distortive effects. The ASCM controls subsidies that affect trade relationship, even outright prohibiting some forms of supports, e.g. most export subsidies. In essence, the SCM agreement represents a consensual balance struck

---

882 Literature on green subsidies and trade is vast, which makes the absence of discussion on export credits even more conspicuous. A sample of the influential literature on the topic, presented here, do not address the issue, Steve Charnovitz, 'Green Subsidies and the WTO' [2014] World Bank Policy Research Working Paper <http://documents.worldbank.org/curated/en/2014/10/20290817/green-subsidies-wto> accessed 25 October 2020; Bradly J Condon, 'Disciplining Clean Energy Subsidies to Speed the Transition to a Low-Carbon World' (2017) 51 Journal of World Trade 675; Ilaria Espa and Gracia Marín Durán, 'Renewable Energy Subsidies and WTO Law: Time to Rethink the Case for Reform Beyond Canada – Renewable Energy/Fit Program' [2018] Journal of International Economic Law; Luca Rubini, 'Ain't Wastin' Time No More: Subsidies for Renewable Energy, The SCM agreement, Policy Space, and Law Reform' (2012) 15 Journal of International Economic Law 525; Gary Horlick and Peggy A Clarke, 'Rethinking Subsidy Disciplines for the Future: Policy Options for Reform' (2017) 20 Journal of International Economic Law 673.

883 Since the tussle between Embraer of Brazil and Bombardier of Canada pursued by the respective governments in the early years of the WTO, the provisions relating export credits have not been much contested. One exception the *Korea – Measures Affecting Trade in Commercial Vessels* (DS 273) dispute decided in 2005.

by the WTO members between distortive subsidisation and domestic interest protection. As the bargain is politically struck, the rationale underlying the agreement is not always economically optimal. It is especially true with respect to the areas where existing market failures justify subsidisation from an economic point of view, but the current rules will prohibit such steps.

Initially, the SCM agreement had a framework resembling a traffic lights approach, protecting certain subsidies from being challenged,[884] while outright prohibiting certain others.[885] In between, there were subsidies that could be challenged in a dispute provided that those resulted in some form of 'adverse effect'.[886] Since the lapse of Article 8 of the agreement there are no protected subsidies (i.e. non-actionable subsidies).[887] While the prohibited subsidies can be challenged in a dispute by any members, the 'adverse effects' can be challenged by the members who are impacted thereby.[888] In addition, the member into whose territory subsidised products are imported, can also initiate an investigation to determine the margin of 'injury' to the domestic industry. Upon a positive finding, the aforementioned member is allowed to impose a countervailing duty (CVD) against the exporting member.[889]

While the proposed measure in the previous section is motivated by the importance of public financial support for low-carbon technology diffusion, the WTO law must play a role to make sure that the supports do not become an excuse for unnecessarily distortive industrial policies, in particular harming the growth of new industries in the developing countries. As a result, it is important to retain the essence of the earlier mentioned balance in the SCM agreement between public support and trade distortion. To do so, while allowing for opportunities to promote clean technology transactions, is a quest to find a threshold beyond which a capital market failures resulting in lingering common concerns should be intervened by the governments. Where that threshold

---

884 Article 8, Non-Actionable Subsidies, Agreement on Subsidies and Countervailing Measures (n 434). It should be noted that the provision did not save subsidies that were designated as prohibited.

885 Article 3, ibid.

886 Articles 5–7, ibid. The categories of adverse effects are: (i) injury to domestic industry, (ii) nullification or impairment of benefit accrued under the GATT 1994, and (iii) serious prejudice.

887 Article 8 was the outcome of a successful bargain driven by the EU, Canada and Mexico. It lapsed in 1999, along with the other part of the bargain, i.e. Article 6.1 of the Subsidies Agreement. See Coppens, *WTO Disciplines on Subsidies and Countervailing Measures* (n 440) 187–188.

888 Articles 4.1 and 7.1, Agreement on Subsidies and Countervailing Measures (n 434).

889 Article VI, General Agreement on Tariffs and Trade (n 426); Articles 10–11, Agreement on Subsidies and Countervailing Measures (n 434).

would lie depends on the extent to which the current subsidy rules allow or prohibit the proposed steps. Following paragraphs elucidate that point.

A *The Key Questions*

The key sticking points regarding the compatibility of enhanced ECA support for clean technology finance with the SCM agreement can be ordered in accordance with the structure of the agreement itself. At the outset, the question would be to what extent the envisaged ECA measures would come under the coverage of the ASCM. Second, with regard to the transactions that may fall within the agreement's scope, the issue would be how the agreement may deal with those.

The coverage of the ASCM is determined by Article 1 of that agreement. Simply put, the provision holds that any 'benefit' conferring 'financial contribution', coming from the government or a public body, or private entities 'entrusted or directed' by the former are within the scope of the agreement. Whether the SCM rules would cover the matters regarding promotion of LCTs or not would primarily hinge on the question whether such measures are considerable as conferment of benefit upon the recipient. If so, then rest of the Agreement provisions would come into play. Another issue would be the dividing line between trade and investment, raising the question whether identical measures promoting investment rather than export would also fall within the SCM agreement's scope or not.

ECA support measures that fall within the boundaries of the ASCM raise two further questions. One is the extent to which the agreement would altogether prohibit support measures of such form. The agreement clearly disallows subsidies that are contingent, either in law or in fact, upon export performance.[890] While compliance with the OECD arrangement by a support measure provide limited cover from the prohibition,[891] the question would be whether that is sufficient or useful at all. Furthermore, even when an ECA support for LCT diffusion is not found as manifestly illegal and subject to immediate withdrawal, there is the possibility that third-party WTO members may challenge such financial supports on the ground of those being 'specific'[892] and resulting in price distortions or displacement of the share of their exports in the receiving country market.[893]

---

890 Article 3, Agreement on Subsidies and Countervailing Measures (n 434).

891 The second paragraph of item 'k' in the illustrative list of export subsidies, Annex I, ibid.

892 Article 2, ibid.

893 Serious prejudice, as per Article 5, ibid.

Given the fact that the proposed approaches attempt to facilitate LCT related exports and investments in a mutually beneficial fashion, it is not foreseen that the receiving country itself may object to such actions by the incentivising country. However, in the absence of a shared understanding to that effect, in case such measures are found as a subsidy, they may also be challenged by the receiving country in a dispute or through an injury investigation followed by the imposition of CVDs. As it is not considered forthcoming, we will refrain from that analysis.

The following paragraphs elaborate on these questions.

B *Scope of the Agreement*

The subject-matter scope of the SCM agreement is determined by the definition of a 'subsidy' as laid out in Article 1.1 therein. Accordingly, a subsidy exists when a benefit is conferred either by a financial contribution, or an income or price support. With respect to the measures under analysis, i.e. export credits and guarantees in different forms, the pertinent questions are, first, whether these are considerable as financial contributions; and second, if so, whether they confer benefit within the meaning of the ASCM.[894]

(i) Financial Contribution by a Government or Public Body [...]

Among the different avenues of support that are listed under Article 1.1(a)(1) of the SCM agreement, one explicitly covers credits and guarantees. The first item of that list is, "a government practice [that] involves a direct transfer of funds (e.g. grants, loans, and equity infusion), potential direct transfers of funds or liabilities (e.g. loan guarantees)". Different forms of export credit support for LCT diffusion would exactly fit this description.[895] Direct support measures such as export credit or interest rate support would be considered as actual transfer of funds. For example, in the *Japan – DRAMs (Korea)* the Appellate Body (AB) opined that the transactions that are similar to the ones given example of in the list are covered by the list scope.[896] In the *Brazil – Aircraft* dispute that involved interest rate support payment made by the Respondent to the institutions extending the export credit, it was not even contested that such

894 We do not explore the income and price support route because it is arguably a long stretch, for reasons below, to think that credit or guarantees would be found as such instead of financial contribution.

895 Dominic Coppens, 'Disciplines on Export Credit Support for Non-Agricultural Products', *WTO disciplines on subsidies and countervailing measures: balancing policy space and legal constraints* (Cambridge University Press 2014) 361–362.

896 *Japan – Countervailing Duties on Dynamic Random Access Memories from Korea* [2007] Appellate Body Report WT/DS336/AB/R, DSR 2007:VII 2703 [250–252].

supports are subsidies.[897] Pure cover supports, e.g. risk insurance or credit guarantees would be considered as a potential transfer of funds. Furthermore, to be considered as a financial contribution, it is not required for such transfers to be actually carried out.[898] It should also be noted that it is the actual measure by the government that fall suspect. So, in cases where the ECAs directly extend the support instead of going through a financial intermediary (e.g. a bank), then the transaction itself can be considered as a financial contribution. Similarly, in a situation where the government supports an intermediary to provide a guarantee or credit, it is the government support and not the credit itself that falls under the coverage of subsidy consideration.

Additionally, the subsidy definition requires that the putative financial contribution must also have a linkage with a government apparatus. Therefore, among the different types of export credits and guarantees supplied in the market by the private financial entities, multilateral development banks, as well as public institutions, which will fall within the scope of the SCM agreement depends on the wording of the provision on one hand and actual characteristics of the transaction on the other. Article 1.1(a)(1) specifies that the provider of support must be one of the three following – the government itself, or a public body within the domestic territorial domain, or even a private entity that is required by the government to provide such contribution as part of the governmental activity. Keeping this in view, support by the ECAs is indeed considerable as provided by the government or public body.[899] Support by private financial institutions would not automatically be so considered, as long as the private institution has no relationship with the government. However, it has been decided with respect to one dispute that the extent to which government or public support enables a private financial institution to supply export credits, the support itself would be considered a financial contribution.[900]

897 *Brazil – Export Financing Programme for Aircraft* [1999] Panel Report WT/DS46/R, DSR 1999:III 1121 7.12-7.14; For more, see *United States – Measures Affecting Trade in Large Civil Aircraft (Second Complaint)* [2012] Appellate Body Report WT/DS353/AB/R, DSR 2012:I 7 616, 620.

898 *Brazil – Export Financing Programme for Aircraft* (n 900) 7.13; *European Communities and Certain Member States – Measures Affecting Trade in Large Civil Aircraft* [2011] Panel Report WT/DS316/R, DSR 2011:II 685 7.302.

899 *Canada – Export Credits and Loan Guarantees for Regional Aircraft* [2002] Panel Report WT/DS222/R, DSR 2002:III 849 [7.62, 7.66]. The Respondent Canada did not dispute that financial support provided to Bombardier through its ECA, i.e. the Export Development Corporation (EDC) amounted to financial contribution within the meaning of ASCM Article 1.

900 *Brazil – Export Financing Programme for Aircraft* (n 897) para 7.12–7.13. Although the exporter received support through financial intermediaries, the Panel did not find

While in most cases, as mentioned above, the finding of official export credit support as a financial contribution would be straightforward, some ambiguous questions can indeed arise. One such is the issue of characterising the nature of support extended through state-owned enterprises (SOEs) or state-owned commercial banks (SOCBs). While such entities are not government itself, they could be considered as a 'public body'. However, such characterisation, according to the Appellate Body, must comprise of a careful and detailed, fact-based exercise to determine whether the entity "possesses, exercises, or is vested with governmental authority".[901] There must be "formal indicia of government control, [and] evidence that such control has been exercised in a meaningful way".[902] In absence of such evidence, the entities, even if substantially owned by the government, cannot be considered as a 'public body'. Mere policy pronouncements or situations where the private entities conduct is a by-product and not a result of government action is not sufficient.[903]

To sum up, export support activities by the ECAs would in most cases, in a straightforward fashion, be termed as a subsidy within the meaning of the SCM agreement. While covering government support, the agreement will, in all probability, also bring under its cover the activities of state-owned commercial entities, when providing similar natured supports to spread LCTs across borders. Whether the latter would be the case depends on various surrounding factors pertaining to the relationship between the government and the entity in question. There may be some opportunity to hide a support measure behind

it worthwhile to specify how it amounts as a subsidy. According to the Panel, the contested measure 'fulfils the definition of a subsidy because there is a government practice, whether it involves a direct transfer of funds -- as Canada believes -- or a potential direct transfer of funds – as Brazil believes. As soon as there is such a practice, a subsidy exists, and the question whether the practice involves a direct transfer of funds or a potential direct transfer of funds is not relevant to the existence of a subsidy'. [para 7.13].

901 *United States – Definitive Anti-Dumping and Countervailing Duties on Certain Products from China* [2011] Appellate Body Report WT/DS379/AB/R, DSR 2011:V 2869 [317, also 288, 290, and 310].

902 ibid 318. Also note para 319: "[i]n all instances, panels and investigating authorities are called upon to engage in a careful evaluation of the entity in question and to identify its common features and relationship with government in the narrow sense, having regard, in particular, to whether the entity exercises authority on behalf of government. An investigating authority must, in making its determination, evaluate and give due consideration to all relevant characteristics of the entity and, in reaching its ultimate determination as to how that entity should be characterised, avoid focusing exclusively or unduly on any single characteristic without affording due consideration to others that may be relevant".

903 *United States – Countervailing Duty Investigation on Dynamic Random Access Memory Semiconductors (DRAMS) from Korea* [2005] Appellate Body Report WT/DS296/AB/R, DSR 2005:XVI 8131 114.

non-transparent relationship between the government and an SOE, but this will not be sustainable in the long run.

(ii) Determination of Benefit

The finding of benefit being conferred as a result of financial contribution is an examination that compares different situations of the recipient before and after the contribution. The pivotal question to be answered is whether the financial support has rendered the recipient better off than the entity would otherwise have been. Whether the provider has incurred costs in doing so is irrelevant. With respect to export credit practice, one of the very early WTO panel dealing with the issue opined that when government support enables a domestic producer to offer better terms of finance to the purchaser, benefit can be considered to exist *prima facie.*[904]

Also, the exercise of benefit analysis takes place in the context of the existing market conditions. In the *Canada – Aircraft* dispute the AB endorsed the Panel finding that a financial contribution confers 'benefit' when "it is provided on terms more advantageous than those that would have been available to the recipient on the market".[905] Markets, according to the AB are "the area of economic activity in which buyers and sellers come together and the forces of supply and demand affect prices."[906] Defining the bounds of the relevant market, and finding an appropriate benchmark therein has, over time, emerged as a crucial point of determination.

Regarding the abovementioned use of a benchmark, Article 14 of the SCM agreement, detailing benchmark calculation guidelines for CVD investigations, is relevant as an interpretative context of Article 1.[907] It provides for different methods to determine the benchmark in the various settings of financial

904 *Brazil – Export Financing Programme for Aircraft – Second Recourse by Canada to Article 21.5 of the DSU* [2001] Panel Report WT/DS46/RW/2, DSR 2001:IX 5481 41, 42; Coppens, 'Disciplines on Export Credit Support for Non-Agricultural Products' (n 895) 363.

905 *Canada – Measures Affecting the Export of Civilian Aircraft* [1999] Panel Report WT/DS70/R, DSR 1999:IV 1443 [9.112]; *Canada – Measures Affecting the Export of Civilian Aircraft* [1999] Appellate Body Report WT/DS70/AB/R, DSR 1999:III 1377 [157, 158]. The standard latter became know as the 'private market test'.

906 *United States – Subsidies on Upland Cotton* [2005] Appellate Body Report WT/DS267/AB/R, DSR 2005:I 3 [7.1236]; *European Communities and Certain Member States – Measures Affecting Trade in Large Civil Aircraft – Recourse to Article 21.5 of the DSU by the Unites States* [2018] Appellate Body Report WT/DS316/AB/RW 1259.

907 *Japan – Countervailing Duties on Dynamic Random Access Memories from Korea* [2007] Panel Report WT/DS336/R, DSR 2007:VII 2805 7.275; *Canada – Certain Measures Affecting the Renewable Energy Generation Sector / Canada – Measures Relating to the Feed-in Tariff Program* (n 500) para 5.130.

contribution. Three of the four methods supplied in Article 14 cover equity support, loan and loan guarantee relate to Article 1.1(a)(1)(i) – the list item covering export credit practices.

a) *Identifying the Relevant Market: Simple Conclusion*

A possible straightforward conclusion regarding the finding of benefit can be that it exists any time official support is provided to complement the capacity failure of private financial markets in facilitating transactions involving LCTs.[908] The underlying argument is that these are transactions that would not otherwise take place in private market terms. We can also recall that the key reason behind our proposition is to enable exporters to engage in transactions that are not feasible under the current conditions of the market. If the contexts paragraph (b) or (c) of Article 14, as appropriate, is taken into account, the conclusion would point in the same direction. In both of those provisions, the support in question, i.e. a loan or a guarantee, is suggested to be assessed against the terms of a comparable commercial loan in the market.[909] So, the cases where instances of a comparable commercial support measure do not exist, or in other words, is not offered by any private operators, it would appear conclusive that the terms offered by the government to support LCT transactions are beneficial to the recipient.

b) *Alternate Conclusion: Distorted Market Argument*

In contrast to the straightforward conclusion above, it is submitted that some previous disputes have also taken account of situations where the private market test is difficult to apply due to the absence of an undistorted benchmark. For example, in the *United States – Softwood Lumber IV* dispute, reference prices that could be obtained in the domestic market were found to be distorted. The question was, in context of Article 14 (d) of the SCM agreement,[910]

908 Coppens, 'Disciplines on Export Credit Support for Non-Agricultural Products' (n 895) 366–367.

909 Paragraph (b) provides that "a loan [...] shall not be considered as conferring a benefit, unless there is a difference between the amount that the firm receiving the loan pays on the government loan and the amount the firm would pay on a *comparable commercial loan* which the firm *could actually obtain* on the market."

Paragraph (c) provides that "a loan guarantee [...] shall not be considered as conferring a benefit, unless there is a difference between the amount that the firm receiving the guarantee pays on a loan guaranteed by the government and the amount that the firm would pay on a *comparable commercial loan* absent the government guarantee." [emphasis supplied]

910 In situations where a government supplies goods or services to an entity, the Article 14(d) would mark that as beneficial, by the extent to which the remunerations fall short of

whether such prices should form the benchmark for benefit analysis. The Appellate Body held that under proven circumstances of predominant government role in the market to the effect that private prices are distorted, an investigating authority is justified in relying on out of market prices.[911] Later, in the *US – AD CVD* (*China*), both the Panel and the AB agreed that similar flexibility also exists under Article 14(b).[912] There, in the context of loan rates, it was held that when it is established that government intervention in the market has rendered the interest rates unusable as benchmarks,[913] Article 14(b) would not preclude establishing a comparable out-of-country benchmark,[914] as long as it is well approximated.[915] Such jurisprudence may help establish that in a given situation existing private market reference rates for credits, insurance or guarantees, or absence of such rates therein would call for out-of-market, constructed benchmarks to be used.

While developing a similar argument with respect to the proposed ECA based support measures, one key distinction ought to be made. With respect to LCT incentives, the market situation is different from the exampled disputes. While in the abovementioned situations the government influence distorts a benchmark that could potentially exist, in the current case there may not be any pre-existing benchmark as the clean technology spreading transactions would not otherwise take place at all. Especially in the latter situation, as previously argued, the government intervention is proposed to cure a private capital market failure to allocate an optimal level of resources to facilitate LCT diffusion. In sum, while the proposed promotion of LCT transactions by the

being adequate. It is to be noted that the provision dictates the adequacy of remuneration to be determined 'in relation to' the prevailing market conditions.

911 *United States – Final Countervailing Duty Determination with Respect to Certain Softwood Lumber from Canada* [2004] Appellate Body Report WT/DS257/AB/R, DSR 2004:II 571 [103.]. The conclusion was arrived at by the Appellate Body based on the finding that with the phrase 'in relation to' in Article 14(d) the drafters did not intend to exclude the possibility of using alternate benchmarks [para 88–89]. This was a conclusion, which according to the AB was supported by the intent and purpose of the SCM agreement [93–95]. Surprisingly the AB analysis began by an agreement with the Panel that provision in question does not call for comparison with a purely free market [87].

912 *United States – Countervailing and Anti-Dumping Measures on Certain Products from China* [2014] Panel Report WT/DS449/R, DSR 2014:VIII 3175 [10.40–10.45]; *United States – Countervailing and Anti-Dumping Measures on Certain Products from China* [2014] Appellate Body Report WT/DS449/AB/R, DSR 2014:VIII 3027 [489].

913 *United States – Countervailing and Anti-Dumping Measures on Certain Products from China* (n 912) para 479.

914 ibid 480.

915 ibid 482–483. Such approximation comprises of various factors, including the repayment terms, time of the loan, maturity, size, and currency [paras 475–476, 486].

ECAs is indeed a positive intervention in the financial market, it may have an effect of establishing a new benchmark standard, rather than distorting and existing one.

In connection with the above, it can further be argued that the financial market space where the intervention takes place is already distorted, as it does not allocate resources in an optimal fashion. Therefore, any positive intervention to alter such a situation shall not be automatically considered as conferment of benefit to the recipient. Instead, such interventions should only be compared to similar situations. This position can be substantiated drawing support from the AB decision in the *Canada – Renewable Energy* dispute. With respect to Article 1, and in context of Article 14(d) of the SCM agreement, one of the questions in that dispute was whether the remuneration provided by the respondent government was 'more than adequate'.[916] The Appellate Body clarified that to define the scope of the relevant market in which a benefit is considered to have been conferred, one ought to take into account all available evidence, including supply-side considerations, and government demand preference, if any.[917] The Appellate Body further mentioned that finding of the appropriate benchmark in the relevant market should not be considered as thwarted by government intervention, more so in situation where the market itself is an outcome of such intervention.[918] The AB also proposed that the situations of a new market creation and distortion of an existing one should be distinguished from one another when looking for the potential existence of benefit due to government intervention in any market.[919] Where a new market is created, the benchmark of benefit ought to be found in that market, or by constructing a proxy for comparison.[920] It is relevant to recall that in the dispute, an ideal benefit benchmark to measure remuneration provided to the renewable energy suppliers was eventually considered to be one that takes account of the intended government supply-mix and reflects what a market would yield.[921] The latter or the proxy thereof could be found in administered prices or through price discovery mechanisms.[922]

---

916 *Canada – Certain Measures Affecting the Renewable Energy Generation Sector / Canada – Measures Relating to the Feed-in Tariff Program* (n 500) para 5.159–5.161.

917 ibid 5.171–5.178. To note – "The definition of a certain supply-mix by the government cannot *in and of itself* be considered as conferring a benefit within the meaning of Article 1.1(b)." [Para 5.175].

918 ibid 5.182.

919 ibid 5.188.

920 ibid 5.184, 5.227–5.228.

921 ibid 5.225–5.227.

922 ibid 5.228.

We see that the position taken by the AB in the above dispute bolsters the argument that the market of climate technology related export credits is distinguishable from the general financial market due to a given a specific policy prerogative, domestically or internationally. While measuring the benefit benchmark in the appropriate context of Article 14(b) or 14(c) of the ASCM, it should be remembered that those provisions have the similar flexibility like Article 14(d), as mentioned above. Moreover, nothing in the AB elaboration of relevant market identification indicates that it should only be applicable to situations guided by Article 14(d). With respect to assessing the LCT support activities of the ECA s, the relevant market can be seen as that of finance terms offered by the sellers of LCT s and accepted by the buyers. ECA support for such transaction should not in and of itself be considered a subsidy, only because such transactions would not otherwise take place.

Practical benefit of the above argument can be subject to some scepticism at least. First, the ECAs at present do not operate under a climate protection mandate.[923] Those that promote climate projects, do so due to the unique specialisation of the domestic industries.[924] So it would be difficult to justify an ECA measure as a climate policy-driven market formation initiative. Second, the new market creation argument will not work in situations where there are private financial entities offering support to clean technology exporters and investors, but doing so at a high rate. The offering of better credit terms by the ECAs in such situations has less chances to avoid being seen as a subsidy. Third, success of the market creation argument can prove to be counterproductive, if there are no checks on the public policy motives considered as an eligible excuse for new market formation. If the argument, as employed in the *Canada – Renewable Energy* dispute, is allowed to serve any preferred policy intent by the government, it can hypothetically be extended to everywhere, e.g. saving coal jobs, or ensuring affordable access to power through coal power plants etc. As a result, in the absence of further normative limitations, the AB interpretation in that dispute is dangerous to follow. The potential utility of the

923 We highlight the latter part of a paragraph cited earlier. The Appellate Body, while quoting the Panel, holds that '[c]onsideration related to [the] externalities will often [...] be the reason why governments intervene to create markets [...]. On this point, we agree with the Panel's statement that, where government intervention that internalizes social costs and benefits is limited to defining the broad parameters of the market, "significant scope will remain for private actors to operate within those parameters on the basis of commercial considerations"'. ibid 5.189.

924 The developed countries still remain the leaders in low-carbon innovation. See Chapter 2 III A at pp. 77-79 above.

doctrine of Common Concern to limit the scope of this approach, as well as to find alternate benchmarks are discussed later in the chapter.[925]

To conclude, government financial contribution for clean technology export through the supply of credits or guarantees may not as straightforwardly be construed as a subsidy, as it may seem upon first look. There is some opportunity to argue that a clean technology supporting financial measures belong to an exclusive market and therefore should only be compared with a benchmark therein. If not readily available, such a benchmark should be constructed. While this approach may prevent any such financial support from being considered a subsidy *per se,* it ought to be noted that a detailed, fact-intensive benefit analysis will not always save a measure. Also, making an argument as such requires further opportunity be made available to a dispute settlement Panel to make normative distinctions between policy objectives.

(iii) Incentives Falling outside the ASCM Coverage

There is nothing in the SCM agreement's definition of subsidies that prevent an investment incentive from falling under its scope. However, no such measure can come under the scrutiny of its rules, because it was not the intent of the drafters to expand the scope of the covered agreements to investment activities. This is clear from the Marrakesh Agreement Establishing the World Trade Organization, as well as the earlier GATT. Article XVI of GATT, which is the predecessor of the ASCM, mentions that the provision comes into play only when a subsidy "operates directly or indirectly to increase exports [...] or reduce imports [...]".[926] Later, the Marrakesh Agreement articulated the objective of the WTO as to "provide the common institutional framework for the conduct of *trade relations* among its members [...]".[927] In a rare exploration of the impact of home state measures to promote investment, Sauvant and others have noted that often the home country measures (HCM) to promote OFDI and trade-related subsidies are provided by the same agencies. While the latter frequently came under scrutiny at the WTO court, the authors maintain that HCMs are unregulated.[928]

It is also not likely that supports by the multilateral development banks (MDB), or other international financial institutions (IFI) will be considered as a subsidy. Such supports can neither be attributed to a domestic government, nor a public body within the meaning of the term elaborated earlier. The

---

925 See section III A at pp. 233-234 below.

926 Article XVI(1), General Agreement on Tariffs and Trade (n 426).

927 Article II(1), Marrakesh Agreement Establishing the World Trade Organization (n 226).

928 Box 1, 'HCMs and the WTO's Agreement on Subsidies and Countervailing Measures', Sauvant and others (n 852).

MDBs work at a supra-national level. Furthermore, only a public body 'within the territories' of a WTO member may fall within the scope of the definition.[929] It should also be noted that the Panel in the *EC – Large Civil Aircraft* dispute mentioned that even though services rendered by a multilateral financial institution may conspicuously fall within the terms of the definition, hardly any may be such that can be considered actionable.[930]

Moreover, like the ASCM, which deals with subsidisation with regard to trade in goods, there are no comparable rules regarding trade in services. Although the WTO members have committed to negotiate on the multilateral disciplines on removing the distortive effects of services subsidisation while taking account of the developing country needs in particular, any substantive rules are yet to emerge.[931] As a result, it remains possible to supply services related to LCTs, like education, training, engineering and construction, transport, accounting, and financial services to the developing countries in subsidised terms, without drawing a challenge under the current WTO rules.

In sum, there are no obstacles for the developed countries to incentivise the domestic technology holders in making greenfield investments to technology seeking destinations. The same official public assistance measures as proposed in this chapter can trigger and support investment outflows as well. One way would be to provide incentives to the parent firms when they supply better emission reduction technologies to their developing country subsidiaries. Trade and investment promotion supports of any form, when coming from the MDBs, remain outside the ASCM scope as well. Beyond the scope of the proposed measures, supply of climate technology related services to developing countries can also be incentivised without breaking WTO rules.

C *Export Incentive and Regulation on Prohibited Subsidies*

The structure of the SCM agreement provides one shortcut route to challenge export credit activities. This is by claiming a breach of the illustrative list of prohibited subsidies. The list, appended to the SCM agreement as an annex, is a historic legacy that has been carried over to the WTO rules framework. It was the outcome of the GATT era attempts by the contracting parties to regulate trade distortive subsidies. As a definition of subsidy could not be agreed upon, the best compromise outcome was a list that designated certain circumstances

929 Coppens, 'Disciplines on Export Credit Support for Non-Agricultural Products' (n 895) 362.

930 *European Communities and Certain Member States – Measures Affecting Trade in Large Civil Aircraft* (n 898) 7.888.

931 Article XV, General Agreement on Trade in Services (n 428).

and thresholds in and beyond which government supports are prohibited. As the SCM agreement inherited the list, it serves as instances of clear cases where a subsidy is contingent on export performance. Items 'j' and 'k' of the list lay down threshold conditions for government support made through guarantees, insurances, and credits. Therefore, to the extent the level of official direct credit support or pure cover support goes beyond the suggested thresholds therein, a case of *per se* breach can be made, without even needing to separately establish the existence of subsidisation.[932]

The wording of the paragraph 'k' of the illustrative list also contains a rare exception, one that saves certain export credit measures when those are in line with the relevant 'interest rate provisions' of the OECD arrangement. Since the lapse of the non-actionable subsidies, this provision, known as the 'safe-haven', is the only exception mechanism applicable with respect to export credits.

That apart, government promotion of clean technology through the ECAs are amenable to be challenged as a prohibited export subsidy. As already mentioned, Article 3.1(a) of the Subsidies Agreement prohibits subsidies that are contingent upon export performance, either in law or in fact. Although it intuitively appears that an export credit would be found to be contingent on exportation, we will see that a lot depends on the design and actual operation of the measure as well as the specific characteristics in each instance.

(i) Per Se Prohibition under the Illustrative List

The common element in both the list provisions is that, characteristic to the other illustrative list items, a prohibition of support provided at a net cost to the government. This, except for explicit exceptions, is the main purpose of the list – i.e. establishment of certain clear cases of prohibited subsidies. The list is also unique as all the cases therein are examples of costs incurred by the government, which is a standard that was eventually avoided in the later agreed definition of 'subsidy' incorporated the SCM agreement. Here we take a closer look at the two relevant list provisions and their implication for LCT support.

a) *Item 'j': Pure Cover Supports*

Item 'j' prevents the following-

> The provision by governments (or special institutions controlled by governments) of export credit guarantee or insurance programmes, of insurance

---

932 *Korea – Measures Affecting Trade in Commercial Vessels* [2005] Panel Report WT/DS273/R, DSR 2005:VII 2749 [7.204]; *Canada – Export Credits and Loan Guarantees for Regional Aircraft* (n 899) para 7.395.

> or guarantee programmes against increases in the cost of exported products or of exchange risk programmes, at premium rates which are inadequate to cover the long-term operating costs and losses of the programmes.

A plain reading of the text would correctly suggest that the prohibition is on incurring net costs in the long run with respect to a pure cover support programme. Breach of this provision is only established by evaluating the long-term performance of the program in its entirety, and when proved, the whole program will be considered prohibited.

The immediate question that would arise is whether all forms of insurances and guarantees to facilitate LCT related commercial transactions will attract the involvement of the item 'j', which upon reading appears to be of limited scope. As the text shows, operation of the paragraph extends to programmes providing security against cost increases of exported products and exchange risks. While none of the dispute decisions so far have elucidated what this entails, it is possible to envisage that not all forms of risk supports extended by an ECA with respect to LCT transactions relate to protection against price increase or exchange rate risks. For example, a seller may be prompted to disengage from a potential transaction due to political, or financial risks being involved, or simply due to lack of information, irrespective of the price performance of the export or the prevalent currency exchange rates. Risk sharing programs to assist a seller in such situations seemingly will not come under the coverage of the item 'j'. These can therefore only be dealt with under the general rule on export subsidy under Article 3.1(a) of the agreement.

The nature of the evidence required to establish a breach of the paragraph 'j' may further make it difficult for a complainant to challenge an LCT support program. So far, only in the *US – Upland Cotton* dispute, the Panel was provided with an opportunity to explore that question of evidentiary requirement. The Panel expounded therein that it was not the precise amount of a premium, but the adequacy of it to cover the long-term costs of the program was subject to assessment under paragraph 'j'.[933] To that effect, the Panel's extensive analysis of the respondent's export credit programmes comprised of an assessment of the past performance whether the programmes were run at net cost or not, also of the relevant elements of the programmes' structure, design, and operation.[934] The approach was later endorsed by the AB.[935] In that dispute, data

933 *United States – Subsidies on Upland Cotton* [2005] Panel Report WT/DS267/R, DSR 2005:II 299 [7.823–7.825].

934 ibid 7.841.

935 *United States – Subsidies on Upland Cotton* (n 906) paras 664–674.

ranging for a period of 10 years (1992–2002) was considered by the Panel. Given the confidential nature of the export credit support programmes, producing such detailed data for the respondent is not bereft of substantial complexity for the complainant. In the absence of appropriate measures to protect business confidential information, the respondent may also refuse to supply the data necessary to prove the case.[936]

With special regard to climate change related transactions, yet another question could be whether, or how the financial benefit of avoided emission in the long-run would be factored in measuring the operating costs and losses of a government insurance or guarantee program. If the government program to support clean technology transactions is guided by the motive to resolve a common concern, then the avoided emission is undoubtedly a benefit the government seeks to generate with the support. It makes reasonable sense if the computation of the long-term cost of a program also takes account of the benefit generated by avoiding costly emissions. One problem, however, is that such benefit would probably need to somehow accrue to the provider to be taken into account. These are questions that remain unresolved.

It should also be noted that the OECD arrangement, while providing for guidelines on credit risk premium, obliges the participants to pay at least the minimum rates (MPRs). What is of interest is that Article 23 of the arrangement holds that the "premium rates […] shall not be inadequate to cover long-term operating costs and losses". This borrowed language from paragraph 'j' raises the question of whether the OECD suggested MPRs would *per se* be probative of the absence of net cost support by the credit supplier. While the construction of the MPRs may factually make sure that a pure cover support program by the ECA is not run at net cost, from a legal point of view, compliance with the MPR may not automatically shield from the finding of paragraph 'j' breach, for reasons mentioned in later paragraphs.[937] Such compliance may nonetheless be of factual support when the long-run performance of the program will be assessed.

b) *Item 'k', First Paragraph: Direct Credit Support*

First paragraph of the item 'k' prevents the following-

> The grant by governments […] of export credits at rates below those which they actually have to pay for the funds so employed […], or the

---

936 *Canada – Measures Affecting the Export of Civilian Aircraft* (n 905) para 9.175–9.177, 9.188–9.189.

937 See Chapter 5 II C (iii) at pp. 228–229.

payment by them of all or part of the costs incurred by exporters or financial institutions in obtaining credits, in so far as they are used to secure a material advantage in the field of export credit terms.

The provision deals with direct supports, in the form of direct credits or interest rate supports, either fully or in part. What is prohibited are transactions that result in a net cost to the government. This is also the point of similarity of the current provision when compared to paragraph 'j'. However, the difference lies in the fact that while the previous provision assesses the net cost in the long run, no similar temporal bound exists in the current provision. Therefore, a complainant can challenge individual export credit transactions as being in breach of the item 'k' of the illustrative list.

The general issue, equally persisting regarding the LCT related transactions, is that of determining 'material advantage' as prohibited in the above provision. This remains open for interpretation. In one instance, the Appellate Body held that a rate of interest below the CIRR could raise a rebuttable presumption that advantage gained has been material.[938] This can serve only an illustrative purpose and not more, as the rules of treaty interpretation would not endorse equating the scope of the meaning of 'material advantage' as that going above the CIRR. In absence of an express mention in the text of the provision, the OECD arrangement may only have very little contextual relevance for interpretative purposes.

Arguably, a finding that a technology export promoting measure does not constitute material advantage provided to the producer *per se*, does not make the respondent any safe. Because a complainant, failing to establish a breach of the illustrative list, can nevertheless challenge the subsidy as violating Article 3.1(a) provision. It has however been claimed that the illustrative list provision can be flipped and used as a defence. As the paragraph portrays export subsidy as net cost export credits provided to secure material advantage, Brazil, as a respondent argued in a dispute that if, on the contrary, it is proven that the measure is not taken to secure material advantage, it should be sufficient to conclude that it is not prohibited at all.[939] We look at this *a contrario* claim below.

---

938 *Brazil – Export Financing Programme for Aircraft – Recourse by Canada to Article 21.5 of the DSU* [2000] Appellate Body Report WT/DS46/AB/RW, DSR 2000:VIII 4067 [64, 67]; Coppens, 'Disciplines on Export Credit Support for Non-Agricultural Products' (n 895) 371–372.

939 The basis of the argument lies in footnote 5 of the SCM agreement which provides that – " [m]easures referred to in Annex I as *not constituting export subsidies* shall not

(ii) Interpreting *A Contrario:* "So Far as [...] to Secure a Material Advantage"

The *a contrario* argument is not an example of logical coherence. We recall that the first paragraph of item 'k' provides one illustration of prohibited export credit support, i.e. when provided at a 'net cost' to the government and resulting in 'material advantage' to the recipient. Disproving either, or both of these requirements can only mean that the measure is not prohibited within the illustrated scenario of item 'k'. Falling out of the coverage of this one specific scenario does not logically imply that the measure is absolved of any possible prohibited characteristics. The first paragraph does not lay down anything on situations that "do not constitute export subsidy" as laid down in footnote 5.[940] Therefore this line of argument is unmeritorious.

In the *Brazil – Aircraft 21.5* dispute, the Panel categorically rejected the *a contrario* argument for the first time.[941] Noting that the footnote 5 extends to only those provisions that affirmatively regard a transaction as not prohibited, the panel indicated that the first paragraph of item 'k' is not worded as an affirmative exception.[942] Treating it as such would have taken away the special meaning of the distinctive drafting of the affirmative exceptions in the illustrative list (e.g. safe-haven clause in the second paragraph). The panel also highlighted that such a reading would eventually run counter to the interests of the developing countries, as it would be comparatively easier for a developed country to subsidise exporters.[943] It was also noted that attempts at that time of reforming the SCM agreement proposed modified language for footnote 5 that does away with the opportunity of making such an argument.[944]

However, this issue lingers because the Appellate Body did not follow suit in categorically rejecting the *a contrario* argument. The AB did not endorse it either. While addressing the respondent's appeal in the above dispute, the AB decided that Brazil failed to discharge the burden of establishing the benchmark

---

be prohibited under this or any other provision of this Agreement" [emphasis supplied]. Brazil maintained this position throughout the aircraft disputes.

940 Ibid.

941 *Brazil – Export Financing Programme for Aircraft – Recourse by Canada to Article 21.5 of the DSU* [2000] Panel Report WT/DS46/RW, DSR 2000:IX 4093 10–23; The conclusions were confirmed by the panel in the second compliance dispute as well. See *Brazil – Export Financing Programme for Aircraft – Second Recourse by Canada to Article 21.5 of the DSU* (n 904) 61–63.

942 *Brazil – Export Financing Programme for Aircraft – Recourse by Canada to Article 21.5 of the DSU* (n 941) para 6.36–6.37.

943 ibid 6.57–6.59.

944 ibid 6.39–6.41.

(other than the CIRR) against which material advantage is to be measured.[945] This precluded the AB from addressing the argument that no material advantage was provided. However, the AB mentioned that if Brazil would have discharged the burden of proof, it could have been found that the measure was "*justified* under item (k) of the Illustrative List".[946] As a result, though logically unsound, there remains a sliver of possibility that the *a contrario* argument may be entertained in the future.

Even allowing an *a contrario* reading would not be particularly beneficial to the LCT export incentives. If it develops as a carve-out, it would be a general one. Nothing would prevent the members from using the defence for climate defeating purposes.

(iii) The Utility of Compliance with the OECD Arrangement

The safe-haven, found in the second paragraph of item 'k' of the illustrative list, provides that "if a member is a party to [the OECD arrangement], or if in practice a member applies the interest rates provisions of the relevant undertaking, an export credit practice which conforms with those provisions shall not be considered an export subsidy prohibited by this Agreement". Once again, the wording is reminiscent of so far back a past that at present it gives rise to intractable ambiguities, as well as legitimacy challenges potentially affecting LCT related official support as much as others.

The plain reading of the provision above suggests that there are two points of entry to the affirmative exception of the safe-haven. One is by actual participation in the OECD arrangement, and another by applying in practice the interest rate provisions of the prevailing version at the time. In both cases, the outcome is that the member's export credit practice is safe from being prohibited as long as there is compliance with the interest rate provisions. Therefore, it is a hypothetical possibility that some of the LCT related official support measures will fall within the coverage of the safe-haven.

From a legal point of view, the scope of the carve-out depends on how one understands the term 'export credit practice' in the provision reproduced above. It was initially held that the meaning should in no way be limited to specific forms of transactions.[947] In that sense, the safe-haven may save both direct

945 *Brazil – Export Financing Programme for Aircraft – Recourse by Canada to Article 21.5 of the DSU* (n 938) 23–25.

946 ibid 80. [emphasis supplied].

947 *Canada – Measures Affecting the Export of Civilian Aircraft* (n 905) para 5.81; *Brazil – Export Financing Programme for Aircraft – Second Recourse by Canada to Article 21.5 of the DSU* (n 904) para 5.65–5.66.

credit supports (direct finance, re-finance, and interest rate support) and pure cover supports (credit guarantees and insurances). However, according to later Panels, the additional requirement of applying the 'interest rate provisions' therein would limit the scope of the safe-haven only to those support measures regarding which the interest rates play a role. Taking the interest rates to be the CIRR, Panels narrowed down the scope of the safe-haven to one specific type of support, i.e. direct export credits on fixed interest rates.[948] It conforms with the provisions of the arrangement, as the CIRR is applicable therein only with respect to official financing supports advanced at fixed rates,[949] with a repayment term of two years or more.[950]

While one may nevertheless argue for a wider interpretation of the term 'interest rate provisions', so as to comprise also guidelines on the floating rate credits, guarantees, and insurances, this would depart not only from the literal understanding of the safe-haven, but also the common intent animated in the related illustrative list provisions. At the time of drawing up the list, the concepts of minimum premium rates (MPRs) for risks and floating rate loans were not existing as modes of official support. The version of the OECD arrangement prevailing at that time did not contain any such provisions as well. In those early days, most of the export credit practice comprised of fixed-rate credits. Moreover, the subject-matter term to be interpreted here, i.e. 'interest rate provision', is of particularly technical in nature, which is limitative of a possible evolutionary understanding. Nevertheless, there are indeed instances in trade law jurisprudence, where underlying common intent of the covered agreements has been construed in ways not completely foreseen.[951] Providing a wider scope of meaning to the term 'interest rate provision' may serve to bring the floating rate supports within the safe-haven coverage. But bringing the MPRs within its folds would indeed be overstretching.

---

948 Coppens, 'Disciplines on Export Credit Support for Non-Agricultural Products' (n 895) 380; *Canada – Measures Affecting the Export of Civilian Aircraft – Recourse by Brazil to Article 21.5 of the DSU* [2000] Panel Report WT/DS70/RW, DSR 2000:IX 4315 [5.93–5.106]; *Brazil – Export Financing Programme for Aircraft – Second Recourse by Canada to Article 21.5 of the DSU* (n 904) para 5.102.

949 Article 19, OECD, 'arrangement on Officially Supported Export Credits' (n 865).

950 Article 5, ibid.

951 For example, in the *United States – Gambling and Betting Services* (DS 285), it was determined that commitments relating to trade in services scheduled by a Member would also cover instances of supply over the internet. While well-reasoned, this decision cannot be said to be an outcome commonly envisaged by the Members at the time of negotiating the GATS provisions. For a detailed review, see Sascha Wunsch-Vincent, 'The Internet, Cross-Border Trade in Services, and the GATS: Lessons from US-Gambling' (2006) 5 World Trade Review 319.

Compliance with the interest rate provisions may not provide any special advantage to boosting LCT transactions. As mentioned before, the ECAs themselves are primarily motivated to promote export by complementing the private financial flows. Therefore, any general saving of official support measures by the ECAs is going to be of use for all forms of economic activities, which may end up increasing rather than lowering global emissions. Also, required compliance with the CIRR in the OECD arrangement is only useful to peg the lending rates against the currency of the participants and to prevent a downward competition in that regard among the dominant players.[952] Such prevention may not even be a good idea, as freer competition in export credit terms, especially when offered to the cash poor developing country buyers, may see more public financial resources being invested in facilitating clean technology transactions. While it is not impossible to introduce more flexibility regarding interest rates for LCT related transactions in the arrangement, no such effort is forthcoming. Nor is there any step on expanding the subject-matter scope of the climate mitigation understanding in the arrangement.

Apart from the safe-haven provision, the overall influence sought to be exercised by the participants to the arrangement upon the SCM agreement provision is not beyond criticism. As already mentioned, the compliance with the arrangement provision has already been provided probative value by the AB with respect to legal issues beyond the safe-haven clause. Furthermore, the arrangement language keeps evolving in a fashion that seeks to influence the understanding of other illustrative list provisions, especially the item 'j' therein. Article 23 of the arrangement currently provides that "[t]he premium rates charged by the Participants shall […] not be inadequate to cover long-term operating costs and losses". This opens the possibility that in later disputes, compliance with the MPRs will be taken as presumptive of abidance with the item 'j' requirement. Similarly, with regard to the provision on matching,[953] the wording suggests that a participant would not be found to be in contravention of the arrangement rules when matching interest rates below the CIRR by other participant or non-participant.[954] Therefore, a case of matching can still

952 Article 20, Chapter II, OECD, 'arrangement on Officially Supported Export Credits' (n 865). The (CIRR) are calculated for currencies of the participating members upon request, based on the rate of return on respective bonds.

953 For 'matching', see Box 4 at p. 205 above.

954 Article 18, OECD, 'arrangement on Officially Supported Export Credits' (n 865). It holds that 'Financial terms and conditions provided in accordance with this Article are considered to be in conformity with the provisions of Chapters I, II […]'. Chapter II contains the interest rate provisions of the arrangement.

be found to be consistent with the interest rate provisions of the arrangement while effectively going below the CIRR rates. These *de facto* influences that can be exercised through the arrangement provision, raises a legitimacy question, as the participants to the OECD arrangement is only a handful of high-income developed countries. We will revert to this issue while discussing the possible avenues for reforming the SCM agreement in light of the Common Concern doctrine.

(iv) The *De Facto* or *De Jure* Export Contingency

Subsidies that are contingent on export performance are prohibited under the ASCM. This includes both *de jure,* and *de facto* contingencies. This raises the question of whether any official export credit support, except for those in compliance with the OECD interests rates, can be saved if found to constitute a subsidy. The answer depends on the meaning of export contingency. A subsidy is contingent on export performance when boosting export is a condition to the grant. The distinction between *de jure* and *de facto* export contingency is that in the former case the conditionality can be read from the law explicitly or by implication,[955] whereas in the latter case it is a fact-driven exercise. Export finance instruments, when considerable as a subsidy, may clearly be *de jure* export subsidy as it only focuses on export transactions. Also, with contextual support drawn from the illustrative list, it would be so confirmed.

Even if the ECA supports are not considered *de jure* export contingent, they cannot avoid being taken as *de facto* contingent. The *de facto* export contingency is a well-tuned standard, where the ultimate goal is to determine whether a subsidy under consideration changes the undistorted market performance of the recipient in a fashion that is relatively export boosting.[956] This investigation takes account of the design, structure, and operation of the measure in question, as well as the relevant surrounding features. In the *EC – Large Civil Aircraft* dispute, the AB mentions that one way of finding *de facto* contingency would be comparing the ratio between anticipated export and domestic production after the subsidy and the same ratio before such support.[957] It has been emphasised that the "total configuration of facts constituting and surrounding the grant" should be taken into account. The mere knowledge that

955 *European Communities and Certain Member States – Measures Affecting Trade in Large Civil Aircraft* (n 815) para 1038. The report in turn cited a former AB report, *Canada – Measures Affecting the Export of Civilian Aircraft* (n 905) para 167.

956 *European Communities and Certain Member States – Measures Affecting Trade in Large Civil Aircraft* (n 816) para 1045.

957 ibid 1047, 1056.

the recipient's business is export-oriented in nature does not prove export contingency in itself.[958] Policy intent, however benevolent, would not save a financial support from being seen as *de facto* export contingent. Altogether, it would appear that measures exclusively promoting export transactions of LCTs such as the one proposed in this chapter would be found as *de facto* contingent upon export performance.

The brief discussion above serves to show the difficulty in saving an LCT enhancing official export credit measure from being considered as a prohibited subsidy. There are certain design features that may provide little shelter making a finding of export contingency somewhat difficult. For example, if a measure that boosts domestic, as well as export transactions at similar rates would be difficult to be found as illegal. The proposed measure would require further adaptation to make use of this shelter.

D *Other Challenges to the Export Promotion Incentives*

(i) Specificity

Apart from the prohibited category, subsidies can only be challenged when those are specific. Finding a subsidy as specific can eventually be a factual determination exercise unless the support is legally constrained to specific entities, enterprises, or industries. The factual consideration in this regard includes the characteristics of the recipient enterprises, the manner of the grant by the authorities, as well as the time period of the grant etc. The specificity requirement highlights that the design of the incentives would play a role. Open-ended, transparent, and industry-wide availability of such support would help the finding of non-specificity. For the same reasons, it may as well be difficult to find official export promotion supports as specific, as these programs tend not to distinguish between industries, or sectors. The same applies to LCT diffusion support as well. Any official support measure should be made wide enough so that relevant mitigation technologies in any part of the destination country's economy can come under the coverage.

(ii) Actionability

Even though a technology export credit is saved by the safe-haven provision, it is not saved from challenges under other parts of the SCM agreement when found to be specific in nature. This is despite the mention in the Agreement that measures the illustrative list declares as not constituting prohibited subsidy shall not be so construed under any other provisions.[959] The Appellate

958 *Canada – Measures Affecting the Export of Civilian Aircraft* (n 905) 167–173.

959 Footnote 5, Agreement on Subsidies and Countervailing Measures (n 434).

Body chose to read the relevant language narrowly, construing that the expression only related to the determination of the prohibited nature of the subsidy and not determination of the actionability altogether.[960] The reading opens the possibility that even the arrangement compliant official export credit supports can be challenged multilaterally as an actionable subsidy or unilaterally countervailed.

Earlier we have assumed that it would be less plausible that the countries gaining access to new technologies as a result of official support, would launch a countervailing duty investigation or challenge such measures in dispute on account of adverse effects to domestic industries. Even in absence of such challenge, it is probable that third parties, e.g. WTO members having a competing industry in the technology sector in question may bring a dispute against the member extending the export credit on account of 'serious prejudice'.[961] According to Article 6.3, a member can be seriously prejudiced if, *inter alia,* subsidies displace or impede its exports in a third country market; or if the subsidy results in significant price undercutting. In cases where export credit support goes to a foreign sector facing competing export interests (e.g. export of solar panels) from elsewhere, it can plausibly draw complaints from the competitors.

III Looking Forward: Role of Common Concern

The foregoing section made a detailed explanation showing that the extent to which official support for LCT exports come under the SCM agreement, they could be challenged in disputes, except for the supports provided at fixed interests rates in line with the OECD arrangement. Looking forward, two avenues appear. One is to avoid support options that draw challenge under the SCM agreement. This means support through the non-governmental institutions, as well as concentrating incentives to domestic companies for OFDI activities involving clean technologies. Another avenue is to look at whether the doctrine of Common Concern supplies any suggestion towards saving the export support measures within the ASCM scope. This section further elaborates upon the second avenue. It explores the implications of the doctrine with respect to

960 *United States – Tax Treatment for 'Foreign Sales Corporations'* [2000] Appellate Body Report WT/DS108/AB/R, DSR 2000:III 1619 [93]; Coppens, 'Disciplines on Export Credit Support for Non-Agricultural Products' (n 895) 387.

961 Article 5(c) read with Article 6.3, Agreement on Subsidies and Countervailing Measures (n 434).

the *status quo*, and also takes a close look at the possibilities of moving forward in circumstances where the current paradigm provides no solution. While the former calls for finding a favourable reading of the existing rules, the latter would require examining the opportunities for reform.

A As an Aid to Interpretation

The doctrine of Common Concern can be of aid to further structure the reconciling position taken by the AB with respect to measuring benefit in the context of subsidy determination. We recall that the AB decision in the *Canada – Renewable Energy* endorsed the possibility that the governments may, driven by policy reasons, create heretofore non-existent markets.[962] It has been explained earlier that although policy considerations found a way into the determination of a benefit benchmark, so far no normative criterion exists to evaluate the preference of one policy goal over another. Without any limits, such an approach can fall prey to arbitrary designations of policy goals, resulting in unabated subsidisation.[963] Instead of being all-out critical of the AB position like most scholars, it is submitted that if public policy motivation to intervene in the existing market is given overriding precedence only in cases marked by the necessity to address otherwise intractable market failures, a reasonable distinction could be created between favourable government interventions others. The Common Concern doctrine will be helpful to that effect.

Within a recognised frame of Common Concern, as laid out in Chapter 3, official support measures for higher exports of LCTs would be seen in a favourable light. In the context of the proposed narrative therein, resolving the failure of private financial markets to channel adequate resources for transactions favouring LCTs is an obligation that must be discharged through complementary public support. Common Concern, therefore, strengthens the policy position that governments can and should take measures to boost technology supply for internalising emission externalities across borders, by enabling realisation of new export transactions that would not take place under current market terms. Such new transactions, made possible through official technology support should not be deemed as subsidies *per se*. Rather, whether

962 See p. 218 above.

963 Luca Rubini, 'ASCM Disciplines and Recent WTO Case Law Devlopments: What Space for "Green" Subsidies?' in Thomas Cottier and Ilaria Espa (eds), *International Trade in Sustainable Electricity: Regulatory Challenges in International Economic Law* (Cambridge University Press 2017) 330–331; Luca Rubini, '"The Wide and the Narrow Gate": Benchmarking in the SCM agreement after the *Canada–Renewable Energy/FIT* Ruling' (2015) 14 World Trade Review 211, 222–223.

benefit has been conferred in such a situation would call for construction of a benchmark taking into account all the relevant factors. While the nature of relevant information may vary from case to case, some recurrent factor to take under consideration can include the necessity of the transaction evidenced by its contribution in resolving a Common Concern, the risk profile of the technology recipient country and firm, cost information of the exporter etc. One concrete approach can be to take the relevant interest or premium rate as suggested by the OECD arrangement, and making further adjustment thereupon.[964] Ultimately, as long as a transaction is necessary to respond to a Common Concern, official support thereof should be considered beneficial only if it results in a more than a reasonable profit to the recipient. The utility of the Common Concern of Humankind doctrine would lie in its assistance to highlight an existing market failure regarding LCT finances and also to construct an appropriate alternative benchmark for analysis.

The doctrine of Common Concern may also be useful to ease the standard to be met under the illustrative list provisions. For example, with respect to supports provided in the form of insurances and guarantees, the net long term operating costs and losses of the program can be determined by setting the accumulated costs against the benefit accrued in the form of avoided emissions due to the transaction. This will justify extending supports at lower rates of premiums compared to transactions involving polluting technologies.

Although interpretative assistance from the doctrine of Common Concern may reduce the chances of an official support measure with climate action motivation to be considered outright as a subsidy, it would not work as surely as if it were an exception clause. The possibility of challenging the official support measures for clean technologies as prohibited or distortive would nonetheless remain. The key challenge is that, as the next section explains, the formal legal language endorsing the need for policy-guided intervention using subsidies does not exist anymore in the SCM agreement. In this respect, one option is to expand the application of the GATT Article XX to the ASCM. Scholarly opinions vary from sceptic[965] to cautious[966] and

964 We note that the CIRR or the MPR are determinant of cost to the government. Adjustments, as mentioned above would be further warranted to ensure that a dispute settlement panel can decide on the conferment of benefit to the recipient.

965 Condon, 'Disciplining Clean Energy Subsidies to Speed the Transition to a Low-Carbon World' (n 882) 685–690.

966 Bradly J Condon, 'Climate Change and Unresolved Issues in WTO Law' (2009) 12 Journal of International Economic Law 895, 903–906; Espa and Marín Durán (n 882) 23–27. The authors in the latter paper share the view that even though Art. XX scope is extended to the ASCM, it would not be of much practical use.

enthusiastic[967] on the viability of any such interpretation of the relevant texts. The optimistic account is based on the role of GATT as the umbrella agreement in the Annex 1A of the Marrakesh Agreement, to which list the ASCM also finds itself. Furthermore, there is an express reference to GATT in Article 32.1 of the SCM agreement – readable as allowing the exception provision to be extended to the latter.[968] Not only such an extension requires an interpretative leap, made even more difficult due to the changing global politics surrounding the WTO, overall implication of such extension is unpredictable.[969] Such an approach would also disregard the fact that the SCM agreement initially had a limited escape clause, i.e. Article 8 on non-actionable subsidies, which the members have allowed to lapse along with parts of the Article 6 of the agreement. Arguing that GATT exceptions were always available to the SCM agreement makes efforts by the contracting parties in entering into such delicate balances to a nullity.

B *As a Guide for Reform*

Before going further into discussion of the needed reforms of the SCM agreement, we ought to recall that the absence of regulatory reform does not block all the options of supporting cross-border supply of LCTs. There are significant avenues that remain outside the scope of the ASCM, which can be immediately deployed. The doctrine of Common Concern of Humankind would demand that those avenues are explored to the best extent possible.

Discussion in this chapter has revealed that the language of the ASCM is unforgiving to the proposed incentive measures, irrespective of how leniently one tries to read its provisions. Thereupon, it is reasonable to conclude that while subsidies remain a key enabler for clean technology diffusion, it contradicts the predominant neoliberal institutional bent and hence generally rejected.[970] This leads to arguably the only viable long-term option,[971] i.e. redrafting the necessary parts of the agreement to legitimise Common Concern

967 Rubini, 'Ain't Wastin' Time No More' (n 882) 559–570.

968 ibid 562–566. The analysis is based on the Appellate Body decisions in China – Periodicals (DS31) and China – Raw Materials (DS394, DS395 & DS 398).

969 ibid 570; Condon, 'Disciplining Clean Energy Subsidies to Speed the Transition to a Low-Carbon World' (n 882) 686, 690; Espa and Marín Durán (n 882) 26–27.

970 Daniel Puig, James Arthur Haselip and Fatemeh Bakhtiari, 'The Mismatch between the In-Country Determinants of Technology Transfer, and the Scope of Technology Transfer Initiatives under the United Nations Framework Convention on Climate Change' (2018) 18 International Environmental Agreements: Politics, Law and Economics 659, 666.

971 Rubini, 'ASCM Disciplines and Recent WTO Case Law Devlopments: What Space for "Green" Subsidies?' (n 963) 331–333.

motivated incentives. The goal would be to introduce a carve-out in the SCM agreement that has well-articulated ends for the promotion of which subsidies will be allowed, and also which are equally useful for both developed and developing countries. This case for legitimising strong policy imperative backed subsidies in general, and official export credit practices in particular, can lead to either calling for the reinstatement of non-actionable subsidies provision (Article 8) in the agreement or proposing an entirely new formulation. The latter is a better option to pursue because not only is the textual formulation of Article 8 dated and focused more upon developed country interests,[972] but actual revival of the provision would still not save the official export credit supports that are currently prohibited.[973]

As far as incentives promoting export of clean technologies are concerned, those that are transparent, bear a clear potential to address a Common Concern, and consented to by the developing country recipient should be exempted from being found as prohibited or distortive under the SCM agreement. A balance must be struck between allowing climate technology-related export incentives and preventing unnecessary disruption in the world market. Inclusion of a necessity test is the time-tested way to attain that balance. The structure of the GATT general exception clause can serve as a guide to the design of a new carve-out. Within this framework, specific exemptions, e.g. trade financing across the renewable energy value chains to promote climate mitigation and technology transfer, can also be included.

To reiterate, first and foremost, the policy objective must be broadly in line with the goal of sustainable development and within that paradigm, may contribute to a Common Concern of humankind. Second, a form of necessity test must be included. Trade distortion resulted from an export incentive should be balanced with the level of its contribution in addressing a concern. The necessity test should also take into account *inter alia,* the appropriateness of the technology in question, and the manifested technology need of the recipient (e.g. the technology needs assessments done under the climate framework). Third, resorting to the legitimate exception should only be available as long as such incentives are provided in a fair and transparent manner.

---

972 For different perspectives on reforming Article 8, see, Charnovitz, 'Green Subsidies and the WTO' (n 882) 60–69; Sadeq Z Bigdeli, 'Resurrecting the Dead-The Expired Non-Actionable Subsidies and the Lingering Question of Green Space' (2011) 8 Manchester J. Int'l Econ. L. 2; Rubini, 'Ain't Wastin' Time No More' (n 882) 570–576.

973 Article 8 was targeted only to save actionable subsidies (Part III of the SCM agreement) from litigation challenges and unilateral countervailing measures (Part IV).

Keeping in mind that multilateral negotiation would be lengthy and complex, if possible at all, an easier yet effective path to follow would be to expand the scope of the safe-haven to all forms of official support measures. One way of achieving this end is to change the safe-haven language to include pure cover supports, as well as those provided at floating rates, or in a hybrid manner. In addition, the coverage of the special rules in the OECD arrangement on official support for climate project should be expanded to include all LCT transactions, and the relevant rates relaxed as long as those transactions bring a clear and direct technology diffusion benefit. As highlighted earlier, influencing the outcome of the WTO rules by modifying OECD rules would suffer from an acute democratic deficit. Alternatively, the key regulations on official support, along with flexible rules for Common Concern guided support measures can be annexed to the SCM agreement and then linked to the safe-haven provision in the illustrative list. A requirement of reporting the terms and amount of support provided can further ensure transparency.

Until any of the above reform efforts are concluded, a periodically renewed peace clause can ensure that clean technology promoting supports are not challenged in disputes.

C *Cooperation and Homework Avenues*

Once again, homework and cooperation remain at the heart of the success of a Common Concern inspired regulatory framework. As mentioned before, the range of official financial support to LCT flow would be fruitful in an enabling policy environment and in the absence of counterproductive subsidies. These issues are better tackled in a cooperative framework. Within the cooperation narrative outlined in Chapter 3, the key task within the WTO is to create well-calibrated and specifically focused policy spaces that can legitimise ECA-led supports for LCT exports. The foregoing sections have already addressed the details in that regard. Outside the WTO, the cooperation at the OECD to expand the scope of special rules on climate mitigation projects to comprehensively cover LCTs, as well as relaxing the applicable interest rate provisions upon the same is of immediate special importance.

At the domestic level, the members engaging in official export credit supports must renew the mandate of the export credit agencies (ECAs) to promote LCT exports, especially to destinations not served, or only sparsely served by the private financial markets. While more resources ought to be dedicated to emission-reducing activities, the same should be channelled away from polluting activities, e.g. coal power plants.

Cooperation is not only important to promote official support for LCT exports and investments, but it is also indispensable for the removal of other distorting subsidies from the market. The WTO in general or the SCM agreement, in particular, cannot provide the basis to tackle all the relevant issues. A framework cooperation agreement in the climate regime should highlight the importance of the activities and assign the roles and responsibilities at different levels, as well as other regimes. The WTO can indeed complement the efforts to incentivise clean technology exports by easing the present constraints along the lines suggested in the previous sections. For example, access to special rates for clean technology export finance can be made conditional upon supplying evidence by a member's adequate action in rationalising domestic fossil fuel subsidies. Bilateral and plurilateral commitments to reduce fossil fuel subsidies also remain feasible. Bilateral agreements between providers and recipients of official support can also avoid in part subsequent challenges of such measures at the WTO.

IV Conclusion

This chapter presented an analysis of the opportunities and challenges regarding official support of exports and investments involving LCTs. In specific terms, it dealt with the obstacles posed by the WTO subsidies agreement in this respect. Furthermore, it discussed the potential contributions by the doctrine of Common Concern in tackling the obstacles.

The WTO and the SCM agreement therein are attracted with respect to a portion of export credits and guarantees. Activities of the private, as well as international financial institutions, fall outside the scope of the rules as long as there are no government influences therein. Moreover, outward investment promotion activities, though taking the same form of those promoting exports, fall outside the WTO purview. While this is promising for the promotion of green investment, there is no safeguard preventing these opportunities from being exploited to expand climate polluting activities.

Although the SCM agreement would apply to export credits and guarantees for low-carbon technologies, in the light of evolving jurisprudence it can be argued that not all supports will be considered a subsidy. Especially with the support of the Common Concern framework, it can be maintained that the governments can and must undertake these kinds of supports for clean technology export. Only because private markets do not find such transactions profitable, would not mean that complementary government supports are beneficial, and hence considerable as subsidies *per se*.

When considered as a subsidy, there is little in the ASCM that can shelter the proposed measures from being considered as prohibited. Only the direct export credits provided at a fixed rate and compliant with the OECD arrangement rules are saved from being challenged as illegal. With the help of the doctrine of Common Concern, a facilitative reading of the agreement would be possible. But at the end of the day, it would not save the measures from all possible challenges. To attain the latter outcome, the ideal option would be negotiating a new carve-out clause in the SCM agreement. The Common Concern doctrine can guide that effort. Until such reforms are successfully concluded, a periodically renewable peace clause can ensure that legal challenges do not prevent the members from promoting LCTs through official supports.

The doctrine of Common Concern would again highlight the need for adequate domestic action and international cooperation in this regard. With respect to augmenting financial support for export and investment transactions in LCTs, cooperation encompasses issues that are beyond the subject-matter scope of the WTO. Therefore, ideally, efforts should be made under the auspices of the climate regime to highlight the expected role of the trade regime. Commitments to reduce distortive subsidies promoting polluting activities (e.g. subsidies on coal and petroleum), made individually or different multiparty setting will also prove useful.

CHAPTER 6

Unilateral Trade Sanctions to Secure Compliance with the Common Concern Doctrine

In continuation of examining different aspects of the Common Concern doctrine with respect to the role of trade in clean technology diffusion, this final chapter deals with the last and possibly the most controversial issue, i.e. unilateral countermeasures to respond to unaddressed common concerns across borders. Consequently, the general theme is the feasibility and consequence of unilateral trade sanctions as per dictates of the Common Concern doctrine to ensure compliance with the proposed narrative of low-carbon technology (LCT) diffusion. There are a number of issues to unpack in this regard, which are taken up in sequence. The chapter begins by sketching out the opposing views on the utility of unilateralism, especially trade sanctions. Like many contested areas of international law, the proponents of the approach see the benefit of sure compliance in sanctions, whereas the sceptics find the threat thereof as cooperation deterrent. To place the doctrine in the midst of the debate, it would be important to clarify how it may maximise the proclaimed benefits while minimising the predicted challenges. Going further, the chapter briefly outlines the grey areas of international law regarding unilateral actions, third party countermeasures in particular, and discusses the advancement thereupon made by the doctrine. Lastly, turning to the trade domain, it is recalled that unilateral sanctions are inherently illegal in the multilateral system, with some avenues to bring *ex post* legitimacy to actions when challenged. One question would be what, if any, additional benefit is brought by introducing the doctrine of Common Concern. Another is whether one should reconsider making such forward-looking suggestions in the currently unfolding geopolitical reality of mistrust and economic warfare. Detailed discussions follow hereunder.

1 The Domain of Unilateral Trade Sanctions

In the vast and varied field of unilateral measures, the domain of unilateral sanctions is only a part. The term 'sanction' is used in this chapter to cover "any unilateral coercive measures taken in reaction to an unlawful act".[974] In this sense, it also includes the legal category of 'countermeasures'.[975] All three words of the term used in the heading above, i.e. 'unilateral', 'trade', and 'sanction' indicate important features that distinguish this sub-set of actions. First and foremost, identifying these measures as unilateral conveys that these are manifestations of domestic political intent, as apart from being executions of internationally agreed obligations.[976] Second and possibly the most discernible feature of sanctions is their punitive design to realise the aforementioned intent.[977] Sanctions operate to impose the expected change in the behaviour of the targeted country through economic restrictions as punishments.[978] As the defining element, coercion is always present in any sanction irrespective of the objective sought to be achieved thereby. Lastly, to maintain the focus on trade, the examination of unilateral sanctions here cover those that are trade-related. Unilateral trade sanctions can entail absolute or widespread restriction on import and export of goods and services with the sanctioned country, as well as possible withdrawal of protection of the intellectual property originating therefrom. However, within this category, trade countermeasures taken by one WTO member against another as a response to the breach of any multilateral trade obligation, i.e. suspension of concessions, remain distinct.[979]

The characteristics of the unilateral trade sanctions are unique when compared to other trade measures with a restrictive impact, commonly grouped as process and production measures (PPM s). While both may be deployed in

974 Alain Pellet and Alina Miron, 'Sanctions', *Max Planck Encyclopedia of Public International Law* (Online, Oxford University Press) para 7.

975 Countermeasures are lawful, unilateral coercive measures other than use of force, characterizable as a breach of obligation owed to one or more wrongdoing sates, taken as a response to the wrongful conduct in question. Countermeasures replace the traditional notion of 'reprisals' in international law. Federica I Paddeu, 'Countermeasures', *Max Planck Encyclopedia of Public International Law* (Online, Oxford University Press); Matthias Ruffert, 'Reprisals', *Max Planck Encyclopedia of Public International Law* (Online, Oxford University Press).

976 Perry Bechky, 'Sanctions and the Blurred Boundaries of International Economic Law' (2018) 83 39; Andreas F Lowenfeld, *International Economic Law* (2nd ed, Oxford University Press 2008) pt VIII.

977 Pellet and Miron (n 974) para 8. The focus on coercive measures leaves out responses that are unwelcome, but legal, i.e. retorsions. See, Thomas Giegerich, 'Retorsion', *Max Planck Encyclopedia of Public International Law* (Online, Oxford University Press).

978 Kern Alexander, *Economic Sanctions : Law and Public Policy* (Palgrave Macmillan 2009) 10; Barry Carter, 'International Economic Sanctions: Improving the Haphazard U.S. Legal Regime' (1987) 75 California Law Review 1159.

979 See p. 258-259 below.

service of the same motive, these two groups of measures would starkly differ in terms of immediate intents[980] and therefore the methods of implementation.[981] In case of relatively commonplace PPM measures, the intent to generate a specific trade effect has a close and objective linkage with the ultimate motive. As a result, the action taken alters when the motivation changes from one to another. To give an example, the motive of reducing carbon emission will be given effect through a PPM measure that intends to curb polluting imports and achieves it through a tax. Similarly, a concern for animal welfare may be responded to by specific product import bans. In contrast, sanctions are fixed tools where the immediate effect intended, i.e. coercion, never changes irrespective of the varying motivations they are connected to. This is because of the conviction of the government that a targeted country will change its behaviour, in any sector whatsoever, when force is applied. For example, the same financial sanction can be deployed with a view to preventing gross abuses of human rights, or against perceived security threat, or to counter blatant disregard for environmental conservation.

Another distinction often-made in the literature relating to extraterritoriality and also having relevance for discussion on trade sanctions is the 'outward' vs 'inward' direction of the measures dealt with.[982] Outward-directed measures are those that seek to address a concern located beyond the domestic territorial limits, whereas the measures inwardly directed are the opposite. While arguably the PPM measures are predominantly grounded on domestic

980 The terms 'motive' and 'intent' are borrowed from the criminal liability setting to indicate the two distinct mental states behind any measure. While intent is the conscious mental disposition to bring about a certain immediate effect, motive is the ulterior goal that is sought to be fulfilled by such action. See for more, Walter Wheeler Cook, 'Act, Intention, and Motive in the Criminal Law' (1917) 26 The Yale Law Journal 645.

981 It is important to highlight this because these two categories are sometimes conflated in the literature. See, for example, Cirone and Urpelainen (n 529) 312–313. The authors considered as sanction any measure that imposes additional costs on producers from lax policy jurisdictions. Such conflation is mistaken from a legal point of view.

982 Steve Charnovitz, 'The Moral Exception in Trade Policy' [1997] Virginia Journal of International Law 689, 695; Sarah H Cleveland, 'Human Rights Sanctions and International Trade: A Theory of Compatibility' (2002) 5 Journal of International Economic Law 133, 144–146. With respect to human rights sanctions, Cleveland identifies three general characteristics – i. outward focus, ii. non-trade relatedness of motive, iii. difficulty to establish effectiveness. All these characteristics are relevant to our discussion here. See also, Barbara Cooreman, 'The (Extra)Territorial Reach of National Measures under WTO Law', *Global Environmental Protection through Trade: A Systematic Approach to Extraterritoriality* (Edward Elgar Publishing 2017) <https://www.elgaronline.com/view/9781786434388/chapter03.xhtml> accessed 25 October 2020.

concerns (e.g. public moral standards),[983] trade sanctions can only be treated as being directed outwards. This distinction bears relevance in the current discussion because of the possible argument that the inward or outward orientation of a measure may determine the limit of the extraterritorial reach of the WTO law. Transboundary effects of inwardly focused trade measure are incidental and justifiable under the existing rules.[984] Whereas the legitimacy of truly extraterritorial trade sanctions targeting behavioural modifications abroad is a candidate for stricter scrutiny, even rejection.[985] It should also be noted that the doctrinal form of Common Concern of Humankind also takes account of this distinction. Despite the indirect extraterritorial effect of the PPM s, they remain an integral part of homework aspect of the doctrine.[986] Truly extraterritorial measures, like the ones under discussion here, only come to play as a means of securing compliance.

The practice of unilateral trade sanctions is not scarce even though the WTO law treats them prohibitively to a degree.[987] In particular, the United States (US) and the European Union (EU) champion the exercise of unilateral trade sanctions, most often done under the banner of human rights protection.[988] Trade sanctions with respect to goods can take forms of import or export restrictions. For example, against Syria, the EU has put in place a range of trade restrictions, including the prohibition of petroleum and crude oil imports,

---

983 Barbara Cooreman, 'Addressing Environmental Concerns through Trade: A Case for Extraterritoriality Shorter Articles and Notes' [2016] International and Comparative Law Quarterly 229; Cooreman ibid. The author gives the example of, among others, the EC – Seals dispute as outward focused PPM, while the issue in Brazil – Retreaded Tyres was deemed as an inward focused PPM.

984 This is addressed in Chapter 4 III C above.

985 Cottier, 'The Principle of Common Concern of Humankind' (n 7) s VII; Robert Howse and Donald Regan, 'The Product/Process Dinstinction – An Illusory Basis for Disciplining "Unilateralism" in Trade Policy' (2000) 11 European Journal of International Law 249, 249; Natalie L Dobson, 'The EU's Conditioning of the "Extraterritorial" Carbon Footprint: A Call for an Integrated Approach in Trade Law Discourse' (2018) 27 Review of European, Comparative & International Environmental Law 75, 78–79.

986 See. pp. 43-45 above.

987 For details on the WTO rules regarding unilateral trade countermeasures, see pp. 258-262 below.

988 Iryna Bogdanova, 'Reshaping the Law of Sanctions for Human Rights Violations: The Potential of Common Concern of Humankind' in Thomas Cottier (ed), *The Prospects of Common Concern of Humankind in International Law* (Cambridge University Press 2021); For more, see US Department of Treasury, Office of Foreign Asset Control (OFAC), 'Sanctions Programs and Country Information' <https://www.treasury.gov/resource-center/sanctions/programs/pages/programs.aspx> accessed 25 October 2020; 'EU Sanctions Map' <https://www.sanctionsmap.eu/#/main> accessed 25 October 2020.

trade in gold and other valuable material, the export of telecommunication equipment, luxury goods etc.[989] Of note can also be the recent rejection of the EU–Mercosur trade deal by Austria due to Brazil's inadequate action to prevent the Amazon wildfires.[990] Sanctions can also affect trade in services in different ways, e.g. prohibition of tourism, refusal of access to payment systems, or targeted sanctions against financial institutions.

One of the most controversial instances of unilateral trade sanctions is the US Section 301 regime. US Trade Act of 1974[991] authorises the United States Trade Representative (USTR), upon direction from the president, to take any tariff or non-tariff-based retaliatory measures within the President's capacity against any foreign government, when any policy or practice of the latter is considered to be against US commercial interests. The law itself does not require any prior approval or endorsement of the WTO for any such action to be taken. Harking from a pre-WTO era devoid of a compulsory obligation to settle trade disputes multilaterally, this law, except for very recently, remained largely dormant since the inception of the WTO.[992] In 2018, pursuant to a United States Trade Representative (USTR) report,[993] the US President imposed retaliatory tariffs on trade with China as a reaction to the alleged

989 'Restrictive Measures Agains Syria' (*EU Sanctions Map*) <https://www.sanctionsmap.eu/#/main/details/32/?search=%7B%22value%22:%22%22,%22searchType%22:%7B%7D%7D> accessed 25 October 2020.

990 'Mercosur Trade Deal Gives EU Leeway to Pressure Brazil on Amazon Fires: Maas' *Reuters* (26 August 2019) < https://www.reuters.com/news/picture/mercosur-trade-deal-gives-eu-leeway-to-p-idUSKCN1VG0LJ > accessed 25 October 2020; 'Austria Rejects EU-Mercosur Trade Deal Over Amazon Fires' *Bloomberg.com* (19 September 2019) < https://www.bloomberg.com/news/articles/2019-09-19/austria-moves-to-reject-eu-mercosur-trade-deal-over-amazon-fires > accessed 25 October 2020.

991 Trade Act of 1974, United States Code, Title 19, Section 2411. While the actual section 301 was repealed, the name remained. For an overview, see, Andres B Schwarzenberg, 'Section 301 of the Trade Act of 1974' (Congressional Research Service 2019) In Focus <https://crsreports.congress.gov/product/pdf/IF/IF11346> accessed 25 October 2020.

992 In one WTO dispute, the Panel has found that a similar provision, i.e. section 304 of the Trade Act allowing the USTR authority to unilaterally determine breach of trade interests, was prima facie inconsistent with the DSU, *United States – Sections 301–310 of the Trade Act of 1974* [2000] Panel WT/DS152/R, DSR 2000II [7.97]. However, the provision was found not to be inconsistent at the end, as the exercise of USTR's power was limited through an administrative declaration.

993 Office of the United States Trade Representative, 'Findings of the Investigation into China's Acts, Policies, and Practices Related to Technology Transfer, Intellectual Propert, and Innovation under Section 301 of the Trade Act of 1974' (2018) <https://ustr.gov/sites/default/files/Section%20301%20FINAL.PDF> accessed 25 October 2020. An update was released on November 2018, coming to the same conclusions as the original report.

Chinese forced technology transfer practices.[994] So far, up to $550 billion of Chinese imports have been brought under the coverage of the measure in four phases.[995] In response, China has so far launched three disputes against the US.[996]

Fuelling a growing distrust in multilateralism, recourse to trade sanctions are on the rise. So are actual trade disputes between countries in that regard. Ongoing hostilities between the Russian Federation and Ukraine have led to both countries imposing trade sanctions against each other. While one dispute settlement panel has already looked into Ukraine's challenge of transit ban by Russia,[997] the latter's complaint regarding the imposition of goods and services trade ban by the former is in the consultation phase.[998] In 2018, Venezuela challenged the trade sanctions imposed by the United States against the country.[999] Also recently, Saudi Arabia, UAE, Bahrain, and Egypt each separately imposed economic blockade, including trade embargoes, against Qatar on the alleged ground of terrorism financing. As Qatar's complaint to the WTO shows, the sanctions imposed involve a near-complete ban on trade in goods and services, as well as restrictions regarding the protection of intellectual property rights.[1000] In a further escalation of the growing trade tension globally, Japan, under a thinly veiled excuse of national security, restricted export of

---

994 Andres B Murrill, 'Tricks of the Trade: Section 301 Investigation of Chinese Intellectual Property Practices Concludes (Part II)' (Congressional Research Service 2018) Legal Sidebar <https://crsreports.congress.gov/product/pdf/LSB/LSB10109> accessed 25 October 2020.

995 'China Section 301-Tariff Actions and Exclusion Process' (*Office of the United States Trade Representative*) 301 <https://ustr.gov/issue-areas/enforcement/section-301-investigations/tariff-actions> accessed 25 October 2020.

996 *United States – Tariff Measures on Certain Goods from China I, II, III* (DS 543, DS 565, and DS 587).

997 *Russia – Measures Concerning Traffic in Transit* [2019] Panel WT/DS512/R.

998 'Ukraine – Measures Relating to Trade in Goods and Services – Request for Consultations by the Russian Federation' (World Trade Organization (WTO) 2017) WT/DS525/1.

999 'United States – Measures Relating to Trade in Goods and Services – Request for Consultations by Venezuela' (World Trade Organization (WTO) 2018) WT/DS574/1. A Panel has been requested by the Complainant on 14 March 2019.

1000 'Saudi Arabia – Measures Relating to Trade in Goods and Services, and Trade-Related Aspects of Intellectural Property Rights: Request for Consultations by Qatar' (World Trade Organization (WTO) 2017) Request for consultations WT/DS528/1, G/L/1182 S/L/417, IP/D/37; 'Saudi Arabia – Measures Concerning the Protection of Intellectual Property Rights: Request for Consultations by Qatar' (World Trade Organization (WTO) 2018) WT/DS567/1; IP/D/40. The UAE responded with a challenge of sanctions imposed by Qatar, 'Qatar – Certain Measures Concerning Goods from the United Arab Emirates: Request for Establishment of a Panel by the United Arab Emirates' (World Trade Organization (WTO) 2019) WT/DS576/2.

certain chemicals to South Korea.[1001] The recent return of the United States to trade unilateralism, coupled with the absence of a functioning Appellate Body (AB) at the WTO is further prompting countries to take unilateral courses of action.[1002]

A *Arguments in Favour of Unilateral Sanctions*

Unilateralism, as an opportunity, is of great value to promote compliance with environmental norms. As Bodansky noted, despite the existing critique of unilateralism as an affront to the sense of community in international relations, the notion itself cannot be fully done away with.[1003] According to him, instead of being considered as a binary choice, unilateralism should rather be seen as a gradient offering different possible solutions of 'less' or 'more'. While unilateral efforts, such as implementing multilaterally agreed environmental standards fall on the lenient side of the spectrum, the extreme cases of sanctions attract most of the criticism.

Unilateral actions can and do push for the development of new rules in the desired direction. The aviation directive of the EU bears irrefutable proof of that.[1004] The directive triggered the first global agreement between the International Civil Aviation Organization (ICAO) member states in 2016 to reduce aviation emission and become carbon neutral over time. Dobson and Ryngaert trace similar development in the regulation of maritime emissions as well.[1005] Another important contribution of unilateral action is ensuring enforcement of the existing commitments with the necessary degree of stringency by all. With regard to climate change, renowned economists often call

---

1001 Keith Johnson, 'Why Are Japan and South Korea in a Trade Fight?' (*Foreign Policy*) <https://foreignpolicy.com/2019/07/15/why-are-japan-and-south-korea-in-a-trade-fight-moon-abe-chips-wwii/> accessed 25 October 2020.

1002 For example, European Commission, 'Proposal for a Regulation of the European Parliament and of the Council Amending Regulation (EU) No 654/2014 of the European Parliament and of the Council Concerning the Exercise of the Union's Rights for the Application and Enforcement of International Trade Rules' (European Commission 2019) 2019/0273 (COD).

1003 D Bodansky, 'What's so Bad about Unilateral Action to Protect the Environment?' (2000) 11 European Journal of International Law 339.

1004 The Directive 2008/101/EC of the European Parliament and the Council modified an earlier emission trading directive of 2003 (2003/87/EC) to bring aviation emission within the trading scheme. Put into operation by 2012, the scheme is provisionally limited to flights within the EEA member states to support development of multilateral rules at the ICAO.

1005 Natalie L Dobson and Cedric Ryngaert, 'Provocative Climate Protection: EU "Extraterritorial" Regulation of Maritime Emissions' (2017) 66 International & Comparative Law Quarterly 295.

for unilateral actions that are credible and impose a big enough cost to induce compliance.[1006]

Though not all unilateral measures are essentially sanctions, the virtue of unilateralism, as depicted, would nevertheless empower the argument that sanctions can prove beneficial to enforce onerous international commitments. While articulating the doctrine of Common Concern, Cottier mentioned that unilateral trade sanctions play an important role in regimes where compliance is not voluntary. As the attention of the United Nations Security Council (UNSC) do not go so far as to take account of the long-term welfare and security challenges arising from issues like climate change,[1007] inequality of income and wealth, or marine pollution, these fields largely depend on unilateral progress, often through restrictive measures, to ensure regulatory development and avoidance of free-riding.[1008] From a political point of view, unilateral trade sanctions can supply political currency to engage in climate mitigation in general, as it would allow the possibility to counteract the initial cost disadvantage of participation by shifting the burden on the non-cooperating locations.

In light of the above, it could be said that a potentially favourable impact of trade sanctions for the benefit of LCT diffusion can indeed be considered, despite the fact that the goal is best served through international cooperation and diligent homework. As declared in the outset of this volume, the role of sanctions as last resort measure to bring countries to the cooperation forum cannot be denied.[1009] Countries that are equipped with the necessary resource and ability, can sanction locations where wilful inadvertence prolongs emission of greenhouse gases. The same approach may also apply to countries whose deliberate non-cooperation stall multilateral progress.[1010] In contrast, in cases where a country cannot gain access to the necessary LCT, appropriate trade sanction against the technology owning destination may expedite the process of coming to an agreeable arrangement regarding LCT access and diffusion. However, as discussed below, there are serious concerns that must be addressed before making any concrete proposition regarding trade sanctions for clean technology diffusion.

1006 Nordhaus, 'Climate Clubs' (n 686) 1346–1352; Barrett, 'Climate Treaties and the Imperative of Enforcement' (n 528) 245–247; Thomas C Schelling, *Arms and Influence* (Yale University Press 2008).

1007 With respect to climate change, the reality may be slowly changing as the issue has found its way into Security Council debates. See, pp. 269-270 below.

1008 Cottier, 'The Principle of Common Concern of Humankind' (n 7) s 1.7.1.

1009 See Chapter 1 V B (iii), and Chapter 3 II E above.

1010 The fossil-fuel income driven economies. See Chapter 2 IV B (ii) at pp. 97-98 above.

B *Concerns Regarding Unilateral Sanctions*

Critics of unilateralism tend to reject the approach for motives very similar to those that sway the proponents to prescribe the use of sanctions. While the sceptics also desire an effective multilateral rule system preserving common interests, it is highlighted that the deterrent effect of a unilateral measure can be inimical to the development of mutual trust in such settings, possibly even driving some participants away altogether from cooperation at the international level. This, in turn, would make impossible the building of a robust and inclusive rule system in the long run. The difficulty to obtain recognition of the necessity and relevance of trade-related response measures in the climate regime is a good example of that.[1011] Global agreements on issues like climate change are complex and incremental in nature, bringing vastly different countries under one system of rules. In such constellations, inclusivity comes at the cost of clear and specifically assigned responsibilities. Also politically, agreement on situations that will legitimately draw unilateral trade sanctions is very difficult to strike, because most countries would foresee it being applied against themselves.

Specific to the climate regime, another objection against unilateral trade measures is that those often fail to reflect the dictates of differentiated responsibility. Even unilateral measures that are unequivocally beneficial for the community, can fall short in taking account of the developing country-specific situations. An appropriate example is the absence of such considerations in EU aviation directive as pointed out by Scott and Rajamani.[1012] As the authors argue, a beneficial unilateral trade measure like the aviation directive can nevertheless lack adequate design and operational specifications relating to differentiation. On the same note, we can also recall one of our earlier conclusion holding that differentiated responsibility is not a first-order rule of the WTO at present.[1013] Later analysis would also indicate that respect for differentiation may even become fully expendable when an apparently WTO-illegal trade measure finds shelter under the cause of national security.

Similarly, unilateralism can indeed further fuel the acerbic North vs South conflicts. Biermann gave the example of the unfolding trade and environment conflict in the early 2000s when attempts to introduce environmental

---

1011 Bacchus, 'What Is a Climate Response Measure? Breaking the Trade Taboo in Confronting Climate Change' (n 3); Frank Biermann, 'The Rising Tide of Green Unilateralism in World Trade Law. Options for Reconciling the Emerging North–South Conflict' (2001) 35 Journal of World Trade 421.

1012 Scott and Rajamani (n 695).

1013 See pp. 49–50, 125–126 above.

concerns in trade rulemaking were decried by some as "eco-colonialism".[1014] A similar conflict also prevents any meaningful clarification from being made regarding the role of trade-related response measures under the Paris Agreement.[1015] Any proposal to legitimise taking of unilateral trade sanction in connection with climate mitigation would intensify that conflict. Cottier has already noted in relation to the doctrine of Common Concern that a unilateral countermeasure can easily be mistaken as a neo-imperialist tool.[1016]

Unregulated license to move unilaterally against other states is unpredictable, dangerous, and potentially destabilising for international law and order. The recent rise of unilateral trade sanctions and related challenges to the multilateral trade regime bear ample examples of that. Also, when considered in isolation, the coercion focused nature of unilateral trade sanctions appears unbalanced. It is true that while sanctions can be a useful threat to prevent non-compliance, they hardly do anything to address the root causes of the problem, e.g. lack of capacity to comply. Also, despite the theoretical availability of the measure to all states, in real terms, only a few rich countries can credibly deploy sanctions – being economically powerful enough to make good on a threat. Therefore, the unconditional legitimisation of such an avenue would raise the concern of further entrenchment of power imbalances in international relations. Lastly, in an integrated world, sanctions run the danger of creating a knock-on impact on the innocent countries situated downstream in a global value chain.

The above arguments may also hold water with respect to trade sanctions for the promotion of LCT diffusion. To address these concerns, trade sanctions in pursuance of the Common Concern doctrine should carefully specify the type of infractions that shall merit such response. We must recall that a Common Concern of Humankind implies a threat to international peace and security and thus has very specific and narrow application.[1017] Hence, the duty to act attaching to the obligation of securing compliance with the doctrine is limited to rare cases marked by paramount loss otherwise. The doctrine cannot and does not proffer unilateralism across the board.

Furthermore, it is also important to make sure that the impact of any trade sanction is calibrated to the specific context of the country targeted, taking into account the principle of common but differentiated responsibility (CBDR). In

---

1014 Biermann (n 1011) 422.

1015 Bacchus, 'What Is a Climate Response Measure? Breaking the Trade Taboo in Confronting Climate Change' (n 3).

1016 Cottier, 'The Principle of Common Concern of Humankind' (n 7) s 1.1.

1017 See pp. 40–41 above.

addition, it should be kept in mind that the legitimacy, as well as the wider acceptance of a coercive compliance tool as such, would depend on its equal availability and utility to the developed and the developing countries alike. Lastly, trade sanctions should not be considered as a complete solution in itself. Appropriate non-forcible means of resolution must take precedence before any opportunity for sanctions can be legally taken under consideration. In the following section, we explore how the doctrine of Common Concern may take these issues into account while suggesting unilateral trade countermeasures.

II Countermeasures and Common Concern of Clean Technology Diffusion

A *Recap of the Doctrine's Position*

A well-structured response action in the form of unilateral countermeasures is a valuable proposition made by the Common Concern doctrine to advance the reach of public international law. In turning this proposition to reality, the doctrine recognises full well the utility, as well as the drawbacks of resorting to this measure for addressing a common concern of humankind. The essential core of the proposition is a duty to act, preventing the perpetuation of unresolvable common interests. This is explained by Cottier as:

> The basic duty to act emerges at the heart of the principle of Common Concern, subject to the principles of proportionality and accountability. It amounts to an essential and defining ingredient of the principle. It is here that it transgresses traditional domains and disciplines of international law. It profoundly adds a new dimension in general international law calling for a reasoned response to violations of community rights. In many instances, action will not be suitable and possible. But the mere fact that such action needs to be considered and options examined renders states accountable towards the principle of Common Concern and thus enhanced compliance with international law.[1018]

Ideally, an unresolved Common Concern entails a duty upon all involved states to act through unilateral countermeasures. It is a last resort option to reinforce cooperative attitude and ensure adequate domestic action by the free-riding parties. By doing so, the doctrine extends the boundary of the customary

1018 Cottier, 'The Principle of Common Concern of Humankind' (n 7) s 1.7.3.

norms of international responsibility of states, which were considered as embryonic[1019] by the International Law Commission (ILC). The ILC position was as follows:

> [T]he current state of international law on countermeasures taken in the general or collective interest is uncertain. State practice is sparse and involves a limited number of States. At present, there appears to be no clearly recognized entitlement of States [...] to take countermeasures in the collective interest. Consequently, it is not appropriate to include in the present Articles a provision concerning the question whether other States [...] are permitted to take countermeasures in order to induce a responsible State to comply with its obligations. Instead, chapter II includes a saving clause which reserves the position and leaves the resolution of the matter to the further development of international law.[1020]

Common interests, even the recognised communitarian norms often end up at the mercy of unilateral protection measures due to the lack of viable alternatives. Especially in duty centred legal regimes (e.g. climate change), compliance mechanisms tend to avoid recourse to adversarial processes like dispute settlement and therefore fall short of effectively tackling non-performance and foot-dragging.[1021] While multilateral sanctions are a possibility, under the current framework of rules, those are the prerogative of the United Nations Security Council, which has hardly been effective even to tackle the traditional security concerns.[1022] The indispensability of unilateral interventions in international affairs provides salience to the proposition made by the Common Concern doctrine. In line with the ILC expectation regarding further development of international law, the doctrine is an opportunity to further build upon the advances already made to structure unilateral action, in particular, the principle of responsibility to protect (R2P).[1023]

1019 International Law Commission (ILC), 'Draft Articles on Responsibility of States for Internationally Wrongful Acts, with Commentaries' (2001) A/56/10 137.

1020 ibid 139.

1021 Yet again, in COP25, leaders of the world failed to agree on making ambitious enough pledges under the Paris Agreement. 'On Thin Ice – COP25, the UN Climate Talks in Madrid, Ends in a Sad Splutter' [2019] *The Economist* <https://www.economist.com/science-and-technology/2019/12/15/cop25-the-un-climate-talks-in-madrid-ends-in-a-sad-splutter> accessed 25 October 2020.

1022 Nevertheless, the security aspects of climate change is gradually permeating into the Security Council's work. See pp. 269, below.

1023 Cottier and Schefer (n 169).

Without doubt, this optimist account delineated above needs to be tempered with necessary caution to tackle the related challenges of unilateralism. Hence, the doctrine of Common Concern should not only be seen as empowering actors but also as installing important checks in the exercise of unilateral countermeasures. It has been regarded that the exercise of unilateral sanctions as part of reinforcing Common Concern must respect the well-recognised principles of proportionality and accountability.[1024] Proportionality would require any such measures to be well-calibrated, regulating the severity of the impact with the importance of the goal sought to be achieved.[1025] At the end of the day, the geopolitical hazards attached to the wanton unilateralism of the powerful should not be a deterrent, rather an encouragement to rally behind the cause of putting necessary checks on such exercise, to preserve the virtue in unilateral interventions. Even with respect to WTO law, as argued later, such checks would be important to structure some of the available avenues of unilateral action.

Below, the contours of Common Concern doctrine-based countermeasures are further specified.

B *Operational Specifications*

Turning to the topic of LCT diffusion, the general conclusion to be drawn from the discussion so far is that unilateral trade sanctions will be helpful to foster technology diffusion in certain specific scenarios. It should be only be permitted as the final straw to address the related shared concern, provided further that the necessary specifications are made. The foregoing discussion has revealed three important aspects that must be clarified in this regard. First and foremost, it is necessary to specify the metrics that would determine the triggering of unilateral measures. Second, in application of a unilateral measure, the standard of differentiated responsibility must be taken into account. Third, the opportunity to adopt unilateral countermeasure must be reasonably available to all the stakeholders involved, so that it is not perceived as a tool for only a few.

(i) Factors Triggering Unilateral Action

Unilateral trade sanctions are not the solution in itself, but they have the potential to drive the uncommitted stakeholders towards it. It then follows

1024 Cottier, 'The Principle of Common Concern of Humankind' (n 7) s 1.7.3.

1025 ibid; Thomas Cottier and others, 'The Principle of Proportionality in International Law: Foundations and Variations' (2017) 18 The Journal of World Investment and Trade 628.

that the trigger for the unilateral actions would be unreasonable inactions, and refusals to cooperate. Under what terms these actions will be framed as a breach would depend on the prevailing circumstances surrounding the subject-matter, as well as the evolution of the doctrine of Common Concern. Two options can be foreseen. For one, it can be argued that non-fulfilment of pledges made by countries under the Paris Agreement is a trigger factor. This is difficult to realise for several reasons. First, the fulfilment of Paris pledges like the nationally determined commitments (NDCs) are voluntary in nature,[1026] purposely keeping it beyond scrutiny from other participants. Second, substantive rules in the Paris Agreement are of flexible content, which cannot be considered as breached in the legal sense of the term.[1027] Also, the compliance mechanism provided for in the Paris Agreement particularly avoids punitive enforcement.[1028]

More reasonably, and subject to the proposed narrative of trade and LCT diffusion coming into existence, persistent non-cooperation, or absence of diligent and relevant domestic measures to facilitate LCT diffusion would call for taking of countermeasures. In this way, threat or taking of unilateral sanctions serve as a second-tier obligation that comes into play only when the first-tier of actions proposed by the doctrine (i.e. cooperation, and homework) are not complied with.[1029] However, for such a unilateral approach to take hold, it would also be important that the outlook towards trade countermeasures at the WTO is shifted significantly, which at the moment is only allowed after prior authorisation of the Dispute Settlement Body (DSB).

The challenges involved in the above approaches do not mean that in the absence of those States are prevented from championing the cause of Common Concern by taking unilateral actions. This may actually be the most practical

1026 Article 4.2 of the Paris Agreement provides – "[e]ach party *shall* prepare, communicate and maintain *nationally determined* contributions that it *intends* to achieve." [emphasis supplied].

1027 Bodansky, 'The Legal Character of the Paris Agreement' (n 271); Ralph Bodle and Sebastian Oberthür, 'Legal Form of Paris Agreement and Nature of Its Obligations' in Daniel Klein and others (eds), *The Paris Agreement on Climate Change: Analysis and Commentary* (Oxford University Press 2017). Note the authors' conclusion (p 103) – '[f]ew provisions of the Paris Agreement are prescriptive and create precise legal obligations, and these are primarily procedural and focused on "nationally determined contributions" (on mitigation) and a core transparency framework, plus collective obligations regarding finance'.

1028 Article 15.2 of the Paris Agreement provides that the mechanism to facilitate implementation and promote compliance shall "function in a manner that is transparent, non-adversarial and non-punitive."

1029 Ahmad (n 163).

outcome that can possibly be foreseen. As discussed later, any such sanction may then need to be squared off with the WTO rules upon challenge.

(ii) Incorporating Differentiation

Common but differentiated responsibility (CBDR) is an indispensable consideration to be factored into every aspect of climate action, including actions taken in pursuance of the Common Concern doctrine. The earlier chapter that outlined the new narrative of trade and low-carbon technology diffusion, also adequately foregrounded the importance of CBDR within that narrative.[1030] Consideration for the specific circumstances of the developing countries is built into the cooperation and homework aspects of the activities. As a result, any plausible ground for inaction by a country must be appropriately tackled in bilateral or multi-party settings, through supports, assistance, and acknowledgement of the situation. These reasonable grounds apart, what remains are behaviour driven by negligence, impunity, or pure self-interest. In such situations, it is argued that the developed or developing countries alike must face the possibility of trade sanctions being taken against them. However, even in that stage, the doctrine would call for abidance by the principles of equity and proportionality to be met. As would be discussed below, the requirement by the doctrine to keep equity and proportionality in consideration is an important check that currently is not in place in WTO rules.

(iii) Ensuring Equal Access to Unilateral Redress

The opportunity to adopt the path of unilateral redress of common concerns under justifiable circumstances would be available to all willing and compliant countries irrespective of their position as suppliers, or recipients of technologies. This can be foreseen to operate against developed countries when they unreasonably deny the impacts of climate change and refuse to engage in a multilateral setting (e.g. the United States), or those that refuse to bring the discussion on the trade front to avoid development of stricter rules (e.g. the oil economies like Saudi Arabia). It can also operate against the developing countries, especially when economic development is used as a façade to continue investing in polluting activities for the long-term (e.g. China). Although any countries can wield the tool of sanction, it is nevertheless true that effective deployment of the same would require some form of economic clout in the global world. In the end, it may come down to a handful of benevolent nations acting out of own interests as well as those of the international community

1030 See Chapter 3 I B (iii), and Chapter 4 III C (iii) above.

and putting unilateral sanctions into operation. This is not altogether new or deviating from the current state of affairs. The doctrine would only facilitate these countries' recourse to coercive measures when legitimate, as well as prevent the capricious exercise of power in other situations.

III Position under Public International Law

This section makes a cursory analysis of the position of the proposed unilateral action in the background of general public international law rules. As the foregoing section hinted, a full-fledged doctrine of Common Concern would be an advancement over the international legal discipline of state responsibility as embodied in the ILC Draft Articles on the Responsibility of States for Internationally Wrongful Acts (ARSIWA).[1031] In particular, the improvement would be with regard to supplying a clearer legal justification for countermeasures taken by a state to protect community interests. The reason behind keeping the analysis in this section limited is that despite trade sanctions are oft-cited in studies involving state responsibility,[1032] the ARSIWA has little bearing when it comes to saving trade measures from legal scrutiny under the WTO rules. The exclusive jurisdiction of the WTO dispute settlement process in matters relating to trade measures between its members means that the laws therein would claim primacy over the general body of rules.[1033] Nevertheless, the discussion here is an ideal starting point to move subsequently to a narrower and further detailed study of the WTO rules in this regard.

Under the current international law framework, a recourse to countermeasures requires satisfaction of twofold requirements, i.e. proving the existence of an internationally wrongful act, and as a result, injury being caused to the state that is taking countermeasure.[1034] An internationally wrongful act is the

1031 Responsibility of States for Internationally Wrongful Acts, Annex to the United Nations General Assembly Resolution 56/83 2001.

1032 International Law Commission (ILC), 'Draft Articles on Responsibility of States for Internationally Wrongful Acts, with Commentaries' (n 1019); Patrick Hamilton, 'Counter(Measur)Ing Climate Change: The ILC, Third State Countermeasures and Climate Change' (2008) 4 McGill International Journal of Sustainable Development Law and Policy 83.

1033 Article 23.1 Understanding on Rules and Procedures Governing the Settlement of Disputes 1994 (Marrakesh Agreement Establishing the World Trade Organization, Annex 2, 1869 UNTS 401); For a detailed analysis, see Van den Bossche and Zdouc (n 756) 168–178.

1034 Article 49, Responsibility of States for Internationally Wrongful Acts, Annex to the United Nations General Assembly Resolution 56/83.

consequence of a breach of obligation attributable to a state.[1035] A breach occurs when state action is not in conformity with what is required of it by virtue of a specific obligation.[1036] A state can be considered injured under the ARSIWA if a bilateral obligation owed to that state is breached by another.[1037] Additionally, breach of obligations of *erga omnes* nature may also render a state injured subject to the condition that it was 'specially affected',[1038] or that the breach prejudices all the other parties to continue performance of the obligation in question.[1039] These states apart, the opportunity to take countermeasures remains closed to all others, including those affected by the breach of a communitarian norm of *erga omnes* nature. In the latter case, response options available are limited to a call for cessation, non-repetition, and performance of the obligation in question.[1040]

Therefore, to make unilateral sanctions valid within the current international law framework, the indispensable path will be to argue that the actions indicated in the previous section as triggering such responses are internationally wrongful, as those contravene the primary obligations arising out of the Common Concern doctrine.[1041] This argument is hypothetical and can be foreseen to take place either as a breach of a treaty obligation subject to the doctrine being integrated into a treaty body regulating the subject-matter of concern. Otherwise it can also be considered as the breach of a customary norm of international law subject to commensurate development. Which of the two may actually occur would depend on the evolutionary trajectory of the concept. Following the above brief description of the ARSIWA rules, it is submitted that the outcome in these two hypothetical cases may be different. When the doctrine of Common Concern is integrated into a treaty regime, it may be relatively easier for a signatory state intending to take countermeasure to argue that it is specially affected due to intentional non-cooperation or domestic inaction.[1042] However, as explained in the next section, success of such an argument will require support from the compliance regulation in the respective treaty regime. With respect to the alternate course, i.e. culmination of the doctrine as a customary norm, a state seeking to act must additionally

1035 Article 2, ibid.
1036 Article 12, ibid.
1037 Article 42(a), ibid.
1038 Article 42(b)(i), ibid.
1039 Article 42(b)(ii), ibid.
1040 Article 48, ibid.
1041 Ahmad (n 163).
1042 Articles 42 and 49, International Law Commission (ILC), 'Draft Articles on Responsibility of States for Internationally Wrongful Acts, with Commentaries' (n 1019).

establish that it was specially affected, to go beyond the confines of the 'lawful measures',[1043] which as explained in the previous paragraph, falls short of expressly including countermeasures within the scope of its meaning.

Along any of the two avenues mentioned above, unilateral countermeasures for the breach of an identified Common Concern must count upon advancement of the current state responsibility rules embodied in the ARSIWA. The issue of whether a non-injured party can be allowed to take countermeasures remains highly debated.[1044] As earlier noted, the ILC, despite finding some state practice, considered those to be nascent and not normative enough.[1045] The reason for such a conclusion can be the lack of generality in state practice regarding taking recourse to such measures. However, the opposing view highlights the growing number of third-state measures over the past decade, and thereupon argue that non-injured countries can and frequently do engage in actions that are actually countermeasures.[1046] Koskenniemi holds the opinion that the problems of codifying third-state countermeasures have proven to be problematic because it is essentially the domain of international politics.[1047]

While a conclusive settlement of this debate may not be forthcoming soon, it should not mean that the relevant rules of international law are set in stone. The doctrine of Common Concern shows the direction in which progress is to be made. Being not only limited to calling for states in a position to do so to be allowed to take countermeasures, the doctrine also maintains that such actions are a matter of responsibility in themselves. This alters the existing narrative of entitlement to that of obligation binding the states.[1048] This is,

1043 Article 54, ibid.

1044 Dobson and Ryngaert (n 1005).

1045 See, Commentary to Article 54, International Law Commission (ILC), 'Draft Articles on Responsibility of States for Internationally Wrongful Acts, with Commentaries' (n 1019) 137–139.

1046 Martin Dawidowicz, *Third-Party Countermeasures in International Law* (Cambridge University Press 2017); Elena Katselli, *The Problem of Enforcement in International Law: Countermeasures, the Non-Injured State and the Idea of International Community* (Routledge 2010); Christian J Tams, 'Individual States as Guardians of Community Interests' in Ulrich Fastenrath and others (eds), *From Bilateralism to Community Interest: Essays in Honour of Judge Bruno Simma* (Oxford University Press 2011).

1047 M Koskenniemi, 'Solidarity Measures: State Responsibility as a New International Order?' (2002) 72 British Yearbook of International Law 337.

1048 International Law Commission (ILC), 'Draft Articles on Responsibility of States for Internationally Wrongful Acts, with Commentaries' (n 1019) 116. Note the ILC commentary that '[p]art three [of the ARSIWA] is concerned with the implementation of State responsibility, i.e. with the entitlement of other States to invoke the international responsibility of the responsible State […]'.

however, subject to an important qualification that in the universe of countermeasures for an expanding variety of *erga omnes* breaches, only those that respond to violations of Common Concerns are proposed to be responsibilities. In this sense, the suggestion is in parallel with the doctrine of the 'responsibility to protect', although unlike the latter Common Concern doctrine has an open scope.[1049] The language of responsibility also ensures that the taking of countermeasures does not become a tool in the hand of the rich and powerful states, only to be used at their convenience. The Common Concern doctrine, therefore, structures the unregulated avenue of countermeasures by supplying both enabling and restricting conditions.

IV Position under the Multilateral Trade Rules

Venturing beyond the general domain of public international law, examination of the multilateral trade rules' position on a Common Concern inspired trade sanction bears special importance. With respect to unilateral trade sanctions, the WTO rules, especially those in the Dispute Settlement Understanding (DSU) on recourse to countermeasures, serve as *lex specialis* to the customary rules on state responsibility.[1050] Therefore, to the extent WTO rules are applicable, recourse to the general international law rules on state responsibility is not available to a member for validating unilateral trade countermeasures.[1051] Here we start from a brief account of the scope and extent of the WTO rules on

1049 Cottier and Schefer (n 169); Cottier, 'The Principle of Common Concern of Humankind' (n 7) ss 1.4.3.3, and 1.7.3.

1050 Article 55, Responsibility of States for Internationally Wrongful Acts, Annex to the United Nations General Assembly Resolution 56/83. The provision holds that the 'Articles do not apply where and to the extent that the conditions for the existence of an internationally wrongful act or the content or implementation of the international responsibility of a State are governed by special rules of international law'.; The European Commission recently came to a similar conclusion. European Commission, 'Proposal for a Regulation of the European Parliament and of the Council Amending Regulation (EU) No 654/2014 of the European Parliament and of the Council Concerning the Exercise of the Union's Rights for the Application and Enforcement of International Trade Rules' (n 1002) 4.

1051 Joost Pauwelyn, *Conflict of Norms in Public International Law: How WTO Law Relates to Other Rules of International Law* (Cambridge University Press 2003) 218–221. Pauwelyn, following James Crawford (cited therein) believes that WTO rules are *lex specialis* to the ARSIWA as it explicitly contracts out from the latter body of rules in terms of the variety of remedies available, as well as regarding the nature of access to and scope of countermeasures permitted.

unilateral countermeasures. Then we move on to assess their implications for sanctions taken to enforce a Common Concern of LCT diffusion.

Countermeasures, known in the WTO parlance as 'suspension of concessions',[1052] is a tightly regulated avenue under the WTO law. The DSU provides that countermeasures are the last resort, temporary solutions; available only when the DSB recommendation and rulings from a settled dispute are not implemented by the respondent member following a dispute.[1053] Unlike the customary rules on state responsibility,[1054] Article 23 of the DSU prohibits unilateral interventions for breaches of trade commitments.[1055] The provision serves as an "exclusive dispute settlement clause", [1056] generally compelling all members to have recourse to the DSU provision when seeking redress.[1057] However, similar to the customary rules, proportionality is a fundamental condition for countermeasures to be granted by the DSB.[1058]

As mentioned above, the rejection of unilateral self-help measures at the WTO is subject to an important qualification. It is confined to breaches of covered agreements. It is clear from the language of the DSU Article 23.1 that compels members to have recourse to the multilateral dispute settlement system when seeking redress of a violation of obligation under the covered agreements. Similarly, Article 23.2(c) compels the members to obtain DSB authorisation when responding to another member's failure to uphold trade commitments. Decisions in earlier disputes confirm this position.[1059]

1052 ibid 229–230.

1053 Articles 3.7, 22.1, and 22.2, Understanding on Rules and Procedures Governing the Settlement of Disputes (n 1033).

1054 Note, in contrast, Article 22 of the ARSIWA, which precludes the wrongfulness of a countermeasure taken validly.

1055 Article 23.1 lays down that Members seeking 'regress of a violation of obligations' under the covered agreements 'shall have recourse to, and abided by, the rules and procedures of [the DSU]'. History of the provision goes back to the Havana Charter. See *United States – Sections 301–310 of the Trade Act of 1974* (n 995) para 4.72–4.73; Also, 'Unilateralism: An Unforced Error' <https://soundcloud.com/user-885686084/ep-29-unilateralism> accessed 25 October 2020.

1056 *United States – Sections 301–310 of the Trade Act of 1974* (n 992) para 7.43.

1057 *United States – Import Measures on Certain Products from the European Communities* [2001] Panel Report WT/DS165/R, DSR 2001:II 413 [6.19–6.20]; It was confirmed by the Appellate Body, *United States – Import Measures on Certain Products from the European Communities* [2001] Appellate Body Report WT/DS165/AB/R, DSR 2001:I 373 [111].

1058 Article 22.4, Understanding on Rules and Procedures Governing the Settlement of Disputes (n 1033). The level of suspension of concession authorised by the DSB must be 'equivalent' to the level of nullification or impairement suffered by the complaining Member. Pauwelyn, *Conflict of Norms in Public International Law: How WTO Law Relates to Other Rules of International Law* (n 1051) 234.

1059 See notes 1056, & 1057 above.

As a result, the question of the legitimacy of unilateral trade countermeasures in response to non-WTO law breaches remain open. While such actions may be valid under the customary rules of responsibility, the DSU remains silent on the matter.[1060] Pauwelyn believes that such countermeasures 'ought to be' valid under the WTO law, and also liable to be found as such when the issue appears before a Panel.[1061] Other authors alternatively hold that the only plausible path for the non-WTO countermeasures to be legitimised within the existing structure of rules is through the cover of the available general or security exception provisions.[1062]

Even if there is merit in the consideration that unilateral trade countermeasures for non-WTO law breaches should be considered valid if challenged before a WTO Panel, the matter is complicated by the limitations in applicable law and the Panel's subject-matter jurisdiction. The applicable law in a trade dispute remains confined to the covered agreements.[1063] While the WTO is not a clinically isolated regime and there are many instances of taking recourse to non-WTO rules for the purpose of finding the meaning of a provision of WTO law, Panels have always refrained from giving direct effect to non-WTO rules through its rulings. One reason behind is that the jurisdiction of the WTO and its dispute settlement process only extends to settling matters arising under the covered agreements and not beyond.[1064] So, despite the fact that a

---

1060 Bianchi and Gardoni holds that the silence cannot be construed as the WTO Members implied derogation of their international law right to take countermeasures. See, Andrea Bianchi and Lorenzo Gardoni, 'Developing Countries, Countermeasures and WTO Law: Reinterpreting the DSU against the Background of International Law' (ICTSD 2008) Systemic Issue Paper Issue Paper No. 5 29–30.

1061 Pauwelyn, *Conflict of Norms in Public International Law: How WTO Law Relates to Other Rules of International Law* (n 1051) 232.

1062 Cleveland (n 982); Gabrielle Marceau, 'WTO Dispute Settlement and Human Rights' (2002) 13 European Journal of International Law 62.

1063 Marceau, 'WTO Dispute Settlement and Human Rights' (n 1062) 766–779. Marceau views the WTO laws as a largely 'self-contained regime' where non-WTO rules are taken into account only so far as necessary to give effect to the provisions of the covered agreements. Note, in contrast, the view of Pauwelyn. Pauwelyn, *Conflict of Norms in Public International Law: How WTO Law Relates to Other Rules of International Law* (n 1051) 456–478. The author argued that in absence of any explicit contracting out of the general body of international law, WTO rules cannot be viewed as a 'self-contained regime'. As a result, applicable law, for a Panel, can span beyond those in the covered agreements. See in particular, p. 466 (note 82) of the cited work.

1064 Articles 1.1, 7, 11, Understanding on Rules and Procedures Governing the Settlement of Disputes; Also see Joost Pauwelyn, Joel P Trachtman and Debra P Steger, 'The Jurisdiction of the WTO Is Limited to Trade' (2004) 98 Proceedings of the Annual Meeting (American Society of International Law) 135.

member's measure is part of a broader affair involving non-WTO laws as well, the Panel only entertains the questions relating to the breach of the covered agreement.[1065] This outcome has been termed as 'salami-slicing' of disputes. It is unavoidable, as Panels cannot be precluded from the assessment of some aspects of the dispute just because the complete dispute involves other questions beyond its jurisdiction, however important.[1066] As a result, respondents whoses action are legitimate due to a non-WTO reason, would find themselves scrambling for additional cover under the exception clauses.[1067]

In the backdrop of the increasing trend of unilateral interventions, one Panel is currently facing the question of the legitimacy of trade countermeasure for non-WTO breaches. The written response of the United States in the trade dispute between itself and China regarding certain retaliatory tariffs essentially argues that the tariffs are a response to issues that are beyond the jurisdiction of the WTO.[1068] As a result, no 'satisfactory' or 'prompt' settlement is possible preserving the rights and obligations of the members.[1069] One claim made by the US in that dispute is that the Panel ought to take note of the retaliatory tariffs as a solution in itself that has been reached between parties and hence not exercise its jurisdiction any further.[1070] This is similar to the

1065 Pauwelyn, *Conflict of Norms in Public International Law: How WTO Law Relates to Other Rules of International Law* (n 1051) 451–452.

1066 *Mexico – Tax Measures on Soft Drinks and Other Beverages* [2006] Appellate Body Report WT/DS308/AB/R, DSR 2006:1 43 [53]. The Appellate Body confirmed that a Panel does not enjoy discretion to avoid exercising jurisdiction in a matter brought before it. It is because access to multilateral settlement of dispute, under DSU Article 23, is a right of the complainant. *European Communities – Customs Classification of Frozen Boneless Chicken Cuts* [2005] Panel Report WT/DS269/R, DSR 2005:XIX 9295 [7.56]. Also, *United States Diplomatic and Consular Staff in Tehran*, ICJ Reports 1980, para 36.

1067 In the human rights context, Marceau presents this as an opportunity to mitigate conflicts between the rule systems through good faith interpretation. Marceau, 'WTO Dispute Settlement and Human Rights' (n 1062) 791.

1068 'United States – Tariff Measures on Certain Goods from China (DS543)' (2019) First written submission of the United Staes of America <https://ustr.gov/sites/default/files/enforcement/DS/US.Sub1.%28DS543%29.fin.%28public%29.pdf> accessed 25 October 2020. Note the opening paragraph of the submission (para1). 'China has chosen to adopt a range of policies and practices to obtain an unfair competitive edge over other Members by stealing or otherwise unfairly acquiring their technology and intellectual property. Where those policies or practices can be addressed through WTO rules, the United States is pursuing WTO dispute settlement. Most of China's practices, however, are not covered by existing WTO disciplines'.

1069 ibid 9–12.

1070 ibid 15. The claim is that, "in accordance with the last sentence of Article 12.7 of the DSU, the Panel should issue a report that is "confined to a brief description of the case and to reporting that a solution has been reached.""

Mexican claim against the United States in the *Soft Drinks* dispute, where the Panel was requested to refrain from exercising jurisdiction as the matter had a non-WTO (i.e. NAFTA) origin.[1071] However, the Panel's inability to refrain from exercising jurisdiction has already been mentioned in the above paragraph. Several subsequent disputes will be influenced by the way the Panels address the current dispute.[1072]

Summing up this discussion, one conclusion to be drawn is that the WTO rules, especially the obligation to take recourse to the multilateral dispute settlement process would step in as *lex specialis* in a scenario where the proposed Common Concern doctrine based low-carbon technology diffusion narrative is integrated into the body of trade rules. Under such a circumstance, the option of unilateral countermeasures, taken in accordance with the existing laws, is impossible, unless changes take place in the legal formulation of the DSU. This, among others, would require tailored exceptions to be placed in the current exclusive scope of Article 23. Any such change, even when well-intended, must be cautiously approached, especially in a geopolitical setting where countries are seemingly warming up to mercantilist behaviour at the cost of the security and predictability of multilateralism.

Alternatively, trade countermeasures can be taken under a self-standing doctrine of Common Concern. The legitimacy of such a measure under the customary rules of responsibility would depend further on the details. In any case, countermeasure taken on the basis of a non-WTO legal justification will be considered as a breach of trade commitments under the covered agreements, triggering the targeted countries' right to seek a remedy through a dispute at the WTO. A compromise way would be to make sure that such countermeasures find refuge under the available exception clauses. To what extent such an outcome is possible is discussed hereunder.

A *Trade Sanctions under the Exception Clauses*

Two forms of exception clauses taken under consideration here are the general and the security exceptions. The GATT, as well as the GATS, provide for general exceptions as Articles XX and XIV respectively.[1073] These two provisions

---

1071 *Mexico – Tax Measures on Soft Drinks and Other Beverages* (n 713) 22–23.

1072 Most importantly, the two subsequent tariff dispute between US and China (DS565, DS587), as well as the Venzuelan challenge of the US human rights sanctions (DS574).

1073 While the current discussion does not extend to cover the TRIPS agreement, for the previously detailed reasons that protection of intellectual property is not the prominent obstacle for low-carbon technology diffusion, as previously understood; it is nevertheless relevant to mention that exceptions in the TRIPS agreement are more type specific, found in Articles 13, 17, 24, 30 and 31 of the agreement. In addition, there is a periodically

are identical in terms of drafting, structure, interpretation, and application, though some details vary. The security exception clauses are there to allow the members greater degree of freedom to act through trade measures in response to security concerns. These provisions are found in Articles XXI of the GATT, XIV *bis* of the GATS, and Article 73 of the TRIPS agreement. We do not foresee the regional economic integration exceptions coming to play to justify trade sanctions. In the following paragraph, we attempt to point out the key factors that would determine the outcome of any effort to justify a Common Concern motivated trade sanction under the general or security exception provisions.

There are several reasons for the conclusion that trade sanctions cannot be justified under the general exception clauses. Without repeating the substantive details of the general exception provisions,[1074] following paragraphs will briefly articulate those.

First and foremost, the punitive design of trade sanctions would work against any argument that they maintain a sufficiently close relationship to a specific policy goal. A close relationship, or 'sufficient nexus'[1075] is important to bring a putative measure within the subject-matter scope of the exception provisions.[1076] Note that in the *US – Gambling* dispute, the AB opined:

---

extended waiver for LDCs from implementing the agreement provisions, except for the non-discrimination obligations, and those arising from other multilateral agreements, provided in Article 66.1 of TRIPS.

1074 This is done with respect to carbon pricing and the GATT. See Chapter 4 III C above.

1075 *United States – Import Prohibition of Certain Shrimp and Shrimp Products* (n 94) para 133. The Appellate Body famously mentioned that '[w]e note only that in the specific circumstances of the case before us, there is a sufficient nexus between the migratory and endangered marine populations involved and the United States for purposes of Article XX(g)'.

1076 *Colombia – Measures Relating to the Importation of Textiles, Apparel and Footwear* [2016] Appellate Body Report WT/DS461/AB/R [5.68–5.77; 5.123–5.126]; *Brazil – Measures Affecting Imports of Retreaded Tyres* (n 779) para 7.40–7.41; *India – Certain Measures Relating to Solar Cells and Solar Modules* (n 4) para 5.110–5.113; *Argentina – Measures Relating to Trade in Goods and Services* [2016] Appellate Body Report WT/DS453/AB/R and Add.1 [6.203–6.205]. Note the AB opinion in Colombia – Textiles (para 5.126) that "[t]he examination of a defence under both Article XX(a) and Article XX(d) requires an initial, threshold examination of the design of the measure at issue, including its content, structure, and expected operation. In the case of Article XX(a), a panel must examine the relationship between the measure and the protection of public morals; in the case of Article XX(d), a panel must examine the relationship between the measure and securing compliance with relevant provisions of laws or regulations that are not GATT-inconsistent. Thus, while the terms "to protect" and "to secure compliance" may differ, we consider that both terms involve establishing the existence of such a relationship" [footnote omitted].

> A panel should first determine whether the challenged measure falls within the scope of one of the paragraphs of Article XIV. This requires that the challenged measure address the particular interest specified in that paragraph and that there be a sufficient nexus between the measure and the interest protected. The required nexus – or "degree of connection" – between the measure and the interest is specified in the language of the paragraphs themselves, through the use of terms such as "relating to" and "necessary to".[1077]

As explained earlier, a trade sanction is designed to inflict costs and as a result, it does not characteristically change when the policy motive is shifted from one to another.[1078] Hence it cannot be said that the 'degree of connection' between the measure and the ultimate motive is so close as to be justifiable.

Second, the exclusively outward-directed nature[1079] of a sanction would fail the test of even-handedness, also possibly the chapeau requirements. Even-handedness is an essential requirement for measures that target conservation of exhaustible natural resources, which sanctions cannot fulfil as they do not impact domestic industries at all. Even when directed outwards, sanctions generally single out a specific entity, thereby adding implementational discrimination to the initial breach of trade rules – something prohibited by the chapeau requirements of the general exception provisions.

Lastly, sanctions are unorthodox measures and not a regular policy option. Making them justifiable under the general exception clauses would require widening the latter's scope to a degree that would allow for rampant protectionism. It is also confirmed by the arrangement of the exception clauses. If measures such as trade sanctions were justifiable under the general exception provision, the security exception provision would be unnecessary and redundant.

Overall, a trade sanction cannot be provisionally justified under the general exception clauses. Cottier also comes to this conclusion summarily holding that the general exceptions would naturally cover only the product-related measures, i.e. those that apply to a product or process regarding which the public policy issue arises.[1080]

1077 *United States – Measures Affecting the Cross Border Supply of Gambling and Betting Services* (n 779) para 292.

1078 See section I at the beginning of this chapter.

1079 ibid.

1080 Cottier, 'The Principle of Common Concern of Humankind' (n 7) s 1.7.2.

The security exceptions, identically available in the GATT, and GATS, as well as the TRIPS, are the ideal space for legitimising trade sanctions.[1081] Compared to the general exception clauses, most conspicuous structural features of the security exception clauses are the departure of a common chapeau, and inclusion of language allowing a greater degree of freedom of action to the members. These apart, like the general exception clauses, the security exception clauses also supply several sub-paragraphs containing specific scenarios when a member can maintain WTO-inconsistent trade measures. Two possible defences can be foreseen. One is to hold that inadequate mitigation of climate change is an emergency in international relations, and the trade sanction is taken by a member to protect its essential security interests in that context.[1082] The other option is to argue that the sanctions are taken in pursuance of obligations under the UN Charter to maintain international peace and security.[1083] After lying dormant for decades, a number of disputes have emerged where the respondents have sought to use the cover of the former avenue.[1084]

(i) Sanctions for a Climate Emergency

The relevant provision of the security exception clause (i.e. paragraph (b)(iii) of the respective Articles), is as follows:

> Nothing in this Agreement shall be construed [...]
> (b) to prevent any contracting party from taking any action which it considers necessary for the protection of its essential security interests [...]
> (iii) taken in time of war or other emergency in international relations [...]

While states' views tend to split[1085] regarding whether the subjective lean of the phrase 'it considers necessary' influences the provision so as to make it judicially inscrutable *in toto*, recently the first Panel tackling the question decided to the negative.[1086] After a thorough analysis, the Panel concluded that the provision is not beyond Panel's jurisdiction. It was found that upon plain

---

1081 Van den Bossche and Zdouc (n 753) 619.
1082 Article XXI(b)(iii), General Agreement on Tariffs and Trade (n 426); Article XIVbis(b)(iii), General Agreement on Trade in Services (n 428).
1083 Article XXI(c), General Agreement on Tariffs and Trade (n 426); Article XIVbis(c) General Agreement on Trade in Services (n 428).
1084 For example, *Russia – Measures Concerning Traffic in Transit* (n 997).
1085 ibid 7.27–7.52.
1086 ibid 7.102.

reading, the circumstances described in subparagraph (iii) above appear to qualify the discretion accorded to the member. Also, the Panel noted that the phrases 'taken in the time of' and 'emergency in international relations' evoke temporal and factual notions that are objectively determinable. Furthermore, looking at the negotiating history of the provision in the context of the Havana Charter, the Panel found out that the original proponent of the provision, the United States, convinced other participants by explaining that the proposition will make sure of a balanced approach:

> We recognized that there was a great danger of having too wide an exception and we could not put it into the Charter, simply by saying: "by any Member of measures relating to a Member's security interests" because, that would permit anything under the sun. Therefore we thought it well to draft provisions which would take care of real essential security interests and, *at the same time, so far as we could, to limit the exception* so as to prevent the adoption of protection for maintaining industries under every conceivable circumstance. (177)
>
> [Original footnote] (177) Second Session of the Preparatory Committee of the United Nations Conference on Trade and Employment, Verbatim Report, Thirty-Third Meeting of Commission A Held on Thursday, 24 July 1947, E/PC/T/A/PV/33, pp. 20–21 (as corrected by Second Session of the Preparatory Committee of the United Nations Conference on Trade and Employment, Corrigendum to Verbatim Report of Thirty-Third Meeting of Commission A, E/PC/T/A/PV/33.Corr.3, pp. 20–21). (emphasis added)[1087]

In addition to finding that the provision in question is not non-justiciable, the Panel recognised that 'some latitude' was accorded to the members in terms of characterising their respective interests–

> [T]he "balance" that was struck by the security exceptions was that Members would have "some latitude" to determine what their essential security interests are, and the necessity of action to protect those interests, while potential abuse of the exceptions would be curtailed by limiting the circumstances in which the exceptions could be invoked to those specified in the subparagraphs of Article XXI(b);[1088]

1087 ibid 47–48.
1088 ibid 7.98.

As a result, the import of the phrase 'which it considers' is limited to the consideration of necessity in the chapeau of paragraph (b), coming into play only when any of the circumstances of the following sub-paragraphs are objectively determined to exist.

Returning to our issue at hand, i.e. justification of a trade sanction taken to trigger climate action, it would involve a two-step analysis, First, it has to be established that the sanction is 'taken in time of emergency in international relations'. Second, the member imposing the sanction should consider it necessary for the protection of its essential security interests.

The first step suggests that a specific temporal characteristic must exist, serving as the context of a justifiable trade sanction. The pivotal point for the present case would be the question of whether climate change can be considered as an emergency in international relations and if so, what would the implications be for the diffusion of LCTs. In *Russia – Transit* dispute, the Panel considered the literal meaning of the term 'emergency' as well as its appearance in the provision in conjunction with 'war', and the context of sub-paragraphs (i) and (ii).[1089] It was held that mere political or economic difference between countries is not sufficient to be considered as an emergency.[1090] Rather, term emergency would apply to "a situation of armed conflict, or of latent armed conflict, or of heightened tension or crisis, or of general instability engulfing or surrounding a state."[1091] These situations are such that may trigger particular interests (e.g. of defence, security, or of maintaining law and order) of a member. For multiple reasons, this is a standard that the deepening climate crisis would be able to meet possibly now or in the near future. Recent studies indicate that unbridled change of global climate would not only increase the frequency and intensity of natural disasters, but also result in disruption of human societies, and livelihood; resulting in challenges like mass-migrations, aggravation of the probability of armed conflicts in prone areas.[1092] Individually, countries wary of climate change impact are already declaring it an emergency

---

1089 ibid 7.71–7.74.

1090 ibid 7.75.

1091 ibid 7.76.

1092 Ove Hoegh-Guldberg and others, 'Impacts of 1.5°C of Global Warming on Natural and Human Systems' in Valerie Masson-Delmotte and others (eds), *Special Report: Global Warming of 1.5°C* (World Meteorological Organization (WMO) 2018) 244–245 <http://www.ipcc.ch/report/sr15/> accessed 25 October 2020; For a comprehensive review, see W Neil Adger and others, 'Human Security' in Christopher B Field and others (eds), *Climate Change 2014: Impacts, Adaptation, and Vulnerability – Part A: Global and Sectoral Aspects. Contribution of Working Group II to the Fifth Assessment Report of the Intergovernmental Panel on Climate Change* (Cambridge University Press 2014).

to push for further decarbonisation.[1093] In addition, the UN Security Council is also increasingly getting involved in exploring the security threat aspect of climate change.[1094] The status of climate change as a common concern of humankind would also indicate the global nature of the problem. Overall, there is a significant possibility that the proposed measure will satisfy the requirements at this stage.

The second question, amenable to good-faith demonstration of subjective intent, is whether a member taking the sanction considers it necessary for the protection of essential security interests. In *Russia – Transit*, the Panel expressed that essential security interests are those that are quintessential for the functioning of the state, e.g. territorial defence, internal law and order etc.[1095] However, matters that may constitute a threat to essential security interests for a member is left to their discretion,[1096] which is expected to be exercised in good faith.[1097] This subjective assessment of necessity would allow a climate-related sanction to pass the security exception test, while it may fail under the general exception. The fact that the framework of Common Concern requires countries to take countermeasures in appropriate circumstances will serve as an additional argument. Based upon the aforementioned factors that make climate change an emergency, it can be said that the essential security threats can arise from, for example, the risk of hostilities aggravated by climate change spilling over, or the risk of domestic political and societal instability due to intensified migratory pressure. It is expected that any trade measures taken in response meet a "minimum requirement of plausibility", i.e. they are not implausible as measures to protect those interests.[1098] Sanctions, when taken as a last resort measure will surely be successful to some degree to change the target countries behaviour.

(ii) Sanction to Maintain International Peace and Security

The relevant provision of the security exception clauses (i.e. paragraph c of the relevant Articles) hold that:

1093 'UK Parliament Declares Climate Emergency' *BBC News* (1 May 2019) <https://www.bbc.com/news/uk-politics-48126677> accessed 25 October 2020; Joao Vitor Da Silva Marques, 'French National Assembly Expected to Declare "Climate Emergency" ' *euronews* (24 June 2019) <https://www.euronews.com/2019/06/24/french-national-assembly-expected-to-declare-climate-emergency> accessed 25 October 2020.

1094 See the following sub-section (ii) below.

1095 *Russia – Measures Concerning Traffic in Transit* (n 997) para 7.130.

1096 ibid 7.131.

1097 ibid 7.132–7.133.

1098 ibid 7.138.

> Nothing in this Agreement shall be construed:[…]
> (c) to prevent a Member from taking any action in pursuance of its obligations under the United Nations Charter for the maintenance of international peace and security.

Unlike the paragraph (b)(iii) discussed before, the above provision is a justification that may become plausible over time. Paragraph (c) of the security exception operates to clear the way for taking trade measures commensurate with the sanctions regimes established by the UN Security Council (UNSC). The primary responsibility to maintain international peace and security falls upon the UNSC under the United Nations Charter.[1099] Among others, the Security Council determines the existence of a threat to peace, or breach of peace,[1100] and thereupon may recommend for, *inter alia*, interruption of economic relations.[1101]

We consider this notion as an emerging possibility because over the past several years the UNSC have increasingly noted the role of climate change as a threat to peace. In January 2019, the Council held an open debate to discuss the impact of climate change on peace and security.[1102] Since 2017, references to climate change have also frequently been made in the Security Council resolutions adopted regarding several conflict-prone regions in the African continent. In 2017 the Council recognised with respect to the Lake Chad Basin region that:

> [T]he adverse effects of climate change and ecological changes among other factors on the stability of the Region, including through water scarcity, drought, desertification, land degradation, and food insecurity, and *emphasises* the need for adequate risk assessments and risk management

---

1099 Article 24, Charter of the United Nations (n 536).

1100 Article 39, ibid.

1101 Article 41, ibid; See for example, the sanctions regime established against North Korea, United Nations Security Council, 'Resolution 1718 (2006)' (United Nations 2006) S/RES/1718 (2006); For a list of trade embargo that falls within the regime, see 'Security Council Committee Established Pursuant to Resolution 1718 (2006) | United Nations Security Council' <https://www.un.org/securitycouncil/sanctions/1718> accessed 25 Octotober 2020.

1102 'Climate Change Recognized as "Threat Multiplier", UN Security Council Debates Its Impact on Peace' (*UN News*, 25 January 2019) <https://news.un.org/en/story/2019/01/1031322> accessed 25 October 2020.

strategies by governments and the United Nations relating to these factors;[1103]

In 2018, the Security Council requested the UN and the government of Sudan to "*consider* the adverse implications of climate change" in relation to their ongoing programs in Darfur.[1104] Altogether, the UNSC has so far not recommended disruptive action in relation to climate change. But it is not at all unthinkable that in the coming days the non-compliant states will be hit with economic embargoes. The doctrine of Common Concern can structure forward progress along this path.

Overall, the analysis above shows that there is a real and growing possibility that a trade countermeasure to promote low-carbon technology diffusion may satisfy the relevant thresholds of some of the security exception provisions. Most plausible is an argument that times of worsening climate emergency, a trade countermeasure taken by a WTO member to protect itself from catastrophic risks arising from unabated GHG emissions is justifiable. One important shortcoming in this regard is the absence of any proportionality or equitable considerations requirement to condition the access to and application of such measures. As a result, there is no need to respect the principle of differentiated responsibility while justifying a climate minded trade measure through security exceptions. It may be noted in contrast that proportionality is a strict prerequisite for countermeasures that are granted by the DSB to ensure compliance with its rulings and recommendations. Similarly, attention to the developing country interests is a part of the process of implementing the DSB rulings. Developing countries can also take recourse to arbitration to challenge the level of countermeasures implemented against them. The question of whether the doctrine of Common Concern would influence the reading or application of the security exception provisions in a way that takes account of these considerations is discussed hereunder.

1103 United Nations Security Council, 'Resolution 2349 (2017)' (United Nations 2017) S/RES/2349 (2017); The language was then repeated in several subsequent resolutions, United Nations Security Council, 'Resolution 2457 (2019)' (United Nations 2019) S/RES/2457 (2019).

1104 United Nations Security Council, 'Resolution 2429 (2018)' (United Nations 2018) S/RES/2429 (2018); The language was also repeated regarding Somalia, United Nations Security Council, 'Resolution 2461 (2019)' (United Nations 2019) S/RES/2461 (2019); Somewhat similarly, United Nations Security Council, 'Resolution 2423 (2018)' (United Nations 2018) S/RES/2423 (2018).

V Way Forward: Influence of Common Concern

We have earlier presented an outline as to how the doctrine of Common Concern may address some of the common reservations regarding unilateral interventions while ensuring the benefits therefrom. On that basis, it has been proposed that the opportunity to take trade countermeasures shall be strictly limited to matters that merit being termed as a Common Concern of Humankind. Diffusion of LCTs, especially to the developing countries, is one such issue. We propose that negligent failures of countries to cooperate in building the necessary rules and systems regarding facilitation of the trade-related aspects of LCT diffusion in the WTO be met with unilateral trade countermeasures as a response. Similarly, non-compliance with any future multilateral rules in that regard, e.g. neglecting homework responsibilities, shall also trigger similar responses. Beyond that, countermeasures should not be linked to situations that fall outside the domain of the trade regime, e.g. non-fulfilment of Paris pledges by a member. However, members remain free, as always, to pursue any such avenue in practice of their sovereign authority.

Therefore, any language that potentially opens up an opportunity to take countermeasures shall be made a part of any outcome from the cooperation agenda previously detailed.[1105] This way, it can be ensured that the scope of countermeasures remains limited to the issue of LCT diffusion and breaches of commitment arising therefrom. We also recall the earlier discussion on the necessary checks to be applied upon the exercise of unilateral sanctions. As a result, requirements of proportionality, due consideration of the situation of the developing countries, and consistency of practice must be made prerequisites to access the avenue of unilateral trade sanctions.

We recall that at present unilateral self-help measures for perceived breaches of the covered agreements is prohibited under the DSU. While the proposition above seeks to alter that situation, the importance of institutional check upon unilateral exercise of power, especially in an international political environment where mutual trust is waning, is undeniable. As a balance, we suggest that recourse to countermeasures be allowed to avoid a years-long dispute settlement process, but nevertheless be kept subject to the authorisation of the DSB. The following language can be considered as agreed outcome of any trade cooperation for low-carbon technology diffusion:

1105 See Chapter 3 III B above.

> Notwithstanding anything else contained elsewhere in the covered agreements, if there are reasonable grounds to believe that a Member's willful negligence in cooperation frustrates multilateral rulemaking efforts, or when an agreement is reached, lack of domestic implementation efforts by any Member frustrates the attainment of the goals set thereof, any other Member effectively engaged in cooperation and compliance shall be granted authorization from the DSB, upon application, to withdraw concessions in relation to the Member aforementioned. Article 22, and 24 of the Understanding on the Rules and Procedures Governing Settlement of Disputes shall, *mutatis mutandis,* apply to such request.

Another suggested role for the doctrine of Common Concern is to further structure the recourse to security exception clauses by a member seeking to be protected from climate-related risks. The focus is on paragraph b(iii) of the exception clauses, that being the likeliest avenue to legitimise climate motivated unilateral responses. Unlike the foregoing proposition, this one applies to all forms of unilateral measures that members take out of their independent and sovereign authority to enforce the Common Concern of climate change, including that of low-carbon technology diffusion. The purpose of further structuring recourse to the security exception clause is to refine the flexibly worded provision, which allows unrestrained power in the hands of the sanctioning member. It is submitted that as long as a countermeasure is deployed with a climate motivation, the requirements of consistency of behaviour, proportionality, and differentiated responsibility must not be dispensed with.

Hence it is proposed that climate change must be endorsed as an emergency in international relations. Such recognition shall remain in place until the aggregate global mitigation commitment rises up to bridge the existing emission gap. Within this context, countries that consistently discharge their relevant international and domestic obligations, and consider climate change as a threat to its essential security interests, shall have the opportunity to take punitive economic measures against negligent countries to correct the latter's course of action. In exercise of such power, the doctrine of Common Concern shall turn the attributes of consistency, proportionality, and equity into prerequisites. Like before, we suggest the following language to be made part of any forthcoming cooperation arrangement:

> The Members recognize that unmitigated climate change is an emergency in international relations, so long as the aggregate level of global emission remain on a pathway that is unsafe for the planet in the long-run. Any unilateral withdrawal of trade concessions undertaken by a Member

to protect its essential security interest in this context must be proportionate and considerate of the principle of common but differentiated responsibility. Moreover, all Members shall be consistent over time in their recourse to the unilateral modes of action.

VI Conclusion

In the realm of public international law, unilateralism is unavoidable, despite there being views for and against its existence. The idea and application of unilateral trade sanctions are not a novel phenomenon. What this chapter has shown is that, given the opportunity, the doctrine of Common Concern can structure the recourse to unilateral trade sanctions, as well as its application in a way that maximises its virtue while minimising the vice. However, it is impossible to overlook that this discussion is taking place during a period marked by the powerful states' increasing recourse to unilateral self-help for selfish ends, affecting the foundational values of mutual trust and global welfare. Conclusions arrived at in this chapter, therefore, remain subject to the dictates of prudence, and caution.

While this chapter finds that unilateral trade sanctions can be beneficial to address Common Concerns, including that of low-carbon technology diffusion, it limits any recourse to unilateralism to specific breaches of cooperation and homework obligation developed within the trade domain. Moreover, respect for the principles of CBDR, and proportionality is also suggested as paramount considerations to be undertaken when seeking to facilitate climate technology diffusion through trade countermeasures. These propositions indeed go beyond the current framework of public international law, as it enables states that are not injured in the customary sense of the term to take enforcement action in pursuance of the doctrine.

Within the domain of multilateral trade rules, it was highlighted that unilateral self-help measures regarding breaches of the covered agreement provisions are prohibited. Nevertheless, members remain free to adopt trade sanctions for violations of non-WTO commitments. However, the limitations regarding applicable law and subject-matter jurisdiction prevents a Panel from addressing the entirety of any dispute that involves such sanction. As a result, under the current rules, sanctions in response of non-trade issues, even if related to the Common Concern doctrine, has to find additional justification under the exception provisions. The security exceptions, especially the paragraph (b)(iii) is the most plausible defence, albeit providing for a degree of leeway that is more than necessary.

The doctrine of Common Concern of Humankind can influence the state of play regarding unilateralism and trade rules in two ways. To a limited and very specific extent, the doctrine can be used as a basis for creating a direct recourse to the withdrawal of concessions subject to the approval and supervision of the DSB. This path will be useful to engage stakeholders to create multilateral rules for low-carbon technology diffusion within the trade regime, as well as to ensure domestic implementation of the same without a lengthy recourse to the multilateral settlement of disputes. A second way is to further subject the use of security exception provision to the requirements of proportionality, differentiated responsibility, and consistency, when so done to enforce obligations arising out of the Common Concern doctrine. The chapter suggested possible languages to those effects.

Conclusion: Summary and Outlook

If, looking back, the 2010s appear as the era of multilateral disorder for trade and climate change, then looking forward, one must seek the foundational norms for a more sustainable and resilient rule-based international system. In the context of the failure of countries under the Paris Agreement to deliver sufficient pledges required to bridge the current emission gap, as well as the inability to create new market-based mechanisms for mitigation, the shortcoming of the climate regime is a present reality than a mere hypothesis.[1106] We are already witnessing that the progressive agenda of engaging trade policy to tackle climate change is shifting to unilateral gears,[1107] leaving many affected countries without a forum. As conflicts regarding climate-related economic policies continue to spill over to the WTO, the importance of effectively tackling trade and climate change issues is more than ever. If there were any time requiring unprecedented institution building efforts and out-of-the-box approaches, it is probably now.

In the backdrop of above, there can be no doubt that the diffusion of low-carbon technology is a Common Concern of Humankind. To address that Concern, the main goal of this book has been to portray trade law and policy means to bridge the gaps between the expectation and reality of clean technology diffusion. In parallel, it has also been an exercise in the application of the doctrine of Common Concern to resolve cooperation failures regarding transboundary public goods of critical importance. This conclusion will consolidate the principal findings of the research on both fronts. In addition, it would also briefly point out the potential avenues for further investigations.

1106 'On Thin Ice – COP25, the UN Climate Talks in Madrid, Ends in a Sad Splutter' (n 1021); 'COP25: Key Outcomes Agreed at the UN Climate Talks in Madrid' (*Carbon Brief*, 15 December 2019) <https://www.carbonbrief.org/cop25-key-outcomes-agreed-at-the-un-climate-talks-in-madrid> accessed 25 October 2020.

1107 At the forefront of the progressive push is the EU's Green Deal. See, European Commission, 'Communication from the Commission to the European Parliament, the European Council, the Council, the European Economic and Social Committee and the Committee of the Regions: The European Green Deal' (2019) COM(2019) 640 final; At the diametric opposit is the systematic, large-scale rollback of environmental commitments. See, Tyler Clevenger and Matt Herbert, '7 Ways the Trump Administration Is Harming the Climate' (*World Resources Institute*, 21 April 2020) <https://www.wri.org/blog/2020/04/7-ways-trump-administration-harming-climate> accessed 25 October 2020.

I International Trade, Clean Technologies, and Common Concern

In the context of distinct, yet related developments in the trade and climate change fields, technology development and transfer has found very different expressions. The extensive theoretical, factual, and legal stocktaking exercise in the first two chapters leads to a few key messages on the role of international trade rules and domestic trade policy measures for low-carbon technology diffusion. Those can be found below.

First of all, effective and timely mitigation of emission is impossible without the transfer of necessary technologies, especially to the developing countries. Second, although steady efforts are made within the climate regime to facilitate technology transfer, those fall short mainly due to the lack of financial resources available for the mechanisms to comprehensively address global technology need. Third, the key barriers to the diffusion of clean technologies, i.e. high price, lack of finance, and low incentives, are economic in nature, leading to market failures. Fourth, positive policy interventions are indispensable to drive the producers and consumers in the market towards adoption of clean technologies in all sectors. Fifth, low-carbon technology diffusion has an inseparable developmental aspect to it. Transfer of technology under private market terms is not a problem in developed countries. It is so in the developing nations where markets operate under different constraints. Lastly, unlike some widely known sectors like the pharmaceuticals, clean technology diffusion is not primarily or significantly prevented by the protection granted to intellectual property rights.

The doctrine of Common Concern of Humankind serves the important function of supplying a legal form to the claim of involving the trade regime to the steps and processes necessary for low-carbon technology diffusion. Although the doctrine's maturity is a part of an evolutionary process, its proposed normative aspects in the form of duties to cooperate, homework, and ensure compliance, are useful to chart a course of action within the trade rule system. Below are the key findings in that regard.

A *Trade Cooperation for Technology Diffusion*

Although trade policy measures can promote the diffusion of low-carbon technologies, neither the WTO is currently under any mandate, nor are the members thereof under any responsibility to devote themselves to such goals. It is the responsibility of cooperation arising out of the recognition of clean technology diffusion as a Common Concern that serves as the ground for such a new claim. However, for any new claim of cooperation to be accepted by all members, it must conquer the traditional conflicts of views between the developed and the developing countries regarding deployment of market-based policies for climate action. The key contribution of the third chapter of the book is to portray trade cooperation for low-carbon technology diffusion as mutually beneficial. To ensure inclusivity and sustainability, any effort made at the WTO must take into account different interest of the parties, as well as be particularly attendant to the needs of equity and differentiated responsibility. Upon a formally accepted understanding of low-carbon technology diffusion as a Common Concern within the WTO, complementary and interlocking trade policy measures can be designed to be reflecting the interests of different stakeholders. Key efforts would be required to relax market access across the board for the benefit of low-carbon technology goods and related services, also to improve domestic incentives that encourage such flows, and to adopt process and production measures (PPMs) that distinguish and establish preferences for lower embedded emission.

B *Role of Domestic Trade Policy Measures*

Domestic trade policy measures sit at the heart of the trade agenda for clean technology diffusion. Through market opening, as well as other restrictive and promoting policies, governments can trigger both the in and outflow of LCT. The book engaged in two in-depth studies of such 'homework' measures. These provide useful insights into potential strategies, benefits, and drawbacks, especially with regard to the measures' compliance with the WTO laws.

(i) Carbon Pricing

Putting an internationally agreed, in the absence thereof, a domestically determined minimum price on the emission footprint of a product can be one of the most significant homework measures for low-carbon technology diffusion, especially when it is coupled with schemes to utilise the import revenue for technology transfer supports to the developing countries affected by such pricing. Apart from highlighting a new revenue recycling aspect of carbon pricing, Chapter 4 also looks at tariffs, in addition to taxation, as a medium-term strategy to obtain similar results with possibly lesser costs. The revenue recycling is an indispensable part of any carbon pricing measure to take account of differentiated responsibilities, and counterclaims of protectionism. This will be best done through established financial mechanisms like the Green Climate Fund (GCF).

Carbon pricing falls under the general category of non-product related PPMs, which under the current WTO jurisprudence, would be considered as discriminatory. Products are subjected to varying fiscal burden due solely on account of their emission footprint is sure to violate the MFN rule, and may, in cases where comparable domestic production exists, contravene the national treatment (NT) rule as well. While there is ample policy room to justify a carbon pricing measure under the general exception provision, the revenue recycling part would play an essential role to ensure that the measure passes the final chapeau test. It is also found that the requirement of fairness under the chapeau is the only place where attention to differentiated responsibility is required to legitimise the pricing measure.

Alternatively, the Common Concern doctrine may assist in a reading of the non-discrimination obligation that favours the carbon pricing measures. It would mainly be possible if the legal analysis of discrimination is done taking into account the pre-existing distortion of competition in the market that necessitated the intervention in the first place. Under both the traditional and the proposed alternative approach, any carbon pricing measure found non-discriminatory before reaching the general exception provision must additionally be required to the principle of CBDR into account. It is only possible through giving effect to the Common Concern doctrine.

(ii) Export Credit Support

Financial constraint is a key barrier preventing low-carbon technology diffusion. Public financial supports like export credits, guarantees, and insurances can do a lot to reduce this barrier and bring to fruition export and investment transactions that would not otherwise happen. Export credits, especially its role in spreading clean technologies to capital scarce locations do not get much attention in trade law scholarship. It is proposed that the export credit agencies (ECAs) in the technology-rich geographies should extend such forms of support in better-than-market terms to facilitate transactions that benefit developing country firms.

Due to the legal linkages carried into the WTO subsidies agreement from the GATT era, some specific forms of export credits extended at fixed rates in compliance with the provisions of the OECD arrangement can escape the general prohibition on export subsidisation (the 'safe-haven'). While it may sound as good news to support clean technology outflows from the developed countries, in Chapter 5, it is found that the practical benefits are very little. The reasons are the limited scope of climate support projects in the arrangement; the out of date nature of the relationship between the SCM agreement and the OECD arrangement; also the non-democratic nature of the safe-haven clause itself. Apart from that, public financial supports to promote low-carbon technology exports in better than private market terms will be considered as a prohibited subsidy. Saving some of such measures can be possible by altering the OECD arrangement, (e.g. further relaxing the commercial interest rates for clean technology related transactions) and opening up more opportunities to support outflows of LCTs. Ideally, however, a new carve-out in the SCM agreement should be introduced to protect from challenge technology outflow incentives that are necessary, fair, and transparent.

C *Utility of Unilateral Trade Countermeasures*

As a last resort, the final aspect of the Common Concern doctrine, i.e. unilateral countermeasures can be a useful threat against willful non-compliance. But such steps can prove to be dangerous, also affecting long-term cooperation, when not designed carefully. In Chapter 6 it was argued that unilateral trade countermeasures, when prompted by the doctrine of Common Concern, must remain subject to the dictates of good faith, proportionality, and considerations of equity. Some of the aspects of the proposition advance beyond the customary state responsibility rules.

To the extent a Common Concern backed unilateral action is initiated by a member against another involving a purported breach of the WTO covered agreements, it falls under the category self-help measures forbidden by the DSU. As a remedy to this situation, modification of the DSU can be given a careful consideration, to the effect of creating direct recourse to the process of withdrawal of concessions under the DSB supervision. In any case, it would be prudent to avoid full-scale unilateralism – given the tumultuous turn of global affairs in recent times. A WTO member nevertheless retains a great degree of freedom to take trade sanctions against perceived security threats. While unbridled climate change can surely be considered as a threat, it is suggested that use of the security exceptions avenue to legitimise Common Concern inspired sanction must be further tempered by providing for all to abide by the principles of proportionality and differentiated responsibility.

II Lessons Learnt about the Doctrine

The proposed formulation of Common Concern of Humankind, as a legal doctrine, has guided the structure and analysis conducted in this book. As it was detailed in the outset, the role of the doctrine of Common Concern is to address, *ex ante,* the fragmentation between trade and the climate regime on the issue of low-carbon technology diffusion. As the substantive conclusions presented above would indicate, the doctrine can perform that task very well. The normative claims made by the doctrine are idealistic to a degree, but unapologetically so. It remains, as showcased throughout this wok, firmly rooted on the empirically demonstrated need to act regarding creation and maintenance of critically important transboundary public goods. To that effect, the doctrine indeed is representative of "a new and different realism".[1108]

Propelled by the proven urgency of climate response, the most important aspect of the proposed doctrine of Common Concern is the legal impetus it supplies to overcome the otherwise insurmountable barriers to cooperation. It triggers the proposed trade cooperation narrative, which then flows into the other aspects of homework and compliance. The notion of 'common concern' itself is capable of being well-outlined and circumscribed using evidence, thereby preventing any situation of unjustifiable incursion into the *status quo* of the multilateral trade rule system. Moreover, the doctrine is a highly useful tool for the framing of concerted efforts responding to shared concerns. The responsibility to cooperate and homework, backed up by the unilateral countermeasures is a robust structure that can ensure engagement and compliance by the stakeholders on issues of global importance. Within the trade regime, the utility of the doctrine goes beyond the discussed matter of the diffusion of LCTs. It can touch upon other areas of climate change (e.g. adaptation concerns), also issues of transboundary importance.

Although this research has unequivocally found the doctrine of Common Concern to be of important use in public international law in general and in international trade regulation in particular, it is admittedly still too early to pass judgments on its place among the different categories of international law sources. Development of a new norm is not a binary process of transposition from non-existence to being. It will grow in character and dimension over time, during which its content and purport will morph in accordance with the practice and usage. It will be no different in the forward journey of the doctrine of Common Concern. Nevertheless, this volume has treated the doctrine as an emerging principle of international law. The case-studies in particular have demonstrated the beneficial influence its normative content can exercise on the body of international trade regulation.

While conceptualising the doctrine in the structural form of a principle is useful, it will also pose certain drawbacks. A legal principle maintains generality and flexibility at the cost of a strict meaning. The more principled nature a notion takes in law, the more it becomes a guiding thought, finding expression only through the intermediation of an additional layer of precise legal instruments specific to a given discipline. In that sense, the doctrine itself cannot be seen as giving rise to rigid and identical obligations that apply everywhere. The positive aspect of this conclusion is that it makes the Common Concern

1108 Cottier, 'The Principle of Common Concern of Humankind' (n 7) s1.1.2.

doctrine relevant and applicable in a diverse array of subject-matters. In contrast, it also would mean that the legal stringency with which the more forward-looking components (e.g. unilateral trade sanctions) of the doctrine is put into application, would vary across different legal fields. This can put to question the original premise of the doctrine, as it sought, in part, to remedy the lack of options to enforce solutions to Common Concerns. Perhaps the balance would lie in the argument that while unilateral efforts are sought to enforce a concern, not all cases would deserve responses as stringent as a trade sanction. But that, as mentioned in the previous paragraph, remains to be congealed through practice and usage. The most useful conclusion, at the moment, is that the doctrine has a very useful core notion and a robust legal structure, which can be beneficially deployed to resolve collective action failures.

III Outlook

Looking forward, there are several avenues along which the line of research pursued here can be taken further. In this volume, the scope of the studies remained limited to the public international law of international trade and domestic trade policies. Although it was indicated that other areas of international economic law (IEL) can contribute to the overall enabling environment for low-carbon technology diffusion, their nature and extent remain to be explored. Of special importance is the role of international investment regulation, and domestic investment promotion measures upon diffusion of LCTs. Similarly, the commercial terms of the agreements under which the technologies change hand (e.g. technology license) also deserve closer study.

Within the examined area of study, there are more trade policy measures that can be looked into for their potentially facilitative role in spreading clean technologies. Among those, the role of services market access is least understood at present. Also, cooperation and assistance in adopting new green standards relating to products and processing deserve attention. Given that clean technology diffusion has a strong developmental aspect, diffusion of technical knowhows for changing the agricultural practices to reduce emission has special importance, given especially that it relates to the sustainable transformation of the developing countries' agricultural sectors and their food security in the long run. Last but not the least, further research can also be devoted to exploration of any possible obstacle posed by intellectual property protection of technologies beyond the energy sector.

Annex – Scope of Clean Technologies

The list below is generated from the UNEP DTU partnership database on Technology Needs Assessment (TNA). It shows technologies prioritised by 29 developing countries undergoing the tna process between 2011 and 2013.

Sector/ sub-sector	Technology class	Within class varieties
Solar energy	Solar power	Solar homes, PV systems, Lanterns, DC motors for grid connected PVs
	Solar heating/ drying	Solar dryers and water heaters
Wind energy	Wind power	Wind turbines, Standalone and grid-connected systems, On-shore plants, Systems for water/space heating
Hydro power	Hydro power	Micro, small, and large hydro power plants, Pumps to supply water to reservoirs
	Tidal power	
Biofuels	Biogas	Biogas for cooking, heating and electricity, Anaerobic digester, Manure digestion, Compact digester for urban households, System lagoons
	Biomass gasification	Biomass gasifier, Electricity and heat co-generation plants, Direct combustion technology for electricity generation, Co-firing of biomass with coal, Waste to energy
	Biodiesel	Internal combustion, Generating biodiesel from jatropha, soy bean and sunflower, Blending with fossil fuel, Fuel replacement (with conventional diesel)
	Second generation biofuels	Biofuel from sugarcane, Ethanol gel fuel and fuel-based lanterns, Bioethanol from maize, sugar and starch based crops, Ethanol production from agricultural residues

Sector/ sub-sector	Technology class	Within class varieties
Other energy sources	Nuclear	Low power nuclear CHP, Long-term large scale units, Nuclear units of small capacity
	Coal	High efficiency boilers, Pulverized coal combustion (single and double unit), Integrated coal gasification, Underground gasification, Co-firing with biomass, Integrated gasification combined cycle (IGCC) units, RDF production and pyrolysis from coal and syngas
	Natural gas	Natural gas combined cycle, Fuel switch to natural gas at existing plants, Micro and mini combined heat and power (CHP) plants
	Geothermal	Geothermal hot water, Geothermal power technology
Other energy technologies	Combined cycle (CC), and combined heat and power (CHP)	Peat based IGCC, Biogas based co-generation, Natural gas combined cycle, Co-generation by single combined cycle,
	Energy efficient transmission carbon capture and sequestration/ storage	Supply side transmission, Transmission lines upgrade, Smart grids
Forestry and Agriculture	Afforestration and reforestration	Afforestation using machines, scattered tree planting, improving roadside vegetation
	Agroforestry	Soil moisture retention, Mechanization of biomass production
	Crop management	Weed control, Change of crops, Intensive rice cultivation, Wet and dry irrigation
	Forest management	Optimal plantation, Community forest management, Mangrove restoration
	Fertilizer management	Conservation tillage, Controlled application of nitrogen fertilizer, Fixators of free nitrogen, Inhibitors of volatilitization of urea

Sector/ sub-sector	Technology class	Within class varieties
	Tillage management	Replacement of plow, Mini-till and no-till soil cultivation system
	Peat carbon management	Peat measurement, monitoring and remapping, Peat water management
	REDD	Reducing emissions from forest degradation
	Storage and handling	Different storage practices, Decanting, Filtration
	Organic farming	Mirco dose technique, Use of organic manure, Use of sludge from wastewater treatment plants
	Efficient charcoal production	Improved kilns
	Feeding practices	Controlled fodder supplements, Nutrition improvement through fodder processing, Growth hormones
	Others	Land management, Agronomy
Mining and Industry	End-use efficiency	Efficiency in cement industry, Using pozzolans
	Oven and furnace efficiency	Autogenerating crisol oven, Induction furnace, Autorecuperative burners, Forced air furnace
	Efficient brick kilns	Retort, Vertical shaft brick kilns
	Coal mine methane recovery	Enhanced peat / coal-bed methane recovery
Residential and Commercial	Efficient lighting	Compact fluorocent lamps, LED lights, High efficiency lighting systems
	Efficient stoves	Improved stoves (charcoal, firewood, and biomass) for cooking and heating, Mud stoves, Radiation stoves, Ethanol and LPG cook stoves
	Efficient heating	High and medium power heat pumps, Radiant panels, Hydrogen heating systems, Efficient heat, ventilation, and air-conditioning (HVAC) systems, Heat metering, Automatic temperature regulation

Sector/ sub-sector	Technology class	Within class varieties
	Insulation	Building thermal insulation, Wall insulation, Energy protective glasses and pellicles
	Less energy intensive products	Compressed stabilized earth blocks (CSEB), Efficient coolers, Improving battery/ capacitors' power factors, Efficient air-conditioning, Cans with paper bottoms
	Building efficiency	Energy management systems, Prefabricated houses
	Household end-use efficiency	Industrial and commercial end-use energy efficiency, Household end-use energy efficiency
	Carbon footprint of products	Calculating carbon footprints
Transport	Bus rapid transit system	Bus rapid transit (BRT), Transport management system
	Mass transport	Electrification of railway, Integrated public transport, Mass transport collectivization
	Efficient freight management	Repowering, Improved logistics for multimodal transport, Longer v. heavier trains
	Modal shift in freight transport	Railway cargo transport, Technologies to increase use of freight trains
	Electric vehicles	Hybrid elecrict vechicles, Battery powered vehicles
	Energy efficient motors	Energy efficient motors and engines
	Non-motorized transport	Bicycles, Cycle lanes
	Vehicle demand management	Carpool, Four days work and tele-work, Car sharing, Streamlining procedures
	Traffic management	Energy efficient infrastructures, Transport management systems, Speed control of motor drives, Improved traffic signal systems, Improved road infrastructure, Electronic road pricing

Sector/ sub-sector	Technology class	Within class varieties
	Vehicle and fuel technologies	Alternative fuels (hydrogen, fuel cells, blended fuels, CNG and LNG), Promoting import of fuel efficient vehicles, Vehicle emission standards, Sustainable private transport alternatives
Waste	Composting	Composting, Composting in vessel, Vermiculture, Mushroom cultivation
	Reuse and recycle	Recycling of paper and plastic solid waste, Waste reuse, Using organic waste for flour production, Heating technology for recyling tyres
	Waste incineration for energy production	Waste to energy, Co-generation from waste burning
	Landfill gas	Methane capture from landfill, Biomass landfill, Low solid anaerobic digestion
	Biological waste treatment	Mechanical-biological treatment (MBT)
	Wastewater treatment	Biomass wastewater, Biomethanation, Wastewater lagooning, Anaerobic digestion

Bibliography

Abdel-Latif A, 'Intellectual Property Rights and the Transfer of Climate Change Technologies: Issues, Challenges, and Way Forward' (2015) 15 Climate Policy 103.

Adger WN and others, 'Human Security' in Christopher B Field and others (eds), *Climate Change 2014: Impacts, Adaptation, and Vulnerability – Part A: Global and Sectoral Aspects. Contribution of Working Group II to the Fifth Assessment Report of the Intergovernmental Panel on Climate Change* (Cambridge University Press 2014).

Afanador A and others, *Status Report on Nationally Appropriate Mitigation Actions (NAMAs)* (Katja Eisbrenner, Noémie Klein and Xander van Tilburg eds, ECN, ECOFYS 2017).

Ahmad Z, 'State Responsibility Aspects of a Common Concern Based Approach to Collective Action' in Samantha Besson (ed), *International responsibility : essays in law, history and philosophy* (Schulthess, éditions romandes 2017).

Ahmad Z, 'Trade Related Measures to Spread Low-Carbon Technologies: A Common Concern Based Approach' in Thomas Cottier (ed), *The Prospects of Common Concern of Humankind in International law* (Cambridge University Press 2021).

Alexander K, *Economic Sanctions : Law and Public Policy* (Palgrave Macmillan 2009).

Atik J, 'Technology Transfer ' in Thomas Cottier and others (eds), *Elgar encyclopedia of international economic law* (Edward Elgar Publishing 2017) 606.

Auboin M, 'Improving the Availability of Trade Finance in Developing Countries: An Assessment of Remaining Gaps' (WTO 2015) Staff Working Paper ERSD-2015-06.

Bacchus J, 'Global Rules for Mutually Supportive and Reinforcing Trade and Climate Regimes' (International Centre for Trade and Sustainable Development (ICTSD), World Economic Forum (WEF) 2017).

Bacchus J, *The Willing World: Shaping and Sharing a Sustainable Global Prosperity* (Cambridge University Press 2018).

Bacchus J, 'What Is a Climate Response Measure? Breaking the Trade Taboo in Confronting Climate Change' (Centre for International Governance Innovation (CIGI) 2019) 220.

Barde J-P and Godard O, 'Economic Principles of Environmental Fiscal Reform' in Janet E Milne and Mikael Skou Andersen (eds), *Handbook of research on environmental taxation* (Edward Elgar 2012).

Barrett S, 'Climate Treaties and the Imperative of Enforcement' (2008) 24 Oxford Review of Economic Policy 239.

Barrett S, *Why Cooperate? : The Incentive to Supply Global Public Goods* (paperback ed, Oxford University Press 2010).

Barrett S, 'Climate Treaties and Approaching Catastrophes' (2013) 66 Journal of Environmental Economics and Management 235.

Barrett S and Stavins R, 'Increasing Participation and Compliance in International Climate Change Agreements' (2003) 3 International Environmental Agreements: Politics, Law and Economics 349.

Bartels L, 'The Chapeau of the General Exceptions in the WTO GATT and GATS Agreements: A Reconstruction' (2015) 109 American Journal of International Law 95.

Barton JH, *Intellectual Property and Access to Clean Energy Technologies in Developing Countries* (ICTSD 2007) <https://seors.unfccc.int/applications/seors/attachments/get_attachment?code=DM9V7CBIEL8AKG3C1YQLDMFTK64UOLUZ> accessed 28 October 2020.

Besson S, 'Sovereignty in Conflict' (2004) 8 European Integration Online Papers <https://papers.ssrn.com/abstract=594942> accessed 28 October 2020.

Beyleveld A, 'Exploring the Recognition of New Common Concerns of Humankind: The Example of the Distribution of Income and Wealth within States' in Thomas Cottier (ed), *The Prospects of Common Concern of Humankind in International law* (Cambridge University Press 2021).

Bhagwati JN, 'Reflections on Climate Change and Trade' [2008] Brookings Trade Forum 171.

Bianchi A and Gardoni L, 'Developing Countries, Countermeasures and WTO Law: Reinterpreting the DSU against the Background of International Law' (ICTSD 2008) Systemic Issue Paper Issue Paper No. 5.

Biermann F, '„Common Concern of Humankind": The Emergence of a New Concept of International Environmental Law' (1996) 34 Archiv des Völkerrechts 426.

Biermann F, 'The Rising Tide of Green Unilateralism in World Trade Law. Options for Reconciling the Emerging North–South Conflict' (2001) 35 Journal of World Trade 421.

Biermann F, 'The Fragmentation of Global Governance Architectures: A Framework for Analysis' (2009) 9 Global Environmental Politics 14.

Bigdeli SZ, 'Resurrecting the Dead-The Expired Non-Actionable Subsidies and the Lingering Question of Green Space' (2011) 8 Manchester J. Int'l Econ. L. 2.

Birnie PW, Boyle AE and Redgwell C, *International Law and the Environment* (3rd ed, Oxford University Press 2009).

Bodansky D, 'What's so Bad about Unilateral Action to Protect the Environment?' (2000) 11 European Journal of International Law 339.

Bodansky D, *The Art and Craft of International Environmental Law* (Harvard University Press 2010).

Bodansky D, 'The Legal Character of the Paris Agreement' (2016) 25 Review of European, Comparative & International Environmental Law 142.

Bodansky D, Brunnée J and Rajamani L, *International Climate Change Law* (First Edition, Oxford University Press 2017).

Bogdanova I, 'Reshaping the Law of Sanctions for Human Rights Violations: The Potential of Common Concern of Humankind' in Thomas Cottier (ed), *The Prospects of Common Concern of Humankind in International law* (Cambridge University Press 2021).

Boldt J and others, *Overcoming Barriers to the Transfer and Diffusion of Climate Technologies* (Second Edition, UNEP Risø Centre 2012).

Bowman M, 'Environmental Protection and the Concept of Common Concern of Mankind', *Research Handbook on International Environmental Law* (Edward Elgar Publishing 2010).

Brandi C, *Trade Elements in Countries' Climate Contributions under the Paris Agreement* (International Centre for Trade and Sustainable Development (ICTSD) 2017) <https://ictsd.iisd.org/sites/default/files/research/trade_elements_in_countries_climate_contributions.pdf> accessed 28 October 2020.

Brauch MD and Cosbey A, *Vehicles, Availability, and Governance of International Public Finance for Climate-Friendly Investment* (International Institute for Sustainable Development 2012).

Brewer TL, 'International Technology Diffusion in a Sustainable Energy Trade Agreement: September 2012' in Gary C Hufbauer, Ricardo Melendez-Ortiz and Richard Samans (eds), *The Law and Economics of a Sustainable Energy Trade Agreement* (Cambridge University Press 2016) <https://www.cambridge.org/core/product/identifier/9781316137048%23AT-app-7/type/book_part> accessed 28 October 2020.

Brewer TL and Falke A, 'International Transfers of Climate-Friendly Technologies: How the World Trade System Matters' in David Ockwell and Alexandra Mallett (eds), *Low-carbon technology transfer : from rhetoric to reality* (Routledge 2012).

Brunnée J, 'Enforcement Mechanisms in International Law and International Environmental Law' in Ulrich Beyerlin, Peter-Tobias Stoll and Rudiger Wolfrum (eds), *Ensuring compliance with multilateral environmental agreements : a dialogue betweeen practitioners and Academia* (Martinus Nijhoff Publishers 2006).

Brunnée J, 'Common Areas, Common Heritage, and Common Concern' in Daniel Bodansky, Jutta Brunnée and Ellen Hey (eds), *The Oxford Handbook of International Environmental Law* (First Edition, Oxford University Press 2007).

Brunnée J, 'The Global Climate Regime: Whither Common Concern?' [2012] Coexistence, Cooperation and Solidarity (2 vols.) 721.

Brunnée J, 'The Rule of International (Environmental) Law and Complex Problems' in Heike Krieger, Georg Nolte and Andreas Zimmermann (eds), *The International Rule of Law: Rise or Decline?* (Oxford University Press 2019).

Buchner BK and others, 'Global Landscape of Climate Finance 2017' (Climate Policy Initiative 2017).

Bürgi Bonanomi E, *Sustainable Development in International Law Making and Trade : International Food Governance and Trade in Agriculture* (Edward Elgar 2015).

Caney S, 'Cosmopolitan Justice, Responsibility, and Global Climate Change' in Stephen Mark Gardiner and others (eds), *Climate ethics : essential readings* (Oxford University Press 2010).

Castillo-Winckels NS, 'Why Common Concern of Humankind Should Return to the Work of the International Law Commission on the Atmosphere' (2016) 29 Geo. Int'l Envtl. L. Rev. 131.

Charnovitz S, 'The Moral Exception in Trade Policy' [1997] Virginia Journal of International Law 689.

Charnovitz S, 'The Law of Environmental PPMs in the WTO: Debunking the Myth of Illegality' (2002) 27 Yale Journal of International Law 59.

Charnovitz S, 'Green Subsidies and the WTO' [2014] World Bank Policy Research Working Paper <http://documents.worldbank.org/curated/en/2014/10/20290817/green-subsidies-wto> accessed 28 October 2020.

Charnovitz S, 'Border Tax Equalization' in Jagdish N Bhagwati, Pravin Krishna and Arvind Panagariya (eds), *The world trade system : trends and challenges* (The MIT Press 2016).

Cirone AE and Urpelainen J, 'Trade Sanctions in International Environmental Policy: Deterring or Encouraging Free Riding?' (2013) 30 Conflict Management and Peace Science 309.

Clarke LE and others, 'Assessing Transformation Pathways' in Ottmar Edenhofer and others (eds), *Climate Change 2014: Mitigation of Climate Change. Working Group III Contribution to the Fifth Assessment Report of the Intergovernmental Panel on Climate Change* (Cambridge University Press 2014).

Cleveland SH, 'Human Rights Sanctions and International Trade: A Theory of Compatibility' (2002) 5 Journal of International Economic Law 133.

Cole D, 'Climate Change and Collective Action' (2008) 61 Current Legal Problems.

Condon BJ, 'Climate Change and Unresolved Issues in WTO Law' (2009) 12 Journal of International Economic Law 895.

Condon BJ, 'Climate Change and Intellectual Property Rights for New Plant Varieties' (2013) 47 Journal of World Trade 897.

Condon BJ, 'Disciplining Clean Energy Subsidies to Speed the Transition to a Low-Carbon World' (2017) 51 Journal of World Trade 675.

Conrad CR, *Processes and Production Methods (PPMs) in WTO Law : Interfacing Trade and Social Goals* (1st publ., Cambridge University Press 2011).

Contreras JL, 'Standards and Related Intellectual Property Issues for Climate Change Technology' (Social Science Research Network 2012) SSRN Scholarly Paper ID 1756283 <https://papers.ssrn.com/abstract=1756283> accessed 28 October 2020.

Cook G, *A Digest of WTO Jurisprudence on Public International Law Concepts and Principles* (Cambridge University Press 2015).

Cramton PC, MacKay DJC, and Ockenfels A (eds), *Global carbon pricing: the path to climate cooperation* (MIT Press 2017).

Cooreman B, 'Addressing Environmental Concerns through Trade: A Case for Extraterritoriality Shorter Articles and Notes' [2016] International and Comparative Law Quarterly 229.

Cooreman B, 'The (Extra)Territorial Reach of National Measures under WTO Law', *Global Environmental Protection through Trade: A Systematic Approach to Extraterritoriality* (Edward Elgar Publishing 2017) <https://www.elgaronline.com/view/9781786434388/chapter03.xhtml> accessed 28 October 2020.

Copenhagen Economics and The IPR Company, 'Are IPR a Barrier to the Transfer of Climate Change Technology?' (2009) <https://www.copenhageneconomics.com/dyn/resources/Publication/publicationPDF/7/27/0/Are_IPR_a_barrier_to_the_transfer_of_climate_change_technology.pdf> accessed 28 October 2020.

Coppens D, *WTO Disciplines on Subsidies and Countervailing Measures : Balancing Policy Space and Legal Constraints* (Cambridge University Press 2014).

Cosbey A and others, 'A Guide for the Concerned: Guidance on the Elaboration and Implementation of Border Carbon Adjustment' (Entwined 2012) Policy report <http://www.ssrn.com/abstract=2178312> accessed 28 October 2020.

Cossy M and Marceau G, 'Institutional Challenges to Enhance Policy Co-Ordination – How WTO Rules Could Be Utilised to Meet Climate Objective?' in Thomas Cottier, Olga Nartova and Sadeq Z Bigdeli (eds), *International trade regulation and the mitigation of climate change: World Trade Forum* (Cambridge University Press 2009).

Cottier T, 'Renewable Energy and Process and Production Methods' (International Centre for Trade and Sustainable Development (ICTSD), World Economic Forum (WEF) 2015).

Cottier T, 'Improving Compliance: Jus Cogens and International Economic Law' in den Maarten Heijer and Harmen van der Wilt (eds), *Netherlands Yearbook of International Law 2015: Jus Cogens: Quo Vadis?* (TMC Asser Press 2016).

Cottier T, 'The Principle of Common Concern of Humankind' in Thomas Cottier (ed), *The Prospects of Common Concern of Humankind in International law* (Cambridge University Press 2021).

Cottier T, 'Energy in WTO Law and Policy' in Thomas Cottier and Panagiotis Delimatsis (eds), *The prospects of international trade regulation : from fragmentation to coherence* (Cambridge University Press 2011).

Cottier T, 'Introduction: Fragmentation and Coherence in International Trade Regulation: Analysis and Conceptual Foundations' in Thomas Cottier and Panagiotis

Delimatsis (eds), *The prospects of international trade regulation : from fragmentation to coherence* (Cambridge University Press 2011).

Cottier T, 'The Principle of Common Concern and Climate Change' (2014) 52 Archiv des Völkerrechts 293.

Cottier T, 'The Principle of Proportionality in International Law: Foundations and Variations' (2017) 18 The Journal of World Investment & Trade 628.

Cottier T (ed), *The Prospects of Common Concern of Humankind in International Law* (Cambridge University Press 2021).

Cottier T and Baracol-Pinhão D, 'Environmental Goods and Services: The Environmental Area Initiative Approach and Climate Change' in Thomas Cottier, Olga Nartova and Sadeq Z Bigdeli (eds), *International trade regulation and the mitigation of climate change: World Trade Forum* (Cambridge University Press 2009).

Cottier T and Delimatsis P (eds), *The Prospects of International Trade Regulation : From Fragmentation to Coherence* (Cambridge University Press 2011).

Cottier T and Hertig M, 'The Prospects of 21st Century Constitutionalism' in Armin von Bogdandy and Rudiger Wolfrum (eds), *Max Planck Yearbook of United Nations Law* (Koninklijke Brill NV 2003) 261.

Cottier T, Nartova O and Bigdeli SZ (eds), *International Trade Regulation and the Mitigation of Climate Change: World Trade Forum* (Cambridge University Press 2009).

Cottier T, Nartova O and Shingal A, 'The Potential of Tariff Policy for Climate Change Mitigation: Legal and Economic Analysis' (2014) 48 Journal of World Trade 1007.

Cottier T and Payosova T, 'Common Concern and the Legitimacy of the WTO in Dealing with Climate Change' in Panagiotis Delimatsis (ed), *Research handbook on climate change and trade law* (Edward Elgar 2016).

Cottier T and Schefer KN, 'Responsibility to Protect (R2P) and the Emerging Principle of Common Concern' in Peter Hilpold (ed), *The Responsibility to Protect (R2P): A new Paradigm of International Law?* (Martinus Nijhoff Publishers 2014).

Dawidowicz M, *Third-Party Countermeasures in International Law* (Cambridge University Press 2017).

de Chazournes LB, 'Technical and Financial Assistance' in Daniel Bodansky, Jutta Brunnée and Ellen Hey (eds), *The Oxford Handbook of International Environmental Law* (First, Oxford University Press 2007).

de Coninck H and others, 'Strengthening and Implementing the Global Response' in Valerie Masson-Delmotte and others (eds), *Special Report: Global Warming of 1.5°C* (World Meteorological Organization (WMO) 2018) <http://www.ipcc.ch/report/sr15/> accessed 28 October 2020.

de Coninck H and Sagar A, 'Technology Development and Transfer (Article 10)' in Daniel Klein and others (eds), *The Paris Agreement on Climate Change: Analysis and Commentary* (Oxford University Press 2017).

de Sépibus J, 'Reforming the Clean Development Mechanism to Accelerate Technology Transfer' (2009) NCCR Trade Working Paper 2009/42 < https://www.wti.org/research/publications/7/reforming-the-clean-development-mechanism-to-accelerate-technology-transfer/> accessed 28 October 2020.

Dechezleprêtre A and others, 'Invention and Transfer of Climate Change–Mitigation Technologies: A Global Analysis' (2011) 5 Review of Environmental Economics and Policy 109.

Delimatsis P, 'Sustainable Standard-Setting, Climate Change and the TBT Agreement' in Panagiotis Delimatsis (ed), *Research handbook on climate change and trade law* (Edward Elgar 2016).

Dobson NL, 'The EU's Conditioning of the "Extraterritorial" Carbon Footprint: A Call for an Integrated Approach in Trade Law Discourse' (2018) 27 Review of European, Comparative & International Environmental Law 75.

Dobson NL and Ryngaert C, 'Provocative Climate Protection: EU "Extraterritorial" Regulation of Maritime Emissions' (2017) 66 International & Comparative Law Quarterly 295.

Dworkin R, 'The Model of Rules' (1967) 35 University of Chicago Law Review 14.

Ehring L, '*De facto* Discrimination in World Trade Law' (2002) 36 Journal of World Trade 921.

Epps T and Green A, *Reconciling Trade and Climate: How the WTO Can Help Address Climate Change* (Edward Elgar 2010).

Espa I and Marín Durán G, 'Renewable Energy Subsidies and WTO Law: Time to Rethink the Case for Reform Beyond Canada – Renewable Energy/Fit Program' [2018] Journal of International Economic Law.

Fernández-Amador O and others, 'Carbon Dioxide Emissions and Economic Growth: An Assessment Based on Production and Consumption Emission Inventories' (2017) 135 Ecological Economics 269.

Fernández-Amador O, Francois JF and Tomberger P, 'Carbon Dioxide Emissions and International Trade at the Turn of the Millennium' (2016) 125 Ecological Economics 14.

Finnemore M and Sikkink K, 'International Norm Dynamics and Political Change' (1998) 52 International Organization 887.

Finus M and others, 'International Cooperation: Agreements and Instruments', *Climate change 2014: mitigation of climate change: Working Group III contribution to the Fifth Assessment Report of the Intergovernmental Panel on Climate Change* (Cambridge University Press 2014).

Fischer-Lescano A and Teubner G, 'Regime-Collisions: The Vain Search for Legal Unity in the Fragmentation of Global Law Diversity or Cacophony: New Sources of Norms in International Law Symposium' (2003) 25 Michigan Journal of International Law 999.

French D, 'Common Concern, Common Heritage and Other Global(-Ising) Concepts: Rhetorical Devices, Legal Principles or a Fundamental Challenge?' in Michael Bowman, Peter Davies and Edward Goodwin (eds), *Research Handbook on Biodiversity and Law* (Edward Elgar 2016).

Friedmann W, *The Changing Structure of International Law* (Stevens & Sons 1964).

Gallagher KS, *The Globalization of Clean Energy Technology: Lessons From China* (MIT Press 2014).

Gerasimchuk I and others, 'Stories from G20 Countries: Shifting Public Money out of Fossil Fuels' (International Institute for Sustanianable Development 2018) <https://www.iisd.org/sites/default/files/publications/stories-g20-shifting-public-money-out-fossil-fuels-en.pdf> accessed 28 October 2020.

Gillingham K and Sweeney J, 'Barriers to Implementing Low-Carbon Technologies' (2012) 03 Climate Change Economics 1250019.

Global Commission on the economy and climate, *Better Growth, Better Climate: The New Climate Economy Report : The Global Report* (2014).

Green A and Epps T, 'Is There a Role for Trade Measures in Addressing Climate Change?' (2008) 15 31.

Gupta S and others, 'Cross-Cutting Investment and Finance Issues', *Climate change 2014: mitigation of climate change: Working Group III contribution to the Fifth Assessment Report of the Intergovernmental Panel on Climate Change* (Cambridge University Press 2014).

Haites E and others, 'Technology Transfer and the Clean Development Mechanism (CDM)' in David Ockwell and Alexandra Mallett (eds), *Low-carbon technology transfer : from rhetoric to reality* (Routledge 2012).

Hamilton P, 'Counter(Measur)Ing Climate Change: The ILCt, Third State Countermeasures and Climate Change' (2008) 4 McGill International Journal of Sustainable Development Law and Policy 83.

Helm S, Tannock Q and Iliev I, 'Renewable Energy Technology: Evolution and Policy Implications – Evidence from Patent Literature' (WIPO 2014) Global Challenges Report.

Hoekman B, Maskus KE and Saggi K, 'Transfer of Technology to Developing Countries: Unilateral and Multilateral Policy Options' [2004] World Bank Policy Research Working Paper.

Hoekman BM, Maskus KE and Saggi K, 'Transfer of Technology to Developing Countries: Unilateral and Multilateral Policy Options' (2005) 33 World Development 1587.

Holzer K, *Carbon-Related Border Adjustment and WTO Law* (Edward Elgar 2014).

Horlick G and Clarke PA, 'Rethinking Subsidy Disciplines for the Future: Policy Options for Reform' (2017) 20 Journal of International Economic Law 673.

Horn H and Mavroidis PC, 'Climate Change and the WTO: Legal Issues Concerning Border Tax Adjustments' (2010) 53 Japanese YB Int'l L. 19.

Horn H and Mavroidis PC, 'Multilateral Environmental Agreements in the WTO: Silence Speaks Volumes: MEAs in the WTO' (2014) 10 International Journal of Economic Theory 147.

Horn L, 'Climate Change and the Future Role of the Concept of the Common Concern of Humankind' (2015) 11 Australian Journal of Environmental Law 33.

Horn LS, 'Common Concern of Humankind and Legal Protection of the Global Environment' (PhD Monograph, The University of Sydney 2000).

Howard A, 'Voluntary Cooperation (Article 6)' in Daniel Klein and others (eds), *The Paris Agreement on Climate Change: Analysis and Commentary* (Oxford University Press 2017).

Howse R and Eliason A, 'Domestic and International Strategies to Address Climate Change: An Overview of the WTO Legal Issues' in Thomas Cottier, Olga Nartova and Sadeq Z Bigdeli (eds), *International trade regulation and the mitigation of climate change: World Trade Forum* (Cambridge University Press 2009).

Howse R and Nicolaidis K, 'Enhancing WTO Legitimacy: Constitutionalization or Global Subsidiarity?' (2003) 16 Governance 73.

Howse R and Regan D, 'The Product/Process Dinstinction – An Illusory Basis for Disciplining "Unilateralism" in Trade Policy' (2000) 11 European Journal of International Law 249.

Howse R and van Bork PB, 'Options for Liberalising Trade in Environmental Goods in the Doha Round' (International Centre for Trade and Sustainable Development 2006) <https://www.files.ethz.ch/isn/92782/2006_07_Options_for_Liberalising_Trade_.pdf> accessed 28 October 2020.

Hufbauer GC, Charnovitz S and Kim J, *Global Warming and the World Trading System* (Peterson Institute for International Economics 2009).

Humphreys S, 'Structural Ambiguity: Technology Transfer in Three Regimes' in Margaret A Young (ed), *Regime Interaction in International Law* (Cambridge University Press 2012).

IPCC, *Methodological and Technological Issues in Technology Transfer* (Bert Metz and others eds, Intergovernmental Panel on Climate Change 2000).

IPCC, *Climate Change 2014: Synthesis Report. Contribution of Working Groups I, II and III to the Fifth Assessment Report of the Intergovernmental Panel on Climate Change* (RK Pachauri, Leo Mayer and Core Writing Team eds, IPCC 2015).

IUCN, *Draft International Covenant on Environment and Development* (Fourth Edition, 2010).

Jachnik R and others, 'Tracking Climate-Related Export Credits: Existing Official Reporting Practices, Illustration of Methodological Options and Implications through Project Examples' [2017] Working document prepared for the Research Collaborative on Tracking Private Climate Finance.

Jackson J, 'International Economic Law: Reflections on the "Boilerroom" of International Relations' (1995) 10 American University International Law Review.

Jackson JH, 'Sovereignty-Modern: A New Approach to an Outdated Concept', *Sovereignty, the WTO and changing fundamentals of international law* (Cambridge University Press 2006).

Jaffe AB, Newell RG and Stavins RN, 'Technological Change and the Environment' in KG Mäler and JR Vincent (eds), *Handbook of Environmental Economics*, vol 1 (Elsevier Science 2003).

Jaffe AB, Newell RG and Stavins RN, 'A Tale of Two Market Failures: Technology and Environmental Policy' (2005) 54 Ecological Economics 164.

Kasteng J, 'Trade Remedies on Clean Energy: A New Trend in Need of Multilateral Initiatives' (International Centre for Trade and Sustainable Development (ICTSD), World Economic Forum (WEF) 2013).

Katselli E, *The Problem of Enforcement in International Law : Countermeasures, the Non-Injured State and the Idea of International Community* (Routledge 2010).

Keohane RO and Victor DG, 'The Regime Complex for Climate Change' (2011) 9 Perspectives on Politics 7.

Khatun F, 'Trade in Environmental Goods by Least Developed Countries: Issues for Negotiations' (2012) 13 South Asia Economic Journal 157.

Kiss A, 'The Common Concern of Mankind' (1997) 27 Environmental Policy and Law 244.

Klenert D and others, 'Making Carbon Pricing Work for Citizens' (2018) 8 Nature Climate Change 669.

Knoerich J, 'How Does Outward Foreign Direct Investment Contribute to Economic Development in Less Advanced Home Countries?' (2017) 45 Oxford Development Studies 443.

Koskenniemi M, 'Solidarity Measures: State Responsibility as a New International Order?' (2002) 72 British Yearbook of International Law 337.

Koskenniemi M, 'Hegemonic Regimes' in Margaret A Young (ed), *Regime Interaction in International Law* (Cambridge University Press 2012).

Koskenniemi M and Leino P, 'Fragmentation of International Law? Postmodern Anxieties' (2002) 15 Leiden Journal of International Law 553.

Kowalski P, Rabaioli D and Vallejo S, 'International Technology Transfer Measures in an Interconnected World' <https://www.oecd-ilibrary.org/trade/international-technology-transfer-measures-in-an-interconnected-world_ada51ec0-en> accessed 28 October 2020.

Kulovesi K, 'Real or Imagined Controversies-a Climate Law Perspective on the Growing Links between the International Trade and Climate Change Regimes' (2014) 6 Trade L. & Dev. 55.

Lee B, Iliev I and Preston F, *Who Owns Our Low Carbon Future?: Intellectual Property and Energy Technologies* (Chatham House 2009).

Less CT and McMillan S, 'Achieving the Successful Transfer of Environmentally Sound Technologies: Trade-Related Aspects' (2005) Working Paper 2005–2 < https://www.oecd.org/environment/envtrade/35837552.pdf > accessed 28 October 2020.

Lewis JI, 'Technology Acquisition and Innovation in the Developing World: Wind Turbine Development in China and India' (2007) 42 Studies in Comparative International Development 208.

Lybecker KM and Lohse S, 'Innovation and Diffusion of Green Technologies' (WIPO 2015) Global Challenges Report <http://www.wipo.int/edocs/pubdocs/en/wipo_rep_gc_2015_1.pdf> accessed 28 October 2020.

Maljean-Dubois S, Spencer T and Wemaere M, 'The Legal Form of the Paris Climate Agreement: A Comprehensive Assessment of Options' (2015) 9 Carbon & Climate Law Review 68.

Marceau G, 'WTO Dispute Settlement and Human Rights' (2002) 13 European Journal of International Law 62.

Marceau G, 'The Interface between the Trade Rules and Climate Change Actions' in Deok-Young Park (ed), *Legal Issues on Climate Change and International Trade Law* (Springer 2016).

Marceau G, 'Evolutive Interpretation by the WTO Adjudicator' (2018) 21 Journal of International Economic Law 791.

Marceau G, 'Do PPM Concerns Have a Future' in Denise Prévost, Iveta Alexovičová and Jens Hillebrand Pohl (eds), *Restoring trust in trade : liber amicorum in honour of Peter van den Bossche* (Hart 2019).

Marcu A, *Carbon Market Provisions in the Paris Agreement (Article 6)* (Centre for European Policy Studies (CEPS) 2016).

Masson-Delmotte V, and others (eds), *Special Report: Global Warming of 1.5°C* (World Meteorological Organization (WMO) 2018) <http://www.ipcc.ch/report/sr15/> accessed 28 October 2020.

Mattoo A and Subramanian A, *A 'Greenprint' for International Cooperation on Climate Change* (The World Bank 2013) <http://elibrary.worldbank.org/doi/book/10.1596/1813-9450-6440> accessed 28 October 2020.

Maurer C and Bhandari R, 'Climate Notes: The Climate of Export Credit Agencies' (World Resources Institute 2000).

McRae D, *The Contribution of International Trade Law to the Development of International Law*, vol 260 (The Hague Academy of International Law 1994).

Melendez-Ortiz R and Sugathan M, 'Enabling the Energy Transition and Scale-Up of Clean Energy Technologies: Options for the Global Trade System – Synthesis of the Policy Options' (2017) 51 933.

Milne JE and Andersen MS, 'Introduction to Environmental Taxation Concepts and Research' in Janet E Milne and Mikael Skou Andersen (eds), *Handbook of research on environmental taxation* (Edward Elgar 2012).

Monkelbaan J, 'Trade in Sustainable Energy Services: October 2013' in Gary C Hufbauer, Ricardo Melendez-Ortiz and Richard Samans (eds), *The Law and Economics of a Sustainable Energy Trade Agreement* (Cambridge University Press 2016) <https://www.cambridge.org/core/product/identifier/9781316137048%23CN-bp-3/type/book_part> accessed 28 October 2020.

Monteiro J-A, 'Typology of Environment-Related Provisions in Regional Trade Agreements' (World Trade Organization 2016) WTO Staff Working Paper ERSD-2016-13.

Moon S, *Meaningful Technology Transfer to the LDCs: A Proposal for a Monitoring Mechanism for TRIPS Article 66.2* (International Centre for Trade and Sustainable Development (ICTSD) 2011).

Moravcsik AM, 'Disciplining Trade Finance: The OECD Export Credit arrangement' (1989) 43 International Organization 173.

Morin J-F and Jinnah S, 'The Untapped Potential of Preferential Trade Agreements for Climate Governance' (2018) 27 Environmental Politics 541.

Murase S, 'Second Report on the Protection of Atmosphere – 67th Session of the International Law Commission' (2015) A/CN.4/681.

Murase S, 'Washington Conference: Legal Principles Relating to Climate Change' (International Law Association 2014).

Nartova O, 'Assessment of GATS' Impact on Climate Change Mitigation' in Thomas Cottier, Olga Nartova and Sadeq Z Bigdeli (eds), *International trade regulation and the mitigation of climate change: World Trade Forum* (Cambridge University Press 2009).

Neuhoff K, 'International Support for Low-Carbon Growth in Developing Countries', *Climate policy after Copenhagen : the role of carbon pricing* (Cambridge University Press 2011).

Nieto J, Carpintero Ó and Miguel LJ, 'Less than 2°C? An Economic-Environmental Evaluation of the Paris Agreement' (2018) 146 Ecological Economics 69.

Nolte G, 'The International Law Commission and Community Interests' in Eyal Benvenisti and Georg Nolte (eds), *Community Interests Across International Law* (Oxford University Press 2018).

Nordhaus W, 'Climate Clubs: Overcoming Free-Riding in International Climate Policy' (2015) 105 American Economic Review 1339.

Nordhaus W, 'Climate Clubs and Carbon Pricing' in Peter C Cramton, David JC MacKay and Axel Ockenfels (eds), *Global carbon pricing: the path to climate cooperation* (MIT Press 2017).

Nygaard I and Hansen UE, 'The Conceptual and Practical Challenges to Technology Categorisation in the Preparation of Technology Needs Assessments' (2015) 131 Climatic Change 371.

Ockwell D and Mallett A (eds), *Low-Carbon Technology Transfer: From Rhetoric to Reality* (Routledge 2012).

Ockwell DG and others, 'Intellectual Property Rights and Low Carbon Technology Transfer: Conflicting Discourses of Diffusion and Development' (2010) 20 Global Environmental Change 729.

Odell JS, 'Our Alarming Climate Crisis Demands Border Adjustments Now' (ICTSD 2018) Think Piece.

OECD, *Environmentally Related Taxes in OECD Countries: Issues and Strategies* (OECD Publishing 2001).

OECD, *Effective Carbon Rates* (OECD Publishing 2016) <http://www.oecd-ilibrary.org/taxation/effective-carbon-rates_9789264260115-en> accessed 28 October 2020.

OECD and Climate Policy Initiative, 'Climate Finance in 2013–14 and the USD 100 Billion Goal' (Organization for Economic Cooperation and Development (OECD) 2015) <https://www.oecd.org/environment/cc/OECD-CPI-Climate-Finance-Report.pdf> accessed 28 October 2020.

Oppenheimer M and others, 'Emergent Risks and Key Vulnerabilities' in Christopher B Field and others (eds), *Climate Change 2014: Impacts, Adaptation, and Vulnerability – Part A: Global and Sectoral Aspects. Contribution of Working Group II to the Fifth Assessment Report of the Intergovernmental Panel on Climate Change* (Cambridge University Press 2014).

Ostrom E, *A Polycentric Approach for Coping with Climate Change* (The World Bank 2009).

P. Jeffries C, 'A Preliminary Evaluation of the Proposed Text' in Surendra J Patel, Pedro Roffe and Abdulqawi Yusuf (eds), *International Technology Transfer: The Origins and Aftermath of the United Nations Negotiations on a Draft Code of Conduct* (Kluwer Law International 2001).

Pal P and Sethi G, 'Case Study: Technology Transfer of Energy-Efficient Technologies among Small and Medium Sized Enterprises in India' in David Ockwell and Alexandra Mallett (eds), *Low-carbon technology transfer: from rhetoric to reality* (Routledge 2012).

Papaux A and Wyler E, 'Legal Theory as a Source of International Law: Doctrine as Constitutive of International Law' in Samantha Besson and Jean d'Aspremont (eds), *The Oxford Handbook of the Sources of International Law*, vol 1 (Oxford University Press 2018) <http://oxfordhandbooks.com/view/10.1093/law/9780198745365.001.0001/law-9780198745365-chapter-25> accessed 28 October 2020.

Parry IWH, de Mooij RA, and Keen M (eds), *Fiscal policy to mitigate climate change: a guide to policymakers* (International Monetary Fund 2012).

Parry IW, Veung C and Heine D, *How Much Carbon Pricing Is in Countries' Own Interests? The Critical Role of Co-Benefits* (International Monetary Fund 2014).

Parry IWH, 'Reflections on the International Coordination of Carbon Pricing' in Peter C Cramton, David JC MacKay and Axel Ockenfels (eds), *Global carbon pricing: the path to climate cooperation* (MIT Press 2017).

Parry IWH (eds), *Fiscal Policy to Mitigate Climate Change: A Guide to Policymakers* (International Monetary Fund 2012).

Partnership for Market Readiness (PMR), *Carbon Tax Guide: A Handbook for Policy Makers* (World Bank 2017).

Pauwelyn J, 'A Typology of Multilateral Treaty Obligations: Are WTO Obligations Bilateral or Collective in Nature?' (2003) 14 European Journal of International Law 907.

Pauwelyn J, *Conflict of Norms in Public International Law: How WTO Law Relates to Other Rules of International Law* (Cambridge University Press 2003).

Pauwelyn J, 'Carbon Leakage Measures and Border Tax Adjustments under WTO Law' in Geert Van Calster and Denise Prevost (eds), *Research handbook on environment, health and the WTO* (Edward Elgar 2013).

Pauwelyn J, Trachtman JP and Steger DP, 'The Jurisdiction of the WTO Is Limited to Trade' (2004) 98 Proceedings of the Annual Meeting (American Society of International Law) 135.

Perrez FX, 'Efficiency of Cooperation: A Functional Analysis of Sovereignty' (1998) 15 Arizona Journal of International and Comparative Law 515.

Peters A, 'Compensatory Constitutionalism: The Function and Potential of Fundamental International Norms and Structures' (2006) 19 Leiden Journal of International Law 579.

Petersmann E U, 'From Negative to Positive Integration in the WTO: Time for Mainstreaming Human Rights into WTO Law' (2000) 37 Common Market L. Rev. 1363.

Porges A and Brewer TL, 'Climate Change and a Renewable Energy Scale-Up: Responding to Challenges Posed to the WTO', *Clean Energy Technologies and the Trade System: Proposals and Analysis* (International Centre for Trade and Sustainable Development (ICTSD), World Economic Forum 2013).

Puig D, Haselip JA and Bakhtiari F, 'The Mismatch between the In-Country Determinants of Technology Transfer, and the Scope of Technology Transfer Initiatives under the United Nations Framework Convention on Climate Change' (2018) 18 International Environmental Agreements: Politics, Law and Economics 659.

Rajamani L, 'Ambition and Differentiation in the 2015 Paris Agreement: Interpretative Possibilities and Underlying Politics' (2016) 65 International and Comparative Law Quarterly 493.

Ratnayake R, Proksch M and Mikić M, *Climate-Smart Trade and Investment in Asia and the Pacific: Towards a Triple-Win Outcome* (ESCAP 2011).

Raustiala K and Victor DG, 'The Regime Complex for Plant Genetic Resources' 58 International Organization 277.

Roessler F, 'India – Additional and Extra-Additional Duties on Imports from the United States' (2010) 9 World Trade Review 265.

Roffe P and Tesfachew T, 'The Unfinished Agenda' in Surendra J Patel, Pedro Roffe and Abdulqawi Yusuf (eds), *International Technology Transfer: The Origins and Aftermath of the United Nations Negotiations on a Draft Code of Conduct* (Kluwer Law International 2001).

Rubini L, 'Ain't Wastin' Time No More: Subsidies for Renewable Energy, The SCM agreement, Policy Space, and Law Reform' (2012) 15 Journal of International Economic Law 525.

Sampath PG and Roffe P, 'Unpacking the International Technology Transfer Debate: Fifty Years and Beyond' (2012) 36 ICTSD, Issue Paper <http://papers.ssrn.com/sol3/papers.cfm?abstract_id=2268529> accessed 28 October 2020.

Sauvant KP and others, 'Trends in FDI, Home Country Measures and Competitive Neutrality' in Andrea K Bjorklund (ed), *Yearbook on International Investment Law and Policy* (Oxford University Press 2012).

Schaeli J, 'Marine Plastic Pollution as a Common Concern of Humankind' in Thomas Cottier (ed), *The Prospects of Common Concern of Humankind in International law* (Cambridge University Press 2021).

Schefer KN and Arnaiz P, 'Duty to Protect, Climate Change and Trade' in Panagiotis Delimatsis (ed), *Research handbook on climate change and trade law* (Edward Elgar 2016).

Scott J and Rajamani L, 'EU Climate Change Unilateralism' (2012) 23 European Journal of International Law 469.

Seres S, Haites E and Murphy K, 'Analysis of the Contribution of the Clean Development Mechanism to Technology' (UNFCCC 2010) <https://cdm.unfccc.int/Reference/Reports/TTreport/TTrep10.pdf> accessed 28 October 2020.

Shelton D, 'Common Concern of Humanity' (2009) 5 Iustum Aequum Salutare 33.

Soltau F, 'Common Concern of Humankind' in Cinnamon P Carlarne, Kevin R Gray and Richard G Tarasofsky (eds), *The Oxford handbook of international climate change law* (First edition, Oxford University Press 2016).

Stadelmann M, Castro P and Michaelowa A, 'Mobilising Private Finance for Low-Carbon Development' (Climate Strategies 2011).

Steiner M, 'The WTO Government Procurement Agreement: Assessing the Scope for Green Procurement' (2015) 9 *BIORES* < https://ictsd.iisd.org/bridges-news/biores/overview?page=6> accessed 28 October 2020.

Stern DI, 'The Rise and Fall of the Environmental Kuznets Curve' (2004) 32 World Development 1419.

Stiglitz JE, 'Overcoming the Copenhagen Failure with Flexible Commitments' in Peter C Cramton, David JC MacKay and Axel Ockenfels (eds), *Global carbon pricing: the path to climate cooperation* (MIT Press 2017).

Study Group of the International Law Commission, 'Fragmentation of International Law: Difficulties Arising from the Diversification and Expansion of International Law – Finalized by Martti Koskenniemi' (UNGA 2006) A/CN.4/L.682; A/CN.4/L.702.

Sugathan M, 'Winds of Change and Rays of Hope How Can the Multilateral Trading System Facilitate Trade in Clean Energy Technologies and Services', *Clean Energy Technologies and the Trade System: Proposals and Analysis* (International Centre for Trade and Sustainable Development (ICTSD), World Economic Forum 2013).

Tamiotti L, World Trade Organization and United Nations Environment Programme (eds), *Trade and Climate Change: A Report by the United Nations Environment Programme and the World Trade Organization* (World Trade Organization; United Nations Environment Programme 2009).

Tams CJ, 'Individual States as Guardians of Community Interests' in Ulrich Fastenrath and others (eds), *From Bilateralism to Community Interest: Essays in Honour of Judge Bruno Simma* (Oxford University Press 2011).

Thompson D, 'An Overview of the Draft Code' in Surendra J Patel, Pedro Roffe and Abdulqawi Yusuf (eds), *International Technology Transfer: The Origins and Aftermath of the United Nations Negotiations on a Draft Code of Conduct* (Kluwer Law International 2001).

Tolba MK, 'The Implications of the "Common Concern of Mankind" Concept on Global Environmental Issues' (1991) 13 Revista IIDH 237.

Torras M and Boyce JK, 'Income, Inequality, and Pollution: A Reassessment of the Environmental Kuznets Curve' (1998) 25 Ecological Economics 147.

Trachtman JP, 'WTO Law Constraints on Border Tax Adjustment and Tax Credit Mechanisms to Reduce the Competitive Effects of Carbon Taxes' (Resources for the future (RFF) 2016).

Traerup S, Greersen L and Kundsen C, 'Mapping Barriers and Enabling Environments in Technology Needs Assessments, Nationally Determined Contributions, and Technical Assistance of the Climate Technology Centre and Network' (2018) Background paper TEC/2018/17/4.

Trinidade AAC and Attard DJ, 'I Meeting of the UNEP Group of Legal Experts to Examine the Implications of the "Common Concern of Mankind" Concept on Global Environmental Issues' (1991) 13 Revista IIDH 247.

UNCTAD (ed), *Compendium of International arrangements on Transfer of Technology: Selected Instruments* (United Nations 2001).

UNCTAD (ed), 'Transfer of Technology' (UNCTAD 2001) UNCTAD/ITE/IIT/28.

UNCTAD (ed), 'Facilitating Transfer of Technology to Developing Countries: A Survey of Home-Country Measures' (UNCTAD 2004) UNCTAD/ITE/IPC/2004/5.

UNCTAD (ed), 'Promoting Low-Carbon Investment' (United Nations 2013) Series A, number 7.

UNCTAD (ed), 'Transfer of Technology and Knowledge Sharing for Development – Science, Technology and Innovation Issues for Developing Countries' (United Nations 2014) UNCTAD/DTL/STICT/2013/8.

UNEP, EPO and ICTSD, 'Patents and Clean Energy: Bridging the Gap between Evidence and Policy' (UNEP, EPO, ICTSD 2010).

UNFCCC, 'Second Synthesis Report on Technology Needs Identified by Parties Not Included in Annex I to the Convention' (2009) Note by the secretariat FCCC/SBSTA/2009/INF.1.

UNFCCC, 'Third Synthesis Report on Technology Needs Identified by Parties Not Included in Annex I to the Convention' (2013) Note by the secretariat FCCC/SBSTA/2013/INF.7.

UNFCCC, 'Synthesis Report on the Aggregate Effect of the Intended Nationally Determined Contributions' (UNFCCC 2015) Synthesis report FCCC/CP/2015/7 <http://unfccc.int/resource/docs/2015/cop21/eng/07.pdf> accessed 25 October 2020.

UNFCCC, 'Aggregate Effect of the Intended Nationally Determined Contributions: An Update' (UNFCCC 2016) Synthesis report FCCC/CP/2016/2 <http://unfccc.int/resource/docs/2016/cop22/eng/02.pdf> accessed 25 October 2020.

UNGA, 'Transforming Our World: The 2030 Agenda for Sustainable Development' (United Nations 2015) A/RES/70/1.

United Nations Environment Programme, *Emissions Gap Report 2018* (UNEP 2018).

United Nations Environment Programme, *Emissions Gap Report 2019* (UNEP 2019).

van Asselt H, *The Fragmentation of Global Climate Governance: Consequences and Management of Regime Interactions* (Edward Elgar 2014).

Van den Bossche P and Zdouc W, *The Law and Policy of the World Trade Organization: Text, Cases and Materials* (Fourth edition, Cambridge University Press 2017).

Voigt C, 'Delineating the Common Interest in International Law' in Wolfgang Benedek and others (eds), The Common interest in international law (Intersentia 2014).

Vossenaar R, 'Identifying Products with Climate and Development Benefits for an Environmental Goods Agreement' (ICTSD 2014) <https://seors.unfccc.int/applications/seors/attachments/get_attachment?code=FL5IRCXNKHGQDAD6JQULRT67L7A02OHU> accessed 28 October 2020.

Vranes E, 'Carbon Taxes, PPMs and the GATT' in Panagiotis Delimatsis (ed), *Research handbook on climate change and trade law* (Edward Elgar 2016).

Wang J-Y and others, *Officially Supported Export Credits in a Changing World* (International Monetary Fund 2005).

Ward J and others, 'Catalysing Low-Carbon Growth in Developing Economies: Public Finance Mechanisms to Scale up Private Sector Investment in Climate Solutions' (UNEP and Partners 2009).

Watal J and Caminero L, 'Least-Developed Countries, Transfer of Technology and the TRIPS Agreement' (World Trade Organization 2018) WTO Staff Working Paper ERSD-2018-01.

Weil G, 'Incentive Compatible Climate Change Mitigation: Moving beyond the Pledge and Review Model' (2017) 42 William & Mary Environmental Law and Policy Review 923.

Wenidoppler T, 'ECAs Go to Market: A Critical Review of Transparency and Sustainability at Seven Export Credit Agencies in Central and Eastern Europe' (Finance and Trade Watch, CEE Bankwatch Network 2017).

World Bank, *Global Economic Prospects 2008: Technology Diffusion in the Developing World* (The World Bank 2008) <http://elibrary.worldbank.org/doi/book/10.1596/978-0-8213-7365-1> accessed 28 October 2020.

World Trade Organization, 'Implementation of Article 66.2 of the TRIPS Agreement: Decision of the Council for TRIPS of 19 February 2003' (2003) IP/C/28.

World Trade Organization, 'Proposal on the Implementation of Article 66.2 of the TRIPS Agreement: Communication from Cambodia on Behalf of the LDC Group' (2018) IP/C/W/640.

Wu M, 'Why Developing Countries Won't Negotiate: The Case of the WTO Environmental Goods Agreement' (2014) 6 Trade, Law and Development [i].

Wu M, 'The WTO Environmental Goods Agreement: From Multilateralism to Plurilateralism' in Panagiotis Delimatsis (ed), *Research handbook on climate change and trade law* (Edward Elgar 2016).

Wunsch-Vincent S, 'The Internet, Cross-Border Trade in Services, and the GATS: Lessons from US-Gambling' (2006) 5 World Trade Review 319.

Young MA, 'Climate Change Law and Regime Interaction' [2011] Carbon & Climate Law Review 12.

Yusuf AA, 'Technology Transfer in the Global Environmental Agreements: A New Twist to the North-South Debate' in Surendra J Patel, Pedro Roffe and Abdulqawi Yusuf (eds), *International Technology Transfer: The Origins and Aftermath of the United Nations Negotiations on a Draft Code of Conduct* (Kluwer Law International 2001).

Zhuang W, *Intellectual Property Rights and Climate Change: Interpreting the TRIPS Agreement for Environmentally Sound Technologies* (Cambridge University Press 2017).

Index